130   140   0

TERRITORY of NEW GUINEA

ADMIRALTY IS.

NEW GUINEA

ST INDIES

PAPUA

Rabaul

N. BRITAIN

5

Daru

Thursday I.

Port Moresby

Samarai

Yela

10

ST INDIES

CORAL

15

USTRALIA

SEA

8

Gona
Buna

TROBRIAND IS

WOODLARK I?

LAUGHLIN IS

9

D'ENTRECASTEAUX I?

MILNE BAY

10

UA

LOUISIADE ARCHIPELAGO

Samarai

CONFLICT I?

MISIMA I?

11

tralia since 1884

ONE HUNDRED MILES

YELA I?

12

48   150   152   154

NEW GUINEA HEADHUNT

By Caroline Mytinger

HEADHUNTING IN THE SOLOMON ISLANDS

NEW GUINEA HEADHUNT

NEW GUINEA HEADHUNT

by

CAROLINE MYTINGER

NEW YORK
THE MACMILLAN COMPANY
1946

To Margaret Warner

ACKNOWLEDGMENTS

As I go over the names in this section I feel like a miser with his gold spread out before him. Figuratively with each name I pick up a portion of treasure, feel its good weight in my palm and turn it this way and that, appreciating its worth. Each name is that of some person without whose help our painting venture might have foundered anywhere from the Coral Sea to the last page of the story. Many are the names of Britons who, according to one British attitude current at the time of our appearance, should not have inconvenienced themselves for a Yankee. They are proof that among civilized people nationality is a negative factor, that where there is instinctive good will even personality does not count for or against the beneficiary of their kindliness. Because of these Britons in Papua and elsewhere who so unstintingly gave what they had of what we needed most, hospitality, advice, friendship, we owe all Britons a debt of understanding. Because of them we feel in this world of doubt today that friendship between nations and races now antagonistic is not forever unattainable.

For this as much as for the tangible help they gave us we acknowledge our indebtedness to Sir Hubert Murray, to Mr. and Mrs. A. P. Lyons, A. A. Aumuller, Captain Lindquist, Charles Pinney, Mr. and Mrs. C. L. Hall, Captain C. O. Anderson, C. de Lani Harvey, Mr. and Mrs. George Zimmer, Captain John Dean, Ivan Champion, Mr. Bannon, Percy Hinds, Captain Donaldson, Mr. and Mrs. Gordon Rowley and Mrs. Guy Du Boise-St Marc.

We are proud of our fellow countrymen Mrs. Harry Post

of Batavia and Port Moresby's "natural Mason," Percy Leigh, to both of whom we owe gratitude for very special favors. Such Americans abroad are responsible for the good will of other nationals by which we benefited in the friendship of the Chinese, L. Zecha.

Finally we wish to thank those unsung benefactors of book writers, the librarians of the San Francisco and Monterey Public Libraries, especially Margaret Lee Keith of the latter who may have been only performing her duty in assisting me in the research necessary for this book but who put into it such cheerful thoroughness that she has glorified all librarians.

This book is dedicated to Margaret Warner, and though that is doubtful honor in recognition of all she endured in helping to create the material for it, that's all there is.

CAROLINE MYTINGER

NEW GUINEA HEADHUNT

LAST WORD

Though many of the characters in this book are headhunters past or present and the action is hunting heads, there is little blood beyond these first few pages. Our own manhunt in New Guinea was for native models whose heads we wanted to paint in portraits, and it took place in the golden days between wars when anything as sober as this chapter would have been written by a bearded historian. Our picture of New Guinea is therefore just an artist's impressions of a place that may never be quite as funny again.

New Guinea is remarkable for a number of reasons, not the least of which is how much we still do not know about it. But perhaps its most unique feature is that on this island only a few miles from Christian churches and law courts, electric shavers and symphony music coming in over the air from the most sophisticated cities in the world, people are still eating one another and bagging human heads as war trophies, just as our ancestors of the paleolithic era doubtless did. Here too, eons after the real stone-club age has vanished, organized bands of men are still clouting others insensible as the ethical and only conclusive way of winning an argument. But more interesting than these primitive practices is the reason they still endure in a country that has long been under the rule of civilized nations. It is what we call a paradox of conscience. The answer is that the New Guinea "savages" began emerging from their long isolation just as civilization was itself becoming civilized enough—an ambiguity that will be cleared up by the following survey of European occupation of the island.

By the end of the nineteenth century history's ranking imperialist, Great Britain, at last had a bellyful of empire and was not only reluctant about acquiring any more world territory but actively opposed to such policy. Nevertheless in 1884, the year in which the German flag went up over Friedrich Wilhelmshafen (now Madang) on the northeast coast of New Guinea, the Union Jack was hoisted "with prayers" at Port Moresby on the southern coast. This prepared the way for the Australia-owned Territory of Papua and at the same time finished the partitioning of the big island between European powers. The west half of the country from the Fly River on had been conceded as a Dutch possession ever since the treaty of 1814 when England and Holland, after warring for a century over their conflicting markets in the East, drew a line roughly along the equator, the British agreeing thenceforth to appropriate no lands south of it and the Dutch no countries to the north. Conforming with the traditions of the times, the native inhabitants of these countries were not consulted.

The new British possession in New Guinea comprised the

southeastern portion of the island from the Dutch to the German border which latter ran diagonally east and west along the Owen Stanley Range, the central backbone of high mountains. The territory was named after the Malay word for all of New Guinea's aborigines, Pǎ′pū-à, which means woolly-haired. Then, since it was Australia that had insisted on acquiring the new land as a strategic defense for herself, it was handed over to her for administration.

For the next quarter of a century or more the vast hinterland of New Guinea still remained a mystery to its owners. The Dutch with their enormously rich Indonesian islands were content to hold their portion in reserve for the future, German scientists employed by the private Neu-Guinea Kompagnie, long the only colonial administration of that territory, made a few hazardous expeditions up the largest rivers, but those real builders of empires, the missionaries and merchants, devoted their efforts to consolidating positions along the coast. Papua, meantime, was deliberately following a "go slow" policy, new in native administrations; and of this more presently.

One of the reasons for this unprecedented caution or indifference toward the new prize was the New Guinea natives themselves. The Papuans have not remained exclusively Papuan all these centuries by welcoming visitors. On the contrary, from the beginning of their known history, they have shown a disagreeable tendency to greet all strangers, regardless of skin-color, with barrages of rocks and barb-tipped arrows and spears. When callers came at them firing guns they fled into the bush and remained in hiding until the invaders left, or if these proved to be colonizers and stayed, the natives simply remained in hiding and at every opportunity picked off an empire builder, saving his head and eating the remainder of the evidence. The early explorers who penetrated inland usually blasted their way with rifle fire from village to village. But everyone got tired of this, even including the explorers; and anyway as yet no real (commercial) incentive had been found for risking one's neck very far beyond the coast.

Then, about 1908, something happened that changed the whole picture, making the loss of a head or even a whole hide just one of the hazards of fortune. Gold was discovered by Australian prospectors working the Waria River about twenty-five miles inland from Morobe on Huon Gulf. By 1926 it had become a gold rush, and by 1938 the Mandated Territory (old German, now British) was exporting over $10,000,000 worth of bullion a year, most of it removed from the comparatively small area between the coast and Papuan border around Huon Peninsula. The west bulk of this second largest island in the world was still largely unprospected. (Little wonder Japan was interested in New Guinea.)

In this gold rush, normally the most ruthless of white invasions, the aborigines for all their gastronomic fearfulness might speedily have gone the way of other backward peoples obstructing the path of "progress," save for one poetic factor. The powers had developed a conscience toward backward races. This was embodied in Article 22 of the Covenant of the League of Nations, which states that in these countries "inhabited by peoples not yet able to stand by themselves under the strenuous conditions of the modern world, there shall be applied the principle that the well-being and development of such peoples form a sacred trust of civilization." This was delivered as binding along with the German New Guinea territory when it was handed to Australia for administration after the First World War. Put to work, the sacred trust gave the aborigines little more than civil rights in court; but this was something the white man at least understood, and as an inhibiting factor it forestalled some of the out-and-out exploitation and abuses that helped decimate primitive populations in earlier periods. However, even as recently as 1937 members of the Citizens Association of Rabaul were agitating for restoration of the old German system of issuing permits to flog natives. It was claimed that the natives were being flogged anyway, and without a license it was dangerous because most natives had an enlarged spleen from chronic malaria and if the whipping ruptured the spleen a man was up for manslaughter. Whereas with a license . . .

It takes fearless individuals as well as hard laws to make ideals work, and anything as beautiful as Article 22 without such a champion was bound to have rough sledding in the Mandated Territory, where it had everything from strongly entrenched vested interests to the whole caboodle of the caste system to buck . . . just to save the black hides of a lot of savages. It remained for Papua to produce men as big as the concept of the Covenant. In fact Papua had long ago created her own sacred trust to her native subjects, and it had been in force since the early days of Australian occupation. The first Lieutenant-Governor was Sir William MacGregor, "one of the great colonial governors of the British Empire," but of an unorthodox cut of greatness for that era. It is said that "he took up his appointment in Papua because he felt that it was the one spot left where the British had the opportunity to prove to the world that it is possible to rule a native race without annihilating it." It was the Papuan administration through its two champions, Sir William MacGregor and Lieutenant-Governor Sir Hubert Murray, which discovered that the native subject had a spiritual as well as a physical well-being to keep in trust.

It has been found that the decline in primitive populations which inevitably follows the coming of white men to their countries is not always caused by new diseases or abuse alone. There is also a mysterious disintegration of the spirit, a weakening of the will-to-live that gives microbes and bullying a fallow soil to fall on. One cause for this, scientists tell us, is too abrupt a transition from the old culture to an entirely different new one; from the rich old beliefs and exciting customs like headhunting and cannibal raids, the gorging feasts and sumptuously costumed dancing to comparatively vacuous new activities. Say, hymn singing and the monotonous routine of plantation work or pack carrying for the prospector. In other words, the toxins of sheer boredom act on the primitive just as they do on us.

Many of the natives' old customs are genuinely antisocial, and in other protectorates they have been immediately and usually forcefully suppressed. The Papuan administration goes slow. Sometimes it does not go at all. The anthropology department studies the suspected material, often while missionaries and the southern press howl for action together, and when it is found that the custom actually is injurious and not likely to die out of its own accord, then it is weeded out, but as painlessly as possible. For example, cannibals who insist that they eat human flesh not because they are starved for meat but because it imparts to them the spirit-strength of the victim, are persuaded that pork is full of such strength and a lot more expensive anyway—which gives eating it greater prestige. Headhunting raiders within reach of the government patrol who do not know that they are being unlawful are brought in and treated to an education instead of revenge. Others beyond reach at present can wait. The result of this civilized program is that after more than half a century of occupation the native population of Papuan New Guinea is almost the same as if white men had never come to the country. A decline in the more exposed eastern division is balanced by an increase in the west, where the warring tribes who might have annihilated one another in time without European intervention have been protected from one another. Inland there are vast areas still closed to the outside world, still waiting to be taught cautiously that headhunting and cannibalism, terrorism, raids and killing for ethical reason are taboo, at least for them, in the new world.

But today a new kind of manhunt has come to New Guinea, brought, ironically, by the very crusaders who would have made the old kind taboo. Modern warfare with a range of human slaughter that makes even the highest mountain fastness vulnerable has made the smallest human a potential victim. The shock of its impact, the very sound of it to primitives who have never heard anything louder than thunder and fear even that as the voice of demons, the wildest of whom in the past have been subdued by the mere firing of rifles into the air, the effect on these can hardly be calculated. Hill villagers who did not know that such beings as white or yellow men existed have now seen them come plummeting down out of the sky. Enlightened natives who have been so gently but firmly weaned to turning the other cheek now find that the teacher himself can swat back—and with a delivery never dreamed of by the sport-raiding headhunter. Papuans who have learned by painstaking education that the *taubada's* person is inviolable have now seen hundreds of white men die, violently, grotesquely, even as their cannibal victims once did.

Before our war carried to the Coral Sea islands I should have said that the natives there, given rifles and ammunition, would have had a field day shooting the bottom out of everything, including the inviolable white man and his enemy. Everywhere except in Papuan New Guinea . . . for our concept of gratitude and justice dies hard. As it happened the Armed Constabulary of Papua was the only native outfit we have heard from that was trusted to retain its arms after the military took over from the civil government. No one knows what happened among the natives of the Solomon Islands, because the Japanese got there first with the war; but at

Rabaul when an estimated seventeen thousand Nipponese were bearing down on a known force of exactly 1,399 Australians, the only potential help, the native police, were promptly relieved of their rifles and sent out of the area along with all the town indentured natives and prisoners from the jail. One can understand why the Citizens Association wouldn't want them around. Later when the mainland campaign began in earnest with the landing of Japanese forces on the north coast, the Orokaivas, a spirited tribe inhabiting the gold mines district, *did* have a field day, with the blessings of the enemy. After the First World War some four hundred German missionaries were allowed (by signing a neutrality agreement) to remain in the New Guinea protectorates to carry on their work. For some of them—Lutherans, the Catholics say,—this continued to be work for the Fatherland, later the Nazis, which carried right up to the Second World War. Resentment toward the "Diggers" was not hard to stir up among the warring Orokaivas, especially with the gift of rifles. The tribesmen were given plenty of ammunition and spread out through the countryside on a good old-fashioned terrorist raid, killing other tribes that refused to co-operate with the Japanese, spying on Australian activities and generally proving primitives an asset in modern warfare that the Rabaul garrison had overlooked.

Meantime, while the survivors of that Rabaul rout were making their way on foot through the bush and by canoe and launch across to the mainland, Australia's other "strategic defense" was getting ready to be wiped off the map in the same way. At Port Moresby a "handful of kids" averaging about eighteen years who had never before seen action manned two antiaircraft batteries. Singapore had already fallen and the Dutch Indies, the Philippines, the Solomon and Bismarck Archipelago islands, and Darwin and other northern Australia towns were being bombed when the Japanese landed on New Guinea's north beach. This was at the terminus of the track that led through the gap over the Owen Stanley mountains to Port Moresby just one hundred and seventy miles away. Papua was the last northern barrier to be taken by the Japs, and between their mounting concentrations at Rabaul and Australia were just the "kids" at Port Moresby. The kids and those one hundred and twenty armed native police. There were no fighter planes, no bombers, no navy, no other white garrison then anywhere in Papua.

Everyone in Port Moresby those first weeks expected the Japs to take the Papua capital as they had taken Rabaul, softening it up with air raids and then landing troops from the sea. Only with less fussing with bombs, and more speed. All the Australian kids expected to do was to pot away with their A.A. fire until it happened. But the enemy had been cautious at Rabaul, and they were still cautious—unnecessarily —now. While they raided Port Moresby day after day it was from an altitude safe from ground fire and there was no follow-through. Meantime a now thoroughly alarmed Australia was rushing up defenses, at first "only a handful of slow Catalina flying boats and Lockheed Hudson reconnaissance bombers, and a Wirraway lacking one wing" along with some veteran troops of the A.I.F. who had seen service in the Middle East. But eventually a strong garrison and air base began building up at Milne Bay, and by and by bombers and fighters of the R.A.A.F. followed—though still not enough as yet to be of more than nuisance value in raiding Rabaul and the north coast until the Jap land forces came around that eastern "corner" of New Guinea. The Aussies, they say, were praying those days and wondering if the Americans would get there "before"—though no one could imagine how it could be in sufficient force then to change the finale. The sea lanes around New Guinea were stiff with Jap submarines. But the Australian Foreign Minister, Dr.

Herbert Evatt, had already gone to Washington maneuvering for Australia what Churchill had for England in the same kind of emergency. General MacArthur was given supreme command of the allied forces in the South Pacific, and shortly thereafter Flying Fortresses from the Java campaign turned up in Papua along with other U.S. squadrons of fighters and bombers; then hell began a-popping in the Coral Sea. An enormous Japanese armada—transports, carriers, warships and an unknown number of submarines—was reported heading south in the direction of the Louisiade Islands off that eastern corner of New Guinea. The expected invasion of Papua seemed to be shaping up. But at that moment the United States Navy made its surprise attack in the Solomons, the Japanese fleet heading for Papua swung east to lend a hand; and what happened is now ancient history. What isn't generally remembered about that engagement is that Papua was incidentally saved. And for the *second* time. For the Japanese had planned their invasion of the possession for a month earlier and had their minds changed that time by the loss of some twenty ships and countless aircraft destroyed in the north at the moment of taking off by our Papua-based air forces.

The United States Marines in the Solomons began drawing away a lot of the Jap fire from Papua, but by this time the enemy had taken without resistance, and held, all of the Northeast coast as well as an inland airfield at Wau. (Only when they landed at Milne Bay just a few miles north of the Papua port of Samarai were they beaten off by the Anzac land forces and both Australian and American air forces, their very first defeat in the war so far.) And from the concentrations around Huon Gulf the Japanese were swarming up the north slope of the Owen Stanleys, heading for the gap that was the gateway to Papua. The Australians met them at Kokoda, and thereafter for three bloody months the battle raged back and forth in those terrible highlands more than six thousand feet above the sea. This was almost entirely a British show—and a brave one. The Japanese had sent in their veteran jungle fighters who had seen service on the Malay Peninsula, big men, six-footers who were clad in green uniforms that made them invisible in the forest gloom. They were well provisioned and armed, and they outnumbered the Diggers three to one.

When the Japs had pushed the British forces back down the Kokoda track to within twenty-five miles of Port Moresby one of those at-first-inexplicable things happened that made the situation parallel that of the Germans' near-capture of Paris in the First World War and their almost fatal bombing of London in this last war: with no extra resistance put up against them they failed to push over those last two easy ridges and take their objective. The fist of the Jap arm began to go limp and then to wither away. Emaciated bodies of Japanese were found that looked as if they had died of starvation as much as from wounds. Japanese dying of poisoning by bush berries and fruits and from eating the spoiled tinned food that the Australians had left behind in their retreat (the tins of which they had carefully punctured) were picked up. And there were others dying of diseases; scrub typhus, malaria and dysentery, left behind as the enemy retreated northward. The answer is that the Jap arm was being strangled at the shoulder. The U.S. army had arrived in New Guinea, and the allied air forces were blasting the Northeast coast, cutting off the enemy line of supplies.

Major-General George Kenny was responsible for this latest ninth-hour miracle. With the sea route from southern supply bases blockaded, General Kenny organized a gigantic air ferry and transported to Wanigela in Collingwood Bay and other points around Buna not only some 18,000 American soldiers but a million tons of stores and equipment, even including artillery and jeeps, and he did it *in time*. While more troops were still being landed the first American outfits were already closing in on Buna, choking off the life line of the Japanese threat to Moresby. The survivors of the weary A.I.F., who had held on so long and so bravely in the mountains, pressed on down to the north coast past the scattering and dying Japs and took up positions behind Gona. And everyone knows the rest of that story, too.

In the excitement of his own battle the reader may have forgotten all about our primitive manhunters, but we haven't. All the foregoing is just leading back to those one hundred and twenty native police of the Armed Constabulary last seen in Port Moresby. They proved to be the nucleus of a vast unofficial native army whose part in the defense of Moresby, and progressively that of Australia, cannot be estimated in the ordinary way. The first duty of the police was to control the hysteria that threatened to break out in the villages when the bombs began to fall, which might have spread and become a serious obstruction to British activities. Then to be rounded up and induced to return were the couple hundred indentured boys who had fled from the settlement. These too were a potential source of widespread trouble because they would attempt to get back to their home villages, some of them through unfriendly tribes, and would either starve on the way or stir up resentment stealing food. Besides, they were needed in Port Moresby, hundreds of natives were needed for work that the white soldier could not perform in such a climate without serious depletion of strength. And the constabulary went out among the villages and got the necessary "boys." These unloaded freight, worked on roads and air strips under the blistering sun, transported on their backs up the heartbreaking Kokoda track the war matériel that kept the battle in the Owen Stanleys going for three months. And then came back down the trail bearing litters of wounded A.I.F. Many

a sassy Australian today owes his life to the numb endurance
of those "blackfellows." They tended the sick, buried the
dead, sniped with their primitive weapons at the green-clad
Japs hidden from eyes not trained in jungle fighting. They
carried communications through enemy territory, spied on the
enemy positions and led the tenderfoot Australian guerrillas
through the maze of jungle to carry out successful ambush.
And they too were killed by Jap fire and died of diseases
and exposure in the cruel mountain cold but without equal
weapons of defense nor knowing why they were dying with
so little sport in it. The police, who had rifles, went "native,"
conducting little private headhunting raids along the lines of
the best old traditions. They came back to headquarters only
when they needed more ammunition (which they got),
dressed in choice parts of Japanese uniforms and with notches
cut on the butts of their rifles—also an old Papuan custom
executed on the handle of war clubs. They were crack shots
and had better sight in the gloom of the bush than most white
men. And they loved the work.

However, neither they nor any of the other natives who
risked their lives in the defense of Port Moresby were com-
pelled by force to do so. The scrap over the natives in Rabaul
when the war closed in was not repeated in Papua, for what
civil authority remained refused (by argument) to allow the
military administration to conscript natives. Unless all were
given arms they could not be sent into the field of action,
even as carriers. The natives were paid for their work, but
they could have chosen not to risk their lives for pay. That
they did so voluntarily is evidence that the principles of the
sacred trust contained in Papua's native policy can produce
dividends: never to leave behind a legacy of hate for the next
white man who comes that way.

1

It may be that this is the first expedition the reader has ever gone on that moved forward backing up, so it should be explained that we did not choose this form of advance to be like the wee-wee bird who flies backward because he doesn't want to know where he is going—he just wants to see where he has been. It is a style of locomotion devised for expeditions that know very well where they want to go but having in pocket only the price of a ticket home, back up toward the objective bit by bit only so far as newly acquired funds make it safe to go farther from home. When Margaret Warner and I left Rabaul for the mainland of New Guinea we were stretching that native caution a bit, but there was good reason for it this time.

Out at the very end of the Louisiade Archipelago, the chain of islands that strings out into the Coral Sea off the tail of the New Guinea "bird," is an island about ten miles long and half as wide spelled Yela and pronounced Yā'lah. On it lives a "lost tribe" of dark-skinned, woolly-haired primitives. It was these Papuans whose portraits we wanted to paint. The group should interest even a layman, if only as the objects of statistical gluttony because they once managed to eat almost at a sitting three hundred twenty-six-and-a-fraction Chinese coolies who had been shipwrecked on their reefs. It was the remaining fraction of the three hundred twenty-seventh who was rescued to tell the tale . . . only to come to an inglorious end as a bootlegger in Victoria. Once during his career when the law caught up with him the court waived the charge because of the man's harrowing experience with the Yela cannibals.

Why should two young women be after the portraits of such characters? To explain that, it is necessary actually to back up and describe as briefly as possible what we were trying to do, how much had already been done, and what we still hoped to accomplish. (And don't leave us here if you have already read this much in *Headhunting in the Solomon Islands*. While it is still the same campaign that was described in that book, we are now carrying the front to the new locale of New Guinea.) We were attempting to paint the portrait of the Melanesian race. The collection of portraits included, as well as studies of the Melanesians, the subraces like the Fiji Islanders and the race stocks that may have combined to create the present Melanesian type. So far we had obtained portraits of the Melanesians of the Solomon Islands, and as many of the subraces as we could catch. Before us was the last third of the work, that of painting the "ancestors."

No one knows, naturally, the history of the Melanesians, whether the islands around the Coral Sea were once uninhabited and became populated by peoples migrating from other lands or whether the natives were always there in the earth and the pigs rooted them up, as many of the tribesmen themselves believe. For the sake of simplicity we are proceeding on the theory that the race evolved from two primary stocks, one which was negroid and probably the indigenous one, and the other mongoloid and superimposed. There is evidence sufficient for anthropologists to suppose that the modern descendants of the negroid progenitors are the natives inhabiting most of New Guinea, the long-headed, woolly-haired and dark-skinned Papuans. The immigrant mongoloids probably came from the near-by islands west of New Guinea in a series of migrations that extended over a long period of time. Their light-brown skin modified in the

Melanesian descendants the blackness of the aborigine's color, and in some localities there are even Melanesians with straight or wavy hair like the Malays'. There are also both mongoloid round and negroid long heads among the Melanesians. The present-day type representing the mongoloid stock may be found in the natives of the East Indies. These two groups, the native Papuans and the Indonesians, were to supply the models for the "ancestors" of our Melanesian picture.

Looking at a map of the Pacific, it would appear a simple matter for an artist taking off from Rabaul—which, incidentally, is pronounced Rå-bel' in Rabaul—to pop straight

over to the mainland if he wanted to paint a Papuan; New Britain and New Guinea are only half an inch apart on the map, and why travel all the way down to a dinky island like Yela, especially when it meant backing up to it? This is one of the illusions created by the size of the Pacific Ocean.

Even if Rabaul and Salamaua, the nearest port on the mainland, were not half a week's journey apart even on a steamer, between the port and the nearest Papuan there would still be miles of swamp and jungle and heartbreaking mountains to cross on foot—as many Americans now know. For the full-blood Papuans do not live on this coast. Those ancient mongoloid mariners who changed the race type seemed to have come around the north of New Guinea, and evidently the Papuans treated them to the same barrage of rocks and arrows with which they later greeted white men, for it was not until the invaders reached this eastern end of the island that they were able to get foothold. But once the beachhead was established they absorbed either matrimonially or gastronomically the resident Papuans. Then as the centuries went by the now-Melanesian descendants spread out along the coast as far west as Cape Possession on the southern shore of New Guinea. And this coastal band of Melanesians between us and the Papuans presented an unsurmountable obstacle to a female expedition stymied by a delicate financial condition north of New Guinea.

Then at the point of taking advantage of that emergency measure of being faced homeward, we uncovered the Yela Island Papuans. This was a lost tribe if there ever was one. Here for hundreds of years, while the population of the entire island world around them (even as near as twenty miles) was slowly evolving into round-headed Melanesians, this handful of natives on tiny Yela had somehow managed to remain serenely long-headed. Their presence in the east seemed to solve everything for us. The island was less than two hundred miles from Samarai (să'mà-rī), the eastern port of Papua, and Samarai was in the direction of home from Rabaul. (If we *had* to go home it would be shorter instead of farther.) There was just the matter of backing up those two hundred miles from the mainland to Yela.

Before leaving Rabaul we already suspected that it was not going to be easy to reach this island even if we went at it in the conventional way, bow forward. Some old-timers had never heard of an island by the name of Yela, others knew it as Rossel but said there was no transportation they knew of down that way. Apparently the only ships that ever called there were the ones that unintentionally piled up on the infamous Yela reefs that had snagged the Chinese labor ship. (And enough of them had done this in the past to supply the sons of cannibals with cooking pans and metal for knives and spearheads to last them for generations to come.) Our problem seemed to be that of getting onto the island like a lady instead of a Chinese. But if this was to be done by any means but levitation, it still required passage money that we did not yet have.

The reader may well be asking himself at this point (as who was not) what an expedition was doing out in this remote part of the Pacific without ample funds. Why should we be low in funds, Margaret and I occasionally asked one another, when we had the best possible support? There was San Luca, patron saint of artists, who through the medium of a battered old cigarette tin of drawing materials was supposed to produce the wherewithal with which to travel. And there was the little gold elephant called the Heffalump in our purse whose job it was to see that the wherewithal never got down below the price of passage home. To some people this may seem whimsical, but the third charm was practical and so far had made the first two work. This was Margaret, my companion. I have never been able to quite put my finger on an expedition label for Margaret. In fact I usually had to look at her twice to see which end of the horse she was at the moment—the one that was leading the expedition or the one that was keeping the flies off it. I know more definitely what she did *not* do; that was, to paint the pictures. I did that. But Margaret, conspiring with San Luca, even kept me at that. She was also the one who guarded the Heffalump who guarded the ha'pennies. And she did everything else around the expedition, some of it with a ukulele.

Actually fees from portraits—portraits made from the drawing materials in the cigarette tin—of Europeans living along our route to and through Melanesia had supported us all the way from San Francisco; but only to have the system bog down in this largest white settlement in the islands, Rabaul. Whether this was a lack of art appreciation in Rabaul society or a temporary lapse of San Luca was still not certain. We only know that Rabaul kept its gold and let us keep our art—and that Rabaul blew up first.

Perhaps the nervous reader is now asking himself why we did not send home for funds to continue our project, if it were so vital. Surely there was plenty of money available for such a noble work as recording the physical appearance of a vanishing primitive race. But have you ever tried to persuade anyone to finance a headhunting raid? We had our pride. North Pole, South Pole, stratosphere, the depths of the ocean and Wogs, thousands to record these phenomena which we will always have with us; but for the early types of man whom the Lord will soon tire of creating, and even for modern man about whom we could know more still without knowing enough, proportionately little money is available for study.

Anyway, up to this point we had been doing well enough on our own. And we still had a few of the necessary things for an expedition as we backed up toward our new objective. Despite prophecies to the contrary we had our original heads after a year among "those savages" in the Solomon Islands, and in other ways we were fairly intact Americans. And by that I mean we felt impervious though our mortal flesh might be sloughing away here and there with island sores, and Margaret was periodically sick of hearing me groan with malaria. The presumable reason she did not groan with it herself is that she had been taking preventive doses of quinine ever since we had been in the malaria islands. I think this had a lot to do with her charm, because five grains of quinine a day can keep one just dizzy enough to have a certain elusive quality. But you cannot paint pictures with that, and I took my quinine all in a lump when the fevers struck.

Best equipment of all, one of the things that had been lacking at the launching, we felt savvy. It was not so much what we knew as the realization now of how much we did not know: that the real hazards of the locale were not so becoming as a feverish nose nor so quaint and easily recognized as a whooping sorcerer. Probably our attitude when we left Rabaul for New Guinea was just about what might be expected of headhunters no longer ingénue; the swagger of the old-timer cloaking a fearful earnest hope that we might not only reach Yela but stay on the project and finish it by also painting the "ancestors" in the Indonesian islands.

For the present everything depended on Samarai, the port to which we were sailing. *Could* the little government station with a population of less than a hundred Europeans produce enough portrait commissions not only to support us in the hotel while we executed them, but to send us down the Louisiade islands, when Rabaul's white populace of two thousand had only—just—allowed us to remain honest women?

You see what we mean by backing up. You don't have to lose time turning around if you have to beat a hasty retreat.

2

From a distance Samarai looks the way it ought, being a "South Sea isle"; like a big heap of spinach. But that was the only tourist note we took in as the steamer identified it by ignoring all the other little salads floating on the blue water and heading toward the one with the cluster of white at the waterline. That was what was absorbing our attention, that light patch. That, presumably, was our portrait clientele waiting for us, Samarai's white-skinned, white-clad citizens. Island residents usually turn out to see the steamer through, and from the size of this crowd it seemed the entire settlement must be on hand. It couldn't have been better for our plans.

There were more small craft anchored before the island than we had seen even in Rabaul's busy harbor, and there were two large vessels, one of them a slick white yacht with the Union Jack flying. It looked gay, almost like a regatta. We found we were not as blasé as we might have been. There was the same old excitement of coming into a strange port, the happy spirit of exploration and discovery that stirs in the breast of woman at sight of a cluttered bargain table. The sea was like glass, and as the sun sank low in the west all the white boats and white-garbed crowd suddenly reflected pink in the deep blue water. Down at the right of the landing the seminude natives standing in their canoes shone like copper statues. That was a feat, we thought, to stand in the keelless dugouts; we had not even been able to sit in the sculls and stay topside.

We were up on the bridge deck as we came in, and when

the steamer was eight or ten ship lengths from the wharf we saw one of the launches, a high-powered racing type which must have been the only one in the islands, snort out from shore. As it rose on its tail coming toward us, accelerator all the way up, it threw a wash like a submarine chaser. "That damned woman again," said someone vehemently in the chart room. Then everyone leaned out of the window to watch, grinning in anticipation. As the launch roared past, the groups of dugouts and standing occupants keeled over like wheat before a cyclone. Even canoes too distant to get the wake shuddered and "capset," and natives on the outskirts paddled and poled like mad in every direction away from the "flying witch." The pink boats danced on the roughened water and even the yacht swung slowly to port and back. When the launch reached the steamer our own hair rose. Instead of slowing down and coming alongside as we expected island launches to do, it came on still at full speed and then suddenly swung on its left hind leg and cut across our prow, missing it by what must have been a matter of inches. When it came out into view on the other side, butt in the air, we saw a white woman at the wheel and she was looking back, grinning up at the officers on our deck while her speedboat, bit in teeth, headed for our stern.

From then on until our engines cut down the launch circled round us, first risking being diced by our prow, then spanking across our wake. As soon as the steamer tied up, the launch made off after the canoes that were still topside and had cleared out to what they thought was a safe area. The woman sent them over one after another like ducks in a shooting gallery by making a snappy curve and sending her wash at them. This was the spirit of the Anglo-Papuan in a nutshell.

Meantime the gangplank was over, and it was old home week. The Samarai crowd surged on board, hallooing passengers. We got swept along in the tide running into the bar, and for the next two hours until the steamer finished loading and went its way south, we sat fondling a glass with ice in it, thinking this would be the last cold thing we would feel for a while. The usually tomblike bar steamed up and filled with the drone of men's voices, gossiping, "cheering" (buying drinks), and laughing with pleasure at seeing old friends from "the territory" and Papua . . . the local distinction between the two British-mandated territories. Many were doubtless beaming just at being part of a crowd again. Of those who were introduced some had names we recognized as belonging to persons other island friends had asked us to look up. A few introduced themselves because they had been asked to watch out for us when we came along. Everyone was hearty and we had the impression that it wasn't all beer and "sun-downers." We felt in fact like expected and welcome guests who had arrived. Samarai was surely going to be different from Rabaul.

What we were wrong about, just as a start, was ice. There was plenty of it in Samarai. The island has a power plant, and even electric lights that stay on until two o'clock in the morning. But we did not learn this until hot and cold and light and dark seemed as if they would make little difference in our lives in Samarai. We were rendered numb by the discovery that of our welcoming committee, few were local. They were Empire Day celebrators from all over Papua. In little Samarai filling the hotel beds and guest rooms in homes for the next two or three days. It *was* a regatta crowd. And we did not make that discovery until the southbound steamer had disappeared over the sunset horizon bearing away every shoulder we knew well enough to have the vapors on.

In the next homeless hour or so we had a lot of time to catch up on Samarai's scenery. We discovered by doing it rather continuously that an American who still has some of his health can walk entirely around the island in fifteen or twenty minutes by the shore path. It has another name, Dinner Island, which must be taken from the plate by that name, for the outline of the shore is almost circular. Some habitations look loved, and others do not look like anything. Samarai, even in this least sentimental of hours, made us think of one of those little castle-encrusted isles in the European lakes, snug, compact; a lot of love had gone into the luxuriant tropical planting up the slopes of the one hill. This hill is low and off-center, for one face of it is a sheer cliff where the surf climbs high on a wild day, while the other slopes down gradually to the steamer landing. The residences strewn up the long slope are almost hidden from view from the water by the bower of green.

Below on the flat adjacent to the landing are a few corrugated iron trade-stores and warehouses, the two then-overflowing taverns, the movie "theater," bowling green, tennis courts and the inevitable cricket field of the inevitable Britisher. Somewhere there must be a courthouse, because Samarai is a district government station; but luckily that was one place we did not have to locate.

There is no native village on the island, but there are native constabulary barracks, and their location is marked for the tourist by a number of long, foot-wide jetties extending out over the water from the east shore, each high pier with a rustic excretorium on the very end. Again, in this least promising of hours, the possibilities in that arrangement during an epidemic of dysentery struck us as something to live on for. Visiting natives from the mainland and outlying islands are allowed to remain in Samarai only twenty-four hours at a visit, and not far from the barracks is their canoe anchorage. That was something to live for too; it was a place of incessant coming and going of types and costumes out of Sindbad's tales.

Seen from the veranda of the Residency on the summit of the hill, all around for miles the reef-blue water is "studded with tree-crowned isles, and ringed as with a jewelled girdle by mainland hills rising fold on fold, and high peaked islands twixt which come gleams of narrow waterways leading to the outer sea. I doubt if in all the world there is a more beautiful spot, for it is a cameo cut by immortal hands out of sea, and shore, and sky, and ever will remain a very garden of the gods." * This, then, is the place where we could not find a bed on which to lay our bodies.

The one thing we had learned as a free-wheeling expedition in the South Seas was never to interfere with our destiny by forcing issues. Though we had a kind of initiative which I suppose might be called passive insistence. For instance, on each circuit of Dinner Island during which my feet, cramped into store shoes for the steamer, swelled from the heat at the rate of an inch a beat, we stopped in at each of the two taverns and Margaret, in a quiet brave voice that should have broken the heart of anyone who was going to lie on a bed that night, asked if they had yet found anyone willing to double up so that we might have a room. If it had been a case of merely doubling up we might have had immediate results, but if one single room had been vacated it would have thrown at least five Empire Day rejoicers out on the world. Ordinarily Empire Day is in most of the Empire no more momentous a holiday than our Fourth of July is in normal times, but in Papua it is always whoopee. Every resident who can leave his plantation swarms in to this annual banquet and sports tournament, which spreads over two or three days and is accelerated by plenty of iced beer, not to be had at outlying stations. But the celebration is usually held at Port Moresby, the seat of

* Colonel Kenneth MacKay in "Across Papua."

government. Any year but the one we grace with our arrival.

Somewhere along about the fifth or sixth lap of Dinner Island I remarked to Margaret that my feet felt just about sick enough to go to a hospital. "Hospital!" Margaret exclaimed and stopped in her tracks, "Hospital *bed!*"

3

Getting a bed in an island hospital is not the lengthy adventure it is in better regulated countries. For one thing, in this miasmal belt most white residents should be in the hospital anyway . . . or back where their breed evolved, in a temperate climate. At any rate, anyone who voluntarily appears at the door of one is certainly too sick to be elsewhere, for it is the local British custom to carry on until one is carried on. So the applicant is entered without having to put up any money, or remember what his grandparents died of, or even to get the affidavit of a doctor that he is deserving. He is sure to have one or more of any number of diseases, or die shortly, which in either case entitles him to a bed on sight.

The nurse on duty that night ushered us to a room without bothering to take our names . . . we couldn't have got off the island without paying our bill, and she probably knew our names anyway, as well as our ages and everything else there is in a passport; such is bush telegraph. If we were entered on the records it should have been as "cases of desperation." For we were not ill. The facts are that a nice young doctor was called over to the hospital from an Empire Day warming-up party, and after carefully examining Margaret's wide blue eyes decided she could stand some "observation." I was just given a cot in her room in case she died of my feet.

It was an ample room, spotlessly clean and screened and re-screened by a mosquito net canopy over the bed, but it was neither cool nor very private. As in most European buildings, the roof though high was of galvanized iron that held the

28

scorching heat of day through most of the night. In theory the trade winds that livened up at dawn and sunset swept in through the doorless entrances and over the low partitions to the rest of the hospital; but in practice the air went the other way, and it did not blow. It oozed down from the oven roof and in from the gallery, bearing the odors of ether and fever sweat and food, and the sounds of gagging and grunting human beings too ill to maintain any longer the British tradition of understatement. The least one can have in an island hospital is insomnia.

Someone, a woman's voice, was talking to Margaret when I began emerging from that hot sticky cocoon that goes for sleep after the equator sun is up. I did not have to open my eyes to know it was late; the sunlight was penetrating as death rays, bending in under the veranda roof, straining through the mosquito net and piercing my very skin. I was sleeping "in the raw" and had to keep on playing sleep under the sheet until the stranger left, but what I heard was making me itch. The caller, it developed, was the wife of the Resident Magistrate and "this" was her daughter. *That* opened my eyes. There were so few white children in these hot islands that we had held the total childlessness of Rabaul to be partly responsible for our failure there. It was the portraits of people's offspring rather than themselves that had paid our way as far as the islands. The presence here of a youngster of any age would give us our best opening with a "speculative" drawing, for even if there were no more children in all the rest of Papua we would have a tenderly appealing subject with which to introduce our wares. What I saw made me close my eyes weakly again. Standing below the veranda on the path, smiling indulgently, was a "boy," a native fifty years old or more, and on the top step of the veranda was a wiry little white girl of five or six with a cupid-sized bow and a handful of the small arrows that are made from the split midrib of the palm. The little girl was shooting at the boy, and the native was sidestepping and catching the arrows by hand. I didn't have to see the child's face; I knew she had a snub nose, brown with freckles, and intensely blue eyes that would not be fooled by any of Margaret's tricks to keep her sitting still. Her sunlit hair against the brilliant foliage beyond was so orange that it vibrated like red letters on a green ground, hard to look at long on an empty stomach.

There was something else wrong with that picture: the boy. In the islands behind us no Europeans would have risked a girl child to the care of a male nurse, no matter what age. I looked again. The man had a good face, more of it than most natives, for his hairline had receded a little. In other clothing he could have passed as a houseman in some old place around Baltimore. His legs and feet were bare, but a dark blue serge wrap-around *sulu* (sarong) fell below his calves, and the upper part of his body was covered by a low-necked, short-sleeved jumper trimmed with red braid. A garment above the waist was unusual for a native too. But this was Papua, where things were going to be different.

Our caller, meantime, was regretting that we had been obliged to start our visit in Samarai in the hospital. She had hoped we could come to tea at the Residency that afternoon and meet "His Excellency." The government yacht, *Elevara*, was down from Port Moresby and would be leaving the morning after Empire Day for a tour of inspection of the Southeastern Division. This comprised all the eastern islands from the Trobriands to *Yela!* Moreover the Lieutenant-Governor was very partial to visitors who came to Papua with an interest in the aborigines, for his native subjects were almost an "obsession" with Sir Hubert. Frequently he invited such visitors on the *Elevara's* tours of inspection. . . .

More than any other figure in these islands we had wanted to meet, without ever expecting to, Sir Hubert Murray, moral

successor of Sir William MacGregor as keeper of the Sacred
Trust and champion of primitives. Our hero worship of
Papua's governor had begun long ago in Sydney when a rubber planter down on holiday began damning "Murray" for
ruining the possession. He was not opening up the country
fast enough, the "niggers" were being pampered, white set-
tlers couldn't get the land for planting if natives were thought
to need it, there were such restrictions on recruiting that the
plantations were failing for lack of labor. But as the rubber
planter was also damning the Yankees for ruining the rubber
market we listened to the anti-Murrays with an open mind
from then on. It was soon apparent that what "Murray" was
doing was enforcing to the hilt British laws already in existence for the protection of native subjects and instituting new
ones to cover loopholes that developed, and he had furthermore been doing it conscientiously and energetically for almost two score years while two generations of squealing
damning would-be promoters came and went. Here was a
humanitarian who was not just keeping records of a vanishing
race but was preserving the mortal natives themselves. And
here the great man was at the other end of a simple tea invitation.

Only it was not so simple. From bedridden invalids to full
tea drinking health at the Residency by four o'clock gave us
only something like six hours in which to dress. I could take
six hours to tell about it, but a few high spots will show our
progress. The first thing we did after collecting our luggage
from the wharf and hotel where we still expected to stay, was
to blow out the entire electrical system of the hospital.

It all began with that mystical by-law of the islands called
white prestige, which prohibits a woman going down in the
laundry where natives work and ironing quickly and expertly a frock that a washboy will take two hours to ruin.
Anyway any extra boys there were in the hospital were be-

ing borrowed for civic duties that day, and the only iron in the laundry was one of the local charcoal furnaces. This is a metal drum the size and almost the weight of a curling-stone which has to be filled with hot embers, and as it requires an aboriginal's sense of timelessness to keep stoking one of these, withal it seemed a good idea to press our frocks with our traveling iron in the room. For ironing board I intended to hold the bedside tray aloft in the air so that the cord would reach, while Margaret ironed. We never got that far. The iron was a so-called international—but without regard for the voltage of New Guinea. Three of the plugs had no effect, but as the fourth was plugged in the electric fan on which we had been counting to dry us off after the exercise of taking a bath whirred to a dead stop. The curling iron which was to have frizzed up my remaining hairs into a "do" returned to its normal tepid temperature when not connected. (Margaret still had hair, but the periodic high fever of malaria was taking its toll of mine.) For a minute afterward the entire building hung in suspense like the pendulum of a clock that has stopped running, then there were calls of "boy, boy" all over the place followed by an answering thumpity-thump of bare feet on wood as the personal boys of the patients rushed in from under the hospital where they loafed.

Things had just quieted down a bit and we were about to carry on when there was another charge of feet. These were shod and coming up the gallery in our direction. Thinking they were after our scalps, we shoved our chores under the mosquito net of the bed and stuck our heads out around the door screen as a front line of defense. It was one of the nurses and the young doctor. "I say," the doctor greeted unaccusingly, "you're interested in native anatomy. Want to see what a shark can do to it." We momentarily forgot all about shaking hands with the great and followed to the native annex.

The anatomy, what there was left of it, was lifeless. The

shark's victim was a young man, and he had expired while
the doctor was getting to him from the cricket field. He
would have died anyway. Great chunks of strong young
muscle were shredded from the upper legbone and pelvis,
torn away by the very roots of tendons. It was like a cadaver
on the dissecting table with the detached muscles flapped
back, only not so neat.

The interior anatomy was exactly like that of the white
man, but the unmutilated remainder of the body was strangely
unfamiliar even for a Melanesian. This was the first dead native we had seen. The skin of the healthy young native . . .
like that of the orderlies swabbing up around us . . . is a rich
coppery medium brown not unlike that of our Southwest
Indians. And the wiry wool on the head, which is usually
worn the full length of its natural growth by the men, stands
out around the face full of life and almost always full of ornaments. The hair of the dead boy was wet with salt water
and hung limply back on the table like a mop, revealing for
the first time the rounded contour of the Melanesian skull.
And his skin, drained of blood, was blue, the soft gray-blue
of the plumage of the dove.

Taking photographs of the subject blew another three-
quarters of an hour, but we needed the pictures to show to
William Beebe, who maintains that shark are really shy fish.
Of course, we would be lacking photographs of the guilty
shark, but the natives who had been with the victim insisted
that it was a "s'ark." And they ought to know the boy's own
mother. It seems that this mother, who was deceased, had
taken the form of a shark, or her spirit had come to inhabit a
shark; anyway, twice previously she had attacked her son.
With what motive it would be hard to say, except that the
spirits of the dead are always malicious. (This gives the native
something to blame ill luck on, which must be a great safety
valve.) One would think that the boy might have stayed out

of sea water when he knew he was being stalked, but he was not free to choose. He was indentured to a trader, and worked on the man's lugger as a shell diver. A boy's labor contract can be broken only by ill health, and even His Excellency had no laws to make an employer believe in ghosts . . . which reminds us that we were on our way to meet him.

When we got back to our room to continue the ordeal of dressing we found that the electricity fuses had been replaced, and the restarted fan had taken a bite out of one of the frocks we had intended to wear. The motor was moaning just before burning out, and the hot curling iron was on its way down through the bed pad. Wraiths of smoke from the charred cotton were being sucked over the top of the partition. From two doors down we heard the nurse say to a patient who had been expected to die of black-water fever in the night, "You're sure you weren't smoking and dropped a coal on the bed. Something is certainly burning along here." All this hastened us out of the hospital, indifferent to grooming, and up the steep hill to the Residency.

No wonder His Excellency's weary-lidded eyes seemed to sag at sight of us. Besides being wantonly stockingless, we were late. And we discovered yet later that this was our first social error, for it reversed the presentation to an imperial governor by obliging him to rise and curtsy to us as we came panting across the wide veranda. Languidly he did so, somewhat after the manner of a tripod opening. As he rose from the low cane chair one long joint after the other unfolded until he stood tall and lean and straight for all his threescore-and-something years. We were to learn that this weariness of movement was part deliberateness and part the unhurried mannerism of a droll Irishman, but some of it was real fatigue. Yet, where most white men do not last more than ten or fifteen years in this latitude, almost forty had merely seemed to bleach the Murray. His skin, his hair, the whites of his faded blue eyes were all variations of a single color note, tan. The monotone was accented by the whiteness of his jacket, which had a standing military collar and was buttoned all the way up to the chin. (One doesn't have to wear even a chemise under this kind of Dutch tropical blouse.)

We had been thinking in a rather blurred way as we raced up the hill what we should say to the great man after being presented. We might thank him more or less formally, as a visiting expedition, for preserving the primitives for us. From this point we could lead up to Yela and then let fate carry on from there. But we lost control of the situation. We have never discovered any formal way of stanching perspiration flooding out of the face except to swab and swab, and in these countries where the weather won't let you think of anything else for very long the cause of sweating is usually a taboo subject. But there is a lot of weather in New Guinea and someone did mention it. Before we knew what was happening His Excellency had floated away on the tide of it into another conversation, and when he left the veranda half an hour later I was on my third conversationalist and the same topic. Shortly after that, still swabbing, now from the hot tea, we backed down the hill. Back to our charred hospital room and dead hopes for Yela as guests of the Papuan government.

4

There were tennis and cricket matches and teas the day before the great day, a movie that night, and tennis and cricket and tea on Empire Day and a banquet and ball in the evening. Though we were bleeding internally we took it all in. And it all had features not usually associated with these diversions elsewhere.

The cricket can be written off briefly as diluted baseball. (Also see Keith in *Land Below the Wind*.)

The tennis interested us not only because it was "our" game but because it was the first we had seen played on concrete courts in the islands, thereby providing a contrast to the other island tennis we knew. Tennis courts may seem an incongruous note in a Stone Age land, but the larger settlements have clubs and a few of the plantations have courts. And as long as our American health lasted we played on them. Margaret and I had been playing as a team since long before our portrait travels, even in the States, and we had everything worked out to our satisfaction like a couple of old bridge partners. And we had kept right on playing with some satisfaction down the South Pacific until we began to run into the lawn courts first of Auckland and Sydney and then in the islands. From then on we never again won a set until we got back on concrete in Papua. All the period in between we had wet feet. My windmill serve which, whether it went in or not, usually so convulsed our opponents that they were rendered harmless, was hazardous for me on the juicy turf. The only thing it could be compared to is tearing around on soapy sponges. You couldn't get any traction or, worse, stop if you got going. Then the bearded English balls were usually dead from the moisture and heat, and if they once struck the turf they seldom rose again. They just lay still or trickled along the ground, so that there was no second chance at them. The island game was consequently a chop-lob-slice affair suitable for badminton; the British understood it and played it expertly, but it just made us old California backline drivers mad.

Not the least of everyone's handicaps was the flood of perspiration that streamed into the eyes, into the racquet palm and the shoes. There were never any backstops but instead an army of delighted boys who retrieved the balls and threw them back to the players with a girl's motion or, after they had been bawled at a few times, brought them up and carefully placed them in front of the wrong player's feet. Most of the islanders played with gut-strung racquets that were like butterfly nets—from the moisture. We had all-steel racquets, and if they could have been brought into contact with a ball they would have been an advantage. But we just wore ourselves out tearing up long painful furrows in the turf sliding to base. And always the hostess would come out personally in the middle of a hard-fought point, gather up the sod, and replace it on its scalp. Or worse, give it to a ball boy to save. A lawn of real grass is hard to maintain in these islands where everything grows like mad, because the weeds also grow like mad and it has to be cut with a ruler because if sheared too short the sun will kill it in a day.

But our attitude was all wrong for Coral Sea tennis. The British player would stand in the middle of his court and reach. If an opponent accidentally put a ball beyond reach he would say, "Sorry, old man," and the one who had missed would answer, "Well played." Or if he were a purist, "Righto." The thing was not to be too vulgarly interested in getting the ball back, and above all to remain cool. After all this was the tropics, tennis a Sport, and winning only incidental to tea. For us it was a by-product of moral and physical collapse.

But Papuan tennis played by the hard-hitting Australians was California tennis at its fastest. The backstops were high, wide and strong—but native backfielders were also stationed up in the surrounding hills and out on the beach. The sweat of deadly intent flew like a lawn sprinkler, and for every set played a layer of skin was sacrificed from the feet, for the concrete was the temperature of a stove lid. Every now and then someone would fall by the wayside with a heat stroke or blind staggers from the glare, but so long as the beer held out these British carried on, gallantly.

The "picture theater" across from the steamer landing was a long, high-roofed hall about the size of the average side-street store, strategically located opposite the Cosmopolitan Hotel. ("Electric Light; Freezing-works; Best Brands of Wines, Spirits, Ales.") Unlike the Rabaul theater, where the natives sat on one side of the screen and scratched and the Europeans on the other, we all scratched in harmony together in Samarai, the screen being at the end of the house. We sat on tiered seats at the closed rear of the hall where the air was a bit thicker, and the house boys, boat boys and police were on the floor opposite the open door and right up under the screen. There was a "horse opera" being shown that holiday eve. I think there was always a horse opera, or part of one. We never saw anything else, nor an entire one. The reason for this is that our "Westerns" need less editing than films with more sense in them. Nothing harmful to white prestige can be shown. Also the climate does its own editing. The pictures that are shown do a South Sea circuit, and at each theater a lot more of the film disappears from the heat and moisture, and the story with it. Obviously no one cared how the picture was patched together, not the operator, nor the native audience—and least of all ourselves. They were the most entertaining comedies we had ever seen. White men were shot at but never died, custard pies flew through the air but never hit a Nordic, horses and riders would leap back up cliffs, and amorous couples were always reaching out but never met in a kiss. This last was possibly to save the sensibilities of the natives, who would have been infinitely shocked if they had known that such things were going on for all to see. Sometimes we would be shooting up the dirty halfbreeds with the Royal Mounted Police, and end up tearing out of the heart of Texas on a horse that appeared to leap right out over the audience. Then the natives on the floor down in front would scramble out of the way, dogs would bark—and that was about time for the film to break. At which we Europeans filed across the road for a cold drink. It was going to be a long wait. Sometimes we just filed out anyway for a breather, like the audience of a Chinese theater. These were silent movies, literally; there was not even a radio, piano banging or a gramophone. And until they find some way of editing and damaging the sound-track to match the films, I doubt if there will be "talkies."

We never found out what happened to most of the Empire Day ball. The music was supposed to have been provided by dance programs on the radio from Sydney or Hongkong, but even the raucous tropical static thinned out to a whistle and finally disappeared off the air. Then someone sat down at the old upright piano that hadn't been tuned since it was brought to Papua by the pioneer missionaries. He played half of "Dardanella," got warm and went back to the tavern for a beer. But the entertainment committee, being feminine, was determined there should be a ball; and a boy was set at the pleasurable (to him) task of playing a hand-wound gramophone. For a while there was a rise in party spirits. People lured in from the cool night air by the sounds of revelry wandered up to watch at the doorways, where they could still breathe. There would have been few dancing partners for the number of men if the men had not wisely stayed where there was cold beer; only two nurses, two barmaids, two headhunters and ten or twelve miscellaneous "ladies"— as female British islanders are called, possibly to make the distinction from "woman" which is the term for a native's wife. The men who did appear came dressed in dark evening trousers (with a white mess jacket) which after a round or two of the floor began to give off the fumes of moth balls and wet wool that reminded one of a press-while-you-wait establishment at home. The boy at the gramophone must have been new at the machine, and he made native music on it, playing one side of one record over and over again, apparently without anyone being aware of it. But we remember very well it was "In a Little Spanish Town" ('Twas on a night like this). He never did get the idea of intermissions, and "cutting in" hadn't yet reached the Coral Sea. There was no refueling station nearer than the tavern up the road, and when my life partner denied that the British were inconsistent, dancing up the right-hand side of the ballroom when they drive up the left side of the road, then I thought the white woman's burden in the tropics had been carried long enough. Someone . . . the son of a pioneer family of Samarai and a genuine Anglo-Papuan, born in New Guinea . . . suggested that we go out and "ride the rip" to cool off, and we leaped at it, whatever it might be.

Outside we could see the white sulus of houseboys squatting under the shadows of the croton bushes watching the dancing as they waited for their *taubada* (white man or master). Ordinarily no natives are to be seen about a white settlement after nine o'clock, for this is the indentured boy's bedtime and houseboys may not leave the premises, but on a whoopee night a personal boy accompanies his employer to see him safely home. As usual when we found ourselves being watched by primitives we became conscious of and a little embarrassed by our civilized antics. We knew that for all except the most savvy of those quiet blacked-out observers we had been providing the exhibition of a peephole show. The spectacle of the sexes clasping one another in public and so paired waltzing around without any of the usual religious excuses of making the yams grow or bringing rain in a drought must be rather startling to natives who would rather be seen dead than with a hand on the person of one of the opposite sex unless sanctioned by some ritual.

American girls have the reputation with the British of being rather good sports though much too twittery or, conversely, too hard-boiled to really give it flare. We risked our lives for our sisters in four rounds through that rip before we sang out. When we found that "riding" it meant going out in a launch we had visions of a moonlight ride on old Silver Lake, and Margaret sent back for our "wha-whas," the ukulele and guitar. There was a moon, but even that was not the same as the one that brings out the ukuleles at home. Around Dinner Island it pulls up a tide of from ten to fifteen feet, depending on the season. Between the cliff shore of the island and the mainland is a deep channel so treacherous that there is a legend believed by even the white populace that a man who gets into it is gone forever; even his body is never recovered. Through this channel flows a powerful current that runs counter to the incoming tides, and when the moon is full and the tide at its maximum it creates a tremendous rip whose churning seas rise to a man's height above the horizon.

The launch for our initiation was a sturdy eighteen-foot cargo boat with, we carefully noted, a quick-starting steady engine, and at the tiller was the famous old Sergeant Giberi

of His Majesty's Constabulary Service. He had faced death
in the line of duty often enough to qualify him as helmsman
on this purely pleasure cruise. But we never saw a man, native
or white, work harder and faster, nor more seriously than
when we started into the channel rip. The whole scene ahead
was lit by a lunar daylight, and it was awful. Almost instantly the big launch was smashing and bouncing into the
white maelstrom, and I felt a chill as if I were getting an
attack of malaria. Then we began to be tossed from alp to
alp, rudder and propeller skipping the gulfs between. We
dived into black gullies, swung half about in blacker whirlpools; and once or twice even the old sergeant grunted when
we went side-slipping toward the rocky bank of the island.
Along this admittedly "bad" stretch the water near the shore
was littered with huge projecting rocks of coral, and beyond
them the surf charged high up the face of the cliff. It had
none of the dependable rhythm of beach breakers; it was a
constant angry boiling that exploded in every direction with
equal fury. We went through it, tore around the island and
through again. And again and again.

I could give you no better introduction to the spirit of
modern Papua than this harebrained experience. It was such
men as this son of a pioneer who rode the tide rip for *fun*
who formed the New Guinea Volunteer Rifles, and such
men as Sergeant Giberi of His Majesty's Service who stayed
with his *taubada* even through his most half-witted exploits,
men such as those whose audacity held off for three months
the Japanese hordes when they were pouring over the Kokoda
track to take Port Moresby.

It was no consolation during the next few days to have
learned at the ball that we should have been invited on the
Elevara cruise if the cabins had not already been filled with
guests. We thought we knew why. It was because we were
an expedition that did not own a pair of stockings where no

gentlewoman would appear without them. But more because we did not wear whiskers or bifocals, nor even enough years to recommend us as serious company. And that humorless mood lasted until mid-morning of the third day.

It was at eleven o'clock of that historical morning that a "paper talk-talk" was delivered to us from the manager of one of the big plantation and shipping companies. At eleven-five we were swinging into preparations for our trip "down the islands" toward Yela. Not on the *Elevara* but on a copra boat leaving Samarai before daybreak the following morning.

It was a trip without obligations. Mysterious forces had been at work in our behalf. We were to be guests of a company renowned throughout the South Pacific for *not* giving free rides to strangers.

5

When the *Maroma* (which was our name for it) left Samarai that four o'clock of an ink-blue morning, we had no assurance that its itinerary included the island of Yela. It was enough for the present that it was going in the right direction, for there is such a thing as island hopping in boats. But we had learned that there was a planter living on the outpost island, and that meant coconut cultivation and an even chance of the *Maroma* calling for a shipment of copra. However, we were much too savvy now to think of depending on the hospitality of this resident. Plantations will often bed down the passerby in these tavernless islands, but one cannot *ask* them to. We were at last equipped like a regular expedition to house ourselves with a "field outfit."

I think one of the reasons we had not owned such gear before is that privately I was so afraid we would camp if we had the equipment for it. There had been a time when I did not mind eating live insects—nor spending the night sitting up with them, washing greasy pans with sand and cold water —nor becoming a smoke-suffocated sacrifice to every meal; but living the open-air life of the islands had made a softie of me. I had obsessions for perfumed cleanliness and sensuous luxuries that I had never indulged in even when they were obtainable. Margaret was made of sterner stuff, however, so we had the camp gear. But I comforted myself now with the thought that we would probably not use it anyway. There would be rest houses in some of the villages of Yela—the hut built and kept in repair by the natives for the visit of the

Guv'men' patrol officer—and we would simply appropriate one for our use. It would be risky to ask permission in Samarai because it might be refused to unescorted "ladies," and this might even preclude using our own gear. For these frontier countries are not quite so free as we are accustomed to thinking of them, and Papua especially is very careful about the people she allows off the beaten track lest trouble be started with the natives through carelessness or losing one's head in an emergency; both feminine attributes, they tell me. Anyway the average Aussie has such a devastating sense of humor that it was just as well if we kept our plans of camping on Yela private until we had done it.

So from a puzzled "clark" in one of the Samarai stores we bought with all the money we dared risk a field outfit so inadequate that he could never have dreamed that we meant to use it in the field. There was a ten-foot square of canvas for a fly as overhead shelter, a couple fathoms of rope (to hang ourselves with, I prophesied), two canvas hammocks, two "native" blankets (the kind plantation employers are required to provide native labor, so thin you could almost read through them), a tomahawk (island name for a wood hatchet), and a machete for paring yams and clearing ground. For Margaret we bought a wash basin and two sauce pans for something. Our defense "weapons" were still only the heavy flashlight and walking stick that we had carried but never had to use all through the eastern islands.

All the time we were purchasing these things I kept thinking about the "nature man" we had heard about when we were in Rabaul. He was first reported to be roaming the bush trying to live the simple life, equipped for his ghastly business with only his fingernails and teeth. Then the natives brought in word that he was "close up finish," which is about to die. To the great annoyance of the Service, which has its hands full just keeping track of the sane ones, a patrol party was sent out to search for the man. They had orders to bring him in by force if necessary because the court did not want to be obliged to convict any natives on a charge of cannibalism when a white man had dropped himself in their pot. The party finally tracked the fellow down, but he ran and was captured only after a chase. He was in a pitiable condition, naked except for some hair and a layer of island sores, starved and quite daft. He died soon after he was put in the hospital. Indubitably the effects of camping in this land.

Margaret, who had a conspiracy with the Heffalump, kept guiding me away from the tinned-goods shelves, insisting that we could get vegetables from the natives. To which I responded, *"What* vegetables!" Yams, taro root, sago (the mangled pith of the sago palm which we eat kibbled as tapioca), banana, coconut, and perhaps sugar cane; all carbohydrates and not a robust mineral in the lot. A white man would get rickets from what keeps a native at least on his feet. But she did let us have tinned meat. Only, however, after I had reminded her of the itching "fis'-mouth" one gets from eating the wrong kind of fish. For what may be the right kind for an aborigine can give an expedition bubbles at all its vents. She also stocked some tinned milk, all the while protesting that coconut milk was a beverage more tasty than British tea and more sustaining than coffee with cream in it, and that I should learn to love a daily catharsis. The idea of doing without bread was painful to both of us, but it involved bulky and hard-to-keep ingredients as well as some idea of how to make bread. And anyway the price of tinned butter—which is soupy and tastes like anything but the product of an honest cow—was what we then thought staggering; about seventy-five cents a pound. Simple salt completed this most unappetizing of all larders.

Then there was the first-aid kit. When we left San Francisco, we had carried no medicine at all, largely I think because we had our health and there is nothing quite so indestructible-feeling as a healthy American. But also because we did not have any extra funds with which to gamble on being sick. Now we had brews for malaria, for dysentery, for a total absence of dysentery, for eye-strain and foot and ear fungus, for island sores and insect bites, and a big tin of Buzzoff for purifying the very air around our heads. These items luckily did not have to be purchased now all of a lump; they were an accumulation acquired as we had acquired the indispositions they had cured. And to them we added only a few yards of white trade calico from the antiseptic inside of the bolt as the cheapest bandage material available.

A devastating layout which we could not get around was for trade tobacco. "Trade," incidentally, is any "European" goods which is exchanged with the natives, and tobacco was really a conversion of our shillings into local currency. The "tobac" is a twisted stick six or seven inches long of some substance that looks like tarred or molasses-soaked rope. It burns in spite of the perpetual dampness of the climate, but it tastes more like wet skating mittens than any mittens I have ever had in my mouth. The natives elsewhere had preferred it to even their own wife-grown tobacco, and accepted it in payment for both goods and labor. We expected to obtain with it, at a much cheaper rate than honest shillings, help in setting up camp, supplies of carbohydrates, good will and models.

And now having acquired more equipment, the appearance of our luggage got completely out of hand. When we left California we had believed, like tourists with a consideration for the tip, that we must travel "simple." But the tip is no consideration in the South Seas once you get off the big steamer routes. In fact, the planter would then have leaped at your neck if he saw you dropping a month's wages of a couple "bob" into the hands of a Melanesian who had portered your wardrobe trunk on his back. So as we had helplessly accumulated things, we had accumulated other things to put them in. The big cases had long since been discarded because they were often too heavy for even many boys to handle safely over the surfs, and they had been traded with our hosts for smaller and yet smaller cases until now we had for perishables two small sound metal trunks about the size of army regulation which one native can carry on his back for a short distance. Everything else went into labeled duffle bags, which are an article sent straight from heaven to impoverished travelers with no vanity. When we stood in the midst of our gear we looked like Ali Baba surrounded by the jars of thieves.

As expedition equipments go it was still modest enough, but when it had been carried onto the deck of the little *Maroma* and was followed up by more boys bringing the big black "umba-umba" (the beach umbrella for painting under), the "wha-whas," a fat roll of wide painting canvas, our cord of collapsible easel, that repugnant camp gear and finally, at three-thirty A.M., our giddy selves draped with monumental pith helmets and dilly bags of camera and films, notebooks and sketchbooks and crayons, and tins of cigarettes and bars of still cold and hard chocolate . . . then Ali Baba gave way to the Byrd taking off for the South Pole. We rather fancied ourselves, but the *Maroma's* skipper looked like a pink-faced Scandinavian who has just been notified of a death in his family. Clearly he had been expecting two lady tourists with an overnight case. He had had the spare cabin cleared out and perfumed with Buzzoff and . . . appealing thoughtfulness . . . there was even a small trade mirror laid on one of the berths. But we were carrying our own two square feet of mirror by this time, and one sniff inside the guest cabin decided us to store our insensible gear there and ourselves use the wheeldeck outside for bedchamber. The vessel was new for a copra carrier and it had even been built originally for a pleasure yacht, but two years in New Guinea waters had bestowed on it the island flavor which had inspired our name of "m-aroma." It had a Diesel engine, and mingled with its stench of burning fuel oil were the other normal ones of Buzz-off and bilge and the rancid coconut oil of past shipments of copra. These were concentrated in the cabin.

There was still plenty of night left as the vessel cast off, and as we had not yet had any sleep, we turned "in" modestly wrapping our blankets around ourselves and wedging a hip in the gutter to keep from rolling. The Skipper raised his lantern above his head, took one last baffled look at his unnatural "ladies," and then went forward to his quarters with his mouth still hanging open and mute.

We were under way. And if there is any snugger feeling in all the good world than the gentle roll of a small vessel under one as it plows forward in the right direction, then it is not given to headhunting raiders. There is no other way of getting to a place that has in it so much the sensation of going. No other path has the hillocks of seas to rise on, pass over and leave behind. Nowhere else can you lie on your back and watch the marker of mast sweeping past the miles of star clusters, feel the soft passage of moist night wind on your skin, and hear the knots of ocean gushing by the side of your vehicle. All marking space, shortening it. The last thing you see is the black, naked-looking silhouette of the native wheelboy, guiding apparently by some extra sense, for there is no light on the compass and he has no knowledge of navigating by the stars. Nowhere in the blue ahead is there any light, and to us the island landmarks are all floating clouds in a sky that begins at the edge of the deck.

The first day began two hours later, just as the thin red edge of sun was sliding above water still cast in the deep blue of night. Something was stomping up my abdomen. I brushed, and a cockroach the size of a hummingbird flew down

the deck. Margaret and I had stowed away *pied-à-pied* in the
gutter, which is another way of balancing oneself, and we
were still in that juxtaposition; so I had the soles of her feet
to examine as my first view of the Louisiade Archipelago.
There on her big toe was another cockroach, also bird-sized,
munching away at his breakfast. The *Maroma* was crawling.
The Skipper told us later that he slept in special "cockroach
socks" made of layers of mosquito net. He was fastidious, but
the socks were not so much to save his cuticle as because the
roaches didn't know when they had reached the quick, and
their careless nibbling started island sores. After that we spent
our nights in the field hammocks strung up on deck, swathed
like a cocoon in the mosquito nets, just in case the roaches
were the flying kind. And a more reliable means of producing abdominal unrest than a hammock on a ship has never
been equaled in the inventiveness of man.

All the way from Basilisk Island near the mainland to
Misima about a hundred miles to the east, there is no island
on the chart bigger than a pinpoint. But the sea is strewn
with land. Big islands crowned with palm trees and even
some underbrush, and little isles that have only one or two
palms—and some with none. These latter are strips of dazzling white sand that disappear altogether when the tide is
high. The whole area looks like flooded land, with only the
trees sticking up above the water. Or earth in the process
of becoming. This it actually is, for the coral polyps have
built what can be seen, and they are still at work on it.
Everywhere there are reefs. Those near or above the surface are marked by towering lines of crystal-white breakers
that thunder all along the way. Those lurking below for the
keels of vessels show only a change in the sea color from
deep cobalt blue to pale chartreuse. The stark sun penetrating to the very ocean floor shows up the danger spots in
the daytime, but no one tries to sail at night in this coral

field unless he knows his channel well or believes in immortality.

The island of Nari, about sixty miles from the mainland,
was our first call, and we slowed down only long enough to
drop a duffle bag down into the dinghy that came out for it.
That is our authority for dragging this island in by the hair
of its head. But Nari is important to our theme, and it was
our only contact in the east with Papua's experiment in "raising the Papuan to the highest level of which he is capable."
The island is a native Alcatraz, where the bad boys are sent.
Though what constitutes a bad primitive is not the same as
what constitutes a bad white man. It is not merely the untamed native who gets caught once beheading or eating his
fellows, murdering, raping, raiding . . . these things are custom . . . it is the one who repeatedly misbehaves, knowing
very well what makes the Guv'men' "wild." (Angry.)

The convicts on Nari have their liberty restricted by being
confined to the island, but there they are no more inhibited
than indentured natives working on a plantation. And they
do the same work. The whole island is an agricultural experiment station where crops suitable for the New Guinea
climates are being tried out. The prisoners not only work
routine hours in the gardens . . . anything routine being
hitherto unknown to them unless they have previously had
a term on a plantation . . . but learn to grow and rotate
crops that will keep the village in food the year through and
so stave off the periodic famines that have caused the Papuans
to be called "the hungriest people in the world." It is not because the native is lazy that he is hungry; the soil of New
Guinea is poor and level garden land is scarce behind the
coast, water must be carried to the crops (when they are
watered at all), and tools are primitive. They have not yet
discovered even the hoe, and they garden almost entirely
with a digging stick. Moreover the gardeners are the women,

with much of their energy expended on child bearing and toting, and the rest bestowed on raising tobacco and produce that lacks real nourishment. The Government's idea is to develop the agriculturist in these primarily hunting people. They have the philosophy for it. The natives do not think of themselves as owning the land, but of themselves as belonging to it; they grew out of it, and the other things that grow are in some mystical way a part of themselves. It is hoped that they may be guided toward raising crops not only for themselves but for the market, so that eventually they may become economically independent of the white man. It's a long dream, but even if it does not work the natives meantime will have been given some interest to supplant the now outlawed raiding that once provided the vital drive of their existence. And it is the prisoners, the bad boys of society, who are given this training and return to the village bearing the gospel of a better kind of life than one of murder and fear. We hope.

All of the natives on Nari are serving long terms or life terms, but they seldom serve out their full time unless they are psychopathically dangerous. And judging from the samples who came out to the *Maroma* in the dinghy, a sentence on Nari should improve the whole race. There were three cinnamon-brown Melanesians in the boat, and a chocolate brown individual who might have been a black Armenian if there were such a thing. He did not look like any South Sea islander we had ever seen before. The bare hides of all of them were glossy with good eating and live muscles, regular hours and secure nights. For one of the risks of being a freeman in New Guinea is that of finding yourself an angel any dawn that the neighbors happen to come a-raiding. The most conspicuous feature in these natives was their spirit, their whooping enthusiasm for being convicts on Nari. At least they whooped. And our Melanesian crew whooped back at them, but in a refined way since the *taubada* was looking on. As the *Maroma* swung into full speed again the Nari men stood up in the dinghy still calling, jerking their hands and laughing after us until we were too much blinded by the glare on the water to watch them longer. After that we felt better about Civilization. And we had been feeling pretty good about everything before. We were sixty miles nearer to Yela.

6

It was the end of the day when we entered the ship's passage of the twenty-mile-long oval lagoon formed by the little coral islands of the Conflict Group. Panasesa at the far western end was the night's berth. There was not a cloud in the whole sky, and the earth's curve of ocean all around us was as apparent as if it had been drawn with a compass. As the red sun dropped inch by inch dead ahead, it made a gleaming path of coral from horizon to ship's prow in water that was the blue of burning sulphur. We passed down an aisle of little islands that were made symmetrical bursts of rose and livid green by their identical reflection in the satiny lagoon. After fourteen hours of violent rocking and noisy vibration of machinery we seemed to be sailing on ice. It was sheer magic, the holy kind that could transform even the redoubtable *Maroma* into a majestic galleon sailing an astral sea. The planter who lived on Panasesa, we thought, must make his inspections of the coconut tracts in the Group on Pegasus.

"Better you ladies should stay here and get some roses in your cheeks," the Skipper was saying as the anchor chain clanked out before Panasesa, "There is not a mosquito." We smiled indulgently and prepared to go ashore armored in our usual slacks and long sleeves. For it was the itching hour when the night shift of anopheline malaria carriers take over from the big stripe-legged daytime mosquitoes, and they are all on deck together. But the plantation manager who stood on the beach waiting for us had about a square yard of skin

exposed. *"Aren't* there any mosquitoes here?" we called out
to him from the dinghy. He looked dazed for a minute, doubtless at hearing feminine voices coming from the pant-legged
arrivals when he thought the nearest woman at least fifty
miles away; then he laughed. "Godstruth," he called back.
And he swore true. There were no mosquitoes, humpbacked
or striped, anywhere in the atoll.

"There are no sand flies either," the planter was telling
Margaret at dinner: "I fancy you'd enjoy painting here.
Masses of scenery." And he waved his long arm to include the
arc of the earth where there were only masses of water.
Scenically or otherwise there appeared to be nothing whatever to paint on Panasesa. The plantation residence itself was
a masterpiece of architectural lack. It was the usual large
square floor on piles four feet above the insects of the earth,
sheltered by a peaked, exactly square roof of corrugated iron.
The floor became veranda by the presence of clusters of
windowless, ceilingless enclosures sprouting at odd places
over its surface. The two adjoining ones in the exact center
were supposed to be bedrooms but were an office and storeroom. The "house cook" and "house wash-wash" were used
for what they were intended for, but the real living, eating,
sleeping, loafing, was all done on the open veranda. The residence was on the highest point of the island, and where we
sat eating our dinner our heads could not have been more
than fifteen feet above sea level. There were one hundred
and forty acres of sand in all of Panasesa, but the island was
so low and narrow that when we were standing on the lagoon
beach we could see the crest of the surf breaking on the
opposite windward shore.

The vegetation was all palms, coconut palms and again
palms, hundreds of them. But not the familiar wild coconuts
leaning gracefully into the wind. These were cultivated in
righteous straightness, set out in neat rows, every solitary

one of the hundreds exactly the same height because they
were the same age. As far as we could see each long way of
the island the level white sand was evenly patterned with
exploding blue shadows of palm fronds, like a machine-made
cretonne. And at the distant ends of the aisles of shadow-
striped pillars there was the same intense blue of ocean or
lagoon. It could get pretty monotonous. Yet Panasesa was
instantly appealing. We did not know what it was then, but
we do now. It was simple cleanliness. This is the unsung
beauty of the coral isle. No chimneys and exhaust pipes
belching gases and soot and clamor, no mud nor dust, mix-
tures of grease and manure, nor littered paper, tin cans and
bottles, and no dump heaps in the vacant lot. Especially, no
clutter of steaming crowds. Just virginal white sand under
glossy palm fronds; and it is such a snug little piece of world
that it seems to belong just to you. Even the perspective at
Panasesa was not rattling. Stretching out eastward down the
wide lagoon were the crests of the coral castles, reef, isle
and island following in line like beads in a necklace, around
it the clear expanse of blue sea, and sweeping over it the
space-washed trade winds.

It was tempting, but we had no excuse, like that of enjoying ourselves, for stopping off at Panasesa. It lacked models.
For in all this snug little domain there is not a native village.
There are fifteen islands in the atoll large enough to have
names, and most of them have stands of cultivated coconuts
belonging to the Panasesa owners, but there never have been
villages in the group. There is no fresh water. Panasesa got
its soft pure water from the rains draining off the corrugated
iron roof into a big storage vat. There were native boys working on the tracts, but they were recruited from all over the
territory—and a plantation boy is stripped of his village garb
and so loses his primitive identity as a model. (We have seen

types of American Negroes who looked exactly like individual Melanesians; only the races as a whole are distinctly
different, and the styles in ornaments and hairdressing help
to make local distinctions.) "And anyway," I answered the
planter for Margaret, "we're on our way to Yela." At that
our shy, crimson Skipper, who had been sitting silently beaming on and off like a firefly, dropped to low voltage, but his
eyes bugged out like blue Easter eggs. This was the first he
had heard of it. But he made no comment, and nothing more
was said about it. This was because he did not know that we
hoped to travel to Yela on his vessel, and we did not know
that the *Maroma* was not scheduled for the island.

The end of the sunset breeze was rustling the hanging
fronds of the palms around the veranda, and as the moon
swelled above the purple steam of cooling ocean, Margaret
took her ukulele out of its case. Then I took myself for a
walk. It did not seem possible that any girl who looked like
Margaret could be so unaware of herself as to croon with a
ukulele on an island like Panasesa on such a night, and I did
not want to sit and watch the ninepins going down. Even I
could feel a spring tide rising in my atrophied lungs as I
headed for the white beach. The Skipper was going out to
the boat, and as he stepped into the dinghy he remarked with
his usual brevity, which lent mystery this time, "He's a
bachelor . . . a gentleman." To a European a gentleman is
a man who has gone to a "public" school, so I brushed that
aside as an unimportant datum, but what had impelled him
to mention our host's matrimonial status? To me. Well, I
could keep *my* feet on the ground.

The ground, I found as I got a way up the beach with my
sandals off, was sand as fine and evenly white as corn meal,
and it was warm between my toes. Ghost-white fiddler crabs
scuttled along on one edge out of my path, and presently I

began leaping over them. No reason for it; just leaping. There were no mosquitoes nor sand flies speeding me on as was usual at night. Then I was *running*.

The reason this was sensational will be easier to understand with the following supplement. When we were in the Solomon Islands we succeeded as guests at a Guadalcanal plantation a young Yale alumnus who was evidently determined to keep up his Yale form to the ends of the earth. Every morning, to the horror of his Australian host and mystification of the native labor, he did a little track workout around the plantation, muffled in a sweat shirt above and bared in shorts below. Only a primitive could admire this incongruity in costume, but the running round and round, sweating and panting, and the total collapse for the rest of the day established a reputation for Americans that made the natives look at us from behind trees when we first arrived. The Yale man's form lasted less than three months, and then he was shipped home in very bad shape. No one runs in these islands, not even the natives, not even the runners who carry messages; just California tennis players when they get off alone on a coral isle in the moonlight. A minute later I had left my clothing in a heap and was bounding off up the blue-white beach like a gazelle . . . or whatever it is that springs horizontally, perpendicularly and on the bias all at the same time. Natives who have attacks of moon-madness caper this way, and it is not unusual nor very hard to understand. One just feels uncommonly full of air and free of the last vestige of self-consciousness. It feels fine.

There was not a civilized light to be seen anywhere when I alighted on the tip of the island. From this point the opposite shore returned in a straight line to the residence and being on the windward side had no beach. It was a steep bank three or four feet high built up of treasures of sea shells in all the loveliest patterns and shapes and colors a coral

island has to show. Ahead however, just about my swimming distance, I judged, was a white islet with a cluster of palmettoes and some tall coconuts on it, one of the beads on the atoll chain. It was inside the quiet lagoon . . . the protecting line of surf lay off to the right . . . and the young palms were nodding their crowns to me.

I suppose there are many people in the world who have never swum naked. And many more, alas, who will have lived and died without swimming in the middle of the Coral Sea on a moonlit night. Just from a practical angle they will never know how slick and co-operative water can be sliding along bare skin. But also they will never have seen their mortal selves vested in radiance, all gleaming white with phosphorescence, with long luminous streamers trailing off fingers and toes; and behind, a wake of whorls of light. (It's even better when there is no moon and the water is black.) Simply by turning over and floating on the back one can get a glimpse of immortality. The sky over the sea that night was a glittering infinity, a million years of stars so densely strewn across it, so huge and brilliant that the expanse was more light than color. And the moon more substance than light; it was a place. Far out on the reefs the surf droned like

the sound of a distant train as it rolls across the desert in the night, rising, falling, fading away and then echoing on as a dream sound. There was no other note for mortal ears in this vast cosmic silence. There was left just the little core of restlessness that was oneself—and even that quieted down in this world of peace without end.

It seems now that the whole system of living in our "rational" civilization must be bust-behind when we spend a third of our lives sleeping through the time of day when our senses are most acute and our soul, if we have one, is nearest the surface. The primitives know better and when the moon is full they sleep through the heat of the day. Few of us are awake to see the mystery and muted beauty of midnight, the wonderful patterns of black tree shadows, and forms against the sky, the subtle colors and tones, the strange scents that rise from familiar things as they dampen with dew, and the small sounds of night spirits that are drowned out in clamorous daylight. A night on Panasesa makes one feel that we should even be born at the other end. Then we should start life as wise and patient old people who know what things are worth working for, and grow daily stronger and more able to do them, and more lovely and unselfconscious as the twilight comes, finally exiting as dear but unessential infants, honestly regretted as we are honestly welcomed the way it is now. Some day, we decided, we should return to some Panasesa and back up. For nothing, as Don Herold our great American philosopher says, is likely to seem like heaven after this life.

It was farther to the islet than I had judged, another of the illusions created by the tropical night; and my unseasoned muscles were beginning to feel the strain when I thought I felt something sniffing at my toes. Instantly the picture of that mangled blue body of the shark's son flashed into mind and sent me leg-over-arm for the islet, whole schools of sharks in hot pursuit. I just had enough cosmic air left in me to haul myself up on the sand, and there I lay for a long time wondering how I was going to get back to a commonplace life again.

Dream sounds? Above the drone of surf I could hear a nearby something, a steady thump-pause-thump with intervals of longer pauses, like something striking hollow wood. The solution of driftwood being knocked against rocks seemed satisfactory until I remembered that there was no stone on the surface of an islet like this one. And there was not enough force in the low swells that lipped up the beach to strike a log on anything. Then by and by I began to think I smelled smoke. It even had an odor; it was the pungent ammonia smell of briny driftwood burning that suddenly made me think of a beach picnic at home—and I mentally added hot dogs and corn on the cob to the long menu we were compiling for that first meal when we got home.

The smoke odor was certainly an illusion, and the sound must be some bird. Island birds make noises like everything else in the world, and they are so elusive and well camouflaged that we had seen few of the makers of these weird rackets. But now was my opportunity. The palms were low, and if I were very quiet . . . On hands and knees I started crawling forward in the shadow of the fronds toward the sound. What I saw on the opposite side of the grove, then not ten yards off, would have stopped a better dressed girl than I was. It was a solitary native squatting beside a log.

For minutes afterward I had a harrowing time wrestling with the devil to keep from rising up suddenly in all my loveliness and saying "Boo." It would have started a native legend—if it didn't kill the native with shock first. But it would also have interrupted a very interesting business. The boy was chunking and chipping away at the log . . . which must have been driftwood, for there is no such big timber in the small reef islands . . . making a canoe and using an instrument for it that I would not have believed was any longer owned by these metal-conscious natives had I not seen it myself. It was a primitive stone adze. And it was not hard to figure out that the native was one of Panasesa's plantation line, AWOL. It was long after nine o'clock when the gang had to be accounted for in the labor quarters. But this was why I recognized him as a true artist. The rules were for others, and bed the last resort when there was work to do and still light in which to do it. You could have threaded a needle in that light.

The outside of the log was only roughly shaped, and the native was working down a long slot on the top side. Thump-hiss-thump. He held an unlighted pipe in his teeth and in-haled in a half musical note as if a tune were running through his mind, then exhaled with a hiss that blew the chips of wood away. There *was* smoke. It rose in a thin blue wisp straight up in the motionless air from one end of the slot where embers were charring the wood to facilitate chipping. Every now and then the native paused to blow up the coals with a bamboo tube and to add more chips of wood to the blaze, after which he regularly lit his pipe from the ignited end of the bamboo. The scent of the rank trade tobacco in that cool night air was like perfume, and I would have swum through a mile of sharks for a smoke myself. But the boy let his pipe go out as he resumed his work. He was a happy man. A man in two yards of calico with a log and a stone ax with which to make something out of it.

When he finally stopped, my back was aching for him. He rose then and glanced up at the moon, uncinched his sulu and dropped it on the sand, scratched his head thoroughly and then further relieved himself squatting in the water in the center of a pool of phosphorescent light. Without bothering to move to another spot he washed himself all over with the palms of his hands, ran them through his hair to dry them and then waded ashore and stood naked looking at his work as he puffed his pipe up. I knew just how he felt. He couldn't bear to leave it. But the moon was over the zenith, and he finally pushed afloat the outrigger canoe that was nosed up on the beach and hopping into it paddled off for Panasesa. I let him get about half a block away and then slid into the water silently as a crocodile, feeling more secure for the swim back with a "savage" for company than I had with the imaginary sharks.

By the time I reached the tip of the island I had found our excuse for coming back to this bugless paradise for a breather. It was to paint a portrait of the happy canoe carver. But only after the Yela Papuans were immortalized.

7

The blue slip of Sud-est was on the horizon when we got our first intimation that the *Maroma* was not scheduled for Yela. We were looking at the chart, with the Skipper, and saw above the red ink line of the course between the two islands the notation "20." Only twenty miles! "But ladies cannot camp alone on an island," the skipper worried; "you have no protector, no boys. You need boys anyway, and plenty of rice." "That's just why we have no boys," I said, "We have no rice." It was no use. The *Maroma* was not going forty miles out of her way, either for guests or for paying passengers. "Well, it'll be a long swim," said Margaret in her sweet, helpless way. Then we went back to work on the portrait sketch we were making of the Skipper with the charcoal out of San Luca's magic cigarette tin.

Margaret was sitting beside me as I worked, crooning gypsy love songs with her ukulele to keep our sitter amused. He was looking far from amused. For almost three hours he just sat and stared at Margaret's face, the taut skin over his large cheekbones scarlet and his eyes, so transparently honest and blue, looking like holes to the blue sea behind his head. He could handle a vessel and the crew of boogie-minded young Melanesians, but "ladies" made him dumb; he saw so few. When the sketch was finished, its technique determined largely by the motion of the *Maroma*, he looked at it carefully and then put it between the pages of an old *London Illustrated News* and slid the magazine under the cushion of the wall seat in the little salon where we ate our meals. "That

I will send to my daughter," he said soberly, "and tell her
it was made by two American ladies on my ship. She will be
proud of her papa." Then he ordered a tin of smörgåsbord
fish opened and we had it with a thimbleful of Holland gin
and a puritanical washer of Dubonnet. Our Skipper seemed
the most guileless man in the world.

Two shipments of copra had been picked up, and we
understood there was another on Sud-est farther east and
nearer Yela, and here we intended to disembark, bag and
bustle, no matter what the scenery. San Luca would have to
maneuver the remaining twenty miles. Meantime we were
trailing a line astern and hauling in small sharks as fast as the
line could be played out again. They were around twenty-
five pounds and still kicking, and after losing a few hooked
ones to other sharks we didn't bother playing them but gaffed
them to bring them up on deck as soon as the line could be
pulled in. This was feast and fun for the boys, who love
nothing better than to see a fat fish caught, unless it is to
catch one themselves. In the excitement they had no hum-
bler-than-thou attitude toward the *cinabadas* (Motuan for
the pidgin English white "missus") and as we slapped each
"s'ark" on the deck they unhooked it with those Melanesian
gargles of pleasure, and rushed forward to their quarters to
eat it unsalted and barely dead. When they had had enough
we just toyed with our prey, pulling in the troll line quickly
before a fish could strike. Sure enough there would be a
s'ark after it, maneuvering at the chunk of one of his less
fortunate fellows with which the hook was baited. He would
think he nearly had it and would turn over belly-up to strike,
and we would give it a powerful jerk and keep jerking until
we had drawn him up below the stern. The heavy wash from
the propeller did not distract his efforts, but it fouled our
attempts to gaff a shark unhooked, something we thought
might make an angling record.

All this was so absorbing that we did not realize what was happening to the scenery. When we looked around again we were out at sea. Sud-est was going over the glaring horizon. And the guileless Skipper was looking like a pink Scandinavian who had kidnapped two headhunters and was taking them back to Samarai!

It was not fatal, of course; we could still disembark at some other island. Should the *Maroma* call at any more. But guileless! Who, pray, was guileless?

For a long time we had been running parallel with an almost continuous line of surf, and far ahead was a bank of clouds that obscured the horizon. They were not the kind of fluffy cumuli that usually hover over an island at sunset. It wasn't sunset, anyway; it was just past midday. These were rain clouds, sunlit on top, to be sure, but low and horizontal and gray on their under side. The line of surf extended up to and disappeared in the strip of blank shadow underneath them. The Skipper joined us leaning on the rail. "Looks for rain," we observed. The Skipper's eyes were still as round and blue as a babe's "from out of nowhere into here" as he looked at the clouds ahead. "Yela," he announced.

The island of Yela was in actual fact under those clouds. We still could not believe it, not until we saw a solid-looking spot of blue extending about the cloud mass. It looked suspiciously like a mountain, like a picture of Fujiyama. It was a mountain, and it was almost three thousand feet high. No coral castle, this Yela, but of volcanic origin; and it was *all* mountains. Would we hang our hammocks over a cliff?

From then on my new-found optimism at reaching Yela left me at the rate of knots. As we ran under the clouds the sun was blotted out, the strip of glare between clouds and water became narrower and narrower until it was only a line drawn across the horizon. Then we were enclosed in a

low-ceilinged world as bleak and gray as the North Pacific
in foggy winter. Finally it began to rain, and that blotted out
even the surf of the reefs. When we finally came to anchor
in quiet water all we could see of the coast of Yela was a
deep misty gray-green between silvery water and clouds
like shredded steel wool.

Those first few minutes after the anchor chain had ceased
clanking and the engine had given its final throb were the
most strangely silent ones in our experience. It was not the
vast quiet of Panasesa where visible worlds still moved in
their eternal lanes; this was the blank stillness of the end of
all motion. We had arrived, but to deserted, god-forsaken
anticlimax. The roar of the obscured breakers far behind us
just added the note of doom, and from somewhere in the
distance ahead where the wind of the heights was sieving
the clouds into rain, came a rumble of thunder; the mutter-
ings of Wanjo, the snake god of the mountain summit, who
sends fearful storms to punish mortals. Rain, yes, but electrical storms were something we had not counted on. There
had been a comforting absence of fireworks in our island
experiences so far.

Now, we supposed, was the moment for our heroic dis-
embarkation; and we turned an unheroic eye toward the near
land. That was the moment for a low suspicion to enter *my*
mind. There was no place to land! There was even nothing
that could properly be called a coastline. Stretching as far as
we could see in the rain in both directions a dense forest of
aerial roots grew out of the water, rising to six or eight feet
above the surface before they joined into trunks and then
spread out into the limbs of mangrove trees. Nowhere was
there a strip of sand beach or even a mud or rock bank. Nowhere any sign of habitation, native or white, nor even a
canoe. And when the rain lifted we saw that the deep green
of mangroves extended far inland and beyond were mount-

ing waves of gauze-marked foothills without a break in them. The air was like something that arises from a pan of boiling water.

Margaret was "humming a little hum to herself," a sure sign of visceral fidgets and a display of the caballero that always brought out the worst in me. "Remember," I hissed, "how Marko wouldn't even let us sleep on *dry* canvas stretchers because they were miasmic . . . or is it miasmal?" "Plenty of mosquitoes and sand flies, too," contributed the Skipper unnecessarily. Margaret's brave hum turned to a thin peanut wagon whistle as the thunder rumbled again and the rain swept back. "But I thought the bad weather came only during the northwest monsoon," I accused the Skipper. "Always rains here," he answered, "the year around, but now is the time of electrical storms."

We got the use of the whaleboat without protest, and the Skipper even sent us off with two boys to row, but he did not offer to come with us to find a place to land. He watched us go down the ladder with the first expression we had seen on his face. It looked as if it were about to burst at the seams. Then just as we were shoving off he called to us to wait and handed down a gun of Viking vintage, saying, "Better you take this." "What for?" we sniffed. "Oh, maybe you meet one of those cannibals. If not, you meet a pigeon; bring him back for dinner." As we set off he had his last little joke; the steam whistle of the *Maroma* nearly parted the clouds above us, and must have notified all the living Papuans on the island that a boat was in. Wanjo, enraged, answered with a bawl of thunder and released an ocean on our heads.

The two boys, just as interested in this journey of exploration as ourselves, and hopped up now because we had a gun in the party, pulled briskly in toward the shore of mangroves and then swung to port because the water looked "good fella" in that direction. To their nautical eye the slightly opaque yellowing of the lagoon indicated a river, and sure enough, we presently found ourselves going up a funnel-shaped inlet. A short way in, however, the mangrove-lined channel split up into many channels leading off in different directions. We simply told the boys we wanted to "go along village," and let them have their head. The channel they followed presently became giddily serpentine, and alternately widened and narrowed; but it was the main one, for it continued on. Finally it was so narrow that the branches of the mangroves met overhead, and then we were traveling in a deep green gloom between walls of weird roots. And in a stillness that was broken only by the dip and trickling of oars, the drone of rain, and our incessant slapping at mosquitoes which, Godstruth, *were* the most rapacious we had yet played host to. The tide must have been low, for the stench of mangrove roots was enough to pickle your lungs.

Many of the rivers of Yela are taboo to women because coconut palms are grown along their banks, the cultivation of coconuts being one of those exclusively masculine operations (on Yela) that can be contaminated by the female. So the rivers are guarded against women by malevolent spirits which in turn are guarded by the men. This was one of the ways the Yela islanders had of remaining exclusively Papuan. The rivers were an entrance as well as an exit for the Yela stronghold, and while any stranger who appeared at the mouth of one was promptly eaten, the women were also kept away from them. There was little chance of a rendezvous with an outsider, for until a few years ago no Yela women dared set foot in a canoe no matter on what water, and none had ever visited another island.

So far we seemed to be safe from the river ghosts, for there were no coconut palms. But by and by the scene changed. The tunnel widened, and finally a strip of feeble cloud-light appeared above as palmettos and honest earth-rooted trees and

vines mingled with the mud vegetation. The cold overhead
light made the river ahead of us, with its deep shadows under
overhanging bush, look like a ribbon of silver on sable. Presently we came to stretches of sandy mud extending out from
the banks of foliage, and our noses got hot with the scent of
the quarry. The mud was scored with imprints, and to our
Daniel Boone eye that meant that men had passed this way.
Soon there must be a village or a pad leading to one.

Ahead there was a sharp bend in the river where a mud
spit with some logs on it stretched nearly across the stream.
Behind the bar was what looked like a cleared area, the
surface of which was scored every which way with furrows
as if canoes had been dragged over it. This was certainly a
landing, and I was just taking in air to tell the rower to
pull into the mud when we came to it, when the arm of the
boy sitting in the stern behind us shot past our shoulders,
grabbed the barrel of the gun and tipped it forward. We
could see nothing, but the rower sat motionless while the
boat drifted downstream. Suddenly there was a bump as the
keel struck a submerged log or root. It was a muffled bump,
but at that instant the whole river seemed to leap into life.
On the mud spit above, the logs, four of them, rose on fat
bowed legs and plunged into the water. Directly opposite
the spot we were drifting past there was a hiss, and an enormous white gaping mouth materialized in the shadow followed by about twelve feet of crocodile that slid into the
water in our direction. The water was opaque and suddenly
seemed full of spikes. An impression that the rower seemed
to share, for he was digging in for all he was worth. Rowing
still stern first. We sped downstream with the current and
a great splashing of oars and shouting, awakened crocodiles
continuing to plop out of the shadows while we continued
to be obliged to go over the spots where they had submerged.
The river was too narrow to do anything else. We took a

wrong turn and got lost in a labyrinth of roots, and backed and filled in the *culs de sac* while the mosquitoes devoured us and the rain, returning with a vengeance, rained grapeshot down on our changed minds. Nothing in the world we wanted less at that minute than to meet a Yela son of a cannibal. Nor to camp on the infested island, even to record the last living Papuan.

Yela actually is infested with crocodiles. These are the spirits that guard the rivers, and killing them is taboo as it has doubtless been for many generations. The result is that the waterways are literally alive with them, which must make it unsafe for even the men to frequent the streams. After the encircling reefs and the mangrove shores and taboos, the saurians are the Yelamen's fourth line of defense, one that should not be underestimated. There are said to be two tribes of New Guinea crocodiles; in some localities they appear to be harmless, but in others they have even been known to "capset" (pidgin combination of "capsize" and "upset") canoes in order to get at the occupants.

When we finally got out of the woods Margaret found she had been holding the gun muzzle up to receive the rain and still tied to it was the clump of orchids one of the boys had

climbed an ant-infested tree for. (He was our only casualty, and seemed to be taking the ant bites more seriously
than they warranted.) The *Maroma* was parting Wanjo's
hair with another blast . . . music, now, to our ears . . .
and alongside the vessel tied up to the rope ladder were two
empty canoes, strange-looking craft with outriggers and
built-up gunwales. Their owners, six live Yelamen, were
aboard the ship.

8

A Yela islander in the flesh is not the anticlimax one would expect after hearing his record and viewing his habitat first. He is just as miserable looking as he ought to be. These six had come out from God-knows-what hidden hutch in answer to the ship's first whistle, and the first newsworthy thing is that they were on board. Strange natives, even in much traveled districts, are seldom invited on a vessel. And especially Papuans, who are notoriously light-fingered and have been known to lift everything from a missionary's head to a chief engineer's teeth which he was resting in a glass of water. But the men, while still in their canoes, had made motions to leave when the Skipper did not appear to have any further business with them after the usual preliminary present of tobacco, so to hold them until he could get us back (we had heard the *Maroma* tootling) he had let them come on board. Now they were "under control," sitting on the deck listening to but not much entertained by the Skipper's favorite record played on our little gramophone. It was a "Meanderings of Monte" discourse on how "women's silk-k stock-kings must-t come down."

So here were the Yela Papuans we had spent sweat and tears to reach, here the blue-blooded race of races, "probably the purest Papuans living"; hook-nosed, black-skinned, long-skulled and small of stature. Evil-smelling, wet and sullen-eyed and suspicious-looking. This the people who for centuries have refused to breed with other breeds, gorilla-armed, scrawny, pot-bellied and ricket-legged from eating only their own sago. This the ultimate in race exclusiveness, one of Nature's few perfected experiments in human self-sufficiency.

We realized now that the "black Armenian" we had seen at Nari had been a Papuan, but beyond his strong features there was no resemblance to these men. He was a tall man,

and his skin was glossy and a full-blooded brown with health. All six of the visitors had the Yela curse of *kukikuki*, gray scaly patches of itching eczema that made them look like piebald albinoes. All six had blowzy black hair through which the white eggs of the centuries' descendants of lice were scattered. We appreciated now how much the Melanesian's fussing with his "grass" had to do with altering his appearance from the barbarian. His persistent applications of coral lime to his scalp to kill the "walkabouts" which also, incidentally, bleached the hair to all shades of blond, his continual scratching with the long pronged comb that kept the kinky hairs separated and standing up, and the trimming into geometrical shapes and ornamenting with feathers and flowers, all these attentions which we had thought male vanity were only sartorial self-respect. The Yelamen had combs stuck in their armbands or over an ear, but they were used only to scratch the scalp. The coiffure was a wet mess of ragged-end, tangled ropes of greasy wool from whence issued the odor of rancid coconut oil.

Unlike most inhabitants of the islands, these Papuans wore few ornaments and, with a single exception, the few were unimaginative. The man I chose to make a study of had only a clam shell bracelet above the elbow of each arm and the incised lobes of his ears were encased in tiny tortoise shell rings the color of his skin. But he was the one of the group who wore the Yela "pants." (The rest were in faded blue calico sulus.) This loin covering is a harness of palm fiber rope that is wound round and round the hips and allowed to fall in loops down the thighs, somewhat like a Follies girl's didy of pearls. The central motif is a bull's eye of bleached-white pandanus palm leaf that is drawn between the legs and up over the abdomen above the navel, where it is hitched underneath the top rope. It covers everything, or properly should. The bottom loops of our model's pants had fallen sloppily down around his knees, which caused us to reflect on the practicality of such a garment in case of a hasty retreat before an enemy. One loose end, and the Yelaman would find himself hog-tied. The fact that this was the only ornament the native wore and that he wore it where he did might suggest the ultimate preoccupation of an inbred people. It was never meant for modesty at any rate. We bought the pants right off the fellow for three sticks of tobacco, and the only ones present who were shocked were the shy Skipper and the Melanesian hoodlums on board.

The harness was acquired because there was not time to paint more than the man's head and we needed it to use on another model later in order to finish the figure. The *Maroma* had to get out of the lagoon before dusk or anchor inside all night, so while I worked against time Margaret got a demonstration from the other natives on how to don the loops. Later whenever I saw my friend crooking her little finger back as she drank tea in some cultured society I made winding motions around my hips. This reminded her of two smelly naked Papuans . . . they had removed their own sulus for the demonstration . . . winding around her middle the greasy ropes of our model. And it refreshed her memory of the sweaty hour later when she posed, with the rope and pandanus leaf on, over a bathing suit because we found we could not get them on a native model properly.

The original sitting was uneventful because the Yelaman just sat. He did not know what for, but the prepayment of tobacco was enough to persuade him to do whatever was asked. However, he never took his baleful eyes from me as I worked. It occurred to me then that I might have been a little timid if this picture-making had taken place anywhere but on the *Maroma*. The Yela men are not distinguished for chivalry. In the not-so-old days, when they killed it was a gang murder; never less than a crowd of men armed with clubs set on a single unarmed individual, and most of their victims were children. They are no longer cannibals today; but when they were, which is within the memory of living men, their man-eating was only thinly ornamented with the usual excuse of religious ceremony. Nor did they always kill to eat, so it was not entirely meat hunger. It seems that they just liked to kill. When a chief died it was customary to kill and bury someone with him so that he would not be lonely in the hereafter, but there was little warfare between the few tribes on the island, so one of the chief's own subjects, and the more the better, was the sacrifice. Adults could run fast even if they couldn't run far, so it was children who became the victims.

But whether the prey was child or adult, tribesman or enemy, there was one customary way of dispatching him. He was not killed outright, but was clubbed helpless. His arm and leg bones and sometimes his ribs were intentionally broken, after which he was left until needed. If he had not died of shock by this time he was stretched out face down on the ground, and men kneeled on his back over the chest, crushing and smothering the life out. The primitives of the Coral Sea are not usually so imaginative in their methods of killing, and the excuse in this case if it could be traced back to its origin may be merely that of good meat cooks who always try to retain the juices.

The windfall of shipwrecked Chinese was the final orgy of the Yela cannibals, and it gave them a Benjamin's mess for their talents. The French ship that was returning the coolies to their homeland from Australia was wrecked, not on the coast of Yela, but on the girdle of reefs that surrounds it at a place called Heyon Island. It was actually a desert isle, and the survivors who struggled ashore there were without shelter from the sun, and separated by two miles of shark-infested water from food and drink on Yela. But these tribes of Papuans were not quite sporting enough to paddle out and kill three hundred and twenty-seven half-drowned and un-armed coolies. And besides, meat, which is what a dead China-man was to the islanders, will not keep in this humid climate. Therefore, they kept the coolies alive by taking them food and drinking water, but for every ministering trip they brought back to Yela, "on the hoof" so to speak, a batch for the "cooking pot." Actually the classical cannibal cooking pot is not much used in preparing meat in these islands, and when it is used for boiling vegetables, it is still not the caldron of the cartoon; it is a small clay jar, seldom of more than two gallons capacity. Meat, including human flesh, is roasted or steamed, tied up in leaf-wrapped packages.

Such customs as killing people to eat them can be "educated" out of a group in a very short time, but such a degree of insensitivity as the Yelamen reveal in their manner of killing must be an inherent quality which it might take more than a generation of sweetness and light to breed out. There was nothing reassuring about our Yela visitors that made us think living alone among them would be comfortable.

One of the surface features that gave our model, as well as the other men, a strange look was the absence of eyebrows. The eyes of the usual islander are sunken under a full projecting frontal bone and rather heavy eyebrows, which gives him a mysterious "black" look, but the face of the model was naked. Probably the weather of Yela made it possible to do away with this protection from the sun; anyway, the eyebrows had been plucked out and it was a neater job than any of our maidens achieve with tweezers.

The other peculiarity of the model was inside his head. When the study had been carried as far as I could go in the graying light we turned it around for the man to see, to get his reaction. At sight of it the other visitors had burst into strange vocal noises in the native language that "sounds like the snarling of a dog interspersed with hiccoughs," but the model himself gave us a kind of mute horse laugh. He stared at the picture for a minute, chin out, then threw up his head and curling back a loosely attached upper lip, bared his teeth. And held it. There was a curious wheezing sound through the nose. This, we think, is the gayest laugh the morose Yelaman can achieve. Meantime it was worth having seen the inside of the Yela mouth. We were familiar with the sight of natives with lips crimson and teeth badly stained by the juices of betel nut and lime, but the model's teeth were walnut brown and so caked with residue from betel nut that there were no divisions between them. The two solid rows of dentures protruded like the false teeth of a clown, a sign of excess that was once only the privilege of chiefs. On such a small island the supply of betel nut was limited and in control of the chiefs, and any commoner who could get his teeth as badly caked as the chief's was suspected of tapping the royal cache and was consequently broken up in little pieces and eaten. Seeing those crimson-smeared black bones in the prehensile-lipped mouth, one could easily visualize the model "craunchin'" on a chunk of coolie, or even on one's favorite anatomy.

Somewhere the hot red sun was setting as the *Maroma* got up speed and started down the lagoon for the ship's passage. I worked as long as I could see the coastline on a sketch for material to be used as a background when I repainted the Yela figure. The rain had backed into the misty foothills, and the water of the lagoon in the foreground was like a flexible mirror repeating the "long ago and far away" mystery of the outpost island. It was a secret place, this lone mountain in the sea, hidden away under its eternal clouds, fenced in by its girdle of sharp-toothed reefs, guarded by its river spirits and forbidding-looking primitives. I had the feeling as I painted that I was on the outside looking in, not on honest land, but on some lost portion of the world's beginning where dark things had been going on for centuries unknown to the rest of the world.

For a long time after our call at Yela the reason for it, the call, was not altogether clear. We could see ourselves that camping anywhere along the coast where we were taken would have been impossible, but there are plantations on the island and we could not understand why the *Maroma* had not called at one of these, where we could at least have landed on a beach. Then when war came to New Guinea everything seemed to be clear. The Government had expected action in the Coral Sea, we thought, and was at last building up defenses to make the territory a real protection to Australia, and travelers would hardly be invited to look in on them. The Skipper, out of friendliness, was willing to let us have a glimpse at our obsession but without risking our landing.

Yela has some features that are at least useful enough to have interested the Germans in the first war, apparently, for there is a native legend which concerns two "German steamers" that "haunted" the island at that time. If this is pure legend the natives, who presumably had never then witnessed naval action, did a rather realistic job of yarning. As the story goes, the two German ships bombarded the native hero as he was paddling his canoe, first firing with their guns on one side of the vessel and then, getting "tired" in that quarter, firing from the other side. For a layman it is easy to imagine that Yela would have all sorts of advantages to anyone who held it in case of war in the Coral Sea. Its western lagoon, which is almost thirty miles long, is largely free of reefs and has ample soundings and two ship passages that can admit vessels of deep draught . . . a quiet body of water in mid-sea almost equal distances from the seats of government of the three British mandated territories, Tulagi, Rabaul and Port Moresby, and only a little farther from Australia. And in a region where the sun blazes down like a searchlight to the very depths of the ocean floor and even schools of fish may be seen from the air, this island alone with its reef-fortified lagoon is almost the year around obscured by its blanket of rain clouds. Whatever was meant to be hidden there would really be hidden from observation from the air.

But Australia was not building up defenses at Yela or anywhere else in the islands those days. (On the contrary she was helping the United States to build up Japan's offensives

by sending her shiploads of scrap iron.) We were not suspected of being Mata Hari with our sketchbooks and camera.
The Skipper simply wanted to hustle us back to Panasesa. It
seems the plantation company was having trouble keeping
overseers in the atoll, the station being a lonely spot and the
succession of overseers being bachelors or older married men
whose families remained in the south. A bride, it was probably thought, should stay anchored for a while and hold an
overseer at his job. But white brides are not usually to be
found in New Guinea. Then suddenly here were landed right
in Samarai two unattached prospects who even wanted a trip
in the direction of Panasesa. And if our informant was right,
that heaven-eyed Skipper, who was genuinely guileless, was
sent out with sailing orders to play Cupid.

9

The sun along the equator rises the year around at about six o'clock, and this is a time of day for singing paeans. There is a sweet breeze swinging the hanging palm fronds, and the world looks all refreshed by its night with God, as if it were just new and beginning. Down at the labor quarters on Panasesa the yips of the natives assembling for the day's orders sounded like a gang of boys setting out on a Saturday fishing trip. All this quieted down the minute we left the veranda with the *Taubada*, and by the time we reached the quarters the faces of the yippers were composed for white inspection, personalities withdrawn. Which one of those brown boys—who all look equally stupid in a labor line— was the canoe whittler who had whished a tune between his teeth and pipe and so loved what he was doing that he defied plantation rules and voluntarily did an extra shift at night? We could not identify him.

The boys were kept in line for the purpose of locating the carver, and while the questioning was going on our six o'clock spirits sank at the rate of knots. Until this minute of seeing an aggregate of New Guinea Melanesians we had been under the impression that we had painted all the types of natives who could illustrate the race. Now we saw how much there was still to be done. These boys at Panasesa, recruited from all along the eastern coast and adjacent islands, were as different from the Melanesians of New Britain and the Solomons as a Cajun American is from a New Englander or a Minnesota farmer. As different as those eastern Melanesians are from

one another on the various islands. Even among these New
Guinea boys there was a wide variety of types. Wisiki, the
Taubada's houseboy (so named for the well known beverage
[whisky] doubtless under the impression that it was a popular Christian name) was a Motuan from the tribe around Port
Moresby and compared to the other boys present he was out
on the end of the mongoloid limb of the family tree. The
Motuans are not overly fond of hard plantation work and
so do not develop the muscles of other indentured natives, but
they make good houseboys and Wisiki was typical. He was
a familiar kind of thyroid type, not shorter than the rest of
the boys but small-framed and lithe and with a jerky hilarity
that in a group would produce the primitive version of the
"zoot suit" movement. His taupe brown face was round and
flat and soft looking, he had a short upturned nose and even
the juvenile "mongoloid fold" of the upper eyelids. His black
hair was an enormous glamour bob that covered his forehead
and the back of his neck and was still abundant enough to
stand seven or eight inches above his head. Compared to,
say, Iomai he represented a feminine-looking stock.

Iomai, who inevitably became Me-oh-my, was the canoe
carver, and native of Panapompom of the nearby Deboyne
islands. As he stood in the horizontal sunlight against a background of blue lagoon, his muscular stocky body and strong-
boned face seemed as hard and rich in hue as copper. His hair
was an uncompromisingly masculine mound of ocher-colored
wool on the top of his head, tall to protect his brain from the
sun and ocher yellow only because the lime delouser had
bleached it.

There was nothing beguiling about the carver's face, and
at the moment no humor nor any happiness; he only looked
miserable and embarrassed. Iomai, in fact, was blushing a
negroid blush, the normally creamy whites of his eyes flushed
with pink. Wisiki, the hussy, had tattled that he was the one

who was going off in the outrigger every night, and the other boys were making the most of it. It was not open laughter but savvy grins and a kind of clucking like those strange sounds small boys make when they first realize they can do something with their voices besides talk. Iomai was embarrassed—not over being caught disobeying plantation rules but because he was being made conspicuous by the discovery. And to be different from others is a great joke. Everyone had expected the *Taubada* to "fight-m strong fella" (reprimand) for his infraction of rules; and everyone, except Iomai, was disappointed when he only ordered the boss boy to go with the carver to the islet and tow back the log he was working on.

That, so far as the *Taubada* was concerned, finished the matter. It was not thought necessary to explain to Iomai himself that he was to have his portrait painted as he worked on the canoe; he would just be instructed to sit with it when the log was brought in. Pay and reprimands are dealt out by the plantation overseer, but orders are given to the boss boy, and he sees that they are carried out. This is to preserve prestige. But Iomai did not even wait until the *Taubada* was out of hearing to voice his reaction. He was protesting something in a language we thought was his own until it began to run down, when it proved to be pidgin English. His tone was moderate enough but his motions were vehement; he jerked his arms toward the islet, then jerked them toward his chest in the motion I had seen him use with the adze, while the other natives, including the boss boy, stood absorbed as if they were listening to an eye-witness account of a raid of the dread Kukukuku. The *Taubada* returned and listened with a quizzical expression on his lean face, and for a few minutes after Iomai stopped talking there was an impressive silence. Then the boss boy summed it up in one short sentence; "Boy he say canoe taboo." The new canoe, it appeared, was in a delicate stage of its creation where it could not be moved without endangering its career. Very well then, we said, we would go over to the islet with Iomai and paint the picture there. Then the whole truth came out; the embryo canoe was too fragile to be looked on by female eyes. And it was because of such very things as this taboo that we especially wanted to paint the canoe-making!

It all begins, rather remotely I must confess . . . though the reader may presently see the connection between the custom and the kind of paintings we wanted . . . with a tradition of gift exchange, a business called *kula*. In the Southeast Division there is a ring of islands, excluding only Yela and, I believe, Sud-est, around which the natives exchange traditional gifts with traditional co-givers. There are just two kinds of presents, neither of which is useful and both of which are possessed *only* to be given away. One is a heavy clamshell bracelet ornamented with smaller shells and raffia, the other is an elaborate harness of red wampum. Such clamshell rings, unornamented, and the wampum in fathom lengths, are currency ordinarily. The curious feature of the custom is that the two objects are traded for one another, the bracelets traveling only clockwise around the ring of islands and being exchanged for the necklaces coming anticlockwise. Dollars exchanged for even dollars, to all appearances. Most of the bracelets and necklaces in existence are old, for the savvy young natives, while they participate in the functions, no longer make the presents, so the objects traveling the ring today have probably made the circuit hundreds of times.

The gift-making voyages are going on constantly somewhere in the ring, but no one village or, properly, tribe of villages, makes more than one kula journey annually, and receives only one set of gift-bringers. It takes the full year to get ready for the two events. First of all there must be canoes. Men must fell the trees for them, somehow the pig stock must be increased to pay for the making of them and finally weeks and even months are spent decorating them. Meantime the women are planting and cultivating and harvesting and in the end preparing the food for the two big feasts, that which takes place at the departure of canoes and the other when visiting gift-bearers arrive. They must wrest what pleasure they can from the feasts, for it is only the men who make the trip.

On the surface there appears to be no reason for the custom outside of sociability and perhaps the normal human desire to see other faces and eat their pigs for a change. This may be the origin of the tradition, but it has had two far more interesting results. One is that this group of islanders, almost alone of all such geographically related groups in the Coral Sea, are at peace with one another and apparently have been since long before the advent of the white man. The second is so tied up with the first that it would be hard to say which is cause and which result. This is the interdependent economic relationship. Each island manufactures for trading with its *kula* co-givers some commodity which it is best qualified to produce. The Amphlett Islands, for example, have good clay for pottery, so when the men of Amphlett sail for the Trobriands with their bracelets they take along jars and come back with the hardwood food bowls and drums and dance shields that are so expertly carved by the Trobriand men. The stone adzes ground out on Marua and the shell ornaments made along the eastern coast of the mainland, which is also in the ring, work their way around the group in the same way, via the *kula* sing-sings (dances and feasts).

The commodities are traded for one another at a long-established rate of exchange. And I should like to say that it was based on the rate of man-hours employed in manufacture, but I might be suspected of pointing a moral. And

anyway I am not sure. I do know, however, that business
carries on without bloodshed in spite of lacking our supply-
and-demand price-fixing. Meantime, it is an amusing feature
of the custom that the moneymakers of the ring do not belong
to it. These are the Yela Islanders. But the principle of special qualification still applies to them. The red shell that
makes the higher denomination wampum, that which goes
into the *kula* necklaces, is abundant among the reefs of Yela,
and even before these Papuans were on speaking terms with
the Melanesians of the ring, they were laboriously cutting
and grinding the shell into tiny disks, stringing it into fathom
lengths and sending it out on the market via their only friends,
on nearby Sud-est. But there was no gift exchange attached
to this transaction. The Yelamen took fat pigs in trade for
their product.

The red shell for wampum is to be found elsewhere in the
kula ring islands, but it seems to have been recognized that
the Yelamen had the monopoly in working it. And they remained without competition until just a few years ago, when
an Australian living on Sud-est designed and had made in
London a machine for cutting and drilling shell for use as
money. With it he was buying coconuts from the village
natives for making into copra (which was exported for good
King's silver), and was even paying the labor on his plantation with it until the government decided that he was a
competitor of its own and suppressed his activities.

Of all the products of the group by far the most important
is the canoe. It is the vehicle of the *kula* voyages, in fact the
only means of transportation for anyone, and the specialists
are the natives of the Deboyne Group of which Panapompom, home of Iomai, is the second largest island. At this
point we reach familiar ground. The canoe-makers achieve
the nearest thing to a civilized racket to be found in the

system. They are the aluminium trust, plumbers' union, holy rollers and D.A.R. all rolled into one. The manner in which they have the edge on other equally good log-chippers is not that they are organized into a trade guild; instead each canoe-maker has inherited individually a monopoly on certain "in" ghosts, the spirits who have the stuff that goes into an ordinary log, making it a speedy canoe that will stay afloat and topside in a storm. Not anyone can go and knock out a canoe from any old log just because he has an "ackis" (ax) any more than we can get a wrench and hitch up a gas stove and be blessed by the city plumbing inspector. There are rites beginning with the sorcerer-selected tree and continuing down to the launching with charms supplied by the select brotherhood at so many pigs per. The carver is not overpaid for his work, but he uses his monopoly on the spirits to beat off competition—and what should be a public utility becomes a source of power. No one would use a craft that was not properly charmed.

One of the hundred and one taboos in canoe construction is that concerning its pollution by women. No one can tell a woman that this banishing of women during the rites was not to preserve that aura of masculine mystery without which men would surely lose the upper hand in the battle of the sexes. Moreover the making of a canoe is an inspirational business. The carver will work a little while and then wander off and do something else, returning to the job only when he feels the urge. And that is not the way a woman likes to see a job done. So we have such beliefs as that a woman even casting her eye on an unfinished canoe will sink it when it gets into the water. In some districts the carver may not even have sex relations with his wife while he is working on a project. Though all that time she must be preparing him special food which is taken to him by the anxious tribesmen who have ordered the craft.

If Iomai had not raised such a fuss over his driftwood on the island we would not have suspected that he was one of the holy craftsmen. We would therefore not have persisted in painting his portrait, and his canoe spirits would not have been called on to attempt the spectacular revenge they did.

10

Margaret's task in this painting of Iomai was, as usual, to get me set up with my playthings on the beach and then, as was not unusual, to do something about our public. Most artists, I believe, prefer to stand up to paint, so that they can walk back frequently to see how the work carries from a distance . . . and while backing up knock their head on low-hanging branches or trip over a root or electric-light cord. This has the added advantage of keeping a happy expectant look on the model's face. But standing up on the beach I could not even see Iomai's face. He was sitting down in the stern of the outrigger canoe, which was pushed off from shore just far enough to be afloat, and he was hanging his head toward his lap in misery. Since he would not produce his log to be painted (and to have forced him would not have helped the posing) he had been induced (ordered) to deck himself out in "fashion 'long limlimbu," the adornments of the *kula* voyager. And he was now, for the purposes of the painting, setting out in the Panasesa outrigger. Probably in the village these personal decorations would have been much more elaborate, for there is dancing at the feasts, but Iomai did very well for a desert plantation. A bone stick shaped like the Kaiser's mustache and on which there was a delicate incised pattern was thrust through the septum of his nose and in his hair was a big plume of white and gray feathers which have never been identified. All the rest of his ornaments were braided sennit bracelets and leg bands of black, red and yellow designs into which were thrust wads of dried "grass"

which looked like seaweed. This is the tag-end school of
sartorial decoration and is peculiar to Melanesia. Iomai had
his name in upside-down English letters tattooed on his chest,
but it had not been visible until now, with all the colors of
his skin heightened by a liberal coating of coconut oil. On
his face he had painted a double line of red and black running from the forehead down his nose and across one cheek.
The meaning of these lines was not revealed to us then, but
we know now that they were the reason for more clucking
by the other boys which in turn was the cause of Iomai's
sheepishness. In any case, in order to see this face at all I
had to sit down too—and as far down the slope of sand as the
water permitted.

Then, the spot having been selected, we began the lengthy
business of constructing an outdoor studio. The big native
mat was spread over the sand so that when I began scrambling
around in the throes of creative ecstasy I wouldn't be painting
with sand and oil, the umba-umba was stuck up and tried at
different angles in a futile attempt to make it really shade the
painting canvas, ditto the canvas and easel in the hope of
finding some position without reflected glare (with the same
results), and then everything was roped together to keep it
from falling. The last thing was to squeeze the oil paints out
on the palette. Squeeze is an overstatement. The tubes were
hot when we picked them up, and we simply removed the
cap and let the oily pigment drool out . . . and then run off
the palette onto the mat if the ground were not exactly level.
Finally everything was ready, always excepting the model.

All the time this was going on the sun had been rising in
the sky, getting whiter with heat; and Iomai, sitting unpro-
tected under its beating rays, was reduced to semivertical
molasses. Melanesians, for all their living almost on the equator, are not children of the sun when they can avoid it. Their
villages are well shaded by trees, the thatched roofs of their

houses are feet thick and they never walk nor sit in the sun if there is shade. Even the heads of the salt-water natives are insulated by half a foot of hair over their brains. But Iomai's suffering was caused largely by our audience. Wisiki had brought a pitcher of lime juice down from the house and he was still standing holding it in the sun with a catty grin on his face. The two plantation boys who had helped to haul the canoe down into the water and erect the palm-mat sail were waiting for further orders—while hoping that Iomai would explode before they got them—to return to work. The savvy old boss boy was on hand, ostensibly to see that Iomai did what we wanted but really with the expectation of getting a handout of tobacco if the *Taubada* ever removed himself from the scene. The *Taubada* was there just to get stepped on by Margaret apparently. For a member of a society that makes a cult of not standing out from the crowd Iomai was being tortured. Margaret's last duty therefore was to disperse the watchers, and she did it by escorting the *Taubada* back to his work on the plantation, at which the boys followed. Ah, paradise—now to work.

In about fifteen minutes I was bawling everyone back. The sun! This was the first time I had tried to work right out under it, and I was learning some new things about it. It was shining straight through the black umbrella, glaring even through the sized painting canvas, reflecting up from the white sand all around me; and Iomai's oiled and oozing skin was just a mass of glittering highlights against a glittering mass, the lagoon. They came running with a sail tarpaulin, which was thrown over the umbrella, touching the sand all around except for a hoist in the rear to light the painting canvas. Then I crawled inside the coop with my playthings again and was closed in except for a slit on the lagoon side through which to see Iomai. At last, *now* paradise!

After about ten minutes in the hotbox I went up to the house to change from modest slacks into garments suitable for painting portraits on a coral isle, bra-and-shorts and the hell with prestige. Iomai had decided to catch up on the sleep he had lost by making a canoe nights, but my reappearance gave him insomnia. And I don't think it was because I put his mind on gender. It was because I required him to sit out there in the sun and broil while I, perhaps the first white woman he had ever seen and certainly the nakedest he would ever, sat inside a tarpaulin and talked strong fella to myself. He was alert and motionless watching the slit of my coop, and from then on he made a perfect model.

In case the blessed reader has never painted a picture it should be explained that paintings are not built up in pieces. That is, one portion like a figure is not completed and then something else like a canoe finished. One works all over the canvas (so they tell me) carrying all parts along at the same stage of incompletion until some outsider comes along and seeing that the picture will not be improved by any more work, does something to terminate it. So it was that though Iomai's figure was still in the "rough stages," I was shortly faced with the background, which was the lagoon.

The lagoon looked blue now that I could see it, just a simple very intense blue, and I used blue paint. It was as unlike the translucent, opalescent radiance of the real thing as a glass eye is. In fact blue paint on the canvas looked black in contrast to the lagoon outside. I saw that I should have to apply my mind to this, figure out the nature of the thing and reproduce it by illusions. Therefore: the sea was, first of all, a heavy level sheet of something hugging the earth, perhaps the most extensive level of anything on the globe. But it was transparent, and what was under it was not level. The sea bottom was all hillocks and valleys of snow-white sand. That

was why, because of the varying depths, the degree and hue
of blueness changed every few inches in the perspective. But
between the level top and uneven bottom a multitude of
things was happening, and you could see them all with your
naked eye. Ten billion suns blinked on and off on the rip-
pling surface, shooting diamonds into my eyes and wriggling
rays down through the moving depths where they bounced
back off the brilliant white sea bottom, creating more wriggling rays. One facet of the ripples reflected the limitless
blue of heaven overhead, another showed the depths of the
sea bottom, always shifting and yet with changeless organization over the whole. It was like an opal in more ways than
one, the unbeatable one being that neither the opal nor water
has any self-color; they are all refracted light. And it is given
only to God to make light.

However, by a process of painting on and scraping off I discovered what a lagoon was not. It was not an illusion of cobalt
blue, not ultramarine, nor cerulean, emerald, chartreuse, rose,
coral, nor violet. Alone. It was all of these colors side by
side or superimposed. Or something. It was an intangible,
alive with sun as a face is alive with soul.

Salty sweat was in my eyes, soupy paint in my hair and
sand in my cigarette and mouth, and my sitzplatz was wet.
With perspiration I thought. Iomai's orange hair bobbing
slowly up and down past the currently orchid horizon was
enough to upset one's stomach. The boy stared at the tent in
alarm as I began scraping my latest lagoon off the canvas.
The water I had painted looked exactly like a wrecked bakery
truck I had once seen. It had been delivering a load of what
appeared to have once been entirely loganberry pies, for the
white truck itself and the scenery over a radius of fifty feet
was plastered with awful shades of blue. I lay back to laugh,
and sank into inches of water. The tide had crept up and
the studio was afloat. So I crawled out of it on hands and

knees and, greatly to Iomai's interest, kept right on going past him into the lagoon, changing the crawl to a breast stroke when the element demanded it. I never looked back, for I intended to drown myself.

After about a week of this kind of joy-through-creative-work we released Iomai to return to his cooler job of lugging hundred-pound sacks of coconuts on his back, and I tackled the lagoon alone. It seemed especially hot the morning I went to work on it. The sweat rolled in streams out of my scalp, running down into my eyes and dripping off my nose and chin. Wisiki finally brought me a pail of water with a sponge in it, and when I wasn't swabbing with it I had the sponge pinned on top of my head because it gave the illusion of cooling my brain. The air was "thick" and hard to get into the lungs, and outside the coop it was motionless. There was a curious stillness all over the island, as if even the normal sounds of chirping native voices and an occasional bang of a pan in the distant house-cook were not strong enough to get through the pressure. Margaret was on the veranda labeling and labeling her collection of shells, and every now and then when I stuck my head out of the coop for a breather I saw her run her hand over her face and snap her arm, and I knew the sweat was flying.

Margaret had had a lot of misery with her shells. There was a good book of conchology in the house, and guided by it she had collected, cleaned and labeled three or four hundred fine specimens, even discarding old ones when she found better ones. It was a smelly job, because often the shell's inhabitant had died indoors and the decayed remains had to be dug out of the chambers, the shell thoroughly washed and then put out on the hot sand to dry—at which time she did the tedious labeling. One morning she found about half her best nautilus specimens missing, and in their places an identical number of strange shells. Hermit crabs had found the clean nautiluses in the night and had moved in, walking off with Margaret's collection on their backs and leaving their untidy discards. We met labeled crabs for days afterward, and Margaret was brute enough to reclaim her property. The new occupants were stubborn about being dispossessed and only retreated further indoors when she tried to pull them out by a claw, but a few minutes in boiling water did it. Now she had the precious retrieved shells as well as numerous other hard-won specimens, including the conch-shell trumpets she had made herself, lined up along the sunny edge of the veranda ready for crating. Though the house was about half a city block back from the beach, in the stillness I thought I could hear sighing as she lettered and pasted and lettered and pasted.

It must have been almost noon when a curious sound outside caused me to pause in my work. . . . I was no longer referring to the lagoon as a model; I knew what it looked like. My problem was to match it on the canvas. The sound was almost like an airplane flying very high. Above the clouds, a kind of who-ing murmur. When I looked out I noticed the water was one color it had not been before. It was a deep green like northern water. There were clouds over it, though above Panasesa the sun was still blazing. "Looks for a wet," I thought and began cleaning up my palette. It was soon apparent that the sound was wind going through the stand of palms, but a very curious sound indeed. Then there was a bang up at the house and simultaneously the conch shell began grunting. That would be Margaret's "sing out" for *kai-kai*, but it did not speed me. Luncheon would be hot tinned mutton pie with an indestructible Melanesian crust two inches thick—and we had already eaten enough mutton to baa. Then another sound made me shoot my head outside the curtain in a hurry. I just had time to see that the world was black and then everything rose in the air around me.

A blast of sand struck me in the face and after that I saw nothing. I was lying flat on the beach, with a wind going over me that was taking the pins out of my hair.

At that time Nordhoff and Hall's famous blow of the South Seas was mercifully unknown to me, so as I lay there being sandblasted, undressed and scalped I was ignorant of the possibilities of the sea rising and washing over the low slip of land. But I soon could feel and hear enough to get my own idea of a hurricane. The surf on the windward side of the island, from which direction the gale was coming, was not at first booming any louder than usual . . . the sound in the palms drowned out all others . . . but the spray was like hail driving right across the island. The wind in the fronds was a hundred bullroarers, moaning, whining, roaring all together. Pitched high. Coconuts pelting down on the iron roofs and thudding on the sand all through the acres were an all-out bombardment. There was a big crash, and something went banging past me. It could have been the mutton-pie crust but was a sheet of iron siding from the house-cook. Then pans and huge palm fronds began sailing over me, as the booming of the surf rose over the wind. Above it I could plainly hear the insistent mooing of the conch shell, a sound as ominous in this thrashing as a fog horn in a winter storm at sea. It occurred to me then that Margaret must think I had been blown out into the lagoon and was calling for an answer. I nearly had my head turned inside-out when I opened my mouth to shout, and it was instantly filled with sand. I had better make a try for the house before she did something heroic. Anyway I wanted company.

All of that two or three hundred yard trip I opened my eyes only twice. I crawled like a three-legged lizard, one hand cupped over my nose so that I could breathe, and my one alarming thought was that I might miss the house and crawl right over the island. When I looked to see, which was backwards, there were no familiar landmarks. Those tall straight palms were leaning over at a frightening angle, their fronds horizontal, and the air was filled with foreign matter, coconuts, branches, husks, sand and water, sheets of paper—our expedition notes—and even sea shells. It was a dishpan from the denuded house-cook nearly stripping the knobs off my spine that assured me I was still in the lee of the house. If it still stood. I felt seasick and it must have been the pressure on the eardrums for my ears were aching with it.

The second time I looked was when a strange human cry broke through the clamor. It was the *Taubada*. He was making his way in from north-northeast, and he had been bopped on the head by a coconut. The glimpse I got of him was so overwhelming that hysteria finally got the upper hand, and I lay on the sand jerking with laughter until he got to my side. (He thought I was wounded.) He had been trying to get to the house like a British gentleman on two feet by darting from tree to tree, and the instant I saw him he had paused in the lee of a buckling palm and was clinging to it with one hand and holding his injured head with the other.

He was still in his pants, but they were full of wind; and his hair, in need of the barber's touch, and the arms of his shirt which he had tried to bind around his face were standing out on the horizontal like the frond above, pointing east while the planter faced west. He was like a *mae*, which is an amphibious snake of the Solomon Islands that can assume the form of a seductive young girl for the purpose of tempting the young men. The way the young men know which of the tempting girls is a *mae*, if it makes any difference, is by the fact that its arms and legs bend the wrong way.

The blow on the head had made the *Taubada* so dizzy that he was now willing to emulate a plebeian American and crawl to the house with me. When we got around to the lee side of the veranda we thought we had a reasonable chance,

and stood up; but the minute we opened the door to one of
the rooms the wind tearing down into its uncovered top
sailed out the open doorway and struck us in the face with
everything loose.

Inside, my old friend Margaret, whom I had imagined
wringing the skin off her hands in anxiety for me, was standing in a sheltered corner convulsed by her unseasonable
sense of humor. I could laugh too, later; but at that minute
my face was too stiff from its beating and the layer of wet
sand. Besides, I was now becoming thoroughly frightened.
The house sounded like the inside of a boogie-woogie trap-
drum. The whole structure was jerking loosely on its piles
in the sand, and the iron roof, open to the blast underneath,
clanged savagely as if it must rise in the air at any minute.
There were no more coconuts falling, but every now and then
a great heavy frond struck the metal over our heads like a
demolition bomb. But the house held together all through,
and in less than three-quarters of an hour the highest wind
had passed. The sky overhead was still black and racing, but
toward the west horizon could be seen a slender streak of
the sun shining feebly through a yellow haze. Curiously, there
had been no rain. We could only conclude that it had been
raining horizontally and would get down to us later. It did,
in something like a cloudburst. The surf on the windward
beach was a thundering and continuous wall of foam, the
sea behind it white for miles. Before it was over the surf
had torn over a low place down the plantation, sweeping
away a lane of palms and almost making two islands out of
Panasesa. This apparently is the force that counteracts the
coral polyps' work and keeps them from strewing the whole
ocean with islands.

The *Taubada* admitted with typical Papuan nonchalance
that it had been a "dinkie-die blow." Perhaps it wasn't a
record cyclone, but any movement of the air that can fill

your umbilicus with sea shells deserves a braver name than "blow." It must have scalped the reef islands of all their thatched roofs. Ordinarily European islanders do not waste their breath defending their weather, but we could never get anyone in Papua to admit that the region was visited by hurricanes and cyclones such as sweep the China Sea. Nevertheless the Coral Sea is officially in a tropical cyclone belt, the blows originating in the "summer" months (January to March) somewhere along the east coast of Australia and blowing north. Now we understood why Panasesa was so clean. The tall palms were a lovely harp for the normal trade winds to sing through, but without either underbrush or hills there was no protection when a real wind came up. The island was simply peeled of everything loose, including a collection of shells, a picture painting equipment and all the expedition notes, photographs and films that I had been bringing up to date on the veranda. Ah, paradise—alas!

The lagoon quieted down quickly, but the water remained cloudy with sand for days, and until it cleared we salvaged the surface for our belongings, using the launch. On the far side of the lagoon, beached on different islands, we picked up both the wooden easel and the outrigger we had been painting. Iomai was one of the boys helping, and he cast a reproachful glance at the *cinabadas* when we reached the canoe. It was stripped. Sail and outrigger were gone, and there was not left more than a fragment of the vine that had bound the framework to the hull. Our wood-handled brushes were strewn all over the South Seas but we retrieved a few, enough to work with until more could be sent up from Sydney . . . if we stayed in New Guinea. Also our paint tubes were still safe on the spot where last seen. We had only to dig down in the sand to recover them.

The portrait of Iomai was naturally given up as drowned "finish," but that was not nearly so painful as the loss of the painting umbrella. This could not be replaced easily, because we had covered the framework ourselves in the beginning and it had all sorts of mechanical improvements over an ordinary beach umbrella—which it had been in the store. It was mostly in the hope of retrieving the umba-umba that we organized the diving cruise when the water cleared.

It was a lovely day for a water picnic. The lagoon was again as innocently smooth and transparent as a bird bath, and as dazzling with blues and twinkling diamonds. We took three rejoicing plantation boys and Iomai and Wisiki, all salt-water boys, and from the start they were under the water more than they were above it. Tea and coffee pots, pails and saucepans and paint rags, the tarpaulin and our laundry blown off the clotheslines were retrieved from the sea bottom close inshore. Farther out our mat was spotted, and near it a felt hat the *Taubada* had lost in some previous dinkie-die blow.

When the umba-umba was sighted we were over about three fathoms of water, but the umbrella was still open and its round dark form could be plainly identified. I had been stringing along on the end of a rope while we cruised, and I ducked as the boys came off the launch with a whoop. I couldn't descend far (like Herbert Hoover I apparently have bladders on my feet) and as the boys went past me like brown wriggling octopuses, streamers of light-bubbles streaked behind them to the surface, and all around us the rays of refracted sunlight in the agitated water gave the effect of a bursting star. This underwater world was not like the small landlocked lagoon where fish dart like birds among the branches of rigid rose and violet coral trees, and dangerous clams and ugly black bêche de mer litter the sea floor. Here all was uninterrupted neatness in every direction across the sweep of sand. Straight below me, among the writhing white lights reflected down from the surface, was the fish-shaped shadow of the launch and my own shadow that looked like some wog you see under a microscope. Next to it was a brilliant spot of color. The color was geometrical in shape and looked like a huge opal, all luminous blues and violets with rich browns and yellows on one side. Somewhere else I have described the experience of laughing under water, so I won't go into that again. This time I popped to the surface to whoop. Iomai's canoe spirits had not succeeded in avenging him after all. We still had our portrait of him. The radiant jewel-like oblong was the painting, still attached to the umbrella by the guy ropes. And it should have been left down there at the bottom of the Coral Sea, for it never afterward looked so like the real thing as with three fathoms of lagoon over it.

"Goddam," chortled Wisiki, "Boy (Iomai) walkabout 'long *gaydobada* (big water) no catchem *gagaia*." This is the Melanesian "gag," the joke that stretches them out; man is frustrated in amorous intent. Iomai, presumed to be as desperate as most boys in this womanless paradise, had even gone looking about in the sea but still without catching any gagaia. The symbols of his wolving were the red and black lines across his face in his portrait. And the fact that the boy had voluntarily painted them on his own face as a feature of the *kula* voyage suggests that there is another customary exchange around the ring besides bracelets and necklaces. This might help to explain the unusually amiable relations between this group of islanders.

The following reflections on the foregoing may seem strained unless we explain that one of the occupational diseases of the amateur anthropologist is a stretched imagination. One is always discovering in exotic cultures remarkable similarities to one's own, or remarkable contrasts, or highly significant clues which appear to explain peculiar things we do. So it is no feat for us to find the *kula* coition-cum-commerce idea functioning in our society. Almost two hundred years ago when the Netherlands established rule in the East Indies, thus launching among the native populace large forces of wifeless young Dutch soldiers, one of the politic acts of the government was to legitimatize halfcaste children. This extended the blessings of the Crown to inter-racial marriage. The result is a large halfcaste population that has served with marked success as both buffer and link between the alien races. British residents of native lands, on the other hand, seldom marry the girls—even in India, where a large part of the population is Caucasian like themselves. Their failure in India is just as notable as the Dutch success in the Indies. And in other cases, as in Egypt, they have either had to relinquish control of the territory or depend on armed authority to retain it. On neutral ground, as in the markets of South America, it has been nip and tuck for both the British and Americans to get the business where there was German competition because the Germans, despite their reputation for race intolerance, were not averse to throwing in a little kula charm even when there was no extra pressure needed at the moment. Moreover they proceeded vigorously with the idea of fraternization throughout their occupation of Europe during the war. Perhaps one day we will discover in an "Aryan-ized" Continent that the Nazi secret weapon was as much propagation as propaganda. Just a modern application of the ancient *kula* ring idea.

11

"Little Mildred" is the pet name that Margaret and I, by unspoken agreement, immediately arrived at for the small pink-haired daughter of Samarai's Resident Magistrate. This is from the jingle that goes: "Little Mildred in surprise plucked out both the baby's eyes, stepped on them to hear them pop. People cried. 'Oh, Millie, stop!'" It was not that our Millie was a bad little girl, but it was apparent from the first minute of the sitting for her portrait that the debilitating climate that sends most white children South at an early school age had so far left the health of this one unimpaired. Underneath the well disciplined British child's seraphic manners was the average six-year-old's enterprise. But it had had some rather unusual opportunities for development in this Stone Age country. From birth Millie had been surrounded by household servants who had spent their own childhood and youth in the primitive village and who brought to their services all the background lore and the beliefs and attitudes of prehistoric man that persist in New Guinea today. Little Mildred therefore had a slant on life that we had not met before in our experience doing children's portraits elsewhere.

The boy in attendance for the sitting was the same one who had been at the hospital the first morning. His Christian name was Sarli, which is the native pronunciation of "Charlie." And he was not a nursemaid; he was a member of the Armed Constabulary retired from the active list because of old injuries. He had been "shot full of arrows as Saint Sebastian" when his outfit entered a mountain village to arrest the murderer of a sorcerer. Playing nursemaid to a six-year-old girl should have been a humiliating demotion if the girl had been any other than Little Mildred. As it was he was less "boy" than honor guard and tutor in native lore.

One of the hazards of doing juvenile portraits is that the child usually prefers to make the drawing himself to posing for it. He can often be diverted from using the artist's materials, however, by handcuffing him to his chair, nailing the chair down to the floor, and then inserting kneaded erasers into his throat so that he cannot call to his mother for help. The mother has always been sent away from the sitting as being a Bad Influence. But there was no nailing Millie down, and she instantly made the usual spirited attack on my drawing board and then dug her little hand into our sacred cigarette tin drawing box. Sarli stood by smiling proudly. Therefore, to attract the lass's attention back to her chair Margaret took her ukulele out of its "bed" to sing to Millie that whimsical melody about the "little shadow that goes in and out with me, and what can be the use of him is more than I can see." Ping! Clunk! Irreplaceable gut strings, already rotted by the moisture and tuned to the breaking point, whanged apart under Millie's lightning snatch at them. Even this was only the average child's reaction to a ukulele, but when Margaret attempted her next entertainment we got something peculiarly Papuan in response.

Millie had been induced to sit down in her chair and Margaret pushed the low table against her stomach so that she was the next thing to be nailed down, and she then proceeded to show the lass how to make a dear little "porcupine." For this hitherto unfailing child-spellbinder she ordinarily used a potato and toothpicks, the latter being stuck into the former. And taken out and stuck in again, and so on for hours while I occasionally squeaked like a porcupine so that the sitter would look up at me. But this was Papua, totally lacking in raw potatoes, and a British household where the teeth, when there are any, are not picked, at least not with a toothpick. And on top of this Millie knew more about pythons and bats and crocodiles than she did about porcupines. Nevertheless Sarli produced some matches and a ripe custard apple, and Margaret went to work. A custard apple is a black-skinned fruit about the size of an orange that has the interior consistency of heavy farm cream. It is deliciously sweet to eat but one of the hardest things to get out of the hair, next to live ants, that I have ever had on my head. Mildred, quick as light, had let fly the misnamed apple from a palm leaflet sling with which she apparently went armed, using it with a hefty swinging snap that she had learned from Sarli. The fruit hit the top edge of the drawing board and rained cream flak down on the drawing paper and my head on the other side. It was a regular bushman technique and gave one a lucid idea of what a rock so heaved by a serious adult would do in a raid.

By the time I had a new sheet of paper tacked on the board and had got some of the custard out of my eyes Margaret was taking instructions in sling throwing from Sarli, and Mildred had produced another weapon. This was a toy bamboo blowpipe, and our sitter proceeded to show us how she could shoot everything full of holes with little blunt-tipped bamboo shafts blown from the end of the pipe. Natives use this small blowpipe for birds at short range, and Little Mildred's darts might as well have had sharpened tips as usual for any difference in the feeling when she made a hit.

All this time Sarli was plodding patiently around the big veranda collecting ammunition and returning it to Mildred, and as he stooped to pick up the darts Mildred would use his bottom as a bull's eye. Being shot with arrows must have only felt familiar to the old veteran; anyway, he never lost his dignity. Nor his adoring smile. We decided that he must be her usual target and so, in a final effort to keep the model in one location, we induced Sarli to pose as William Tell's little boy while Mildred, with a stack of darts before her on the table, was lowered into her chair again. A new custard apple was nested down in the bushy top of Sarli's hair and our sun glasses were put on his eyes, just in case Mildred's aim improved. The best way to use a blowpipe is to balance the elbows on something, and because the table was low for Millie's elbows, her aim was also low and she consequently got some parts of Sarli's anatomy more sensitive than his face. But he stood it. He even smiled with the encouragement of the tutor when she came nearer the target and nearly stripped off one of his ears. There was something about Sarli, we decided, the sweetness of his nature was in every line of his weathered old face.

Meantime the blowpipe was not advancing art, and everyone took a new breath when Mildred volunteered to show us the cat cradles Sarli had taught her. She was wonderfully dexterous with her baby fingers, but for the next and final hour of the sitting I saw her face to draw it through a screen of fingers and string patterns. There was a laughing baby, a squall at sea, a humpbacked anopheles mosquito, four men paddling a canoe, and something that looked just like it, four white men drinking out of glasses. "Here is woman belong boy, now," said Millie and made a pattern like the laughing baby while Sarli grinned at her banter. Sarli's wife was half his age.

For anyone interested in native lore this seven-year-old was a cache of information. She could tell the Papuan legends of spirits and ghosts as another white child recites the vapid fairy tales. She could converse with a native in two of the Papuan languages, as well as Motuan, the most widely used of the Melanesian dialects. And she addressed us in pidgin English as often as English English. But we discovered that

she did not know pig Latin, and it was in this that we ex-
pressed ourselves at the end of the ordeal.

After the situation had been hauled off to luncheon Sarli
returned to help Margaret pick up the pieces. I still worked
on the drawing, "pulling it together" and trying to remove
the resemblance to a wind cherub on an old map that had
crept into portrait during the blowpipe period of the sitting.
When Sarli paused behind me I glanced around despairingly,
and he smiled. It was approval, but reserved. Still I felt grateful for here was someone who knew the child's face well.
This first portrait in Samarai was such an important one, and
we couldn't have had less co-operation in a picture that was
to show off our wares. So thereafter each time Sarli paused
behind me I looked at his face for assurance that I was im-
proving the likeness. The boy said nothing, but his smile
became more and more approving; and when he finally
looked satisfied, that was the artist's signal of enough. I knew
I had it as near as I was likely to come to the resemblance
in this attempt.

This little native by-play will seem trivial unless it is understood that Melanesians do not do this sort of thing. No native
before Sarli had ever criticized even his own likeness in a
painting. This could be for a number of reasons; perhaps a
lack of critical faculties—the primitives do not seem to pick
at details the way we do—lack of familiarity with his own
features or even an interest in portraiture, or fear of ven-
turing an opinion and displeasing the great white fella
missus. But this was Papua, and Sarli was one of Governor
Murray's Melanesians with years of association with the carefully chosen and trained white men of the Service; and he
had a normal man's self-respect and assurance.

All this was just what we had asked for in primitives, nevertheless when Sarli appeared at our tavern a few days later
bringing his wife whom he offered as a model, obviously with

the idea of possessing the drawing as the Residency did Millie's, Margaret and I had to make apologies to one another.
Our reception of the police boy was a caricature of the more
inflated Empire Builder. I was importantly at work on the
balcony of our second floor room, executing our first Samarai
portrait commission, which was the direct result of Sarli's
assistance with the drawing of Little Mildred. Our patron
was the speedboat demon of "steamer day," who had seen
that portrait and decided that if we could achieve something
human-looking of "that little *guba*" (a squall) we should produce a masterpiece of anyone so poised as herself. But we
forgot to be grateful to Sarli for his help; he was a "boy."
He had left his wife outside the hotel and himself had come
no nearer than the far corner of the balcony, where Margaret
talked to him. "My bloomin' oath!" our patron exclaimed indignantly as Margaret repeated the request. "Yes," I added
absentmindedly, "tell him to raus." "Raus" is German pidgin
English for "scram." Sarli retired.

A few minutes later I had backed up to the balcony railing
to have a long look at my work, and saw Sarli emerge into the
road from underneath, followed a few paces behind by a
native woman, the correct formation for a man escorting his
wife. "Boy, boy," I called after Sarli, and Sarli, just like any
other subservient Melanesian "boy," forgiving as a kicked
dog, returned, bringing his wife. She was a ready-made
artist's model.

12

We have always maintained right in the face of antifaction fire that the reason the Balinese women have the wide reputation for beauty they enjoy is because one sees more of them than is revealed of women elsewhere along the beaten tourist track. And they stage-manage woman's best points by clothing themselves in a sarong right up to but not covering them. Venus de Milo did something of the same sort by starting to dress at perhaps a better point, the low hip line. But the old Balinese women look just like any other old women, and the young ones have nothing that plump young women of other races haven't got. Sarli's young wife was proof apparent that even the notoriously unlovely Melanesian woman can with a little Balinese padding over her garden muscles and Venus' sense of style achieve the same results. She had, moreover, anticipated the American radio's advice and done something about her skin and hair. Her complexion was like an old Java batik, a lustrous cinnamon brown and *blue*. She was tattooed literally from head to heels. Then, instead of the black kinky hair being sheared off close to the melon-shaped skull which is the fashion of Melanesian matrons, hers framed the face as hair is intended to do. The top was trimmed into a modified pompadour, the back left long and cascading down over her shoulders in pencil-thin "ringlets" in the style of a Manet portrait. The impression of an early Victorian lady was accented by the girl's *rami*, which was not the ordinary skimpy "grass" skirt of shredded banana leaves that the "Maries" of eastern Melanesia wear. This was a bouffant of layers of

shredded pandanus palm leaflet half a foot in thickness that
billowed out from the low waistline and fell below the bony
Melanesian knees. The soft shiny fiber was dyed in wide
alternate stripes of creamy gold and violet, really a faded
indigo that was a handsome note with the blue-and-brown
skin. When the girl sank onto the floor of the veranda to
begin posing, a practised movement of the women that keeps
the skirt modestly concealing what it is meant to conceal,
the rami fanned out around her and was like a base for a
prim little porcelain figurine.

Sarli had acquired this treasure of a woman in a rather
unorthodox way. There are rigid rules for matrimony, especially who shall marry whom. The marrying populace is
divided up into, not families or village units or even tribes,
but clans, each of which has a totem, and one may marry only
a member of another totem. Or, depending on the district,
one may marry only a member of the same totem. At some
remote time this restriction must have originated as an attempt to prevent inbreeding, but often today it works in
reverse and can sometimes even oblige one to marry only a
blood relative. There is a custom confusing to artists of
classifying totem members in family terms, as for instance
when a man is a totem "uncle" to someone he is referred to
as an uncle when he may be no such thing. According to
anthropologist W. E. Armstrong, however, the whole system
is very simple. "The rules (for marriage) on the basis of
patrilineal descent," he assures us, "are simple . . . namely
that every class marry the class of sisters, or that every class
marry the class of sister's daughters, or that every class marry
the class of sister's daughter's daughters. (Thus) the grandchild . . . may be an old man, while the grandparent is a
young girl. (So) every man who selects a granddaughter his
own age (to marry) is dooming one of his brothers to marriage with a granddaughter who will probably not be born

until he is dead. The granddaughters, however, will be young when the grandfathers die, and of suitable age for the grandfathers' nephews, and so they become, by a second marriage, the wives of their mother's father's sister's sons, the men, therefore, marrying their mother's brother's daughter's daughter, and their mother's brother's daughter's daughters are passed on to their nephews, so that in the next generation a man's wife is likely to be his mother's brother's daughter's daughter." You see?

What we think happened is that Sarli fell in love. And he married the girl, though she was of the forbidden class. No one knows exactly what would happen to anyone violating the marriage taboos because not enough have done it to establish an opinion; but all taboos are protected by ghosts, and everyone knows that sickness and death not due to old age or injuries are the work of spirits whose taboos have been violated. The girl of course took a chance too, but she had not much choice in the matter if she had any objections to Sarli. She had been married before to a man at whose death Sarli succeeded, as senior male member of the "mother's" totem, to guardianship of the girl. It was then his duty to marry her to someone else and provide the pigs for the wedding feast. But he was widowed too, and an emancipated native, so he married her himself. Like many such marriages in our society condemned by public opinion, life in the home village might have been made intolerable for them however emancipated they felt, but they were married by a missionary and like their civilized counterparts they escaped whatever penalty was due them by leaving the village critics behind and living in the metropolis of Samarai.

There was a generation between Sarli and his wife, but there was nothing of the father-and-daughter atmosphere about it. Outwardly Sarli's attitude was exactly that of every other native spouse in public, highly impersonal. But while

his wife was posing for her portrait he sat a short way down the veranda and watched intently every brush stroke I put on the canvas. He never looked at the girl nor she at him, but in his nice dark face was something so tender and about the wife such a soft air of contentment, absent in most native women, that it did not take any imagination to recognize this as one of those cases of perfect adjustment between a man and woman, the mystical union that is rare in any society.

On the girl's part she had a husband to be proud of, judged by our standards, though doubtless she was unimpressed by his position except in so far as it had provided relief from the eternal gardening that would have been her lot if she had married another village native. But as a member of His Majesty's Armed Constabulary Sarli was a distinguished citizen, at least in European circles. (The police are not so esteemed in native society. Governor Murray tells about some natives who were brought into court on a charge of pelting some of His Majesty's police with rocks and who on being liberated after a reprimand begged to be hanged because as they said if they could no longer throw rocks at the police life held no pleasure for them.) The men of the Constabulary are selected from the best physical specimens among the candidates, and for special personal qualities; self-discipline, courage, and stamina and especially a capacity for loyalty and executing orders. From these the few natural leaders are trained to be V.C.'s, village constables, and return to their communities to be intermediary between government and natives. Those of the ranks who are made corporals and sergeants are the cream of the Service. Sarli was a sergeant, highly respected by the white officers for his record. On the occasion of his being shot as full of arrows as Saint Sebastian it was to drag his wounded officer to safety that he had taken the barrage.

Even ordinary policing of Papua is no routine business,

not the way the Papuan Government does it. "Never leave a legacy of hate behind for the next white man," said Sir William MacGregor, so when news of a murder or raid filters down to the government stations, a detachment of constabulary under a white officer goes out, not to take wholesale reprisal by shooting up the populace, destroying gardens and burning villages (even as the Papuans do themselves in their raids in New Guinea) but to make *arrests*. It is a matter of Service tradition to complete the assignment without fail and without bloodshed. Often a whole village resists the arrest of a single individual with all the ancient weapons, trickery, clubs, spears, arrows and rocks. But there are only two or three occasions on which this sporting government will use rifles against such primitive defense. One is to save the lives of the Service and then the police may fire over the heads of the attacking natives. The sound of it is usually sufficient, but still it takes poise to walk fearlessly into a village where arrows and spears are all ready to let fly when it would be so simple to fire into the air first and eliminate doubt. It is said that the Papuan in spite of a bloody history is a cowardly fighter, and there is some proof of it, but the records of Sarli's outfit show that the Papuan needs only the classical ideal and the moral support of a rifle to bring out classical virtues.

These days the natives who are still raiding live in the hinterland and here, besides the necessary cool-headedness to face primitives who would resist encroachment, it takes moral and physical stamina to stick out the hardships of the terrain. New Guinea is an enormous island, as long from east to west as the United States is from Lake Superior to the Gulf of Mexico; and except for the vast Fly River basin in the southwest and the narrow swampy areas along the northeast coast much of it is mountainous. Not just ordinary hill ranges, but series of tremendous peaks that soar to as high as thirteen thousand feet between gorges and valleys that drop as much as ten thousand feet. Most of the Constabulary are "salt-water boys," as Sarli was, who until they joined the Service had never climbed anything higher than a coconut palm . . . if they had even done that, for the coconuts in these islands are picked up from the ground after they have fallen. Anyway their blood is watery from the coast heat and malaria, and in those icy mountains it rains more or less continuously, water freezes at night and the frigid winds never stop blowing. This is where the evil spirits live; and it takes a sturdy native, however emancipated, to sleep through the bitter nights with the *demoni* howling all about him. Firewood, when there is any . . . for above the timber line the mountains are entirely barren . . . is always wet, so it takes a long time at the end of a weary day to boil the rice. Sometimes the only water is the rain caught in canvas. Sometimes there is no rice. A boy will eat what he carries in a few days, so rations are always tight; and when the rice runs out the party goes hungry if it is not traveling through friendly country where vegetables can be obtained from the villages. But New Guinea is a sparsely populated country, and even unfriendly villages are few and far between.

Then in the lower highlands there are the leech-infested rain forests where everything drips; where feet deep, lividly-green moss covers the surface underfoot, the tree trunks and branches and the great aerial roots. It is like walking on wet sponges; and where it grows across between the aerial roots forming a false surface it is a trap that drops the plodders through. Any injured must be carried by the other, always exhausted, men. No one is allowed to lag. For as a patrol officer once told us, woe betide the injured man who falls by the wayside where leeches abound if he is not picked up in time; he would be sucked dry. It is the burdened carriers who fall by the wayside first, dying of pneumonia or ex-

haustion, but the police and white officers suffer and sometimes die too. That they do not die oftener is the miracle.
(This is the terrain in which the Australians fought the Japanese those months in 1942.) No wonder Sarli could stand
and be popped by blunt blowgun arrows and smile benignly.
His hide had been toughened and his humor mellowed by
years of hardships that would break an ordinary man. And
no wonder he adored his soft doll-like little wife after the
celibate years.

When her figure was at last finished (and we also made
a drawing of her head for Sarli) the old sergeant squatted
down before the painting and looked and looked like a man
who is reading, absorbed. He said nothing, but when he
turned his face up to me I knew the portrait was all right.
That was when we decided that Sarli should also be painted
into the same picture, posed behind the girl in just this attitude of looking. All the preparation that was necessary was
for him to remove his police uniform, the dark blue jumper
that had impressed us when we first saw Sarli. (We understood now that the wool jumper was for warmth in the mountains and for authority on the coast.)

Mrs. Sarli had been a good model because she was shy and
afraid to move out of the pose, but the sergeant understood
from watching the business why one must remain still. At
least he appeared to when he began posing himself, and at
the second sitting he heaped glory on himself by appearing
in costume. Rather, he had left off what he had on before,
the wool sulu, and wore a loin panel of tapa cloth and a
handsome necklace of *sapi sapi*, the coral colored shell money
that comes from Yela. It was a fine color note on his brown
skin, but after we had painted it on his figure we discovered
that it did not belong to him and he did not know its origin.
It was too old. Like many of the best old pieces of local art
it was in the collection of the bishop. Better from the point

of view of authenticity was the lime spatulate he brought. It was from Trobriand, but both it and the gourd lime container with its pig-tusk stopper were the property of his wife. (Police boys are the boy scouts among natives and do not have the habit of betel nut with which the lime is used.) This was the inevitable flaw in the pearl, for the girl chewed betel nut in such excess . . . she had a quid in her mouth all the time she was posing, which may account for her demureness for it is supposed to make one dopey . . . that her teeth in that prim little face were black as a Yelaman's.

The lime spatulate was an insignificant piece to illustrate the work of the finest and most prolific carvers of all the Melanesian islands, but it was typical of the materials and designs and told a story of native ingenuity and the fate of native art. The hard wood used in the Trobriands carvings is naturally a light walnut in color and is made ebony black by soaking it in a concoction of mangrove root. Whether this further hardens the wood I am not certain, but I know from trying a knife on it that it is the next thing to stone. Under strong pressure it flakes up in powder or small chips, and it is so brittle that a thin piece of carving, which is often filigree, will break like glass if it is dropped on anything hard. The designs most often seen are consequently not carvings "in the round" but incised lines on a flat surface, and a striking black-and-white effect is achieved by filling the grooves with a white paste that hardens as it dries and becomes like an inlay. In the not-so-very old days coral lime mixed with some binder was used, but today flour paste, which flakes out at the first bump, is the filler. Also formerly the natives made all of their carving tools, and there was a wide variety of materials and cutting edges; hard stone for adzes and hatchets, knives of bamboo, awls and chisels made from the leg bone of the pig and the cassowary and flying fox, scrapers and rasps of sharpened shell or the skin of the shark, augers of broken-off boar's tusk and, of course, powdered coral rock for a fine pumice finish and coconut oil for the patina. Most of these tools could be resharpened on rough stone or thrown away and new ones made from materials at one's elbow, for there was plenty of time.

But today there is less time in a man's life for creating art, because he is using much of the time earning the money with which to buy European tools that, by assumption, will facilitate production. However the metal in the trade knives and axes is of the most inferior quality and quickly loses its edge on the stonelike wood, and the natives have no way of resharpening such tools even if they were good steel. Carving becomes tedious and the results inferior, and by and by the artist cares less to work, or not at all, and then the children of the village no longer squat about watching the carver, impatient to try their hand on a piece of wood. So the arts die. Perhaps this is the story of our own lost art among the people. Man seems instinctively to get pleasure out of doodling with materials and tools, but somehow we have come to think of this pleasure as the special privilege of professionals. We haven't the time for it because, like the Trobriand islanders today, we are too busy earning the money with which to buy time. (Most of us haven't even the time to go to the museums and look at the fun the professionals have had.) In any case in a few years all such old-time native products as Sarli's lime spatulate will have been shipped out of the country by collectors, and if Mrs. Joe Dokes can get her family to the museum of natural history on Sunday afternoon they will see more fine primitive art than anyone who travels half way around the world will see in the whole island that once produced it.

If Sarli's portrait had been just a picture of himself alone, and if we had not preferred to keep it ourselves to parting with it almost as a gift, it might have stayed in Papua. For

Sarli was slated for the hall of dead heroes, "close up." It is projecting our story to finish Sarli's now, but the finale began when we were still in Samarai. It was after the coastwise steamer *Papuan Chief* had come in that the boy who regularly took care of our room and did other chores for us, a kind of temporary personal boy, failed to appear one morning. We asked about him of the boy who substituted, found he was ill and forgot about him. We had decided to go on to Port Moresby on the *Chief*, and on the day of departure were so busy tying off loose ends that we were a little impatient when Sarli appeared at the end of the veranda. After looking at the confusion for a minute, he asked apologetically if he might look at the portrait of his woman. But the canvas was already rolled up, we said, and why didn't he go home and look at his wife in the flesh if he wanted to see her. Sarli just gazed at us helplessly for a minute and then turned to go. "No got woman now," he said, "Woman die finish." The little dresden doll was dead.

It was an influenza epidemic. Though no one knew it then, and it must have been brought in by the American freighter that had called during the week. The sickness did not get going until we had left Samarai, and ourselves had possibly carried it west with us. Even in the end no one recognized it as an epidemic among the Europeans, partly we think because the symptoms resembled both dengue fever and malarial dysentery, both just routine visitations. No one thinks of going to the overworked doctor for a hot nose and over-active bowels, and most of us who felt sicker than normal simply stoked up with a few more tablets of quinine. This naturally was as effective for hoisting the fever of influenza over the hurdle as a temperature from any other cause. The result is that there was no mortality among the whites, and we only knew that there was an epidemic because of the tragedy around us. The natives in their villages, doctorless and without quinine, with no immunity and no understanding of contagion, less idea of how tò prevent the complications that make influenza fatal, these helpless people were stricken. They died by hundreds, in a few days, before the frantic Government could spread its few trained men through the countryside.

Foreign ships calling at Papua and elsewhere in these islands are given the routine medical clearance required at all ports, but this consists mostly in questioning an officer as to the health of the personnel. No white man is examined unless he is ill when he arrives, so the probability of the American freighter having been responsible for this epidemic is high. The eastern coast of Papua was hardest hit, and among the natives of Samarai who succumbed was brave gentle Sarli. He must have died twice, once of heartbreak and only afterward of the sickness. Not the best will in the world, not all the Hubert Murrays there are can check this scythe with which we widen the trails where no white man's foot has trod before.

13

In each small corner throughout "this great, wide, beautiful world" there is always some local character that expresses in one neat package the sum personality of the place. And such a one was the *Papuan Chief*. Our reasons for traveling to Port Moresby on her will be explained presently. Meantime, the first thing we did as we were boarding her was to step on the face of one of her crew, thus launching our acquaintance with characteristic shock.

The *Chief* was sailing from Samarai at four in the morning, and it was almost three when we got to the wharf, where the dark and silent vessel was tied up. The moon had already gone down, and the night was black as the core of your eye. We were disinclined to use our flashlight because, with the doubtful assistance of Margaret's usual wake of art lovers, we were trying to get on board so inconspicuously that the island would not have insomnia the rest of the night speculating on what we had been doing since two o'clock, when Samarai's lights went off. No one would have believed that we had been participating in an aesthetic analysis of Trobriand Island anaglyphs—least of all ourselves. What we had been doing was taking one last beating "body surfing" in the mountainous breakers that roll up the long windward beach of a neighboring island. Anyway I swung a leg over the rail of the *Chief* and came down with all my ten stone on the face of a night-colored native sleeping on the deck. At the bellow of pain and shock flashlights blinked on all over Dinner Island and the ship rose up as one man—thinking doubtless, as we did ourselves, that one more Melanesian had vanished under the heel of the white man. But I was still in my bathing suit and still wet, and all I did was to shave the freckles off his face as I tobogganed off it. My casualty was a skinned knee; score one for the *Chief*, for this was to become a fat "island sore."

The "ladies' " cabin of the *Papuan Chief* was up in the forecastle. This was a kind of architectural burp that erupted right over the bow housing under it the galley and dining "salon" and, on our deck, the wheelhouse and captain's quarters. For the *Chief* was of a design never heard of in shipbuilding circles. She was registered as a two hundred twenty-five ton "steamer," which was only half of it. Years ago in Glasgow she had been a whole steamer, but the thrifty Scots cut her in two just at one side of the then normally placed superstructure, basted a bow over the wound, and sent that end out to New Guinea under her own steam to run the coastwise traffic between Samarai and Daru at the far west end of the territory. On the way out the chief engineer, a hardy fellow who had spent many years on many ships and seas, threw himself down from the forecastle onto the loading deck, thus ending a life no longer endurable. On our first trip on the ship a fox terrier belonging to one of the passengers was to do the same thing. At least he went overboard, and the last anyone saw of him he was going down in the furious wake with a satisfied smile on his face. The *Chief* was then bounding along like a doughnut in a kettle of boiling oil; that was her gait even in placid rivers and the thing that made life in the fo'castle something like flagpole sitting in an earthquake. We were high above what was going on around us, but still an intensified part of it.

When that first day dawned it was raining, just "general rain," but the coast of New Guinea was obscured and the gray-green seas were running high. It was the kind of weather on shipboard when an expedition catches up on its homework. For Margaret this was mending and again mending our decaying wardrobe, and counting our cash from both ends trying to make it stretch out on paper. There were four bunks in our cabin, two on each side wall with a wide seat along the connecting wall, and soon Margaret had spread out with her labors all over one lower bunk and half of the wall seat. The rest of the seat, a card table and the opposite lower bunk were littered with my chores. Between us were numerous ash trays rapidly filling up and the contents and refuse of a bon voyage basket. The basket still had in it the choice edibles of the island, juicy custard apples, little hen's eggs, over-ripe bananas, a rock-hard pineapple and wizened oranges, as well as a few squashy mangoes and papayas. There were also some tiny native nuts, called *gnali* in the Solomons, which were so delicious that we could not resist nibbling on them though they were dangerously like drinking the oil on the troubled sea. But it was the girls' day at home—and the cabin looked it.

My duty consisted of typing our joint serial letter. This was a kind of endless diary of which I made as many carbon copies as the rusty typewriter would take. Periodically we both sent installment copies to the members of our families and friends who still remembered us. It was an economical way of keeping a record, but there were so many pages that the greatest care had to be taken to keep them in order as I went along, for if they got mixed up the labor of re-sorting the blurred copies was not one of love. And this became increasingly difficult as the day wore on, for the general rain became a "flaming" downpour as the wind rose and sent the seas racing head-on in whitecapped alps.

Margaret makes no claim of never getting seasick, but there is something about her manner when I do that implies superiority. She says with a kind of Buddhist calm that it is all a matter of relaxation; so she lies down. And she was lying

back on her boxes of needles and pins looking as if she were
laid out for good when toward nightfall I went out to do
my own kind of relaxing over the rail. It was a bitter sight outside. The black rain was thrashing down with such violence
that the white sea seemed to rise up in indignation, the silly
Chief meantime being tossed between the two masses of water
as if neither would have her. When I started back to the cabin
I was still ailing somewhat, but reaching the door health returned in a flash as I saw Margaret's relaxed body zooming
to port with the card table. Then as I stood there clinging to
the doorway the *Chief* started over to starboard with Margaret, card table, typewriter, orange and banana peels, cigarette stubs, about five hundred pages of serial letter, the ink
no longer in the bottle and the hens' eggs no longer in their
shells. The upper air was filled with flying custard from the
custard apples, *gnali* nuts, needles and pins, thumbtacks and
egg shells, hairpins and cigarette ashes. And finally Margaret
coming back to port. On the next trip they took the contents
of one of the open trunks on an upper berth newly packed
with shoes and the shoes with camera films. It would have
been like going into the teeth of a buzz saw to have ventured
into that room to try and save my friend, and anyway nothing in the world would have moved me to bring order to such
a picture. I could see that Margaret was still alive, because as
she passed me from time to time on her face was still that expression of imperishable good humor with which she will
probably be buried. This in fact was the reason that she could
not save herself; all her muscles were being used for laughing.

But before the *Chief* came out of that spasm I bore scar
No. 2. The door came unhooked and swung around with such
force that it nearly guillotined me on the doorjamb to which
I was clinging, and the result was a purple shiner that, as it
happened, was much admired in the right (native) circles
later. Margaret had black eyes all over her, naturally; but

nothing, I complained bitterly, ever happened to her fault-
less face. Anyway, nothing had until we traveled on the
Chief.

Admittedly the *Chief* is an unusual craft, but her eccentric
behavior is largely a reflection of the locale. New Guinea is
in what is called a monsoon belt, which means sand in the
cylinders that grind out weather. Normally in this latitude
there are the same two simple changes of season that all torrid
climates have; the southeast trade winds shift to northeast,
and there is a corresponding shift from wet to dry weather,
or, more precisely, from wet to wetter. But God does not
seem to regulate these things in New Guinea. The winds
from the icy highlands sweep down to the steaming sea, the
hot air rises and the rain falls according to the local draught
in each place. Thus while Samarai is having its heaviest rainfall between March and May, Port Moresby in the Central
Division is having its driest weather. West of "Port" in the
Gulf Division, the wet months are from May to September,
and farther west around Daru the heavy rains come at the
same time as those of Port Moresby. Each little local change
of seasons is attended by its false equinoctial winds, which
means that by traveling along the coast on the *Chief* one can
remain in a continuous change of seasons, always on a rough
sea with a high wind. Moreover, the farther one goes westward toward the bottleneck of Torres Strait, where Australia
and New Guinea close in and almost meet, and the Coral Sea
becomes the Gulf of Papua, the rougher the water and higher
the wind. And the more convulsive the *Chief*.

Yet with all her rough treatment the old demi-ship holds a
special place in the heart of those lucky enough to get off her
alive and not too battered. The one nearly flawless thing about
her is her master, Captain Anderson, another rose-pink, blue-
eyed Scandinavian who brings to the lonely outlanders the
gossip and news of the steamer ports, receiving in exchange

live chickens and eggs for himself, and for the ship's table fresh vegetables and fruit. He is the totem father of all tribes and his one flaw is that he thinks of the *Chief* as a whole steamer. But the ship does deliver mail and long-awaited supplies, poking up the yellow rivers for plantation produce and, like the Toonerville trolley, stopping anywhere for a whistle. We made sixteen calls along a two-hundred-ninety-mile stretch of coast—and took five days for it.

Our excuse for proceeding to Port Moresby when our finances were in worse shape than when we had arrived in Papua may seem pretty thin to the cautious. But caution, as Margaret pointed out when we were debating the move, is only a matter of degree. Carried to its ultimate one might spend his life in bed because of the dangers of being abroad. That logic won me over. But I was easy winning. The hurried studies of the Yela Papuan we had made, the model selected from only six representative of the group, was far from adequate. We had to get to western Papua somehow, and to paint numbers of Papuans as we had painted the Melanesians. And one way was to take a gamble on Port Moresby. The seat of government had a population three times that of Samarai, and portrait commissions in Samarai had almost paid our expenses there. But not quite, and inasmuch as we should have had to dig into our reserve fund anyway, to tide us over until the Sydney steamer came along, we decided to do it for passage to Port Moresby instead. But the compensation was the chance of a sweepstake, the possibility of a real portrait commission there, a life-size, full or three-quarter length de luxe oil painting of Governor Murray.

In the Papuan Government there is an advisory board called the Legislative Council which is made up of first citizens from all over the territory. Apparently they are much like a chamber of commerce, meeting only periodically, on state business. A member of this board in Samarai approached us as

unofficial spokesman on the matter of fee for a painting of
His Excellency. The council wished to make a gift of such
a portrait to the Territory. This is the sort of picture that any
sane artist paints just for the honor. But there was Margaret
with her adding pencil, and there was the Heffalump; and
after a few tense hours of debate I left the amount of fee up
to her. The report was that the board member would convey the information to the others and let us know. So we
were proceeding to Port Moresby, largely on my private
resolve to paint His Excellency whether the portait was ordered or not. I was pretty sure that we should be paid satisfactorily for it, if the legislators could see what they were
buying. That is, if I did the best work I had ever done in my
life. And keeping in mind what we could do with that fee
should make me, if San Luca were still on our side.

14

Some one has said that it is possible to walk all the way from Samarai to Port Moresby with only a walking stick, by which he probably meant that it would be safe to do so. We question even that. To be sure there would be little danger of getting lost if the traveler stayed on the well beaten government tracks that run from village to village, and no danger from the natives—who are at least as well beaten as the tracks. But unless he were equipped with pontoons and the stick had an umbrella on it he would have a very wet time of it indeed. He might even find himself bogged down without a peasant nearby to pull him out of the mud. The track zigs and zags all over the countryside, inland up the mountains and back down to the coast; everywhere there are rivers to cross, and not always a village near at which to get a canoe, for even the coast settlements are few and far between.

The rain clouds hung low over the land, but whenever they lifted we could see the misty blue foothills of the Owen Stanley Range that in some places crowd down to the very beach of the southern coast. There is so much rain in those highlands and the watershed is so precipitous that most level areas along the shore are delta land formed by the silt of the flooding rivers. Sand bars spread far out into the sea, and these as well as high surf and a fairly continuous chain of reefs kept the *Chief* anchoring from one to three miles off shore. The plantations are up the rivers well above the flood area, and copra comes down on rafts which are punted or towed by launch out to the *Chief*. Loading was a regular Winslow

Homer business in this weather. The big log rafts piled high with wet brown sacks of copra would come tossing out of the gray rain, and all the near-naked boys punting against the heavy swells would be posed in dramatic attitudes like figures in Géricault's "Raft of the Medusa." Colors and tones were intensified by the wetness. Sharp blue-white highlights slithered over the brown working skin of the natives, silver highlights rose on the deep-green seas, while the brownness of the drenched bags and logs of the raft were flat rich masses. The sacks were loaded into a rope net on the raft and hoisted on board by the screeching crane. Everything rocked and swung in all directions, the *Chief* threatening to crack down on the helpless rafts when they were swept too close. Once the loaded net, rising to the deck, swung out as the *Chief* rolled back, tearing the guide rope from the hand of the boy. Coming to, it caught two natives on the raft and knocked them into the sea, stiff as ninepins. Occasionally a miserable planter came out with his first load stubbornly dressed in drenched white clothing, still stubbornly refusing to wear a raincoat and carry an umbrella as he does in civilization. He usually had a cup of scalding tea while devouring the news. And sat looking at Margaret as a freezing man looks through a window at a warm fire.

We were not so warm ourselves, not because the air was cold but because our blood was adjusted to heat and refused to accommodate us for anything less. And we were saturated; we inhaled water and slept on sheets so moist that if you ran your hand across them the skin glistened with water. Whenever the loading was going to take an hour or two Margaret and I went ashore to "work." That is, we went equipped for it; but what I did was sit under the umbrella and enlarge the vocabulary of any Melanesians present with some good old Yankee terms. The drawing paper was a wet rag, the charcoal and crayon slipped around in my moist fingers, and a permanent pearl of dampness tickled the end of my nose. The paper of cigarettes became stained with the moist tobacco and would not stay lit, and no match of civilization would strike. It was even useless to take photographs of our subjects; not only because the light was too feeble for a snapshot (and one can't count on a native holding still for a time exposure) but because the films inside the camera became so saturated before they could be developed that they were pockmarked.

To diverge for a minute on a subject that may be of interest to camera addicts: good photographs are often hard to obtain, even when the equipment is ideal, because the humidity is high in the dry season as well as the wet. Instantly the films are out of their metal containers they begin collecting moisture, and printing paper and developing chemicals no matter how tightly sealed will also deteriorate in a short time, for the same reason. Then there is the matter of obtaining water cool enough for developing. No water in a storage tank that stands in the burning sun the day long is anywhere near as cool as 65°. We always did our darkroom work on moonless nights when water set out in pans would cool to 70° and there was less of a problem with light—and the usual problem with insects. To prevent bugs sticking to the wet films as they hung up to dry we at first used a mosquito net, but this also being damp delayed the drying, so we rigged up a fine wire netting cage in which several films at a time could be hung. But this could never stand where there was a draught, lest the breeze blow the films against the wire and stick them there. Actually the films were seldom dry for very long because the gelatine continued to absorb moisture unless they were packed away immediately. Not the least of our night insect troubles were anopheles mosquitoes, which would gather by hundreds into any darkroom we rigged up. Usually Margaret was on duty more to wave a palm frond at my legs than anything else.

To arrest the deterioration of exposed films until they could be developed we kept them in a metal fishing-tackle box the tray of which contained lime to absorb the moisture in the air. This was the ordinary lime used with betel nut; it was made by the natives by burning coral rock. It was not very successful, and probably commercial lime would have been more so if it could have been obtained, but the stores did not carry it—for the same old reason, dampness.

When we went ashore it was really to snoop and because the *Chief* was even less endurable at anchor than when in legitimate motion. Frequently there was nothing new to see, neither natives nor any sign of habitation in the lonely coast country. And those settlements we found were not permanent dwelling places. They were sago camps, and the natives came from inland. The sago palm thrives best in the warm saturated lowlands, and the hill villages make periodical migrations down to the coast to fell the palms and make supplies of this staple food. (It is the pith of the trunk that is scraped loose, washed with fresh water and packed into hard cakes which, when dry, keep for a long time; it is eaten in some form at every meal.) Many a little war has been fought in the past over some infringement of a tribe's sago patch. But where these feuds have been brought up to the present day the Government has helped settle claims of ownership. Anyway when we came, near the mouth of a river, onto a group of huts having no sign of life in them it did not mean that they had been abandoned permanently. And when we encountered natives like "the three graces" it meant that a sago camp was somewhere back up the river.

It was late afternoon and raining only general rain again when we started for shore at a place where the copra shipment had been left stacked on the beach for the *Chief* to pick up when she came along. There was a plantation boss boy in charge with three of the *Chief's* boys to help him; and by the

time they had punted the heavy raft the two miles to shore,
reloaded and disappeared seaward again the season was changing. The rain slackened, and we were left standing on a spit
of mud that formed one bank of a yellow river that flowed
along parallel with the shore as far as we could see it. It was
a godforsaken spot without even the sound of surf to give it
life. For the sand bars and reefs that kept the *Chief* two miles
out sheltered the beach. Nevertheless we rolled our slacks
high and set out down the spit, wobbling drunkenly in the absence of the *Chief's* deck and retrieving each leg separately
from the deep gray gumbo. We were getting the exercise
we were after.

At first there was no vegetation; then the strip of land widened and, toward the river edge, began to have underbrush
and finally a thin screen of trees. And we were mushing along
on the ocean side of this when a miracle began to unfold on
the opposite, or river, side. First the rain stopped altogether.
We could see it backing away to the east like a screen being
withdrawn, revealing as it did so the heavy jungle on the
opposite shore of the river. Above the treetops a sky gradually
appeared, a long thin strip of the weird yellow light often
seen along the horizon under snow clouds in our winter skies.
But nothing in our middle-way land could approach the green
of that rain-sodden jungle wall below it. It bled green, radiat-
ing into the surroundings and making colors out of tones.
The yellow sky looked lemon, the dull steel clouds were violet and the wide muddy river became a flat sheet of green
gold. Then into this gold and green and violet setting came
the one thing it needed, human beings. A long slender canoe
with an outrigger like the legs of a dragon fly slipped out
from under the shadow of the far shore and started across to
our side. In it were three women. Two of them were seated,
naked and brown from the waist up but each sitting in a
billowing mound of grass skirt the long loose strands of which

floated out along the sides of the canoe like the flower gar-
lands of Cleopatra's barge. The third woman was standing
to punt—and she was a model for Galatea. Her *rami* was full
length, covering her feet (and those bony Melanesian knees)
and it was of unshredded white leaves, a pedestal for a heroic
torso. The woman seemed to be intentionally posing. Though

it could not have been for us, for we were disguised as two
palmettoes in the strip of vegetation. She thrust the long pole
forward into the golden water, and then with exaggerated
grace pivoted the column of her wet brown body in an arc
as the canoe slid ahead of the pole. It was like the slow posturing of a modern dance, all pictures. It was hushed magic,
people out of the dim past moving silently along our horizon.
   When the near bank was reached the canoe was poled parallel with it. Then, still silent, the two seated women reached
forward and lifted to their heads enormous green palm baskets loaded with garden produce, clumps of bananas, green
papayas, brown yams and taro root. They rose slowly,
straightened themselves and posed for a minute like ca-
nephorae, arms up to their baskets as they got their balance
for the wide step over the side of the canoe. Then with a
high lift of the foot that parted the long sheaths of petticoats

away from the thigh, they were over on the satiny bank. Off up the shore they went in single file, long skirts trailing, hips swinging slowly in a wide hula-hula to maintain the balance, three graces in a Greek frieze silhouetted against the golden river.

We watched until they were well up the beach, and then Margaret let out a large happy sigh like a tire going flat, and sank to her knees. I never found out whether she had been going to pray or just to rest her legs. Instantly she bounded up with a shriek. I couldn't see anything. Whatever was the matter. "Ants!" she grunted, beating herself, "ants . . . ants!" They were all over her bare legs, and as she slapped her legs they were on her arms, then on her neck and face. They had their jaws fastened in her skin. And they couldn't be killed. They seemed to leap from the earth, for when I tried to help they were on me, a million hot stinging hatpins. Like flowing acid. We rolled in the mud and then tore for the river and threw ourselves in. When we came out they were still on us, some of them alive and still biting. Margaret's hair was full of them.

Bulldog ants were something we had not even heard about before. But as so often happens after you have discovered a thing for yourself, we found they were such a commonplace hazard that, like people who live in acres of poison oak as we do in California, no one had thought to warn us. Margaret had apparently dropped right on top of the ants' nest . . . and now we knew why the native who had gone up the tree after our orchids on Yela had made such a rattle about his ant bites. We were poisoned, Margaret so badly that she was nauseated through most of the night. The bites stopped stinging by the next day, but by then they had become pustulate and itched so that we scratched them open in our sleep in spite of tying socks over our hands. Then they became infected, turning into the old familiar island sores that take so long healing. And Margaret's beautiful face became a satisfactory companion piece to mine with its yellow-green shiner.

But our trip on the *Chief* was not yet finished. At Hula we picked up a Service officer and his wife, and their party of police boys and carriers, and that was to complete the disintegration begun by the *Chief*.

Hula is a large mission station with a school for natives at the mouth of the Vanigela River, and to pick up the government party the *Chief* dropped anchor outside the entrance of Hood Bay about three miles from the settlement. The launch was put over for the trip ashore because there were eight or ten halfcaste children to be delivered to the mission, so we went along with our usual excuse of making sketches. It was one of the blackest and wettest of Papuan days, and a long dreary trip to the station, with the rain obscuring everything and the drenched and seasick children lopped around us like the fifteen men on the dead man's chest. And when we reached Hula we found that the government party had not arrived. They were finishing a patrol, so it was necessary to wait a while for them. To leave without them would have meant that they would have to beat it on foot all the way in to Port Moresby. Not that a Service officer isn't accustomed to doing everything on his own feet, but often when he has finished an assignment he is ready for the hospital and may have with him native prisoners or two or three carriers and police with spear holes in them. In any event the accommodating *Chief* does not abandon passengers if they do not appear exactly at the appointed time. The missionaries asked us to stay to dinner and the supercargo, who was with us, accepted. So the wet afternoon blackened to wet night and with it our mood. Margaret ducked out once during the evening with the flashlight. I thought it was for a bit of vice in the form of a cigarette, but when she came back in she was mud to the knees and dripping. "Heaven help a sailor on a night like this," she mumbled to me. "It's raining doorknobs. But the gas tank's full." Testing the gasoline tank of launches we were about to embark on was a routine precaution now, for running out of fuel on the high seas was the weakness of island launches. Especially in weather like this.

So when we finally left, without our passengers, around ten o'clock it was not lack of gas that made the launch engine stop somewhere between the station and the *Chief*. Just which haven we were nearest was doubtful, because we could see the lights of neither in the black downpour, and anyway we had both the swift current of the flooded river and an outgoing tide to change our position by the minute. Off came the hood of the engine and in went the doorknobs of rain onto spark plugs and wiring, but neither spinning the fly wheel, priming nor cursing did any good. I felt around in the darkness for an anchor, and luckily finding one, dropped it quietly overboard, playing the rope out delicately to see if I could feel when it caught. I felt nothing. (Putting an anchor over when the launch engine stalls is another aversion of the rugged Empire Builder.) Then we began to ship water, the seas coming over the stern; and when the "super" dropped the flashlight into the water in the bottom of the boat we were in total darkness.

There was one native boy from the *Chief* with us, and he and the "super" then broke up the engine hood and while Margaret took the tiller we three paddled with the slats from the cover. After about half an hour of this churning without seeming to get anywhere, I remembered the anchor and quietly pulled it up. Meantime the aft seas were still coming over, and though it was hard to tell because of being wet all over, it felt as if there were about a foot of water in the bottom of the launch. Margaret was whistling that peanut-wagon whistle and I knew she was thinking of the surf over the reefs ahead between us and the *Chief*. As a swimmer

Margaret is at best a slow-moving floater. If we missed the narrow channel we would be up against the surf—and no turning back then with three-inch slats against the tide and river current. "We'd better go back, we'd better go back now," I kept chanting inwardly with each dig of the slat that was helping us forward. I had a feeling this forward was not in the direction of the *Chief*. My homeward-guiding eel instincts told me we were being swept down the west coast of the bay (I was right) and I thought of the waist-deep mud that forms the shoreline of these rivers when the tide is at ebb, mud that sometimes extends far inland. We couldn't land even if we were washed to shore.

I do not know why it seems so much worse to drown on a dark night than in the daylight, but when I heard the sound of surf and still could not see it, all the air went out of my midriff with a sudden "bump" and was replaced by a sensation that had never come in the daytime when we had been caught in equally tight places. "I fancy we'd better do some bailing now," said the "super," and he sounded breathless too. There was nothing belonging to the launch to bail with, naturally, so Margaret and I used her raincoat between us—which, incidentally, is quite a feat when you cannot see whether your co-bailer is heaving or dipping. "There's nothing like fun," said Margaret as we counter-heaved and dipped; but it sounded pretty pale to me. After that there was silence on board for a small eon, just the splashing of water going overboard and more coming on board, and all around us the beating of invisible rain on invisible water that was so rough we could not keep our balance. And that fearsome rumble of surf seeming to come nearer and nearer. Then suddenly the boy, who had been mute up to this point, burst into a flood of pidgin English. We knew he was jerking his arms because they always do with such vehemence. He saw the lights of the *Chief*. Anyway he saw a light and insisted it was the "siteamer." We could see nothing, not even the way he was pointing; so he took the tiller and we took our slats, and from then on the launch rocked sideways and took the seas from port while the ominous sound of surf came from starboard. And we paddled and paddled.

When Margaret interrupted her whistling to announce excitedly that she too could now see the light midway between up and down in the blackness I could not look. I had my eyes clenched shut and was groaning like a she-oak in the wind. The palms of my hands seemed to be in ribbons and I thought I could feel streams of warm blood running down to my elbows. The rest of me that had any feeling was one big cramp. The fact that I now sit dry and eased, telling this tale, is proof that we did not have to go through the reef breakers —for if we had we should surely have capset. And with my locked muscles I should have been as helpless in the water as Margaret. We learned later that the launch had a metal hull and with any more water in it would have gone down like a pie tin. But we ran parallel to the breakers and in about three-quarters of an hour and a lifetime came to the surf-free passage with the rain-blurred *Chief* almost on top of us.

Then, the anticlimax to end all anticlimaxes was to be greeted when we were hauled up on deck (with ropes) with the accusation of having held up the sailing with our "swagging it" around on shore! The government passengers were on board and had been there since early afternoon. They had heard that the *Chief* was in as they came up the coast from the east, and rather than turn back inland to get to Hula at the apex of the bay, they had proceeded out to the east cape and got some native canoes to take them across to the *Chief*.

The ant-bitten Margaret was having paroxysms of hiccoughing and palsy, and I and my black eye were contorted with cramps like the hunchback of Notre Dame when the now-contrite Captain introduced the Service officer and, of

all things, his wife. But we shook hands like little gentlemen
and thereupon had transferred to us the final blight that was
to deliver us in to Port Moresby semi-invalid. The officer had
a cold and his *cinabada* was getting one, and they gave us
handfuls of it. It may have been the influenza that was sweeping the coast, for most of their police boys and carriers were
sick or were to become so, and one of them later died.

A *cinabada*, in case I haven't explained it before, is, literally
translated, a big toe—and this is the Motu name for a white
woman, who is usually a wife. The patrol officer's wife was
a very big toe indeed. Time was when a man in the Papuan
Service was not even allowed to have a wife, because it was
thought that with an anxious little woman back in the white
settlements an officer was less willing to take the risks that
"outside" duty then involved. Today in advanced Papua a
wife may even accompany her husband on routine patrol if
she wishes to subject herself to the bed of thorns. But the
cinabada was the only wife we ever heard of taking advantage of the license. We never heard of any white woman
like her in the islands, in fact. Physically she was a runt; she
could stand under the outstretched arm of her husband, but
the difference in size was just an illusion. She could lick the
living tar out of everything on the landscape and wink while
she was doing it. The whole outfit, man and wife, police boys
and carriers, had just come over from the other side of the
Range, where the *taubada* had been building an aerial track
. . . a foot-wide bridge of hand-hewn planks laid end to
end on piles . . . over miles of swamp. The marshes were
full of crocodiles and water leeches, and the air with mosquitoes "the size of cows." The men had been in the water
to their waists most of the three months it had taken, and
this was where the first noses began to run. The *cinabada*
meantime had kept the home fires burning in camp on the
nearest solid land.

When she saw our hands she shouted for boys and in a jiffy had us packed into our damp berths with hot-water bags, bandaged and anointed and drunk as lords before the *Chief*, again on its hell-bent way, could take another crack at us. I remember going to sleep in the middle of hysterical laughter. The *cinabada* was telling about the night not long before when they were on the track to the south coast and the *taubada* had been called out to investigate some trouble in a nearby village. The *cinabada* was left alone with only the mess boys, and in the middle of the night a white man whom she knew staggered into camp and collapsed at the bottom of the rest-house ladder. The *cinabada* thought he had black-water fever and had the boys carry him to another hut and then went to attend him. He was having hallucinations in which he thought he was dying. In his lucid moments he insisted on the *cinabada* giving him a benediction, which she did, not once but every time he had a lucid moment. And after each final prayer for the dying he would fold his arms on his chest and compose himself for the end. Only to start up an instant later shrieking, "Tigers! Snakes!" and "Poison!" when the *cinabada* tried to get some hot tea into him.

The *cinabada* and her husband had originally come to Papua as missionaries but, as the *taubada* said, they had seen the light and soon got out of that vendetta and into the Service. The *cinabada*, therefore, was unequipped by experience to recognize delirium tremens. Especially since a scotch breath is not a matter of degree and, anyway, a more or less normal halitus in rugged Papua. When she finally found that part of a case of whiskey was still in the man she ordered the boys to add castor oil to it. Then she went back to her own bed, thinking she was washing her hands of the mess.

A few hours later she was awakened by shrill cries of a man in mortal terror, and thinking the guest was murdering one of her painstakingly trained houseboys, she grabbed up her rifle and tore for the hut. Coming to her ears as she ran was, "Flour, flour, flour, flour. My god, my life's blood is running away. Flour, flour . . ."

We were to live with the *Cinabada* and *Taubada* in Port Moresby, which was not a thousand but a hundred and one nights' tales like this one.

15

One of the startling things that can happen to a traveler along this coast of New Guinea is to arrive at Port Moresby. One night we went to sleep on the romping *Papuan Chief* in the same gusty downpour that had enveloped us all the way from Samarai, and the next morning we woke in still-ness and brilliant sunshine with our nostrils stuck together by the sudden dryness of this strange desert in the tropics. Port Moresby, a scanty cluster of weathered wooden build-ings, trailed over the low hills of a peninsula following an indentation that led from the harbor to the outer shore. Dry yellow grass covered the hillsides, and there was not one life-sized tree to be seen in the whole panorama. It was only eight o'clock, but the residents of Port Moresby could have made waffles on their corrugated iron roofs. The water in the wide bay was no longer the stormy leaden green of farther east, but the intense luminous blue of a deep and almost landlocked bay into which no flood-yellowed rivers run. (British warships were based in Fairfax Harbor during the First World War.) Around the bay the low, almost bar-ren hills in the distance were like the "iron" mountains of the Utah and Nevada deserts, violet and rust-red, ocher and hard prussian blue, colors never seen elsewhere in these tropical countries. Nowhere in all the baked landscape were any of those soft steamy blues and vibrant greens of the saturated East.

A yellow wind—which we soon discovered seldom ceased blowing—was sweeping down over the peninsula road bearing out to us the long-ago odor of dry dust. The heat in it was like something coming from a vat of molten metal. We felt like fish out of water, our scales curling, eyeballs singed, and smeared coconut oil on our shriveling skins, praying for rain.

The explanation for this desert belt which extends about a hundred miles along the coast of the Central Division does not seem clear enough even to the experts for us to repeat with any authority. It has something to do with winds and mountain barriers, and just the general contrariness of New Guinea weather. The district has an annual rainfall of about forty inches, high for a temperate climate, but here it falls all within three months; and a month after it has stopped raining the intense sun has dehydrated the whole district. Around this arid region the precipitation runs up to as much as eight yards a year, but the adjacent saturation does not affect the air of Port Moresby.

The air of Port Moresby, on the other hand, does affect its citizens. For one thing it intensifies the Anglo-Papuan characteristics already mentioned, and the site was probably a good choice for the seat of government. (Incidentally, it was named for Captain Moresby, father of the writer L. Adams Beck, who is better known in the United States as E. Barrington, the author of such magazine serials as "The Gay Perdita.") Among the first residents we met was a family with four children in it all of whom had been born antiseptically right in Port Moresby. Ordinarily despite hospitals and doctors white women must return to Australia for their confinement because of the danger of septicemia. But at first we thought we were too miserable to live because our hides were long accustomed to steaminess. Then as the dehydration continued some of the benefits became apparent. Our colds retreated, at least from our noses; the infections of our ant bites and hands shrank, and our lank hair began to stand on its own again. But the drying out did not stop there. The first warning was when our ukulele and guitar began to crack up—and before long we were going the same way. After all, this was only ten degrees below the equator, without even the cooling effect of foliage around us. The first invigoration developed into "nerves," and the nerves into insomnia that banished sleep even during the now-very-necessary midday siesta. Soon Margaret had dropped more pounds off her already slenderized hips and I was taken with seizures of creative fits when I felt, but did not paint, like Van Gogh.

But all this was in the future. We were still wet-nosed and covered with black eyes and bites when we moved into Villa Viper with the *Cinabada* and the *Taubada*. While still on the *Chief* we had discovered that they were to be as homeless as ourselves when they reached Port Moresby, so we rented a vacant house together and set up housekeeping with our combined camp outfits supplemented with packing cases. The only thing we had plenty of was servants; we had the entire line of carriers, ten or twelve boys. The house, which we had considered ourselves lucky to have found even unfurnished, was perched up on the slope of the first steep hill above the bay, and the boys used the area beneath it for a dormitory. We were like geological strata of civilizations, Stone Age below and Jazz Age above with only a thin wood floor with wide cracks between the dried-out boarding separating us. This had something to do with our insomnia when it was upon us. For the one dominant characteristic of Stone Age men, we now discovered, was that they seldom cease making sounds and they make no distinction between night and day for their kinds of sounds as we do. When there was no moon they slept like ordinary mortals, but then they snored and had nightmares. When there was a moon they talked and laughed. Or sang. One voice would start droning out a monotone, something about his village and homesickness for it, usually with a lot of roast pig rather than a girl providing the love motif. The solo would go on indifferently for some time while the others listened, then by and by another voice would join in moaning the tune . . . we could visualize him with his big mouth hanging open . . . and finally the first singer would yield him the solo about *his* village and *his* homesickness and the pig *he* remembered so dearly. During this the rest would be warming up by moaning. Until it became a round and went on and on, sometimes until daybreak or until the *Taubada,* who was a vocal sleeper himself, woke up and tried to put a hole through the floor with his foot. Then we would hear the *Cinabada* over the partitions say, *"Don't* put your bare foot on that floor. You'll get bitten."

Whenever we heard chuckling below, Margaret and I shamelessly raised the mosquito net so that we could hear better; for we have a primitive sense of humor. A description in pidgin English of how the young blades of the village spread out through the bush when some modest old woman went seeking a place to relieve herself and of how one of them popped out into view every time she thought she had found it had the Jazz Age and the Stone Age united at last. In obscene laughter.

One of the sick boys had "sinakes" and now and then would rise up in the dark of the night with a great scuffling and croaking right under our cots and go bellowing off down the hill with his snakes in hot pursuit. Some of them may have been real, for snakes are a prominent feature of New Guinea and Villa Viper was not so named out of poesy. The things we had were the reason the house was vacant and available for twenty-five dollars a month. In contrast to most island dwellings there was not a screen anywhere and the building was not raised entirely off the ground on its piles. The whole rear or road edge of the veranda on the higher side of the hill rested right on the earth, with the result that any wild life whose habitat was New Guinea did not distinguish their home from ours. Besides the usual lizards and rats and spiders in the bare rafters we had a hundredfold the number of other flying and crawling things, mostly mosquitoes, fleas, cockroaches, ants, sand flies, horse flies, house flies, meat, bluebottle and fruit. Every kind except tsetse, I think. People said they were bad during the rainy season.

We figured out that the reason all these God's creatures came into our house was because we had water and the rest of Port Moresby accessible to them did not. So we set the legs of everything, including our stretchers, in tins of water and then put water troughs all around the Villa so that they would come no further. But it would have taken a moat to handle the multitude; and anyway the ants could walk right over the surface tension of water in a pan. The ants, however, had a function: they carried off each night's casualties among the other insects. And except for the night the whole tribe got into my hair when I had it soaking in coconut oil, we all preferred the ants to the centipedes.

Our centipedes were the inspiration for the name "Viper." The Villa was crawling with them. They were in the toilet down the hill and in the shower stall at the south end of the veranda, and in the *Taubada's* slippers when he was careless enough to leave them outside his mosquito net one night. They were in tea towels and hand towels, in spite of persistent search by the *cinabada-harried* staff of boys, and even in our clothing and on the grass skirt of a model I had sitting for us one morning. Every now and then would come from under the house a vehement "Ugh!" or "Yah!" followed by batting sounds; and we of the Jazz Age above would smile complacently at one another without having to say how happy we were that another of the long brown vipers was out of this world.

One bright morning . . . and note the adjective, for the morning sun on the bay side of the veranda was like a spotlight . . . we were all going innocently about our various occupations; the *Taubada* still drinking his waking-up tea in the shaded north corner of the veranda, Margaret taking a shower at the other end with a stream of water pouring from the floor to the ground ten feet below to show how she was getting on, and a squad of boys moving dazedly about the floor with implements for cleaning. I was pounding away on our non-stop letter while waiting for the shower in order to get the installment up to date. For the southbound steamer was calling in that day. All was peace and quiet, save for the hot buzz of our flies. "When the house is being cleaned in the morning," I wrote, "our little *Cinabada* sounds like Gracie Fields singing about the biggest aspidistra in the world. Primitives cannot understand the fundamental principles of dirt; that it is misplaced matter. I just heard one boy imply that to another down the side veranda. This thing the *Cinabada* calls dirt, he said, is everywhere, but the *Cinabada* was always making him pick it up and put it somewhere else. Now if she would just leave it alone, that on the floor would fall through the cracks of . . . There was a sudden half-human squawk that brought everyone to a standstill. Instantly out of the shower into the spotlight sprang Margaret, undraped and ungarlanded, and came leaping around the veranda spraying water and batting her wet arms about her body, the while emitting sounds that I did not know she had in her. The squads gazed with dropped jaws and the *Taubada* rose with his prune-shaped, "Oh, I say . . ." I was inclined to laugh— though Margaret usually did not go this far with her clowning. But the *Cinabada* knew instantly, and knew the Papuan thing to do. She seized Margaret's arm . . . the centipede bite was on the tip of the middle finger . . . and gave it a sharp whack on the ulnar nerve at the elbow with the side of her palm. It is not for nothing that this nerve is called the crazy bone. The blow anesthetized the arm all right, for the combined pains put Margaret completely out.

Before nightfall the finger was white and swollen, and the pain so great that even morphine injections failed to relieve it. And in the agonizing days that followed the toxin traveled into the hand and the lancing followed it until the glands in the armpit were affected. It was our first major casualty, and it came at a time when we were least fortified to meet it.

I feel as if I were indelicately regretting the expenses of a funeral (as who, sometime, has not) to touch on the cost of this accident. But the island doctors' fees are on a Park Avenue rating, and we were using camp salt for tooth powder these days to help the Heffalump. So far we had heard nothing from the Council regarding Sir Hubert's portrait, and we had done all we could to bring the matter to a decision. His Excellency, pretending not to know what it was all about, had contributed three hours of State time to sit for a portrait drawing. This was to show our wares. Now all we could do was to wait.

16

The doldrums while we waited for portrait commissions from the white populace was usually a profitable time for the native portrait. For it gave us leisure in which to snoop about and absorb into our pores . . . that first stage in the mental process of a painter . . . the essential pictures of the new locale. Now as we sat on orange crates at breakfast on our lofty bayside veranda all the wide stretch of Fairfax Harbor was spread out before us to absorb. Heat was rising from the iron roofs of the houses below us "shivering like wheat in the summer field." Along the waterfront road there was not a living soul passing, for all the traveling had already been done in the cooler hours. Far down the billboard-blue water at a small point on our side of the harbor was the marine village of Hanuabada, its cluster of dry thatched roofs like a heap of gold nuggets against the purple of the low hills behind it. With the *Taubada's* field glasses we could make out the peculiar structure of a vessel anchored before the village. It was the largest craft we had seen in the Coral Sea, actually a catamaran. Twin hulls of long dugout canoes were lashed together and decked over, but the peculiarity was the two big sails which were shaped like crab claws. Normally the "nippers" pointed up from the deck; but at the moment, the vessel being at anchor, they were dropped at horizontal. All around the outline of the rigid sail framework, up the guys of the masts and hanging along the edges of the deck were long streamers of grass fluttering in the wind. It looked gay as bunting, but the vessel was lifeless and actually in mourning.

This vessel, called a *lakatoi*, and important enough to have its portrait on the Papuan postage stamp, was the most significant single thing to be seen under that hard hot sun. Around the *lakatoi* revolve all the neighborhood doings of the local Motuans that wind up annually in a business called *hiri*. Hiri means literally to sail. Once a year when the winds are blowing from the southeast a whole fleet of such vessels sets out for the timber and sago lands of the western Delta Division. They sail laden with cargoes of the dull-blue and copper-red pottery jars that the Motu women have made during the year out of the clay of the district. At the rivers in the west the jars are traded for a year's supply of sago (the sago palm does not grow around this dry region) and for big logs that have been floated down the rivers from inland. The men remain there to shape the logs into catamaran hulls and to build new *lakatoi*. They then load up with the sago, by which time the trades have shifted and blow them back to Hanuabada.

A voyage of any kind of vessel is a perilous undertaking in this part of the Coral Sea (as our trip on the *Chief* should have demonstrated) so for weeks before the *hiri* there are all sorts of observances to insure a safe journey. The sorceresses conduct seances to get the hiri spirits in an amiable mood, test races are held to determine the seaworthiness and speed of the *lakatoi* and finally, just before sailing, there are days and nights of dancing and feasting on the decks of the vessels, a highly questionable ceremony called *siu siu*. This is the season when the missionaries have a frightful time with their flock. In our missionary-compiled dictionary *siu siu* is translated as obscene dance. The dances are performed by the maidens of Hanuabada, and from the photographs we have seen of the dancing maidens, it would appear that the

missionaries may have a case. The picture we have in mind
was taken from below the deck of the *lakatoi*, evidently from
a launch, and there is a row of little Motu bottoms facing the
camera with the flying rami of the dancers completely obscuring their upper body. However wicked, this was the

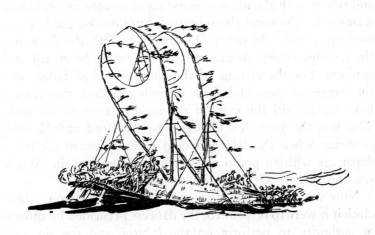

picture we decided to paint of the Motu Melanesians; the
final godspeed on the *lakatoi* with flying skirts and laughing
boys stowing away the blue-and-copper pottery, but most
of all the *lakatoi* itself with its picturesque sails. All this
symbolized the graciousness of the vanishing culture: the
frivolity that ornaments an economic necessity so that it becomes something beyond mere working-to-eat and eating-
to-work with a movie on Saturday night and a drive on
Sunday.

By sheer luck we had arrived on the scene in the proper
season, when the wind was shifting to the south. But that was
the end of our blessing, for there was to be no *siu siu* this
year. Every now and then the storms take a toll of the *hiri*

and the preceding season on the return to Hanuabada the entire fleet had been swallowed by the Gulf with the exception of the lone *lakatoi* out on the bay. Many of the men were drowned and the year's sago was lost. The Government was rationing out rice to tide the people over until the surviving men could sail the *lakatoi* west again, make new crafts and return with the life-sustaining sago, months away. While waiting for the wind the solitary *lakatoi* out on the bay lay motionless under the hot sun looking like a little lost duck, her tired wings folded down and her wayward heart sad and penitent. For the charms of the sorceresses had failed, and the fringes of grass and shells on sails and deck that should have warded off the evils of the sea had been of no avail. This was the year that belonged to the Lord and his missionaries, when the *lakatoi* would make a decent Christian departure without pomp nor mirth nor even any sin. And it was the year of our deep disappointment.

Now we would have to reconstruct the *siu siu* from whole cloth if it were to be painted, the dancers persuaded by money or authority to perform on the *lakatoi*, and the sin, and doubtless the mirth, provided by our imagination. We had tried this creative tactic before, and it was a limp business that needed a lot of preliminary building up. Nevertheless we now went to work on it, starting on our imagination by participating in the races of the "Port Moresby Yacht Club." This was with the excuse of getting the "feel" of the test races of the *lakatoi*. But just between us, we did it partly because the Port Moresby yachtsmen were so set against it.

The yachts of the yacht club are ordinary native-made outrigger canoes with the difference of having a canvas sail instead of pandanus palm mats. They are manned by a native crew, and only "navigated" by the white owner. Actually the canoe races are the Papuan colonial's substitute for the Australian horse, largely something to bet on, and races are run off every Saturday that the wind is "right." But the club is something more than a yacht club. It is a male secret society. There are no women members and, conforming with native taboos, women are not encouraged to do more than look at the goings-on from a respectful distance—as spectators at the races or food providers afterward. But like the native women the ladies are well content with this role—for reasons I was to discover for myself.

Our first task, therefore, was to locate an unsuperstitious yachtsman; and it soon became apparent that this was going to be difficult if not impossible. Still, for art, we persisted. From the minute it became known at the "pub" (the bar being the club house) that we had decided to go in the races the following Saturday, the owners of canoes would dissolve on sight. But finally one sportsman was trapped by not being nippy enough, and when accused of primitive narrow-mindedness he endeavored to explain why women in the races were taboo. They were a crimson (polite for bloody) nuisance. And it was dangerous. Half of the canoes were dumped on the course as a normal thing, and on a tough day all of them. The men sometimes got hit by a flying outrigger or boom, and when they were dunked they had to swim around for hours, days, sometimes years before the pole boat got to them. The bay was alive with shark and barracuda and groupers, and a strong current ran across the course beyond the end of the peninsula. But worst of all, women got seasick. That, our sensitive stomach, was the gallant yachtsman's trump card. In this gentlemanly dispute no one thought to mention the real reason women were not welcome, which was that they were non-functioning ballast on the light crafts where every pound made as much difference in the speed as the extra ounce on a race horse.

Finally, however, powerful political forces were brought into action on our behalf, and on Friday night a paper talk-

talk was delivered from a depressed yachtsman which we translated as an invitation to sail with him on the morrow. (He was in government service, and the *Taubada* claimed that he had been threatened with his job if he failed to take us on.) The invitation closed with a note of hope for our host; he said he expected very bad weather indeed.

It did not look like bad weather when we woke that Saturday morning. The sun was boring everything full of holes as usual, and the whole sky was a flawless blare of light. But if the man had prayed for it he could not have got more wind. A modified kind of "blow" was tearing over the peninsula, carrying the ocher dust of the main road far out over the bay. "Top-hole sailing," observed the *Taubada*, and put his tongue in his cheek. But he blew out both cheeks when I appeared dressed in only a swim suit. Curiously, in this land where half-naked women form most of the traffic on the roads, any woman, lacking that density of pigment which so ably garbs the native, who appears in public with less than the usual costume is inviting comment. I hid under a raincoat until I got past the fringe of spectators lined up along the beach (Margaret's ailing arm eliminated her from this adventure) but out on the canoe the heat and the-hell-with-it made me discard the coat—whereupon a regular tidal wave of shock rolled over the racing canoes and up the beach. I must confess that my Nordic expanse was like a searchlight even under my own nose in this company of almost naked brown crews and fully dressed white men. And to add to my appearance of undress I was wearing gloves. They were the *Taubada's* rubber gloves that he used when treating infectious diseases among the natives, and they were bound tightly at my wrists to keep the bandages on my hands dry. The sores were not yet healed. My skipper took one baffled look at the gloves and hid his head like an ostrich, pulling a sweat shirt on over it. Then he was fully dressed

even with a felt hat. Our crew did their own native kind of
ostrich, pretending not to have noticed me while they cinched
already-cinched guys at the far ends of the canoe. It was then
that I first noticed Pakosi's back. He was tying a bottle of
whiskey to the mast and had it, the beautiful back, turned
to me.

Somewhere else we have said that the Motuans are an
effeminate-looking tribe of Melanesians. But either we had
become accustomed to the slight stature, or the fluffy hair-do
and profuse tag-end ornaments had given us that impression.
There was nothing feminine-looking about this crew, and
particularly Pakosi. The boys were stripped for action. Pakosi's big mop of hair was skinned to the top of his head and
tied in a pom-pom with a bit of rag, and his crimson sulu
was rolled up snugly about his loins like a diaper. Otherwise
he was naked and without ornaments. He was a fine-looking
specimen of anatomy. His back was straight as a plumb line
from the base of his skull to buttocks, and at this latter point
so slender that his Motu shoulders looked broad. Every strong
young muscle was as sharply defined as if he were skinless.
But he had a skin, and it had the lively color and sheen of a
sorrel colt in pasture. "Pakosi," we discovered, is the Motu
word for scissors. And I decided immediately that young
Scissors should pose for some of the gay lads setting out on
the *hiri*.

Six uncontaminated entries punted out to a start ahead of
us, and each crew as it passed cast back on our miserable five
that look of grinning contempt which the male the world
over reserves for his fellow who has a woman anchored to his
neck when there are big things in the offing. But no one could
have been happier making others miserable than I was. And
when we got the signal to pull out the boys forgot me in their
own happiness. Until we got past the pole boat and into the
wind two of the boys punted and the three others were sta-

tioned at the rudder paddles. These were huge paddles five or six feet long over all with a blade about a yard long and eight or nine inches wide. There was no oar lock, not even a noose of vine. The paddles were thrust down into the water through the outrigger framework next to the gunwale, and were held in position by the boy's feet. There were no Royal Yacht Club rules controlling this Papuan event, and I understood each entry could carry as much sail as the yachtsman wished to risk, but the hull could not exceed thirty feet. Ours was about twenty-five, and we must have had almost a hundred and thirty square feet of canvas. The "fastest sailing canoes in the world" they are called, and with skillful handling—and luck in a good wind—they can do up to twenty-eight knots. That's fast. Even for a power boat.

There was only one outrigger on our *Mulukwasi* (meaning "flying witch,") and it extended off the windward gunwale. The float on the outside edge of the outrigger looked lighter than usual, and there were certainly fewer cross pieces in the framework. Even then I was beginning to regard that outrigger relatively. If I had to skip around on it as I understood the crew did—and I was now one of the crew, for a boy had been left ashore to make way for me—I wondered if my legs were long enough after all to span the gaps.

As we left the spectators behind, the skipper strengthened himself from the bottle at the mast, after which he began explaining what I had to do to be as little of a crimson nuisance as possible. The course of the race was triangular, with the first tack running parallel with the peninsula and beyond to an islet some two or three miles out in open water. We were to skirt this and run back into the bay to a buoy opposite Hanuabada, then home. Two laps of it. The "tough spot" was just beyond the end of the peninsula, where wind and current hit from the same direction.

During this introduction we were skimming along under

sail like a surfboard, the outrigger flying about a foot clear of the water. (In the water it acted as a brake.) The skipper was continuing with deadly masculine patience to explain what would happen when we got to the tough spot. "You see," he said, pointing ahead. The lead canoe was just clearing the promontory into the wind-whitened seas, and everyone on board had shifted over to the outrigger side. They stood on the gunwale and had one leg stretched far out on the outrigger, their bodies bending in that direction. The rudder boys pulling on their huge paddles were braced hard against the wind. "Just watch!" As the wind-filled sail bent over the outrigger started to rise in the air, and the men leaned farther over it. Then suddenly, quicker than it could register, the outrigger swept up, smacked the seven men like a bat, the sail spanked clean over followed by the outrigger, and the air was sprayed with superstitious yachtsmen. Prettiest thing you ever saw. "They weren't nippy enough, you see," grinned the skipper, and had another drink. I had one too this time, because I didn't see. "By the way, put that cork in tight," added my host; "we'll need the contents more when we get in the water. Shark never touch a man with good scotch on his breath."

When the second canoe smacked over, I was beginning to see a little better. It didn't explain much about a *lakatoi*, but I was beginning to get a good idea of Motu outrigger sailing. This craft we were on was nothing but a keel-less log with no "down" that gravity preferred, but it had an enormous sail that the wind did. To counterbalance that wind on the sail all on board had to throw their weight on the outrigger and then maintain a nice united adjustment of pressure and release to meet the gusts of wind and seas. And still keep the outrigger from braking in the water. It was manned something like an iceboat, but lacked that balancing runner on the leeward side that made all the difference.

We watched interestedly as the third canoe ran out. It was like a gull teetering undecidedly in a gusty wind. "That was a honey!" exclaimed the skipper as seven more sportsmen sprawled through the air. Even the boys were laughing now, and I tied the expedition's raincoat securely to the mast by the arms. Followed some instructions on how to be swung off an outrigger. Just relax, I was not to hold onto anything but let myself fly and then drop into the water as deeply as fate sent me in order to give the canoe time to settle. For sometimes the mast swung under and bopped a yachtsman on the head—and then a scented breath didn't help him.

When the fourth canoe spanked over, the pole boat had chugged past us and was hauling our rivals out of the way. And I had begun to hiccough as if my breath were on an elastic. But the two remaining canoes ahead of us ran in luck. They got out past the X-area with their wings in the air, and after wagging dangerously for a minute got away with such speed I gave the race to them. But the leading canoe had not gone a hundred yards when the flying outrigger suddenly dropped. And everyone stretched out on it slowly sank beneath the waves. I missed Margaret at that minute. No one else could so have enjoyed with me this peaceful elimination of a faction which had looked on our gender with aloofness.

It was our turn now.

I had taken up a sporty stance, standing spraddle-legged in line with the skipper and boys, but this way I had nothing to hang onto and as the outrigger started jerking up I changed to a less becoming pyramid position, bending over from the waist and gripping the outrigger framework with my hands. At the same time I noticed I was wasting potential tentacles, and slipped off my tennis shoes. The boys had their toes wound around the framework like hands. We cleared the cliff and started into the whitecaps, passing a lot of people we knew. They said the swimming was fine, and they would be seeing us. We thought so too, and I relaxed my grip so as not to hang onto anything by instinct. Nothing happened. The outrigger was flying along just clear of the seas, held in this perfect position as if suspended on wire. I had the most exultant feeling of being swung on a string myself. The

water was rushing under my face going past, not at the rate of thirty knots, but seeming twice that fast. A bird in the sky could not get nearly the same sensation of flying. Spray swept over us, and every now and then a wave nipped up at the float; and we had to work fast backing and filling to keep clear and yet not swing too high. I whoopee-ed and the Australian coo-ee-ed while the wet naked crew posed like the "Argonauts of the Pacific." No color nor sex nor stratum of civilization mattered at this high moment. For we were out in the steady wind, safe, wings in the air soaring toward the island.

The islet was surrounded by reefs, and no punting was allowed here. The boom was swung around, the stern thereby becoming prow; and it was slow business getting under way again. But we got off before the one canoe which had been ahead of us, and in passing I slipped them our national salute. Victory entered my mind at that moment. There were five canoes still in the race. Was it possible that the Flying Witch *could* win—with a female on board? What a revolution that would cause in superstitions! The moment was short-lived. It was unfortunate that I had one hand to my nose and the other was in a slippery rubber glove, that there were cramps in my legs and a whopper of a wave should have lopped up just at that minute. The outrigger dropped out of my hand and the next thing I knew I was riding suspended by my knees and armpits with my bottom dragging in the water, the Witch slowing to a standstill. I had never before heard natives express disapproval. It was a sound something like driving on a flat tire; eye-a-eye-a-eye-a. While I was being hauled up, the canoe we had passed flew by with its leg in the air, thumb to nose.

But this was purely a race of survival. To be a runner-up all one had to do was keep sailing, and to do that one had only to pray. And as is always the case, the prayers were answered impartially as to the merits of the pray-ers. We passed the "grandstand" in the suddenly windless lee of the promontory, running a neck-and-neck race with one of the last contenders to start, at the rate of two or three knots. We were like floats in a parade, and the spectators cheered and blew a car horn to speed us up. I was busy trying to rub the cramps out of my legs, a business which informed me, incidentally, that I had a sunburn. We were lucky again getting out past the tough spot, and we finished—but in what place I never remembered to ask. That second lap I was a crimson nuisance most of the way, especially to myself, for my legs were again locked in an agony of cramps. I couldn't walk when I was set ashore, and had to be carried up the hill ignobly seated on the clasped hands of two of our disgraced crew. One of them was the muscular Scissors, and I could have sworn that he pinched me purposely as they cast me off on the veranda. Though I do not believe the American pinch on the backside is ordinarily a primitive practice.

These muscle cramps, which were to become chronic in my case, have a rather more involved explanation than the same thing when it occurs in a temperate climate. When muscles freeze it is because not enough oxygen is getting to them in the blood supply. Either they have been overworked and the system is tired of feeding them, or slowed circulation, as in old age, during sleep or from cold, causes a local anemia. Pinching or beating up the affected muscles, breathing deeply to increase the supply of oxygen in the whole system and moving around to increase the general circulation will take care of the average case in a short time. But in the hot islands, when severe cramps are unusually commonplace they cannot be budged by "reeling and writhing." A woman who had had children as well as "tropical cramps" told us that of the two kinds of cramps she preferred those of labor because though they were equally agonizing the one kind gave at least periodic relief during a siege. But she did not know the cause of the tropical cramps, nor did anyone else we asked.

We finally figured out for ourselves what the great minds in the medical corps of our armies arrived at when they were faced with heat stroke cramps in the South Pacific—though we did not reach the solution in the same way, nor did our antidote, which was the same, have the same effect. Steel-mill workers, we remembered, are subject to cramps if they are not given a saline solution to replace the salt lost from the system in profuse sweating as they work around the hot furnaces and vats. And losing our salts this way was one thing we had been doing rather steadily for some time. We tried to drink salt water and had to give that up involuntarily, and anyway Margaret never had an attack of cramps. There was no difference in our environment, none in the food we ate or in what we did; but there was an important difference between us in the fact that I had malaria. And this, I humbly submit, for it is not scientifically substantiated, might be the explanation of tropical cramps.

The coloring matter in the red blood corpuscles is the vehicle of oxygen in our systems, and when one has had malaria over a fairly long period there is a deficiency of red blood corpuscles which must reduce the supply of oxygen so necessary, apparently, to lax muscles. We didn't have any cure for that, even when we had risen to the heights of guessing at it.

This first severe attack of cramps was short-lived however compared to the after-effects of having been tied in a knot for so long, or compared to the new symptoms that the treatment for them developed. Someone suggested that we put my legs

As *Anopheles* bites it injects into the blood stream malaria sporozoites which (1) invade the red blood corpusle. (2) Parasite developes, feeding on cell until (3) entire cell is destroyed. Incubation period is about two weeks, when the first attack of fever is felt. The cell ruptures, liberating into the blood stream a new tribe (5–6) of male and female parasites which start to work on fresh red cells, after which they are ready for the bite of another female *Anopheles*. Taken into the stomach of the mosquito, the sex phase of the cycle takes place, producing a new generation of sporozoites. These migrate to the salivary glands of the mosquito, from whence they are injected into the circulation of the human host.

in a gasoline tin of hot water, and it was this first aid that revealed that I was *pataka-pataka*. This is a term usually applied
to yams and a careless cook, and means boiled to a rag. My
hide was literally in a soupy state of sunburn. For a long time
we had thought that the local custom of always being covered
in the sun was simply a precaution against sunstroke. We
never saw a sun-bronzed Empire Builder like the movie version, and supposed that the equator sun did not tan for some
reason. We were right and now we knew why. It just removes the whole skin, pigment, pimple and even some of the
fur.

While growing a new pelt we reached the conclusion that
posterity would have to get along with something less than a
portrait of a whole *lakatoi* and *siu siu*, perhaps just a quiet picture of Pakosi's muscles painted in some shaded nook out of
the wind.

17

The month of August even began auspiciously, for on the first day of that month we acquired a model "negotiator." He would seem to have come straight from heaven in answer to our persevering prayers; but the paper talk-talk he brought bore the crest of the Government on it. The note said that the bearer, Ahuia, was a court interpreter who had worked with "other anthropologists," and that he should be useful to us in explaining customs and procuring models in authentic costumes. He was someone we had been needing for two years. Furthermore we were not to pay him, for he was a government employee, though we might give him a present of tobacco occasionally if we wished.

There was something about Ahuia's bearing and garments that suggested that the tobacco meant was not the ordinary trade stick, so we gave him a cigarette to start with while we explained the portrait business. Ahuia accepted the cigarette, reached inside his white shirt and took from the tight-plaited bracelet on his upper arm a long black hard-rubber nozzle that had once been part of an enema bag. Into the threaded end of this he inserted the king size cigarette, put the other end in his mouth and lit up from our automatic lighter without so much as blinking at its sudden flare. Ahuia was a full-blown flower of that level of civilization to which the Papuan Government was raising the primitive. He even wore a mustache.

The interpreter was barefooted and hatless and wore a

calico sulu like any native, but his ironed white shirt would have identified him even without the mustache. In Papua the ordinary native is not permitted to wear garments above the waist, and no missionary may persuade his flock into such clothing. This is for reasons of health. For the Papuan has never worn upper garments, does not need them for protection, and does not know how to wear them. When he puts a shirt on it is for decoration, and it stays on night and day unwashed through rain and shine until the last thread has parted. When it rains the shirt, unlike his skin, stays wet. He catches cold, the colds become chronic—and the next step is tuberculosis or pneumonia, which raises the mortality. In the other Coral Sea protectorates European clothing is not encouraged simply for reasons of maintaining white prestige, just as the natives are not persuaded to learn straight English when it would be as easy for them as pidgin; eliminating these differences would diminish the arm's length. Our war in these islands will have changed all this. Today hundreds of primitives who never before wore more than a g-string are sporting G.I. shirts and complete Japanese uniforms; and until they have worn out, both the health of the native and the prestige of the Empire Builder are going to suffer. In any case, in Papua only super-natives, the police, teachers in the mission schools and government employees like Ahuia are to be trusted in European garments, and then the shirt is a badge of authority, behind it Government permission which commands respect from the naked.

Our first request of the interpreter was Pakosi, and he appeared to promise to produce the boy. But first there was a good sound financial agreement about the model fee. This came as a slight surprise to us, who had been getting the services of models for everything from old garters to trade tobacco. But Hanuabada is a native metropolis, and we were to learn that the Motuans had a well developed commercial sense even before the round-the-world cruisers began coming with their trippers paying silver for services and curios. The model fee was to be two shillings a day (a month's wages for a plantation boy elsewhere) with *kai-kai,* boiled rice, at noon.

But when Ahuia appeared promptly next day, a surprise in itself, he did not have Pakosi with him. There was no explanation, and the substitute models he did bring took our minds off asking. There was what appeared to be a whole clan, women of all ages with infants in arms and toddlers, all washed and polished Christians and eminently civilized colored folk like Ahuia himself. Yet, they were too interesting to reject for that reason and until Pakosi should appear we accepted them. But from then on Ahuia produced only such natives. And each model was accompanied into town from Hanuabada by the nearest clan relatives.

Most of the reason for this, we thought, was that Viper Villa had an extraordinary mirror. It belonged to Percy Leigh, the "ambassador" from New Orleans, and was consequently the biggest glass in New Guinea, so large in fact that it had to be set up on the veranda, where we all used it. The clans would gather in front of this treasure, one behind the other, and with the help of the savvy houseboys point out parts of their anatomy that they had not seen before. Some of the girls would part their rami and examine the tattooing on their bottom, all with the detached interest of a fish discovering that he was being followed by a tail.

The safari usually arrived at the Villa around ten or eleven o'clock, when the heat under our low roof was enough to make prunes of your eyeballs. They did not like it. Their thatched huts over the water in the marine village were cool, and the unaccustomed idleness in the heat made them sleepy after they had satisfied their curiosity about the big fella *varivari.* So they napped while the model "posed," and if Margaret managed to keep the sitter awake by tom-tomming on the ukulele the girl sulked because she was socially alone and bored. None of our juvenile entertainment could interest these savvy natives for very long.

At twelve, after about an hour of actual work, the clan woke up and went below the house to eat bushels of boiled rice. Rice cost only a dollar and a half for twenty-five pounds, and that much boils up into bushels, but such quantities were going into the clan maws that we thought we must be supplementing the government rations and that a different set of relatives were coming in with the same model each day. It was costing more to feed them than it was ourselves. Then when finally the guests returned to the veranda after an extended siesta they brought a lot of loose rice in their petticoats and were followed by trains of ants. But this did not bother our immaculate *Cinabada* so much as the mothers' habit of holding an infant over the veranda rail to relieve himself, just as they did in their huts over the water. Occasionally one would let go where he was playing on the floor, and the day it ran through onto the belly of the "cookie" who was day-dreaming on his stretcher below was the day we all decided that what I needed was a studio. Away from the house, someone suggested. Out at Hanuabada, I said, because at four o'clock, just as it was getting cool enough to work with any enthusiasm, it was also cool enough for the model and her duennas to make the two-mile trip back to the village in comfort. So they departed forthwith, critically examining the "s'illings" for which we ourselves had given someone our blood.

Hanuabada, however, was also two miles away for us, a four-mile walk, round trip, in this heat, two of them after six or eight hours' work. When we first arrived in the islands that would have been nothing, but we were over two years younger then. It would have been a stalemate except for August being our auspicious month. For each problem as it developed came bringing its solution behind like the tails of Mary's lambs. The Government lent us a horse. To be sure it was only one horse, but the first day we used it to go to the village Margaret rode out with the gear while I walked, and when we returned I was stretched out on the horse . . . mud to the knees and my tongue hanging out. Working in Hanuabada had done this to me.

Our first impression of the marine village was one of unreserved delight. It was like the creation of an artist, something out of a Walt Disney fantasy. The chubby little thatchroofed houses were like birdhouses hoisted up in the air at least twelve feet above the surface of the water on a forest of knobby white piles standing at cockeyed angles. There were irregular streets of houses connected with one another by narrow bridges that ran under the floor of the huts and on down to the shore. Each little blond one-room house had its veranda, with here and there a clump of fish net draped picturesquely over a cross pole above the doorway. And tied up at the bottom of the ladder to the veranda was the family transportation, a spider-legged canoe. All the piles were bleached bone-white; and the whole "meaty" business, a hamlet housing some two thousand natives, was reflected identically in the blue ebbing tide.

The thing that would have continued to puzzle us about this village if it had not been for Ahuia was how the natives had managed to get the piles of their houses upright without the aid of cranes or any leverage to start from. The largest of the posts were fifteen or twenty inches in diameter, about like a telephone pole, and they were heavy hardwood that would take many men to lift even if the log were prone. These come from inland and are floated down the rivers and picked up by the *lakatoi* in the west, but many of the piles are heirlooms which have supported the homes of generations. Ahuia said that the best of them were about twenty feet long, and to erect them takes hard work as well as magic. At the time of lowest water, which is ebb tide during full moon, a deep hole is dug in the mud or coral. The large end of the log is chopped to a point, and guy ropes are attached to the other end. Then the pointed end is directed into the hole, the log is pushed and lifted up with the aid of fork-ended poles and the guy ropes, after which it is sawed back and forth by the guys until it is worked well down into the mud. Sometimes a foothold is built on the top end and two or three men stand on it, adding their weight as an extra drive. Always there is a feast when a house is finally up, and frequently the daughter of the new home owner will have something tattooed on her skin to commemorate the event.

In the days when raiding was the principal diversion along the coast the marine village was a defense measure. Raiding bushmen could not swim and did not know how to handle canoes, nor would it have done them much good. For when attacked the salt-water people simply retired to their verandas out over the water, where they could sit with a supply of rocks handy and at leisure shout insults at the wild men on the beach. But the marine village also has a hygienic function that the missionaries discovered after they had persuaded some of the saved to build new villages on shore like civilized folk. With the Government punishing raiders the water protection was no longer necessary, it was argued, and it would be handier for the soul-savers if all the heathen were snugly on shore. Those natives who complied naturally built the same kind of huts they had always lived in, putting them up on piles. And they still relieved themselves at the edge of the veranda, pushing their dirt through the cracks of the floor and throwing their garbage over their shoulders. The twice-daily tides had taken care of these things before. And they still kept their dogs and pigs in the house on the same floor where the babies crawled. But now the dogs and pigs were filthy from foraging around in the muck under the house, and the feet of the residents were no longer washed clean at the beach as they had been when they had water to cross to get into their houses. Soon the people began to sicken and die in epidemics, mostly dysentery. So the Government ordered the bewildered natives to rebuild their marine villages. And the missionaries turned their brotherly love toward some other form of salvation.

We had made an early start for the village with the idea of trapping Pakosi ourselves, and it could not have been after seven-thirty when we made the turn in the shore road at the near end of the settlement. There were some children already bellyslamming in the slope of tide mud between the bridges, and they saw us from a distance. Instantly they charged. And as they came on, hopping and shrieking, others appeared from out of the houses and tore down the bridges to shore, little naked boys and little girls in flying white rami that made them look like milkweed fluff blown along by the wind.

We were inclined to be charmed by this reception and more than ever pleased with Civilization and His Excellency's good work, for the shy pickaninnies of other villages had usually run the other way at sight of us, and if held back screamed their rage or fear. Sometimes it had even seemed that they had been taught to fear white faces. But another and better reason is that often the awesome masks that the men of the secret societies don to impersonate spirits and ghosts are painted white, and the association caused the alarm. There are no such ghosts around Port Moresby. "Sissypenny, sissypenny," the young Motuans were chanting. "Sixpence, sixpence"—the tourist legacy. Children of Melanesia, too reticent even as adults to ask anything of their employers, were begging for cash like any little Mediterranean port pest. In a cloud of dust and hullabaloo they eddied us along to the one hut of the village that was on shore.

This palm-thatched building was about the size of a one-car garage and was really no more than a small pavilion, having open sides except for a three-foot-high palm mat wall. But it was up on piles, and we went up the entrance ladder to escape the little beggars as much as for shelter from the sun.

The children did not follow us. Instead they shinnied up the piles and clung to the outside of the partition with their grinning faces over the top. "Go fetch-em Pakosi," we ordered regally. "Sissypenny, sissypenny," they chanted; and not one face dropped out of sight. We hadn't any money, for it never occurred to us that any could be used in a Melanesian village. "Go fetch-em Pakosi?" Margaret asked and held up a stick of tobacco. Hands reached out and the stick disappeared—but the faces remained.

A long table with a number of kitchen chairs around it filled the center of the floor, but we could see that we had found a perfect studio, or at least as far from imperfect as is likely to be found in New Guinea. We were just about to clear the center space to make way for our easel when there was a sudden silence, and the faces around us dropped out of sight. A minute later a native man came up the ladder. One could not conceivably call him a "boy." He was elderly and of dignified bearing, with the grave and rather sad and weary look of a Cordell Hull. A large brass disk something like a dog license hanging from a brass chain around his neck proclaimed him a government attachment of some sort, and we assumed he was the village constable. He knew Pakosi, naturally, and we asked him to find him and bring him back to us. And here was a present of tobacco. The native accepted the tobacco, nodded his head in understanding or agreement, and then calmly seated himself in the chair at the head of the table. While we stood gaping. In a few minutes, however, this unprecedented behavior was explained. Up the ladder one by one came the Hanuabada equivalent of our "nine old men." We had butted into the village council chambers, and court was in session. With Gomai, the elder we had ordered to go chasing after Pakosi, presiding.

We were not invited to stay, but we did for about half an hour, to see how this quorum conducted the affairs of state.

The village council is one of those attempts of the Government to restore to the primitives who have had their old idea of justice restrained some of the self-respect that comes with having a hand in one's own destiny. There were actually twelve old men on the Hanuabada board, and they were held entirely responsible for the sanitation and repair of the village and the orderly behavior of the citizens. Cases of serious offense were a matter for the Port Moresby court, but the elders heard all minor cases like the contended ownership of pigs, reports of sorcery ("black" magic, which when there was sufficient evidence of harm done were passed along to the Central Court), adultery and clan squabbles in general. Gossip, which we might consider a minor offense, came under the damaging heading "spreading of lying reports." This was serious enough for the higher court. Samples of it cropped up when our war was occupying the district. The military, not being aware of the local tendency to romance, welcomed native assistance in watching for enemy action. More than once a native would come tearing into headquarters reporting that he had seen troops, presumably enemy, landing at such and such a place down the coast. Scouts would be sent out to ascertain the position and strength of the invasion, only to find that the informant had heard it from someone else or himself had dreamed or imagined it. "Sleep and find out," is a Motu saying. What a native dreams, sleeping or awake, is just as real an experience to him as anything that actually happens, and in recounting it he does not think to qualify it. So to the victims of his romancing (who are usually white because the natives themselves seem able to distinguish which is fact and which fancy) he becomes a liar and guilty under the law.

When the Hanuabada council was first instituted it had the power to levy sentences and fines, and probably it was the only judicial board in existence that functioned according to the letter of the law. Modern laws were written for, and apparently by, angels, allowing for no human frailties like forgetfulness, carelessness or susceptibility to temptation. Moreover every citizen is presumed to be intelligent enough to comprehend the laws of his hamlet, state and nation; and unless the layman is as well informed in them as the orig- inators he may be penalized for a slip. Luckily for those of us who have been caught our jurors are human anyway, themselves subject to any imperfection from pity to stupidity when judging by those inexorable laws. But the Hanuabada councillors were up with the angels. They were informed in their duties and exercised them to the hilt, never handing down anything less than the maximum penalty for real guilt and not allowing for any innocence if there was the slightest evidence of guilt.

That is the Papuan's own idea of justice. For this reason the victims of the council's rigorous decisions seldom re- sented them. And by the same token when the Central Court was lenient there was some suspicion of its omnipotence. In any case the judgments of the village council were so often too severe for the offense that the Central Court, which kept an eye on proceedings, was continually being obliged to rescue the victims of its laws, until finally this end of jus- tice was removed from the board.

One's conclusion about the matter is that the common de- nominator of mass thinking in civilization is exactly on a level with that of the individual primitive. When groups plan for groups they show all the unrealistic reasoning that marks the harsh justice of the primitive. When masses act it is most often with the vengeful insensitiveness of the Stone Age man. (It takes years to unite the people for a reform movement, but for a lynching or a war of any kind . . .) However when civilized men think and act as individuals they reveal the milk of human kindness and, at times, approach real god- liness. It would be a neat trick to get people to think like men.

Today the council itself has been abolished. This was at the elders' own request, and the official explanation is that they decided it, the Guv'men', could handle "such things" better. Probably behind the failure is the native's distaste for individual responsibility. The tradition of thinking and acting as a group is so strong that in searching for individuals with enough authority to act as village constables for the government the tribal chiefs were almost the last to be considered. Their power is insignificant. In fact during times of emergency such as a period of intensified warfare the chief is likely to be only one of the fighters under the leadership of a group of war chiefs. So since there is little personal power there is not its twin, personal responsibility.

A modern parallel to this primitive phenomenon is our labor unions, which exercise plenty of power as a group but whose members renounce any personal responsibility, especially in case of error.

However our ideal of competitive individualism cannot help but appeal when it percolates through to a people who have been expressing it, group against group, for generations. As recently as 1937 the Government was debating the advisability of giving awards for good gardens in an effort to improve them by stimulating the spirit of competition. "Progress" was the desired result. But just what is progress? Has it been achieved in our case by encouraging individualism, or in spite of it? In a few generations the energetic native personalities developed by the government's proposal would be leaving the group behind to shift for itself. There would be chiefs with real power, the snobs and the snubbed and the rich and the poor—the way we have it and apparently like it.

The council members at Hanuabada that morning did not look very different from any similar body of men anywhere except that they were naked above the waist, and dark-

skinned. They were taking themselves very seriously, doodling their hands busily on the table, on their faces that mixture of adult determination and small-boy bewilderment
which distinguishes men making big decisions. Gomai, the
chairman, had a bad case of ringworm, and so was able to
keep busier than the others scratching his ribs. But this was
the only activity; and since the presence of the councilmen
eliminated the place as a studio for us, we moved out.

Until Margaret located Pakosi I intended to busy myself
painting some section of the marine village as material for
background of some portrait in the future. The sun was
mounting in the sky, which meant heat—and the need to get
on with it if I expected to accomplish anything. As we gathered up our painting gear and started for the nearest bridge
the children assembled again and formed a convoy ready to
do whatever we were going to do. At the beach Margaret
made an attempt to control the situation. But she made it in a
Motu phrase which she thought meant, "Call your companions and *go*." What she said must have been that other
one, "Call your companions, and let us go." There was a
whoop of delight, everyone called his companions, and together they shoved us up the bridge. Well, there was still the
chalk taboo line for unwanted spectators that had never failed
so far.

"Bridge" is not a very exact name for the thing we were
walking on. It was really a kind of subway jetty connecting
the long row of houses with one another and the beach. (In
the whole village there were eight or ten of these strings of
homes extending out from shore.) It ran along under the huts
about four feet below the floors so that an adult had to bend
at right angles to walk. The surface was an end-to-end stretch
of heavy planks that were laid, without fastening and rounded
side up, on cross scaffolding between the house piles. And

the piles were loose in the mud. As our tribe got going up the bridge the whole "street" swayed far out to the end house. The tide was low and still running out, so at that moment the bridge was eight or ten feet above the water. We expected to go overboard into it before the day was over, but couldn't have guessed then how it would come about. For the present it seemed the loose planks must be joggled out from under our feet by our convoy. The suction-footed children were tearing back and forth past us, ducking under the floors of houses and dodging one another without a slip or a collision. The convex planks were waxy with years of dripping coconut oil and pig grease, and polished to a high patina by generations of bare feet. We finally got down on our hands and knees and crawled, dragging our gear after us. The little Motuans got down on their hands and knees and crawled, whooping so that residents of the lanes on both sides of us popped their heads out of doorways and stared unbelieving.

When we thought our glands had reached their maximum output we stopped and I said this was the scene I would paint. It was at a point about halfway down the street, where the bridge widened to four planks under a hut and we looked across the water to another string of houses. Margaret helped me spread our mat over the planks, so that my playthings would not fall through, and then we roped the painting canvas to the piles, for the wind was rising. That done, she shooed all the little Motuan ants around on the shore side of us and laid down the taboo line. This was simply a chalk line or circle with dots or crosses or sometimes "No Trespassing" scribbled across it. Anything on our side of the line was taboo to outsiders. Sometimes when we wished to leave our things on the beach or even in the center of the village overnight, we used the native's own materials for the same purpose; a stick with a flag of coconut fiber attached, a circle of stones, or a pile of them. Nothing was ever touched, no one ever crossed the line; for the spirits in our control were guarding the property. But blackboard chalk was something these bright little Motuans *ate*. There was a mission school on the hill above the village, and the chalk used on the blackboard there had to be tied to it. Anyway a chalk line on the village bridge was just a hopscotch frame for the enlightened.

Margaret delayed going after Pakosi, at least until I was settled down to paint, and in about fifteen minutes I was moaning at her to *do* something. The children had settled down behind us, as much as children can settle down when there is a scaffolding they can climb around on to get a better view, but brushes and tubes of paint were leaping around on the mat and finally a round tin of precious cigarettes went overboard. There was now mud below us, and the children slid down the piles to retrieve the cigarettes; and then all shinnied back up, wobbling the piles so that everything else we could not grab plopped over. The wind was banging away at the sail-like canvas, and the row of huts opposite us that I was trying to paint looked like a two-story centipede in the wind-roughened water. "Try popping *them* in the mud," I suggested seriously. Margaret tried it, and the hooligans loved it. They came back for more. Finally she took her ukulele out of its case and at the risk of her neck, since she had to walk bent over and use both her hands for playing, she started for shore singing her Cossack marching song with the shrill whistle at the end of each verse. In five minutes she had swept Hanuabada clean of every last hellion. The last I saw of her for hours was when she disappeared, walking fast over the crest of the nearest hill, followed like the Pied Piper by a long line of children and a cloud of dust. After that my only trouble was pigs.

"Cherchez le porc," says the Governor of Papua, if you want to find the seat of any trouble in the village. And to that I can add my testimonial. My first intimation that I had pigs was when the bridge behind me began to vibrate. The next was when pigs started going over my lap like a train of coal cars. There were only three of them, but they were long and almost head high . . . and I noticed then that the

New Guinea swine does not have the wholesome sty odor of our brand. These three lived in or belonged to a house further down the lane, they scavenged in the tide mud, and their B.O. was that of decayed shellfish and so forth. We had seen many pigs before this in the villages, but had been unimpressed except by the fact that they seemed to be very long-legged—which we attributed to the leanness of their bodies. But face to face this way, there were some features that did impress me. Though their eyelashes were amazingly long,

perhaps an inch and a half, the eyes had an aggressively bel-
ligerent expression, emphasized by the fact that their ears
stood straight up like those of a police dog. And at the end
of the unusually long and unusually loose nose were protruding fangs that added a superior sneer to a face that I did
not like so close to mine anyway.

The sense of superiority was genuine enough. It was produced by being the most esteemed of island dishes, the highest denomination of currency and the most pampered of
citizens; ranking only with children for being beastly spoiled.
The pig lore is endless, and it is curious that there is so much
of it and it is so widespread, because before Europeans introduced them there were no pigs in New Guinea. Yet there is
no other animal, domesticated or wild, that receives such
esteem. For one thing the pig is the only animal which is not
taboo for eating because of being a clan totem. Yet it has a
spirit, and in some localities there is belief in a kind of pig
purgatory not attainable even to men. The native who trades
away his pig will retain its spirit, carefully wrapping it in a
leaf to keep until he can bestow it on a piglet to be born.
Elsewhere, the malicious spirits in a sick man can be transferred to a pig, much as Christ drew the evil from the body
of the sinner and cast it into the swine—and there is every
reason to believe that this is an independent invention and
not taken from a missionary source.

The possession of many pigs is the only evidence of wealth,
the only currency that will procure wives and heaven too—
for the sorcerers are often paid pigs to placate an offended
spirit. Many an age-long feud has started in the past by the
killing, accidental or not, of a single pig, and many a raid has
been averted by the payment of a pig in reparation for the
killing of a man. Natives have been known to try and buy off
the government in this way when the Service was hot on

the trail of someone wanted for murder. Valuable bracelets and neck pendants are made from the big curling tusks of the wild boar, and the skulls of pigs decorate the ceremonial houses as mementoes of the great feasts that have taken place there. Finally, fresh pork sells for the King's silver around Hanuabada (something like thirty-five cents a pound before the war); for pig is meat, the largest hunk of meat available to the aborigines, and this accounts for all the rest.

No one apparently ever tries to argue with a pig—nor did I more than once of the half dozen times these three passed back and forth between home and shore. That once I was in the midst of a creative moment and absent-mindedly waved my bamboo maulstick at them as they were coming up from the beach. The three, one behind the other, stopped and the first in line stared at me indignantly, long ears forward, the bisonlike neck behind seeming to bristle. When I struck out again, this time in fright, the two rear pigs wheeled . . . they could even *run* on the glossy rounded planks with their little sharp hoofs . . . but the first in line came at me. I saved myself by a gymnastic that I didn't know I had in me, and the triumphant pig trotted through, poking holes in our precious mat with its Chinese lady feet.

Finally, while I hung by my hands from the floor of the hut above me, two of them came through abreast, wiping off the day's painting with a bulging bristly side; and when Margaret returned, still followed by her enchanted children, she found me lying with my face to the incoming tide. A centipede had dropped down onto my short sleeve, and before I realized what it was it had progressed to my bare arm, over which it strolled, tail up, all ready to strike if I so much as twitched a pore. The lane of houses was swaying in the rising tide, the smeared canvas was banging in the wind and I was seasick.

An hour later, when the missionary passed by on the way to his home on the hill after a hard day missionizing, he saw something that must have chilled his good heart. It was two barefooted *cinabadas* with their slacks rolled up to their thighs standing calf-deep in the border of mud between the dry beach and water. Out in the water about twenty feet off were the little lambs of Hanuabada lined up in a row, just the tops of their bodies above the surface. The ladies were teaching the children an American game to develop alertness, called sock-the-nigger-baby. Big dangerous balls of wet pottery clay which the students had enthusiastically provided were being socked. And though the idea was that the "nigger babies" should dodge the mud balls by ducking in the water, the American team had been pitching since early youth while the Hanuabadans had been dodging for less than half an hour, so we were running up our score. And every time we saw a pig we aided it in developing alertness too. I might add that in any preceding generation the results might have been in the Motuans' favor. Until the use of such weapons became obsolete in the district it was a small boys' game to learn to dodge arrows and spears.

In the midst of this pleasant pastime the person we had been stalking, Pakosi, poled down the waterway between the huts in an outrigger. There was another lad in the canoe with him, and they had pounds of fish net but no fish. It was a bad year for food all around. So when Pakosi hesitated about coming into town on a business we could not very well make clear to him, in our unpractised Motu, we said we would pay him a tin of meat a day for just sitting still. This should have brightened his eye, for a boy working on a plantation gets only one tin a week. It was about the equivalent of the cash fees we were giving the women models. Pakosi agreed to come, but of course he didn't. Nevertheless the reader may now lean

back and relax for a few pages. For by the following week
we had acquired a private "studio" within stone's throw of
the village, and a natty red roadster in which to get to it daily,
and we were painting the most exciting pictures of the New
Guinea chapter so far.

18

Before the War there were less than two hundred miles of road in all of Papua, and only a small portion navigable by motor, even if there had been cars to run over them. About fifty miles of the road ran out of Port Moresby in three directions. One was the terminus of the mail carrier track that led up the mountains crossing the Laloki River, on over the Owen Stanley Range to Kokoda and down to the north coast, that section of the country that was to run with foreign blood a few years hence. At Rouna Falls on the Laloki the road stopped and the lonely track began. The first thing we did when we acquired a car was, not to drive to work, but, typically, to take a Saturday trip up to the Falls.

The presence of a car in such a roadless country perhaps needs explaining. And that is easy; there was an American in Port Moresby. He was the same "ambassador" from New Orleans who had lent us the mirror, and we came by the car in the same way, simply on our merits as being fellow countrymen. But, as many a desperate American has learned in the past few years, a car will not run on will-power alone. Before we had time to find out that "petrol" cost about twenty cents a quart, even the problem of fuel was solved for us. We were attempting to repay the "ambassador" for his kindness with some sort of painting or drawing. It seemed as if it were going to be difficult at first, because he did not want a portrait of himself nor of any member of his family. But after a few days of pressure he admitted that he would like an enlarged picture in color of a postcard he kept tacked on his desk down in his machine shop on the water front. No, it was not the photograph of a secret love, nor of the old homestead in the South, nor even his deceased mother. It was a print of Old Glory grasped in the claw of a fierce-looking eagle. That was something we could understand, for like the "ambassador" we had learned to love our country the hard way, by living outside it. We made the biggest crayon drawing we had paper for, putting in it the meanest-looking bird not created by a taxidermist ever portrayed, and the gayest flag we had colors for. It was much too successful, for it piled up more obligations. After that the red car was delivered from the shop each morning, polished and full of petrol; and for this there was no listening to arguments for paying for it. Percy Leigh was what a resident called a "natural Mason," high praise coming from a Britisher.

The same Americans who have learned what it is to be carless for the first time in their lives can now appreciate how Margaret and I felt that Saturday morning when we set out on our first day of driving. After two years of navigating on our own clay feet, it was to regain wings over the world. It was to feel cool in blistering heat and see speeding by scenery that had so far been so motionless that by its very stolidity it had seemed to overwhelm our feeble human efforts to move through it. This feeling of release lasted for only a few miles out of Moresby, where the rubble road was still level and in good repair . . . the native prisoners are kept outside working on the roads instead of locked up in jail. Then we began to climb, and from the way the engine suffered from breathlessness and the heat we now know what those Australian troops and the burdened carriers later experienced on this Kokoda track.

Most of the first ten miles was a gradual climb up through the low coast hills, but those hills were barren save for the tall yellow grass and sparse scrub, and when we stopped pe-

riodically with a boiling engine there were no rivers of cold
water with which to refill the radiator and no shelter from
the boring sun. The last couple of miles was a precipitous
serpentine climb in low gear up to a thousand feet above
sea level, to come out suddenly on a sight that must have been
manna to the hot dusty troops of the A.I.F. It was a roaring
column of water high as the sodden jungle around it which
fell into a deep foaming pool and cascaded away down a
gorge as green and cool as an Eden. We were in another of
New Guinea's climates, the cool one of the hinterlands. Mist
filled the air, and rain clouds darkened the high mountains
to the north where the jungle poured down over the slopes
like a green torrent.

Rouna Falls is to Port Moresby what Baguio is to Manila,
a retreat for the heat-weary residents. But there the resemblance ends. There are a number of small wooden cot-
tages around the Falls (among them one belonging to
Beatrice Grimshaw, the writer of South Sea tales), but no
one lives there the year around. There is no store, no gasoline
pump and there were no other visitors the day of our first
trip. And it was unbelievably lonely, a feeling accentuated
by the eternal booming of the water and weird cries of birds
hidden in the dense bush. In spite of the loneliness of the
coast between white settlements, it is in the mountains that
the unpopulousness of New Guinea is most impressive. It is
borne through the stillness and the sameness of hill after hill
rising away to the horizon with nowhere a break in the mass
of green treetops to indicate human habitation. Yet, in less
than an hour after we left the Falls we were in a throng of a
thousand or more natives. Drunk on sheer transportation,
we drove out to Hanuabada that night.

It was a moonless sky when we started out around the bay
road for the village, but the night was so light with stars that
we turned the headlights off, put the hood back so that we

could breathe it in and see it; and then, to be thoroughly incongruous in this Stone Age land, we turned on the radio.
The usual static was grunting and sawing, but after a minute
an Aussie voice somewhere broke through announcing to the
equator the virtues of Anthony Hordern's, where one could
buy a pair of suède-finish fabric gloves for "three and eleven."
It sounded like a good buy, and when we reached the bend
in the road before you turn in past the village we stopped the
car, the better to listen to this forgotten world of warm
gloves and wonderful bargains. "And," said the voice complacently, "use Ausoline's cockroach destroyer. It . . ." As
I switched him off the sound of drums came across the water
from the village. We could see beyond the piles of the huts
two bonfires going on the beach, the silhouettes of legs moving back and forth in front of them. On the other side of
the bay the electric lights of Port Moresby, pink in the blueness, blinked on and off in the steam still rising from the hot
water. Back there sleepy exiles were stretched out around
their hot radios drinking in this rare static-free program
about Ausoline's cockroach cure. And from the other side
the sound of chanting had joined the drums. We got out of
the car to walk the rest of the way to the village, conscious
as we did so that the key could stay in the lock and the car
in the middle of the road and we would find it there with all
its tires and gasoline even if we did not come back for a
week.

The minute we cleared the bend in the road it was apparent that something was going on in Hanuabada this night
. . . and why hadn't Ahuia told us. There were natives
standing about all over the beach, and above their heads we
could see the tops of enormous headdresses that were concentrated in a group between the two fires. The chanting had
trailed off, but the drums were still booming spasmodically,
and there was an irregular clacking sound that we discovered

later came from the bundles of big hollow nuts tied on the drums, and the anklets of the dancers.

There was no dancing at the moment, and to remain inconspicuous we went around behind the crowd and seated ourselves on the rise above the beach. But by stepping on a few we found that there were natives sitting here also. They paid no attention to us. In fact there was a curiously detached atmosphere about the whole assembly, a kind of dream quality that made us feel as if we were on the outside looking in. There was little talking, and though there were children near us, the same little blisters of our first morning in the village, they sat or stood silent and motionless. This was not exactly the attitude of a waiting crowd either, with attention focused on the befeathered nucleus between the fires, but more as if whatever had assembled the crowd had already happened, and they were gathering their wits to disperse.

Even when the business began it was not sudden but so gradual that afterward we could not recall any opening signal. I remember there was an irregular hollow booming going on for a long time, big bamboo tubes with nuts on them being bumped on stones. This had no effect on the natives, who still stood facing aimlessly in every direction. The next thing we were aware of was that the idly thumped drums had gathered into the tempo of the tube-booming, and together they were growing in volume. The irregular line of headdresses began moving about, but still nothing organized happened and occasionally even the "sing" dwindled away, only to start up a few minutes later. If the mosquitoes hadn't been gnawing on us we might have napped like the infants around us stretched out over their mothers' crossed legs.

Finally after a long time something definite did happen, perhaps what everyone had been waiting for. The marine village behind the scene, which had been a flat silhouette

against the darker water, suddenly glowed light. Off to the
east the thin curve of a brilliant moon was sliding up behind
the clean edge of hill. Almost simultaneously a soft wordless
droning began in the vicinity of the headdresses. This took
up the tempo of the drums for a minute, rose in volume and
then, maddeningly, died away altogether. The drumming
kept on. But we weren't sleepy now. We were sitting forward tensely waiting, waiting for the sudden dramatic thing
that should have happened after such suspense. It never came.
The whole white moon rose above the horizon, and the scene
changed as if gods were stirring and pouring. The light
flooded over the scene, making the fantastic village out over
the water look like an opera village against a back drop of
blue. Then the strip of blinking Moresby lights seemed more
artificial than they actually were, like pinholes in a painted
curtain. The dark figures of the crowd took on anatomy and
cast black shadows on the white sand. Slowly one by one
they sank down on their haunches or moved back to the
slopes above the beach. Then we saw the chanters.

It is impossible to describe briefly or simply an aggregate
of Melanesian dancers, for they are so unlike anything familiar that there is no simile to get off with. Confusion about
covers it at first glance; and this was superb confusion. In two
long at-first-irregular lines that faced one another and extended between the fire were dancers of both sexes, maidens
and youths. To our surprise the girls were in the lines with
the boys, stationed alternately and clasping hands behind the
boys' backs. Mixed dances, and especially in such close proximity, are certainly not commonplace in Melanesia. It was
only the youths who wore the magnificent headdresses, great
aureoles of feathers that looked black and white in the moonlight but were parrot-green and red and yellow as well. And
each boy was similarly decked out with a hand drum fringed
with dried grass and nuts, a long nose-stick and a loin panel

of decorated tapa cloth. The uniform feature of the girls'
dress was a big black sphere of hair spotted with starry white
flowers . . . frangipani borrowed from the mission grounds
. . . at the throat, a wide crescent of gleaming mother-of-
pearl and starting low on the hips the long silky rami, white,
rust, orange or deep brown in daylight. And that was the end
of uniformity. All the rest was confusion; heaps of necklaces
around necks and crisscrossed around the body, necklaces of
dog teeth, glass beads, shells and black seeds, pendants of
boar's tusk, clam shell and nacre, armbands plaited and carved
and stuffed with fresh leaves, fragrant herbs and streamers
of dried grass, big black nuts on anklets and bracelets and
bangles with spiky tufts of feathers and stuff hanging from
and sticking out in every direction over the mass of glistening oiled anatomy.

It is surprising that we recognized Pakosi in the maze of
spotty black and white. The curiously aimless chanting had
begun again, and Pakosi's loose Melanesian mouth was hanging open making sounds toward the sky with the rest, the
same dazed look on his face. Probably the reason we noticed
him is because the rest of the lines had straightened and his
section was still irregular. The little girl on his right was
crowding him. It was no accident. We watched, and every
time Pakosi stepped away, squeezing into the girl on his left,
the little one moved up, making a gap between herself and
the next dancer. Curiously un-Melanesian behavior, to show
such preference in public. Then the dancing began, and we
forgot all about the two for a long time.

"Began" is not a very exact verb. At first this did not seem
to be a dance at all. There was no united beginning, not with
steps. The chanting had taken on a definite tempo, highly
pitched young nasal voices, something like those of a boys'
choir, intoning over and over again five or six weird part-
notes that even the musical Margaret did not memorize so

that she could repeat it afterward. Slowly, different parts of the lines began dipping slightly but still with no perceptible movement of the feet. Then presently the lines were united in the dipping and began moving sideways in solid formation. The two "slid" in opposite directions toward the fires and then reversed, sliding back. The faces of the dancers were expressionless save for the strain of chanting in such a high key. Gradually the tempo slowed, the girls began sawing their arms lengthwise of the lines, the dip in the step increased; and while one line lifted up, the other dropped. The shiny skirts of the girls were now swaying from left to right in unison, the two lines in opposite directions. The moon grew in brightness as it rose in the blue space, and on the white sand in front of the formations two rows of shadow figures with swinging rami, sawing arms and lifting and dropping headdresses lengthened and contracted with the dipping, sliding countermoving dancers. On and on, slowly, persistently, never altering the tempo, pitch or intensity, the nuts clacked and drums thumped with the bamboo tubes and high young voices. Here the precision and impersonality of a complex engine with rows of driving pistons and arms and wheels, with the same unvarying sound. We were hypnotized.

The dancers themselves seemed hypnotized, and if the audience was not asleep it too was in a trance, for no one moved or made any sound. Those around us sat absorbed, but with the rather stupid expression of watchers from whom no response is expected. There was no climax. Every now and then one or two of the dancers would drop out of the formation, the line would melt together to fill the gap, and returning dancers would fall in at the ends with no pause in the performance. No one took any notice of departing ones. Except ourselves. We noticed when Pakosi left, promptly followed by the little girl. Perhaps the missionaries who would suppress these dances because they are "obscene" (and are prevented from doing so by the Administration) are right in their interpretation, but to us who had seen dancing everywhere from Hollywood nightclubs to college proms the keynote of this show was superb restraint. By all the laws of physics these lads should have burst into flame long before this, if only from the friction of the girls' arms sawing across the back of their bare waists. We stayed until long after midnight, when the moon was high and the lights of Port Moresby had blinked out, when there was nowhere to be seen any evidence of authority to inhibit the performance, but there was no change in the dance, none in the glazed attitude of the young dancers.

It was not easy to understand or appreciate this performance nor to rationalize the curious spell it cast that has lasted and is still vivid when more spectacular sing-sings have long since faded out of the picture. One obstacle is that we and the primitives set out from different poles toward the exhibition. Our dances and music—in fact, all arts—are designed to stimulate, either the imagination or the muscles. And as these have a saturation point we demand more and more stimulation until we arrive at something super like the jitterbug, "Freudian" ballets, combustion symphonies, Gertrude Stein and picture frames containing wads of shaving paper with the whiskers still on them. Collapse is the only thing that could possibly stimulate after such a spell of creation. And perhaps "modern" art is itself that collapse.

The consciousness of time passing that speeds us does not enter the native picture at all, neither that of the spectators nor that of the performers. There are no names and numbers for days to repeat themselves, the sun and moon rise and sink in almost the same place in the sky throughout the year, and only the changes in wind and rain recur to mark the passing of seasons. Even meals are not eaten at the same time each day, nor even every day. (The native gorges himself when there is game and when he gets hungry again, perhaps the second day afterward, he goes hunting.) Night and day are the same, and the natives can and do dance straight through without stop for several days on end during the big sing-sings. The pace and gymnastics of our dances and the sound effects so long continued would send the undernourished primitive to an early grave, as many a better fortified prom trotter who is now an angel could testify to. But the very monotony of the Motu performance has its own kind of stimulation, something like that of Ravel's Bolero. The sameness is maddening, yet you cannot look away or stop listening because you have not yet got satisfaction. Something has to give. Obviously what that is in a primitive is not the same as for an expedition. Our bottled-up contents when we left the village were in a turmoil planning a new picture of Pakosi, this one a superbly restrained young Motuan in dance feathers. If we could just catch the Scissors.

The car was still there in the middle of the road, but not the same as we had left it. The Melanesians in this most advanced settlement had spoiled their record by lifting a red silk kerchief we had left on the seat. It was the first theft in a thousand miles of unlocked trunks and unguarded bags and the most tempting carelessness with our belongings.

19

The "studio" lent us was the last European house on the shore road to Hanuabada, and the location at the bend before the settlement provided an intimate view of the water end of the village as well as all traffic that passed from it to town. The owner of the house was in government service, so we had free use of the place from nine until five daily. Thrown in was one of those "zoot suit" Motuan houseboys whose name was Biah (beer), and who was joyous because there was no *cinabada* in the house to keep him overworked. For his master was an island "bachelor" whose family lived in the south more or less permanently. The woman's touch that remained in the establishment was an enormous modern electric refrigerator that stood like a cemetery monument of snow-white marble in the first room off the front veranda. The rest of the room was typically "island," partitioned only part way to the roof with dark wood and lighted by only the two doorways from the veranda. (Interior gloom becomes a haven after the eyes have been battered by the glare outside.) Bare two-by-fours stretched across the top of the room, where a ceiling would have been if ventilation were not more necessary to comfort. It was these beams that created a situation. For we had planned to paint in this room, and had not yet begun to do so when we discovered that the rafters were haunted.

Our host had thoughtfully stocked his electric refrigerator with all sorts of delicacies for luxury-starved headhunters; chocolate bars (which become chocolate beverage when not

on ice), tomatoes and lettuce, cold lime juice and exotic
fruits like apples and peaches, all straight from the refrigerator of the southern steamer. There were even fresh frozen
meats and vegetables, and once there was some real milk. And
we had been invited to help ourselves. But a refrigerator in
New Guinea had other uses. The first morning we arrived

for work we went straight to it to cool off in front of the
open door. And we were standing there with our mouths
full of frosting, bellies bared to the icy draught and thinking
what a wonderful thing progress was after all—when the
household cat started into the room. Her tail was up af-
fectionately but she had not come a yard when that tail at
horizontal had disappeared, following the cat off the veranda.
A minute later we did about the same thing. Hanging down
from the rafter above the refrigerator was about a yard of
snake and at least another yard of it was stretched out along
the beam above our heads. In response to our yelps Biah
came out of the house-cook, heard that there was a "sinake"
in the house, and grinned. The snake was a household attach-

ment, even named Adolphus (until it produced young, after which it was called Adolphine), which was allowed to roam about unmolested because it kept the place free of rats. This was all very well, but the non-poisonous Adolphine had a midriff diameter of about three inches without rats in her and she looked like a python to us. We redecided on the veranda as the place to paint. But from then on we ate cold chocolate bars only at the risk of indigestion, for we discovered that one of the snake's favorite loafing places was the top of the ice box. Either she liked the vibrations of the motor or, as I believed, even a snake could not stand the heat of Port Moresby and for once sought cold. Also there was a very good chance of someone having fed Adolphine from the refrigerator.*

About two hours after the introduction to Adolphine and an hour after we had given up Ahuia as just another irresponsible Melanesian after all . . . he was to have appeared with Pakosi decked out in dance feathers . . . we saw a vision coming up the road from the village. It was Ahuia himself, decked out in feathers, magnificent feathers towering twice as high as the headdresses of the moonlight dance, and carrying a hand drum and two of the tall bamboo dance "sticks." He had thought of everything, everything except Pakosi . . . and we were beginning to wonder about *him*. "Something of long time before," Ahuia explained the feathers. This was an old-time headdress of the sort no longer made, for the significance has been deleted. Almost everything

---

* In case anyone is curious about our having planned to paint in such a dark place as the "refrigerator room," it should be explained that we had intended trying it as an experiment. I found that in painting outdoors, even on a shaded veranda, I had been unconsciously loading more and more color onto the paintings, attempting to reach the intensity of light around us. The eyes soon tired in the glare, and failed to register accurately. It produced nothing but "rawness," a fault that was very apparent when the paintings were seen later in the colder light of our country, and especially the all-too-revealing top light of the average museum gallery.

in the aureole was symbolical of something outlawed. Several years ago, before the Government was restraining such forms of uplift, the missions persuaded the natives to make a huge pyre of these "symbols unbecoming to a Christian." In cold cash thousands of dollars' worth of bird-of-paradise plumes went up in thin smoke that day. "They sang as they burned," said Ahuia, who had heard of it from the old men. That bonfire was comparable to heaping up all the Purple Hearts and campaign ribbons and badges of honor and glory in our community and setting fire to them. They were feathers that had to be earned by the Melanesian concept of "outstanding heroism."

The idea of wearing something to show what you have done works in reverse among this group-minded people in that *every* man must win the right to wear certain decorations. It is the native who cannot sport an honor who is distinguished from his fellows, for his cowardice. And it is the "moms" of Melanesia who have kept the practice going. Where we esteem the decorated warrior, the *haniulato* laughs at the youth who has not won his trophies. He cannot get a wife or have any self-respect so long as he delays the business, and you may be sure the normal youth hustles out early after his *heera.*

"Heera" literally translated means personal decorations, but it is also the word for the code of symbols. Most of the decorations are won for assassination, and sometimes as credits for men killed in legitimate warfare. In Ahuia's headdress there were six great flaring copper-red bird-of-paradise plumes, each of which represented the tongue of a victim. Where more than one man was engaged in the business it was the man who struck the first blow, the brave man first in attack, who won the right to put a feather in his bonnet. The red-feathered "sticks" in the center of the aureole topped by tufts of white feathers and jetlike tips are fairly realistic representations. Each symbolizes the "conquest" of a woman. This is a little puzzling, for conquest implies resistance, and on that score few Motu maidens could be considered a conquest. Though a matron or a woman of another tribe might put up featherweight resistance.

The green, black and white cockatoo and parrot quills in

the main structure of the aureole represented "wealth." The connection seems remote, but perhaps the reason is that in this treeless and waterless country of the Central Division there are few birds and feathers must be obtained from inland or far down the coast. Parrot feathers are even "imported" from Australia, working their way from village to village by trade. All this puts a commercial value on the size of the quill section of the headdress. Another *heera* which had worked its way a long distance to Ahuia's arm and was valuable for the same reason was the bracelet of clam and cowrie shells he wore above his elbow. This was either a kula bangle from the Louisiades or an exact copy of one. But to continue with the headdress: there was an extra bandeau that went over the head in front of the big fan which was made of the hide of the cus-cus, a New Guinea relative of the opos-

sum, and this represented the skin of a victim. The "hair" of
another was the thin fringe of cassowary plumage that went
around the back of the head, and some unfortunate's "fingernails" were symbolized by the bandeau of sea shells across
Ahuia's forehead. His costume entirely lacked the "nose" of
victims, however. To represent this feature the enormous

beak of the hornbill, a bird that is responsible for much of
the jungle racket, is used and many headdresses sport four or
five of them. Ahuia brought with him a bone nose-stick which
he said was the "nose" of someone who had lost a duel, but
he could not wear it because his own civilized nose had never
been pierced. Anyway it was not won in a knightly duel.
The one who lost was usually slugged from behind while on
his way to slug someone else in order to win his "fingernails"
and the girl. However, without counting up, we find that

Ahuia, had the headdress been his own originally—which he denied—would have had to his credit some half dozen clean-cut murders, three rapes and eight or ten gang killings from which he had won "hair," "nose," "skin" and "fingernails," not a bad campaign record for one man.

The drum Ahuia brought was his own, some of it his handiwork; and it was fairly saturated with supernatural business. Between a man and his sing-sing drum there is a mystical at-

tachment so strong that the only place an expedition could obtain one in this land of plentiful drums was from the cache of a missionary who had given salvation for it. The one we got was better than Ahuia's, for it had a fine natural curve, something the spirit-guided carver looks for when he chooses the tree in the forest. The right curve gives a good "sing." But the hollowing out is important too, for the thickness of the walls must also be exactly right, and only the spirits know about this. Only the servicing does not need paid spiritual supervision, and an owner may do this himself. In time the lizard tympanum wears out with thumping, not only the thumping given it in the sing-sings but that which it receives as an outlet for the emotions. Whenever a man is too deeply moved for any other expression, grief-stricken or enraged, or just full of grasshoppers, he will go off in a corner by himself and beat the living hell out on his drum. Ahuia was so composed that we suspected he must have replaced a lot of drumheads. In any case he knew the process thoroughly. Several lizards were usually caught before one having just the right quality of hide was found, then without killing the lizard first it was skinned and the hide quickly transferred to the drumhead so that it would "grow" there. It grew because the skin was still pliable enough to be stretched tightly and after being bound over the drum it was firmly stuck by the fresh blood and dried so hard over the shape of the wood that the bindings could later be removed. Lozenges of black tree gum were added to tighten the tympanum and protect it from wear under the beating fingertips.

Ahuia as he posed was holding tightly onto the framework of his headdress, on his face the expression of a man watching a woman sharpen a pencil with his razor. Margaret was practising Motu on his drum. One of my aims in the portraits of primitives was to make them look like normal human beings, which they are, and not like the savages some people have reported them; and I was just about to speak to Margaret when she stopped of her own accord. She was sitting behind me on the steps and after a minute came: "My-y word, wha' name dis fella!" which meant she was addressing Ahuia. She was looking down the road at two figures passing toward town. One of them was obviously a maiden, for her hair was worn like the men's in a big fluffed ball, and she walked with the approved alluring wig-wag of the hips that swung her lustrous skirts in a wide arc. The other figure also wore a rami, but there the clues to the gender ended. The upper part of her body, head and shoulders, was obscured by some kind of dark hood, and suspended from the head down the back was a long string sack, the bottom of which rested on the shelf of her rump and bulged as if it contained coconuts. The piercing nasal voice of a scolding *hahine* came from the pair, and as the hooded figure was the one jerking her arms about, a necessary adjunct to Melanesian languages, we concluded she was that woman. Ahuia gazed down at the road for a minute and then in his most refined English informed us that this was Kori Tabora the sorceress, her daughter Ninoa and the pickaninny of the latter. We saw no pickaninny even when the couple had been brought up to the veranda, but the girl Ninoa we recognized instantly; she was the little one who was always under Pakosi's feet at the sing-sing.

It will be a dull day indeed when all the magic has been scoffed out of the world and one can no longer sit on his front steps with a witch and chat about the ancient mysteries. Kori Tabora and her "mountain vapor," Ninoa, came to pose for us when Ahuia's portrait was finished; and by accident they sat for figures in the same painting. We had planned to do a companion piece to Ahuia's portrait, using the girl in her sing-sing decorations, and Kori got into the picture because she couldn't be kept out. She was all over the place, superintending Ninoa's toilette, messing her fingers in my palette and telling me how to paint in a language not a word of which I could have understood even if I had been a lip reader. For I could not see her face. The covering which we had taken to be a hood was the witch's hair worn in the fashion that distinguished the sorceress in the district. No other "do" could have carried so much conviction. The kinky black wool had been matted with a paste of brick-red pottery clay and coconut oil, and it hung straight down from her crown all around in fat heavy ropes that were flexible only because the dried clay had cracked in joints. Actually the ropes were strings of little bricks connected by hair. The mess was never washed out nor cut off because water can dilute a sorcerer's power. (For the same reason he must never, never bathe.) But Kori had been rained on, and the hair on the top of her head was clayless and frowzy; and in the parts

between the ropes were unhatched millions. The witch was rancid.

Throughout the painting of the two figures we never once saw all of Kori's face. At first we painted her just as she was, but the figure with a perfectly normal body entirely lacking a recognizable head was so unconvincing that we finally attempted to get some profile in it. Kori would not let us touch her sacred ropes with our hands to pull them aside, but she did let us use the bamboo maulstick, which we preferred to anyway, and the slit of face that emerged was the model for all witches from time immemorial. Two little button-bright black eyes set close together with the overhanging upper lids that physiognomists say indicates volubility peered out of the curtain of bricks above a mouthful of teeth that looked as if they had just been stuck in for the effect. Actually there were only about six teeth left, brown with past betel nut and gory with the present quid. They struck out at all angles, and were so long that the upper lip covered them only with difficulty. When we painted the profile with the mouth open, which was normal, the malformed upper jaw protruded so far beyond the small nose that it still did not look a human face. And to make things really trying, Kori's mouth was never motionless.

The sorceress had in abundance that first requirement of successful witches the world over, the gift of gab. That was just what we wanted in a Melanesian witch, because there were a few little items of magic we wanted to find out about. Ahuia had called Kori a rain sorceress (producing rain still being within the law), but even if we only learned how to bring rain to arid Port Moresby it might come in handy. However, a sorceress who can legally make it rain knows some illegal magic, like the mechanics of birth control and how to commit murder without coming into contact with the victim, always nice information to have at your fingertips.

It was exasperating that Kori could not or would not do her gabbing in pidgin English.

We called in Biah to interpret for us, and Kori never even let him finish the first question. She was the kind of conversationalist who even interrupts herself. We waited for a while, thinking she would run down; and then just as we were opening our mouths to ask Biah what she was saying she would sense that she was going to lose the stage, and would raise her voice in a fresh flood of vehemence. We finally got out of Biah that she was denying that she was even a rain sorceress. So we called in Ahuia, thinking that just a slight pressure of government authority would be enough to stanch some of the flow. And anyway it was Ahuia who said that Kori was a witch. But either Ahuia had no authority, official or masculine, or he did not wish to interpret what he heard. He would ask our question briefly, and Kori would answer at length; and after about ten minutes of monologue during which Ahuia's face would become more and more expressionless we would cut in and ask, "What does she say?" And Ahuia, after listening five or ten minutes longer, would answer, "Nothing yet." We could have knocked their heads together.

This infernal wall of languages! When one reflects that speech is about the only vital difference between men and the apes, and that we deliberately erect barriers to communication between one another by stubbornly clinging to the language of our clan fathers—not because it is richer or easier to learn or more consistent—it seems that the descent from the trees was in vain. How can we ever hope to understand and exert our charm over peoples who express themselves in unknown sounds and letters when we often fail in the bosom of the family, where even our thoughts can be read? There had been times on this headhunt and others in foreign lands where we would gladly have been limited to

monkey chirping if it had enabled us to communicate with
our fellowmen as well as the apes do. And this moment was
one of them. Even the *taubada* of the house was helpless with
Kori, for perversely his presence was the one thing that could
dam her flow of talk, possibly with fear lest she reveal knowledge of something illegal.

So for a while our education remained at a standstill. Until
the day it occurred to my able companion, Margaret, to pre-
tend that she was a sorceress herself. She got Kori's attention
focused, a trick in itself, by showing her a sixpence piece, then
she closed her hand over it, opened the hand and the sixpence
had disappeared. She showed Kori her empty hands, palms
and backs, closed her fingers, opened them—and there was the
coin again. Then she made it disappear. Kori was leaning
forward, silent for the first time. Margaret reached up in the
air, took the coin out of it, and handed it toward the witch.
But Kori wouldn't touch it. Sucking and clicking noises were
coming from the loose lips behind her hair, and when the
sixpence disappeared again, this time into the air, the woman
did something that we had not seen since the old French
films; she put her thumb to her mouth and snapped the
thumbnail on her teeth. "The *cinabada* will give thee this
magic . . ." said Margaret in Motu. The intimation was
clear; if Kori would reveal some of hers, an acceptable
Melanesian transaction. The answer was a vehement up-
jerking of the head that made the mop fly and revealed shrewd
little eyes glinting with acquisitiveness.

All this time the mountain vapor, Ninoa, had been sitting
mutely on the sidelines, as becomes the offspring of an over-
powering personality. Her expression for the most part had
been the sweet vapid look of a pickaninny doll, except when
we asked her a question and her mother cut in with her un-
intelligible answers. Then an appealing rather anxious smile
would light her round little face for an instant. If we had

not seen her trampling Pakosi we might have attributed this to shyness, but we checked the girl off as not understanding what was going on, even the reason for her posing. At least she was not bright enough ever to make the sorceress that her mother was—though she would inherit all the magic formulas and the box of "medicine." Now, when Kori agreed to reveal some of her hocuspocus we were again faced with the problem of interpreter, since obviously the secrets could not be conveyed through a layman. And it was then that Ninoa spoke for the first time. In straight English that was better than Ahuia's she said that she would "talk" for us! Her childhood had been spent in the mission school, and she could even write English script, though without much regard for spelling. (The mission schools are subsidized by the government entirely out of taxes paid by the natives, and while attendance is not compulsory both adults and children are encouraged to attend. Students are not required to be converts of the mission.)

The reader will doubtless find it more useful to know how to make it rain than how to prevent conception, so we shall begin with the former. For obvious reasons no charge is made for bringing rain to Hanuabada even if the charm works, but should there be such an accident one may give the magician a small present. The surest method known is for the sorceress to stay indoors once it gets started raining on its own, and come outside only when the village has had enough and wants it to stop raining, for her emerging into the open will send the clouds away. But, chronic dryness being the district's trouble, Kori had more commissions for producing than for stopping a rainfall. With her kit of "medicine," shells, stones and tree roots having magical properties, she goes to the parched garden, where she first claps together the glistening nacre shells—which stimulates lightning in the sky. Then to inspire thunder she beats the stones with a tube of bamboo. Finally a small fire is made of the roots, which are of a tree known only to us witches, and as the smoke rises to the sky it forms clouds which release the long-needed rain. "Rain fall, oh rain fall down," is repeated several times in several different juxtapositions of the words and perhaps over a period of several weeks. If you are a good rain sorceress you can string it out, without losing the confidence of your patron or his present, until the rainy season gets there.

Magic, like modern medicine, is a profession of specialists; and though Kori had numerous sidelines, her specialty was gynecology. She was called in on a confinement, however, only when the family got into difficulties. In normal cases the members of the woman's own family act as midwife. Labor takes place in her home or that of her mother, and if things don't go right it reaches almost the proportions of a community affair. For normal childbirth the woman in labor squats on a coconut husk on the floor grasping a hemp rope that hangs from the ceiling rafters and leaning back against one of her midwives (usually a sister) who sits behind her, holding her firmly about the waist. Two more female relatives squat before her, and each has charge of one of her flexed legs, bracing them to her pressure. Her own mother is stationed in front to receive the child when it is born and to cut the umbilical cord with a sliver of bamboo. The afterbirth is retained in a jar, which the mother herself next day disposes of in the sea. This is probably to prevent its falling into the hands of an enemy.

Ordinarily in Melanesia men—and especially the man most interested, the father—are tabooed company for this little drama, but if the labor is dangerously prolonged the husband is sent for. He raises the lid of the camphorwood box which is in almost every Motu household, then seats himself on the floor and removes the binding that holds his hair in a pom-pom and takes off the plaited bands that he wears above his elbows. This ritual relieves the restriction that is preventing the child from being born. If it fails the woman's brother is called in, and he removes anything that is binding him. The last resort is magic. The sorceress' specific is a bark the odor of which would cause a miscarriage even without magic. This is chewed into fragments by the witch and then spat over the abdomen of the patient, after which the sorceress clasps her about the waist and exerts pressure. Should the woman die no fee is charged, otherwise it is a sizable amount.*

Divining the sex of a fetus is a nice practice, about comparable to professional treatment for a cold, no risks involved and sometimes nature co-operates. It is also simple if you have the rocks for it. Two kinds of stone are used, a male and female, and both are placed on the abdomen of the expectant woman as she lies on her back. There are incantations and when a rock eventually dislodges itself the one remaining is the same gender as the infant to be born.

Birth control magic comes under the heading "black" and dispensing it is punishable and expensive for the customer, about the price of a good hex on your worst enemy. Kori was careful to make us understand that she no longer carried this line, but there was a day when she could get three baskets of yams, a fishing net and from ten shillings to a pound for a successful abortion. One contraceptive is an herb available to anyone but not efficacious unless obtained from the sorceress, properly charmed. Such "medicines" have been analyzed and found to have no property in themselves that could be effective for the intended use. It is the way in which they are employed, especially the mangled root, that may sometimes achieve the desired result for it is the same simplest of techniques dispensed by our clinics. Moreover as the matter for which they are used generally takes place in or near

* From Dr. C. G. Seligman, Melanesians of British New Guinea.

the gardens . . . there is some association in the idea of fer-
tility . . . and as the woman shortly continues working,
the charm has a maximum chance of doing its duty. Nevertheless either the methods are genuinely effective or primitive
women do not conceive easily, for their families are as small
as our own with a widespread use of scientifically determined
controls. The attitude toward large families is that they are
disgusting, comparable to a litter of pigs. The hazardous food
supply may once have been the reason for controlling the
size of the family; but, though this is no longer a problem in
the coast areas because of the Government's watchful care
that none shall starve during famine, the birth rate still lags.
To stimulate it, actually with a view to preserving the race
for its own sake and not just to solve the labor problem of the
future, a baby bonus is paid, out of the natives' own taxes.
Infanticide is punishable naturally and is fairly easily appre-
hended because of the government headman in each village
who counts the heads, present and expected. Still, birth control and magic to produce sterility give the Guv'men' a
headache. They are punishable—but who can prove that the
magic was guilty?

A meal of charmed turtle bones will produce sterility in
both men and women, but the abortion trick is a little more
involved, requiring co-operation on the part of the principals
in the case; and it is not always successful because of the
fallibility of this help.

The first item to be obtained is a female centipede not
less than two inches long. This is the deceased maternal aunt
of the man involved in the case. (Kori admitted there were
signs by which she could pick out the right centipede, but
when we tried to pin her down, we got lost in the jungle of
interpreting.) In any case the centipede is kept between bi-
valve shells during a period of instruction when it is also fed
special food known to please the aunt. On the final day Kori

hides herself on the path regularly used by the pregnant woman, and as the latter approaches she rushes out, flinging open the shells as if to cast the centipede on the girl. Sometimes she actually does if the patient does not appear sufficiently shocked by the motions. And if this does not produce the desired results it is because of one of two goods reasons; either the spirit of the deceased aunt has been offended by the violation of some taboo, or the girl has made a mistake in whose nephew it was. A good job will net not less than three months in jail if it is discovered. Most abortion magic has an accessory of downright pummeling to make it worth the price.

Almost any adult knows what these medicines and the objects used in magic are, and many even know the verbal and manual procedure of the formulas, but only the sorcerer knows what makes them work to the desired end. This is less knowledge than conviction that they do work. It has many of the features of artistic talent; the person who has it doesn't know why he can draw a cow to look like a cow, any more than the person who cannot understands why he can't and the other fellow can. Sometimes the sorcerer tries to explain himself and says that he received some formula in a dream— he dreamed where he was to go to find a certainly magical rock; and when he wakened, there it was. Oftenest he says that the procedures and objects and the mystical conviction were given to him by his father, who in turn inherited them from his father. In the case of black magic this talent just sounds, to a skeptic, like good hearty wishing. As an example: smothering, crushing and burning are popular in black magic. The victim is not killed in any such torturous fashion, but his effigy is subjected to the treatment his enemy wishes for him. A sorcerer hired for the job will place the man's effigy under a special stone for just this purpose, and sits on it, rocking back and forth as if to crush the object underneath—groaning the while, and writhing and shuddering to simulate the agony coming to the fellow. Or the effigy substance may be put in a bamboo tube to slowly bake and shrivel suspended over a fire while the sorcerer moans like the mourners at a funeral. Shortly thereafter the victim will feel himself feverish, not an uncommon thing in this malarial country, and knows that someone has had him bewitched.

The use of magic is not confined to specialists, however; nor, for that matter, is it confined to primitives. Just as we knock on wood, cross our fingers, treasure some object belonging to one we love and breathe a prayer in an emergency, there is a kind of half-casual everyday magic used by most New Guinea natives. As the peasant shoves yam eyes into the loosened earth with his toe he mutters his own wordless charm for their growth, or he places in the hole where he is planting taro shoots a certain kind of leaf that resembles taro leaves but grows much larger. This is, in a manner of speaking, crossing his fingers. But whereas we stow away the precious lock of hair because we were fond of the producer the native will obtain the hair of only persons to whom he wishes to do harm. This is one of the objects on which a sorcerer can work evil. Equally good is a quid of betel nut the intended victim has been careless in discarding or just the spittle. The effigy can be the dirt and sweat of his skin, of which there is always an available quantity that would never be missed, or semen provided by some betraying woman. It can be any object that the condemned one uses; any of the things we treasure because we love their former owner the native will treasure the native equivalent because he hates. Either way it is a belief in magic.

There are many known vegetable poisons to be found in the bush, some of which accidentally eliminated a few hungry Japanese in the war, but for some unaccountable reason these are not used for actual killing in black magic.

Nor are they often used by non-professionals who have a little job of their own to do. The only exception we can think of at the moment is the use of belladonna and the poisonous gall of a certain fish which are slipped into the food of unpopular citizens in some of the Louisiade islands. The so-called poison put on spear and arrow tips is usually only putrefied flesh. However, brews made from fruits, flowers and the bark and roots of trees which in themselves would be deadly poisonous if taken by mouth are mixed with effigies in black magic and work by remote control. There is a vine called New Guinea "dynamite," the root of which when put in the water where there are fish can be as effective as real dynamite in stunning the fish and could kill a man in a short time. But, curiously, this is used only for suicide. On the whole there seems to be some unwillingness to take or give things by mouth. Even in curing magic few if any of the treatments include taking substances into the stomach. The Government and plantation managers at first had the greatest difficulty persuading the natives to swallow medicine. In some cases they had to be paid to do it. This is all the more curious because the Indonesian cousins of the Coral Sea islanders are specialists in upsetting stomachs and will feed an enemy anything from bamboo slivers to chloroform in his soup.

Not all spells are meant to be fatal, however. For example, a hex popular with wives who get mad at their husbands is a kind of casting away in which the sorcerer shoots the effigy of the husband up into the top trees of the bush by means of a spring stick. This won't kill the husband, but it can make him mighty uncomfortable. A frequent cause for marital displeasure is that the husband has been doing a little extramural tinkering around the neighborhood, or has been showing favoritism toward one wife where the wives are multiple, and in some way known only to the sorcerer this catapulting of the effigy into the air neutralizes the man's efforts. Without, however, doing the same thing to his ambitions.

It is to be seen that the idea in black magic is largely torture, something the average native is himself either not brave or imaginative enough to act on when he wishes to injure an enemy. So again, in sorcery he has wisely provided himself

with a safety valve for the emotions that give civilized folk shingles and psychiatrists.

Kori's practice was all honest medicine—or as honest as the profession can ever be without telling a patient anything. The pharmacopeia in her bag of tricks, which was a tin cash box, was a collection of rubbish from all over the countryside and adjoining ocean. There was the skull of some small animal, and the headless skeleton of a snake, crumbles of an edible clay from the Gulf district (where the natives actually do chew it during times of famine), a section of root vaguely resembling a dog's head, sharp pointed "needles" made of bone or shell and cutting edges of bamboo; there were little parcels held together with plaited net ornamented with tufts of feather or sections of shell. There were crocodile teeth, cassowary toenails, small chunks of quartz (one of them a prism of crystal), shirt buttons and safety pins and the glass stopper of a perfume bottle, a legbone of some bird and a dried claw, fish scales and pebbles and stones, some with holes in them, some painted red; about the kind of collection one would find if he emptied a small boy's pocket. One of the things in Kori's box that we wished we had got a prescription for was the section of a vine stem. Rubbed on the skin disease called *kukikuki*, it was supposed to relieve the itching, and probably did. Then there was the bark of some tree that prevented infection in a wound, ginger leaves to be used as a pack like mustard plaster for bad spirits hiding under the skin, and a very large glass bottle of a small amount of white "sap" which could make either a pig or a human fertile if properly applied. With every compound went a liberal dose of hocuspocus.

In surgery there were two techniques, one actual puncturing of the skin and the other a bloodless form of "extraction." To provide an exit for the bad spirits and an entrance for the patient's own spirit, which leaves his body during illness, holes are poked into the skin with a sharp pointed flint; a form of bleeding. The other method is to place hot rocks, heavily charmed, on an aching place to draw out the malevolence, and if this does not actually banish the basic trouble at least it refocuses the sufferer's attention on another stratum of his anatomy and temporarily convinces him that the first spirit has departed. On the same principle of counter-irritation the remedy for headache is to release bulldog ants onto the forehead. Believe me.

Another of Kori's treatments we know to have a certain effect is the use of coral rock ashes (lime) for compound fractures; in our case a damaged coccyx. When our coccyx was damaged we were hundreds of miles from a doctor, we remembered Kori's lime charm and used it with some rather original results. A pack of lime is applied to the affected part, moistened slightly by sprinkling (usually by mouth) and then quickly held over the hot smoke of a fire. Smoke is a disinfectant in itself; and this, with the heat penetrating through the lime, bakes, disinfects and anesthetizes all at the same time. But as anyone knows who has tried to get rid of a corpse, lime will do it. Our skin wasn't even punctured by the original accident, but we are convinced that no matter how deep-seated the malevolent spirit might be, he would come hopping out with this exorcism.

The odds in favor of failure in Kori's practice seemed to be high; but inasmuch as an entirely unsuccessful practitioner is first out of customers and then out of business, it may be assumed that she got some results and had good excuses for failures. It is not always wise in New Guinea to be a one hundred per cent successful medicine man anyway. When anyone dies unseasonably it is usually attributed to black magic; and as someone must pay with another life for such a death, who better than the sorcerer known never to fail? Hence the qualifications necessary to a magician, those of fearlessness and shrewdness. Kori in her perfectly legal practice functioned on two or three qualities that we recognized; good sound horse sense, a highly developed hunch bump, and a sense of the theatrical. Plus gab. But she also had some knowledge. She knew her weather signs and human nature. In her medicine she practised according to long-established principles in the healing art, using stinking herbs and massage and heat for all they were worth, made the patient feel that he was in charmed hands, and left the other seventy-five percent of the cure up to Nature. When Nature co-operated, Kori socked on a large fee; but if the patient died, she merely increased her prestige by not charging anything, for by this maneuver she declared in effect that the sorcerer who had bewitched the patient in the first place had spirits in his control too powerful to combat. Probably the most effective knowledge that Kori had was her belief in her own powers, for this has the feature of convincing others. But also she was actually predestined by nature for her calling. No one could have looked so witchlike by design alone.

The foregoing, it should be explained, is nowhere near an accurate description of native magic nor anything like the shape in which it was delivered to us. Accuracy is possible only when the examination is conducted by a specialist who uses the natives' own language or, through a good interpreter, questions and cross-questions not one but many informants. When we asked a question of Kori it went through a half dozen transmutations by the time the answer reached us. Ninoa interpreted to herself not only our English but our meaning, passed her version along to Kori, who gave it a whirl and tossed back to Ninoa answers that had to be figured out and sorted into English. Finally with the failing of the reasoning animal we had to rationalize everything—when magic is itself based on irrationality. The results cannot help being faulty, but they are *our* version, and I believe are generally descriptive.

20

Though Ninoa in her portrait does not look even adequately clothed the fussing to attain this degree of undress took longer than it does a modern girl to get ready for a dance. First the girl's entire body had to be oiled to make it shine and to bring out the rich color and contrast of her skin and blue tattooing. This was done by shaving up a coconut in its shell and smearing the shredded meat in handfuls over the skin. Then both Kori and Ninoa wiped their hands by running them through the girl's hair, which also heightened the glitter in the black wool. After this the scalp had to be thoroughly scraped with a long-pronged wooden comb, and the hair was combed and combed upward and forward until it stood out around Ninoa's little face like a halo of smoke. Then while the girl tied on thick layers of finely shredded grass petticoats, a brassy gold one over a henna brown, and on top of that an apron of two-inch-wide white leaves, adjusting and readjusting the tie until the layers would all open at the same place and show her thigh when she danced . . . while this was going on Kori fussed with the flowers. Into each hole of the girl's ear lobes she inserted a clump of the pungent purple herbs that are like the smell of cheese to a mouse for the youths of Hanuabada. Then three starry fragrant frangipani blossoms were placed exactly so in the black coiffure, and finally came the necklaces. Clumps of black seeds, glass beads, shells and dog's teeth and, last, the radiant crescent of mother-of-pearl, one of which every girl must own, were draped around Ninoa's neck until it seemed the oiling of her skin had been in vain. She was submerged. Had I painted her this way, the most important feature would not have been visible. That was the tattooing which decorated her entire body. To increase its importance, it was all Kori's handiwork; for she was also in control of the spirit stuff that makes an artist. In fact it was not until she saw me painting the tattooing into the portrait that the sorceress acknowledged me a fellow craftsman. In any case most of the necklaces were removed for the pose; and if I had had my way, Ninoa would have been painted in the nude.

I once had a frock that was designed in repeated patterns of a fairly exact map of Paris. It was sometimes risky to wear it, because persons familiar with dear old Paris would go sightseeing around me, poking at landmarks they recognized and forgetful of my anatomy underneath. This was about the treatment Ninoa was subjected to when we discovered that her tattooing was "writing." It was not writing in letters or even pictures but as symbols of events in the girl's life. The location of the units of design and number present told the story, for the patterns are standardized. Natives knowing the code can tell at a glance just how many landmarks a woman has passed. Around the age of five the arms are tattooed from the hand to just below the shoulder, a year or two later the front of the hips receive a design, and the armpits, the breasts to the nipple and the throat are patterned at ten years. Then there is a pause of two or three years during which the old markings are freshened up; and at the first menses the large patterns on the back of the shoulders and thighs and the buttocks are applied. The diaphragm is tattooed when the girl is betrothed, which happens when she is anywhere from thirteen to sixteen years of age; and when she marries she receives the "varsity V" running from the shoulders down between the breasts. Each tribe has its own peculiar patterns, and the people had to be very inventive or very tough, because any infringement of a design was once considered ample excuse for a war.

After we had witnessed a tattooing "sitting" we could understand why tradition has limited the amount of design

to be applied at each session and why there were two-year and three-year periods of rest between them. The girl being tattooed in this case was receiving the V, and she lay on her back with a brace of log under her neck and another at her feet. She also gripped short clubs of wood in her palms; but I forgot to put them in the sketch. The tattooer traced the entire V design on the skin, carefully but without measuring for symmetry, using a stick with a frayed tip dipped in a solution of oil and soot (from the bottom of a cooking pan).

This was then stippled into the flesh with a needle-sharp thorn fixed to the end of a stick, it being tapped by a leaf-padded mallet. I found by trying a section myself that there was quite a trick to the tapping. If I struck the thorn too hard the girl yelped because it went too deep, and if it were not struck hard enough the tattooing was likely to be feeble and perhaps would wear off with the cuticle of skin in a

short time. The native artist worked fast and completely finished the unit of design before the girl showed signs of having had enough. Blood and lampblack and perspiration were streaming from the decoration, which at the moment looked like a pattern of ground meat; and though the tears of travail had rolled out of the girl's tight-shut eyes, so long as the tattooer worked there was no sound from the victim. A large quid of betel nut inside her lower lip perhaps explained some of her stoicism, but it was an ordeal even for us. It did not seem that the little mountain vapor could have had the stuff to go through such a session as many times as she had.

Besides the conventional designs Ninoa's *reva-reva* told many another little story. There was a unit commemorating an obscure "brother make water" which the reader will have to figure out for himself. The designs on her lower legs from knee to ankle told of a big feast for the completion of a new *lakatoi* of which her father was captain. Then there were fill-in patterns representing, but not even remotely like, crocodile tracks, canoes, dog teeth, houses and so on. The unit that surprised us was the presence of the marriage V, for we had assumed the girl to be unmarried, because of her uncropped hair. Ah, so she was married to Pakosi. That made everything respectable—but for some reason much less interesting. But Ninoa was not married, she informed us, and left us there pondering the inconsistencies of the Stone Age society where everyone is bound by inviolable rules not the same for any two villages.

Then to further befuddle us Kori traced out the symbols for maternity. Ninoa had no husband but she had a child. Whose child then? and where, for that matter, was the picka-ninny that Ahuia had mentioned?

Every morning when the two women appeared they brought with them, one or the other wearing it suspended from the head, the same long net bag that looked as if it had shelled coconuts in the bottom of it. The string sack is a usual accessory of both men and women, the latter lugging vege-tables in their large ones and the men their betel nut makings and toilet sets in smaller kind hung from the neck or shoulder. We always snooped (with permission) into the bags of our models because the trinkets we found there, carved lime spatulates and containers, combs and spare neck-laces and arm rings, could be traded for a few sticks of to-bacco. But we never got a chance at the Tabora bag. It in-vited more than usual curiosity, too, because it had a familiar but unidentified odor about it, and while Ninoa was posing it hung from a nail on the wall and occasionally it dripped. Later on we recalled that Ninoa always took it with her when she went on a "walkabout" (rest) around the house. Yet all this time until we came to the tattooing on Ninoa's abdomen and discovered that she really was a mother there was no indication by sound or movement that the "coconuts" in the string sack were a live baby, the missing pickaninny.

There was no intended mystery about it. When we questioned the tattooing Ninoa took the sack from the wall, laid it gently on the floor, and rolled back the net, revealing a little

tan *karukaru* no bigger than a "mama-doll." It was all folded up compactly as it must have been in the womb, having been held that way by its own weight in the sack. It was a kitten of a pickaninny, certainly one of the best-natured on record. Instead of bawling when it finally opened its mouth it yawned, and then began working the squashy little lips for *su-su*, which it instantly got. At this point we noticed Kori. She was behaving strangely for a grandmother, not saying a word, just sitting quietly under her bricks of hair with her hands lying idly in her lap. That was not only unusual for the sorceress, it was unnatural for a Melanesian grandmother. This relative will not only sit and snuffle at the skin of her grandchild as long as he will let her—sniffing being the Melanesian kiss—but if you admire the child she will tell you that it is hers, entirely ignoring the intermediate generation. Their adoration, and consequent spoiling, of the babies is the one recognizable and lovable trait of these people who do not otherwise inspire much warmth of personal feeling. Yet here was Kori, a highly keyed emotional woman, practically denying any relationship to the cherub. It was the first hint we had got of a "situation."

One morning when the painting was in the finishing stage we saw with our spare eye which was reserved for the road a figure passing by in the direction of town. Ninoa was posing and she did not turn her head but her eyes followed the passerby so intently that I finally looked around. I recognized Pakosi and thought again how stunning the brown of his young pelt was against the blue of the bay, and of how we must trap him for a picture. I almost called out to him, but just then he did an odd thing. He was alone; if he had had company it would not have been conspicuous. He leaned over a little and without looking to left or right or pausing he began to slap a tattoo on his thighs. Still without looking up at the house he continued on up the road, leaving off the slapping after a minute. This might have looked like a mere exuberance of spirits if there had not been an ominous silence behind me. After a minute Ninoa rose and without any excuse, which was usual however, went down off the veranda. But this time she did not take the sack. And she never came back. She must have gone straight over to the village—where they found her body hanging from the rafters inside one of the huts.

We should like to give a logical explanation for this tragedy, but such things make even less sense in print than they do in New Guinea. Our very rationalizing stands in the way of understanding. However there are a few end-facts by which the reader may arrive at his own wrong conclusions until we give the natives' explanation. Everyone knew that Pakosi was the father of Ninoa's infant, but an illegitimate birth was not disgrace enough alone to have caused the suicide, not even enough for Kori to have called on her unused talents to prevent in the first place. The attitude toward bearing children out of wedlock is about the same in Hanuabada as in Middletown; everyone knows it happens now and then, and so long as it is not flaunted about it is accepted as an unfortunate accident. In any case it was not shame for the child that had driven Ninoa to hang herself.

Frustration could have been the cause if this had not been Papua. Though Pakosi did not have a wife, Ninoa could not marry him because he was even farther removed by having a fiancé. In many Melanesian tribes a wife is chosen for a boy by his guardian, frequently when both boy and girl are children, at which time the dowry is paid for the bride-to-be, but among the Motuans the lad and maiden make their own choice of mate. Both are free to do any amount of experimenting with any number of partners before settling on one. There is no attempt at secrecy, for the girl receives her lover in her parents' house, spending the night with him—though it is conventional for him to enter the hut after dark and to depart before daylight. However when finally after a period of this trial marriage the youngsters decide that they have found the right mate there is no backing out, for the announcement of it involves the clans and the conventions. Presents of tobacco and betel nut are exchanged every which way. The boy brings one lot to the girl, another to her relatives collectively, and a third to her brother or senior clan guardian, the latter being the formal request for the girl's hand. The brother then communicates this news to the girl, and if she hasn't changed her mind since last night he takes the betel nut and tobacco to their father, who broadcasts the news to the rest of the relatives.

When all the clan has assembled they debate the proposed marriage. If they decide against it the betel nut is returned to the candidate; but if there is no objection the nuts are chewed, in which case the boy has to go through the whole thing again a few days later, beginning with the present of more betel nuts to the brother and so on. Meantime he is hurrying about collecting from his own clan relatives the marriage dowry. In the old days the average bride price was about forty clamshell bracelets of various sizes, three pigs and enough dog teeth to make a necklace, around a hundred. The modern equivalent is two bush knives, four hatchets, the same number and kind of bracelets and two hundred red glass beads. After all the betel nut giving and chewing and the squeezing for and receiving of bracelets and teeth only death could save a boy from marrying the girl to whom he was betrothed.

However, having kept the contract, Pakosi might have obtained a divorce in the European court by sacrificing the marriage dowry if he had wanted to marry Ninoa. Or the girl might have moved in with the newlyweds as wife number two or as a concubine. (The missions do everything they can to discourage polygamy, but the government has not yet outlawed it where multiplicity of wives has always been the custom.) At least the fact that Pakosi was already taken was not the unsurmountable obstacle that might make one of us at Ninoa's age feel that life was intolerable.

It was Biah who first led our reasoning away from sane channels. He was a bosom pal of Pakosi's, as well as one of the busiest little spreaders of reports in the countryside, and he intimated that the whole thing was a clear case of *davana kori*, punishment or revenge. Instead of killing Pakosi Ninoa had killed herself as the meanest thing she could do to him. It seems that before Pakosi's betrothal he and Ninoa had been experimenting for some time, until finally she decided that he was the right one. It is always the girl who proposes marriage, and she does so in the night, when it is the proper thing for the boy to accept, whether or not he has any intention of marrying. Should he not wish to do so it is customary for him to send a friend a few days later to inform the girl, after which she does not receive him at night any longer. This is the way it is supposed to work; but Pakosi did not immediately send either the acceptance betel nut or the friend, and because Ninoa was in love with the young Scissors she continued to receive him at night. And he continued to accommodate her, because, as Biah said, Pakosi was bewitched. Then Ninoa became pregnant—which is not according to custom.

When a married woman becomes pregnant there is no cohabitation from the time the nipples darken until the child is walking, a period of two years and sometimes more; a violation will cause the infant to sicken and die. But Ninoa was now apparently determined to have Pakosi, and Kori brought into play in her daughter's behalf all the high-powered love cantrap she had in her kit. Potent leaves were always being brushed on Pakosi's skin whenever any of the Tabora clan could get near him, the powdered ashes of a shark skull were slipped into his box of betel nut lime, and crumbs of dried umbilical cord were put into his tobacco.* And of course Ninoa herself was kept charmed up to the hilt, buttocks smeared with the inside of a fresh snake skin, pungent herbs in earlobes and countless other spellbinders rubbed into her

---

* To bewitch an indifferent girl a boy will hide on the path regularly used by the girl and as she passes he works a spine of a sting ray back and forth through the eye of a coconut. Or he will wear where she can see it pendent from his neck an object supplied by a sorcerer, a human penis enveloped in clay.

hair and skin. However, Kori had apparently overdone it, for
the love magic was so strong that Pakosi had succumbed all
over the lot with half a dozen similarly anointed maidens
until, as Biah said, he was like a bau-bau, empty save for the
echo. Ahuia confirmed this much. It seems that the male
population of the district had been so depleted in the wreck
of the *lakatoi* fleet the preceding season that it had caused a
crisis among the maidens, and Pakosi had had more temptation than any lad could stand. He had just spread himself
around, but to such a liberal extent that he had been called
before the village council on the complaint of the mission.
This had resulted in his betrothal to the latest of his playmates.
In any case, we suspected that Pakosi's public censure was the
reason Ahuia had been unwilling to produce the boy to pose
for us. He did not approve of the Scissors as a representative
of his people, and probably did not wish to signify any approval to the lad himself by bringing him to us. For Ahuia
had learned snobbery.

But what did the interpreter think had caused Ninoa to
take her own life? Ahuia had a moment of looking like
Adolph Menjou adjusting his tie. A great weight rested on
His Majesty's servant. He wanted to make native behavior
appear rational according to our lights as he understood them,
yet he also wanted to be exact and honest. Finally he dropped
his hands in a gesture of helplessness and said, "Boy laugh at
girl."

That was actually it. Pakosi had laughed at Ninoa. In slapping his thighs he had ridiculed both her and her plotting
mother. And to be jeered at publicly is the disgrace intolerable to a people who are almost neurotically sensitive in
some directions. However in taking her own life Ninoa's
spirit settled down to a happy existence of bedeviling Pakosi.
When he caught no fish it would be Ninoa who steered the
schools off, when a squall at sea stripped the palm mat sails

from his canoe that would be Ninoa, and when there were
big rents in his sennit net or he couldn't find his betel wood
comb and heard coming from somewhere above and behind
him the little sip-sip, sip-sip sounds like the geckos make—
that would be the ghost mirth of the girl he had laughed at.
All the aches and fevers and itches and frustrations and sores
and sorrows would be the pleasure of the little mountain
vapor so long as Pakosi lived; and when he died, it would be
Ninoa who saw to that too.

Suicide, according to a Papuan government official, is
"not uncommon" in the parts of the country that are known.
The most frequent means is to jump from the top of a coconut palm, with hanging second in popularity and taking
poison 'way down the ladder. One original and rather
courageous method in use in the old days was to depart alone
for a hostile village where the man who did not want to live
was quickly satisfied. This had the added merit of causing
a great deal of trouble afterward to the suicide's tribe. For
however unpopular he may have been it was necessary to
avenge his death, even though the enemy had merely obliged
and everyone knew it.

Psychologists tell us that suicide is usually motivated by an
unconscious desire for revenge, against individuals, institu-
tions or even oneself. Even with that limitation, could the
ratio of suicides to the mortality in a group be an indication
of the degree of success of its system of living? Where there
is hope there is life. When you have an organization that is
livable for human beings of a certain temperament in their
peculiar environment, one especially that inspires participa-
tion in it, there are likely to be fewer maladjusted members.
Personal problems may be minimized by the prevailing feeling of hopefulness. No one knows naturally whether suicide
was "not uncommon" in pre-white New Guinea nor whether
it is a frequent way out today in the parts of New Guinea

that are unknown. There are even no statistics to show whether it has increased since white occupation in the districts.

A few of the known immediate causes for suicide among the primitives are the same that motivate self-destruction among civilized folk. Frequently it is frustration in love affairs—indicating that the "savage" has a capacity for some of the stuff we like to think is exclusively the discovery of higher types of men. For mere sex is even more accessible to him than it is for us, and he would feel little frustration if his attachment amounted to no more than this. Loss of face, disgrace in the eyes of his fellows, the mortally wounded self-respect, this is the commonest cause of suicide. But inability to provide for the family, which drove many of our men to take their own lives during the depression, is not one of the causes for primitive loss of face, because the social system is such that no one member is sole provider for the family. The whole clan feeds the clan, and when one is hungry all are hungry, including usually the entire countryside, for famines are the result of drought. Despair over ill health is never a cause of wanting to end it all as it is often with us who have the benefit of thousands of doctors, nurses, hospitals and the results of years of scientific work. Nor are there those unbalanced individuals who swell our statistics, for insanity was pretty well weeded out in earlier days by the practice of dispatching the unfortunates in youth. Sheer loneliness, the pitiful hunger for company or understanding that causes many a tragedy in the shifting, individualistic life of the progressive culture is almost impossible in classless and stationary New Guinea society. One of us could better understand the native taking a chance on the hereafter in order to escape all the family, clan and tribe company that is in his hair from dawn to death—understanding him so well that he can't get away with anything original.

The inescapable fact that remains, however, is that the New Guinea primitives do commit suicide, which seems to indicate that there are some flaws in their design for living too. But when such things continue to happen in places like Hanuabada it is probably more the hysteria of upheaval. In two generations the people have been hoisted up from the Stone Age into the Combustion Age; and however gradual the government might wish such a transition to be, this could not be controlled in a settlement so exposed to European influence. Hanuabada is in that critical stage between Kori's specialty and Ahuia's, between Ninoa's dependence on charms to hold and then to avenge her love and Pakosi's flouting of them. A few years ago no one, least of all a youth, would have had the audacity to ridicule a witch. He might kill her, but he would not expect to go scot free after publicly insulting one, especially after driving her daughter to suicide. Nor did Pakosi get away with it now.

21

Old Gomai was posing for his portrait, sitting cross-legged
on the floor in the doorway of the "refrigerator room." He
looked as if he had been sitting there for centuries, his fine
old statesman's head lopped a little toward one shoulder and
his eyes "wrapt back on some far place," blind to the things
around him, one of which was a wide semicircle of dandruff
that he had scratched off his ribs. The thin skin of his body
was patterned in gray whorls like watered silk; the result of
a bad case of *kukikuki*. This is a highly contagious skin fungus called *buckwa* in the eastern island and more accurately
if less elegantly described by our Coral Sea veterans as jungle rot. Some of these skin molds, which thrive in moist warm
climates, are pustulate and attack not only the skin but the
hair and nails. They are all hard to cure, and the white skin
seems to be especially susceptible to contagion. However if
one must have jungle rot the most becoming is the *imbricata*,
for the scales grow in concentric patterns that look like the
Chinese "cloud" pattern on an old brocade. Gomai's *kukikuki*
itched in the heat and kept him scratching nervously, so that
whenever he dozed I left him resting still sitting upright.

It was almost noon, and the old councilman and I were
alone in the house, with the possible exception of Adolphine.
Biah had gone into town for stores, and Margaret was out
covering the waterfront looking for the "puzi." When we
arrived that morning Adolphine's last year's skin was lying
at the bottom of the steps and as the pussy had just then
emerged from under the house Margaret had done what any

hearty soul would do, tossed the snakeskin over the cat. And the puzi had thereupon done what any hearty cat would do, started off in a series of deer-high leaps that took her out of sight in an instant. For a very good reason cats are rare in the islands; they are meat, and can purposely be mistaken for a cus-cus, which is a cat-sized 'possum. If this one remained at large he ran a good chance of ending up as game instead of

the *taubada's* "family." So Margaret had gone off in search of it, baited with fish which Biah had handily netted off the beach below the house. All morning long I had heard first near and then far her "puzi-puzi-puzi" as she wandered over the burning dunes. (Margaret usually came back from such tasks with a collection of bugs for examination.) In any case her absence was the reason I had worked less on Gomai's portrait than at finishing up the canvas of Ninoa and Kori.

It was one of Margaret's jobs to keep our "savage" models, not so much tamed as awake and reasonably alive looking. The combination of hookworm, a quid of betel nut and sitting still in the heat with my hypnotic eye on them had a somnolent effect. Margaret's ukulele always worked for a while, but after about half an hour of tom-tom the native would settle back with that all-day-and-all-night expression with which he listened to his own sing-sing music, and then she had to turn to something else. This had been no problem at Hanuabada, however. All Margaret had to do was to keep handing the model blocks of cube ice from the refrigerator. The natives here knew about ice, but not many of them had seen or felt it, and if the novel experience of watching solid turn into liquid did not stimulate them the extreme cold in their hands at least kept them from sleeping soundly. I might have kept old Gomai thus stimulated myself, except that even dozing he looked too venerable for such low jinks. And anyway I did not like the harrowing trip to the refrigerator. So he napped and I spent most of the morning daydreaming myself or "pulling" Ninoa's portrait into shape.

There is no way wholly to convey how still a windless noon can be in these unpopulous islands where even the few inhabitants retire indoors through the heat of the day. The smallest insect is not too insignificant to watch because it is something moving in a world that seems otherwise to have come to a standstill. This day there was no sound whatever, and not the slightest movement in the air. The big palmated leaves of the papaya tree below the veranda stretched on their long stems looking like property leaves in a show window, lifeless for all their spirited form. The sun beat right through them, so that they seemed to be made of yellow cellophane. The only motion in the whole panorama was the artificial sparkling on the hard blue bay. Out there the *lakatoi*, still at anchor before the village, looked more than ever like a beaten duck. Even the little heathens of Hanuabada had retired. To limbo, I hoped, though more likely they were still alive and in school. The odor in the air was the dry dusty smell of hot wood that came from the steps I was sitting on. It was a parched, deserted world that the sun had taken over for the rest of eternity.

When I first recognized them I thought I must have dozed off myself and was dreaming. There were two figures, one behind the other, coming up the road from the village, the woman in front and the man a short distance behind. This formation indicated that they were not traveling together, for a woman being escorted usually limps along about three yards behind the man. In a minute I recognized Kori Tabora, from her hair and the sack of pickaninny she was still toting, and then to my surprise I saw that the other figure was Pakosi. I shouldn't have thought one road was big enough for these two. When Kori turned up the path toward the house I fully expected to see Pakosi keep on going toward town. But the boy was bewitched. When he came to the path he followed Kori, though he came only part way. When she reached the veranda he stopped where he was, the same distance behind her, as if he were on an invisible double yoke. And while I was still rather dopily contemplating this doubtful performance something happened. Or it didn't happen; I'm not sure even now. One thing is certain; Kori had not known Pakosi's "uncle," Gomai, was present. She came forward talking inside her hair as usual, and as she stopped at the bottom of the steps she gave her customary greeting of "*Cinabada*," with the questioning inflection. Her voice woke Gomai and he leaned forward peering around the big canvas of Ninoa and her mother that had been hiding him from the witch. Instantly the talk stopped. And just that way they all remained, motionless; Gomai peering down at the sorceress, no sign whatever of what was going on under Kori's curtain of hair, and Pakosi "waiting" in the sun. While Ninoa sat smiling her winsome half-sad little smile out of the canvas toward him. We all seemed spellbound.

Kori Tabora, I had reason to recall, was hardly a timid spirit. Cautious perhaps, but if she had any idea of reprisal and could manage it secretly she would certainly try. But

Gomai was an old-timer too, and if she were up to something he would be the first to suspect it. He was the native equivalent of a plain-clothes detective besides being Pakosi's "uncle" and naturally interested in protecting his welfare. How had Kori induced the boy to come with her? And why bring him here? I had time to think of all of this, and more, before anything moved in that oppressive heat.

Then it happened. With an explosion that was like a blockbuster behind Gomai and had almost the same effect, the refrigerator tore into action, turning liquid into solid by the magic of luminiferous ether. Above the rhythmic frenzy of the motor could be heard Margaret's weary distant voice calling "puzi-puzi-puzi." Out in the house-cook Biah began banging pans for luncheon, yodeling in a high cracked voice those strange unfinished notes of the sing-sing chant, and if at that moment Adolphine had snaked her head over the partition and yoo-hoo-ed, it would have fit in. For I was laughing. The tense tableau before me had just quietly dissolved in the manner dreams have when they are getting dangerous.

For Americans steeped in the heartening roar of gangsters' automatics, and tires and heroines screaming around curves, this little Motu drama will seem very pale indeed. Yet it was a climax; it even had some of the elements of "good theater." After the long conflict between good and evil, dark superstition on the one side and sweetness and light on the other, the decisive moment had arrived—and the refrigerator had won. Kori got a week in jail in which to reflect on the modern rewards of racketeering. For Gomai duly reported her. The charge was probably the spreading of lying reports, and the basis of it was a rumor Kori had set going to the effect that our portrait of Ninoa had something to do with the girl's death. She may even have believed it herself. In any case it was useful to have others, and especially Pakosi, believe it. By some means she had induced the boy to accompany her to the "studio," knowing that we had been trying to catch him to pose for us and believing doubtless that when we had painted him Ninoa would take care of the rest. Pakosi's own inherent superstition would credit the first accident that befell him afterward to a spell and, with luck, his superstition would make it fatal. The fantastic part of it is that Kori guessed right in generalities and even in one particular, that of our being dangerous company.

After the explosion of the refrigerator the sorceress struck off diagonally for the road, leaving Pakosi standing unbewitched in the middle of the path. He came up to the veranda willingly enough when we beckoned him, and now that he was trapped, readily agreed to pose. Yet until we had set Ninoa's portrait inside the room he did not come up on the steps. But now that we knew so much of his record, all the glamour had gone out of painting him. He had his hair pulled up into a great pom-pom on the top of his head, the way we had first seen him on the sailing canoe, but now there was a long-handled comb for scratching stuck into it and his relaxed muscles and glossy skin looked soft and feminine in the way that Wisiki of Panasesa had struck us. He just looked like what he was, a trifling young buck who needed his little buttocks solidly kicked. I looked at him a few minutes trying to recover my inspiration, then told him to go below the veranda and wait; and I returned to painting Gomai. In a few minutes Biah, still in his *kiapi* like a slatternly housewife . . . the string net nightcap is worn to protect the ball shape of the hair during sleep . . . came sidling around the house with his bamboo pipe, all ready to help Pakosi smoke the trade tobacco we had given him. The two squatted down in the shade of the papaya tree below the veranda, Biah rolled up a cigarette of the tobac' in a piece of the Sydney *Morning Herald*, stuck it in a hole toward the end of the bamboo and then drew a mouthful of smoke into the tube, after which he

handed the pipe to Pakosi. Pakosi inhaled the smoke, blew it out and then politely refilled the tube and handed it back to Biah for his draught. And that business, which went on so long as we supplied the tobacco, became "The Motu Smokers."

The only thing we know to be suspicious about this canvas is the branch of papaya tree that fills the upper half of the composition. It was painted exactly as we saw it, with plummets of fruit hanging down and waxy white blossoms extending off the end of the branch. But there is something the matter with that, our papaya expert tells us. The pawpaw is unisexual, and we seemed to have picked out of all the possible normal trees there are in the South Pacific the one hermaphrodite he had seen in Papua. However, the tree should not have been painted into the same picture with Melanesians anyway, for the original papayas were brought to the country by Europeans, probably missionaries from the Polynesian islands.

The "pay-off," when it came to Pakosi, must have given Kori Tabora a deep gratification after her week in jail, and it should have given Pakosi a few weeks of serious thought concerning the risks of abandoning the old code of ethics before he had full protection in the new. We harbored a few doubts ourselves after the thing happened, because the first act of revenge was inflicted by our own car—and when it was at a dead standstill.

The car had an automatic starter, but it often failed to work, because of a conspiracy against the battery. In the first place the car wasn't driven enough to charge it, then the primitive who looked after it didn't believe in batteries yet, and the cells dried out so fast in the intense heat that the total result was so little "juice" that stepping on the starter just killed it "finish." Coasting to start was out because there was no nearby slope, but there were two alternatives, cranking or pushing—both of them hot, which was the reason Biah did not care much for the job.

The day the "Motu Smokers" was finished we stacked it and Ninoa's portrait on the rear bumper of the car to take them into town, and then found that we could not get started. Biah came down from the house and gave the crank a cautious jerk or two, but being a gentleman's gentleman his Motu muscles were even softer than they looked, and without trying again he shouted down the road after the departing Pakosi to come back and help him push. But Pakosi thought he would try the crank first. Ninoa must have been waiting . . . or the carburetor had been flooded, and the short wait until Pakosi returned was just time enough for it to drain to the right amount of gas. Because the minute Pakosi pulled the crank up Ninoa let him have it. She not only smashed his wrist, she flipped him over on his beautiful back in the road and then tried to run over him. *I* don't know why the car was in gear. A few days later Kori dropped in on her broomstick to have a look at Pakosi's portrait, but the canvas was already in town and all she did was run into Gomai again which sent her on her way yammering under her bricks.

The old councilman had eased quietly out of the picture when we began painting the Smokers, and it was with evident relief to find himself free. For by the time we wanted him back to finish his portrait Pakosi had become our second victim, and Gomai was so reluctant to risk his health posing for us that Ahuia had to use a little pressure (scoffing) to round him in. That morning when they finally appeared together, standing side by side in the sunlight below the veranda, I thought they represented something more than just two village dignitaries. They were allegorical figures in the pageant of peoples, one a soap-polished colored man with an executive's mustache and a shirt made on an electric sewing machine, smoking an English-made cigarette in a hard rubber

holder; beside him the gentle-faced old Gomai, clothed only
in his fungus, his ancestral dignity and a mulberry bark apron,
his grizzled head filled with spooks. There was no doubt
about which kind of man would survive "under the strenuous conditions of the modern world."

It had been an exciting fortnight for us, and these two men
had played their characteristic parts in it. About ten days
before a large party of bushmen had been brought in from
the westerly mountains to the Central Court to stand trial
for so successfully raiding an enemy tribe that not one adult
villager remained alive to give testimony against them. A few
children who had escaped into the bush were the only state
witnesses. No less than half a dozen interpreters had to be
used, because the language was unlike that of any other tribe;
and Ahuia was the final efficient link, translating into English
for the court the testimony he took in Motu from a native
who knew one Papuan language, and who in turn took it
from another—and so on back to the mountains. One would
think that the evidence would have arrived out in the air
pretty well garbled, but the bushmen simplified that. They
not only admitted their guilt but boasted of what to them
had been a flawless success. They were brave and clever
warriors, because they had attacked their enemy in the middle of a moonless night when all the demons were abroad
instead of waiting for dawn, the customary time. While one
of the strange-looking Papuans . . . tall, very dark-skinned,
big-nosed and almost naked . . . stood excitedly describing
how he had set fire to the communal house where the speared
bodies had been thrown, the rest of the bushmen squatting on
their haunches on the wooden floor nodded and smiled in
corroboration and applause. They thought they had been
brought down to the white man's country just to tell about
it. It had been a great day, and they re-lived it vividly in the
telling; but now they wanted to go home, for some other

tribe might be raiding their village, and they feared for their pigs.

When we got back to working on Gomai again we were still full of the lust for blood and wanted to get from him some first-hand tales of the old raiding days around the bay district. He seemed reluctant to remember anything, merely claiming that his people (the salt-water Melanesians as distinct from the inland Papuans) had never fought like these savage bushmen who ate their victims, ravished women, looted and destroyed gardens and then burned the village. But what his people *had* done we could not get out of him and after a while we stopped pestering him. He must have been mulling over the theme, however, because when he finally spoke again he seemed to be finishing the sentence left off an hour before. "More better now," he said slowly, and explained why. In effect he said: I am an old man, and I am still alive, and that is good. In the days before the Guv'men' came there were no men alive so old as myself. The men were killed by our enemies long before my age, and those who survived longest became the *taubadadia* (elders or leaders) of the village. It was these men who remembered the insults and incited the youths to retaliatory raids. The young men loved the attacks for their own sake, and none ever thought of not joining in them, because there was always the laughter of the women ready for the "lazy." Nor did any think of how short the time for enjoying the rewards of victory—which were those same women.

But the raid was purely revenge, an insult to repay insult. It never decided who was right or wrong; just who was stronger. And it was always the attackers who were stronger—partly because it was not the custom to give battle. The villagers, always surprised in their sleep, simply ran for their lives, swearing vengeance. And when they were strong again they rose up and themselves attacked. And won, right or wrong. So it had gone on since "long time before," raid following raid and revenge being heaped on revenge; the men died young, and none ever thought of the Guv'men's way. "Talk-talk-talk-talk," said Gomai, "all-a same *taubada*. Him-he more better fashion." The white men, Gomai well knew, never killed one another, nor allowed his people to. When there was trouble they talked and talked and talked; and now the men lived to a ripe old age, like himself and the Lohiabada, His Excellency. That was more better.

"White man savvy everything," Gomai might have added then. That was his commentary, later, on an illusion no less fantastic than that we never killed except after talking a great deal. (Natives who murder white men are executed but even that, naturally, is always preceded by extensive talk-talk.) It happened this way: On Monday Port Moresby had received the first arrivals of a U.S. agricultural expedition that had come to Papua to collect specimens of New Guinea pest-free sugar cane which it was hoped would renew the health of or replace our ailing southern stock. A schooner had been chartered to carry the expedition equipment up the rivers to the collecting fields, and a local man had been engaged as boss factotum. That was how so much information about the outfit got into circulation. The stories the *Taubada* brought home from the "pub" about the equipment of this *real* American expedition made Margaret and myself exchange Steig grins; that is, with only one small corner of the mouth. Finally, on one of the mornings Gomai was posing, the expedition airplane arrived. It was a seaplane, and after making a few survey turns over the bay it glided down onto the water near the village right before us and then taxied across to Port Moresby. Margaret and I were thrilled. For one brief instant the streamlined plane had posed nose-and-nose with the anchored *lakatoi*, dead duck of the vanishing age. Then the plane roared ahead, and when it came to the steamer landing, the pilot and passengers stepped out onto the pontoons and transferred to the waiting dinghy. We were seeing it, we thought, with the eyes of natives; and it looked like a miracle. But Gomai, the real native, was sitting there watching like the weary-eyed Secretary of State, savvy, unemotional, infinitely sated with miracles.

Toward noon it was blowing a gale hot enough to give one a permanent frizz. All our pores were wide open, losing salt, and Gomai's *kukikuki* was causing him to scratch until he sat in a regular shower of flying dandruff. We heard the starting roar of the seaplane across the water, and knew the pilot was going up with a crate of beer to cool off. Or he should have been. The plane swept so low over our side of the bay that Biah, who always raced to the front veranda the minute he heard it, ducked his head. Then it was gone with our envy into the glare of sky, and a minute later there was not even the sound of the motor. It was some minutes after when Gomai spoke. "*Cinabada*," he said with the rising inflection that always made it sound like a question, "*Cinabada*, long time before me look-m dis fella s-i-teamer; him-he no got-m sail, no got-m paddle. [But] Him-he go." A steamer sounded irrevelant, but Gomai continued, "By-m-by me look-m dis fella cart; him-he no got-m *hosi* [horse], no push-m, no pull-m. Him-he go. [The automobile.] Now me look-m dis fella he fly 'long sky all-a-same pigeon. Him-he go 'long water all-a same s-i-teamer, *taubada huaia* [carried pick-a-back]. Tch-tch, white man him-he savvy everyting." But there was more. After a long reflective pause he started again with his "*cinabada?*" "By-m-by," he said slowly and indicated himself, "boy die finish. (But) boy no savvy which way he go. White man savvy everyting. *Cinabada . . . Cinabada*, which way man go for die all-a time?" (*Cinabada*, *you* know; tell me your secret of where men go when they die.) We would like to have told him the truth (but didn't), that this was just the thing that made us all even; we knew no more than he did about the only thing that mattered to any of us; what became of us in the hereafter. His guess was as good as the savviest white man's.

Kori's comment after looking at her portrait had been that I was probably born with the umbilical cord around my neck which was a compliment because that's what it takes to make an artist. Gomai gazed impassively at his picture and finally pronounced it a *laulau*, a likeness, a reflection, a shadow or spirit. We think he meant mostly the first, because we parted friends. After we had given him his shillings and explained that he need not come again, this was goodbye, he thrust out his hand as if to have it shaken. I think he forgot himself, but we didn't give him time to remember that we were of the exalted race. Handshaking has become popular among the savvy natives, but not even the most emancipated had ever extended to us this gesture of equality, though we had fairly broken the back of white prestige to attain their level. We grabbed Gomai's hand delightedly, and gave it a regular old Rotary Club pumping.

And Gomai gave us his *kukikuki*. As a parting gift from a Melanesian there could have been no better bouquet than this blight that hurts and itches at the same time and can break into ulcers if you break down yourself and give it a good digging. Still, as Margaret always said when she was raking up a new crop of sores, scratching is the best of the few pleasures to be had in New Guinea.

22

All these weeks the commission for the portrait of Governor Murray had been performing like a wad of soot in a glass of milk. Turn the glass any way you wish, and the speck is still in front of your mouth, but just try to pick it out and it becomes possessed of a maddening agility. Most of the news that came into our household arrived via the *Taubada*, who was a regular pipeline to and from the "pub." Here apparently between the hours of five and seven daily all the affairs of state and society were discussed and settled, among them the progress of the portrait affair. So it was from the *Taubada* that we first heard that our "bid" had been accepted and that "they" were now approaching His Excellency on the matter of sitting time. That night we celebrated at Villa Viper, extravagantly. And prematurely, for a few days later we heard that the thing was off. "Why," some devout national had asked, "do we have an American paint this portrait?" And the answer had been, aye, why? The painter of an Australian statesman should be at least British. Or a Catholic! (The *Taubada* never missed a chance to take a "crack" at his old rivals.) So our temperature dropped to zero. But how different, we reflected clammily, from the American attitude where any quality of foreigner's work is preferred to the domestic, even at twice the price.

We went hot and cold a few more times before the issue was settled. Hot when we heard that the Governor had come out for us himself, and in my enthusiasm I made a "layout" of the portrait I thought suitable for the administrator of a tropical country: the usual white clothing, background of mountains and blue water and plenty of sunlight, you may be sure. Cold, when this very layout was used as an excuse for rejection. Who ever heard of a statesman—and particularly a knighted dignitary—being painted in anything but his robes of office or court with plush drapes and marble pillars behind? Warm, when it was reported that Sir Hubert would be damned if he would take those things out of mothballs and sweat in them in Port Moresby. Then finally cold as ice when the matter of fee came up again. This settled it, for added to the general depression a big gold dredging company that had been operating in the east had folded up and the waves of hyper-depression following the withdrawal of the company's enormous trade were shooting through the country like the throbs of neuralgia. The low price that Margaret had submitted was now too high. I broadcast that I would do the portrait and take whatever "they" wished to pay after they had seen the work, and it could be rejected if it weren't entirely satisfactory. That cinched it; there was some slick Yankee trick behind all this. The glass of milk, soot and all, was gone for good.

Our future meantime was being quite satisfactorily solved in another quarter. Those very persons who in their semi-official capacity had been making such an issue of an oil portrait were with the greatest charm ordering drawings for themselves. This was what the chalk sketch of His Excellency had done. A strongly Catholic community, which this one was, means children, no matter what the climate; and in healthful Port Moresby there were families with two, three and even five children who were turned over to us wholesale for pictures before they were sent south to school. They were all little Mildreds under the skin but we did not mind giving blood for this mess of pottage. The pound notes were crowding the Heffalump in the purse. Port Moresby was the first normal opportunity for work we had had in the islands, and we had received the commissions. I do not know what this proves, except that even temporary security can give head-hunters trembling delirium. If no more centipedes crossed our path, if the cost of passage across Torres Strait were what it should be, judged by the mileage, then we should be able to get to Thursday Island after painting the Papuans in the west. And the East Indies, home of Melanesians' mongoloid ancestors, would then be before us. That would mean we could *finish* the job we had set out to do, something we had not dared to think of until this moment. The money we had made in Port Moresby would not last out for the remainder of the program, but as soon as we got back to normal "family" communities such as Australian Thursday Island and the Dutch cities should be, it would be easy sailing. Just like Port Moresby. Now all we had to do was check up on boats across Torres Strait before going west.

"Keelhauled" is a good old-fashioned term that means to be hauled under the keel of a vessel by ropes, which was once done to seamen by way of punishment, a kind of wet "being pulled through a hedge backward." That was the way we felt when we had finished checking up on boats run-ning across Torres Strait, both keelhauled and bush-hauled. There were no passenger boats, not even *a* boat.

We were faced again with the Octopus of the Pacific. From Daru, the government station and farthest-west white settlement in Papua, to Thursday Island at the tip of Cape York of Australia it is exactly one hundred and thirty air miles. Great Barrier Reef, that extends all along the north coast of Australia, terminates in the Strait and between the two mainlands the water is so shallow that if it subsided only sixty feet one could walk across. Yet to reach Thursday Island from anywhere in New Guinea that South Pacific steamship line known as the Octopus, because of its virtual

monopoly of transportation, proposed with a straight face
that we in Port Moresby should return to Samarai for the
Rabaul-Sydney steamer, go down to Australia and there transship for Torres Strait, a Pacific cruise of some two or three
thousand miles, costing the price of a comfortable launch. Yet
there was no alternative.

We went through a throe or two, and then prepared to go
west anyway. And while finishing up the Moresby work we
learned that there was a trader (whose name was not Mr.
Goodfellow) with a launch who lived in Daru and he occasionally made the run over to "T.I." with recruits. The
captain of the *Chief* was promptly commissioned to find out
on his next run whether Goodfellow expected to make the
trip any time in the next two months. Two months would
give us time to get our Papuan studies in the west. The
captain came back with the censored information that the
trader would see somebody in hell before he would carry a
couple of women on his boat. "Go back and tell him we're
American women," we told the captain. "He says that's just
it," the captain reported back, "and anyway his boat's up on
the beach having a hole in her bottom repaired. He ran over
some coral when . . ." "What's he got against Americans!"
we snorted. But we knew; it was that "American millionaire
yachtsman" again, the one we heard about from one end of
Papua to the other.

Some twenty years before, the prudent owner of this
American yacht had tried to hawk his empty gasoline tins
along the coast for a shilling apiece. And for some reason,
probably the fact that the tins are usually acquired painlessly by being paid for with the fuel, this was regarded as
the height of Yankee cupidity. The traders themselves got
two shillings apiece (in coconuts or labor) from the natives
and anyone who had bought the yacht supply would have
made a hundred percent on his investment, yet the American

had been obliged to sail on with his empties. It had been hard for us to live down. "Well, you just keep an eye on the work on that launch as you call at Daru," the captain was told, "and when it's close up finish let us know."

"Now where are you going to stop when you do get to Daru?" the captain had asked on his next stop in Moresby. Goodfellow's boat was almost ready to go in the water. "There's no Palace Hotel on that island, and there are only ten residents when they're all at home. Including Goodfellow." "We'll be living just the way we are now," we said, "using our camp gear, with only the difference of not having bats in our hair." "Well," he laughed, "then you'd better store some mousetraps. Daru has so many snakes they have to keep a town snake catcher. The boy got sixteen last month right around the store, all . . ." "Deadly poisonous," we finished with him.

Rain. We woke on the *Chief* in another of Papua's seasons, and from that first morning on traveled in a downpour with the seas getting higher the farther into the Gulf we went. Beyond Yule Island we entered a new world of people as well as weather. The land of the Papuan aborigine at last. Anyone interested in the subject has read frequently about this curiously abrupt division of the New Guinea races that occurs in the vicinity of Cape Possession. Here within a few miles east of an invisible border there are only Melanesians and to the west are only Papuans. It is hard to understand until one is on the scene, for there is no chart explanation for the sudden change of physical types; no political boundaries, no insurmountable mountain or water barriers. Why was it that these two "savage" peoples did not long ago tear into one another and as a by-product of meeting create one of those border sub-races that mark even our aloof boundaries?

By the time we reached Orokolo in the Vailala River we knew at least one answer to the question. This is the Papuan woman, the sight of whom would take the luster out of even a satyr's eye. Whenever the *Chief* anchored for cargo, which was now usually up some river, half a dozen sapling-decked outriggers appeared out of the rain to trade vegetables with the cook, coconuts with the supercargo and game (small birds) with the crew, always for tobacco. The venders were women, but each canoe had aboard a man or two as ornament and someone to reach for the tobacco. After the petite giggling little Ninoas of Hanuabada with the sun always glinting on their waxed batik-ed skin and colorful rami, their becoming mops of hair and fragrant herb decorations, these Papuan matrons looked like jointed stewed prunes. They were exactly the color, just as wet and almost as baggy; and on top of this, "prunes" in personality. Glum-visaged and suspicious, their cucumber-shaped skull revealed in all its negroid unloveliness by a crew haircut, their unwomanly thighs bared in a brief drab rami, more fore-and-aft panels of fringe than a petticoat, its waistband held up behind by a nature-bagged rump and pushed down in front by a sago-bagged abdomen, long arms dangling in apelike simplicity, petulant lower lip ditto, baggy knees knocked and big flat muddy feet toed in, short-necked, waddy-nosed . . . you kept running your eyes up and down over them, hoping for one redeeming feature, some soft feminine something by which you could identify the creatures with your sex. And you always arrived back at that dark face that can only be described as aggressively uninviting.

The men, as is so often the case among the naked, had come off a little better. At least they were not baggy, and the long limbs and big joints and features just made them the more masculine. *They* wore the becoming mop of hair ornamented with a feather-tipped comb, and they had the small girdle-bound waist and the pouter-pigeon chest. And it was they who laughed, if not charmingly at least readily, as we handed down tobacco in exchange for what little clothing they wore. They stood on their outrigger decks in the rain with spraddled legs, straight of spine and head up with the cocky air of the male who has not only won the battle in the home but has the entire neighborhood licked as well. It is possible that the Papuan men were one reason few of the soft Melanesians of the eastern coast had crossed the line into Papua proper. But what still can't be explained is why, when there were those other softer little Melanesians across the border, the Papuan men stayed at home.

Not all Papuans look like those of our first encounter. There is a wide diversity of physical types among them, and a variety of languages and dialects. Such differences could arise only out of a very long period of watertight isolation of the different tribes one from the other. This suggests that the Papuans have shown no less antagonism toward one another than they have toward all outsiders. The only features the tribes seem to have in common are the stage of their culture and their negroid hair and elongated skull. There are some Papuans as light-skinned as the mongoloid Melanesians, others are as dark as the chocolate-brown Australian aborigines. The natives around the mouth of the Fly River, that region nearest Australia, are also as tall as the Aboes. But in the western mountains there are Papuans, not Pygmies, who are shorter than the Melanesians. All the Papuans we saw and painted were as tall as the average white man, and often taller. They were all very dark, and had the nose which appears to be typical of south coast Papuans, beaked or waddy-tipped, and always large.

We had been told that we should expect to find a difference in temperament between the two New Guinea races. Whereas the Melanesian was emotional and impetuous—the childishness that would inspire a man to burn his house down or kill his mother-in-law because the code of behavior forbade his striking a child that had infuriated him—the Papuan would be stoical and morose. Something happened as a starter at a village up the Vailala River that gave us our own impression of what difference in temperament there was.

On board the *Chief* was a Catholic brother whose station was miles inland, who was to be dropped at the Vailala village and would complete the rest of his journey on foot. We did not envy him. The settlement was some distance up the river, and all along the way the banks were hidden by dense dark jungle that stretched out over the water, draped and festooned with creepers that streamed with rain. The site of the village was the first cleared area we had come to, and here the shore was mud. Gray slimy mud that was soft yards down, and impassable even for the villagers themselves. And herein, incidentally, in the ooze lay another good reason for what Papuan homogeneity there is. An invasion from the sea still depends on the simple existence of something to set your foot on ashore, and this is hard to find in the Delta region of New Guinea. Actual terra firma is far inland of the apparent coast. Throughout the low Gulf basin the country is riddled with water, rivers, swamps, tidelands and delta islands, until it cannot be said which is river-cut mainland and which silt islands. This character of the country proved to be one of the greatest handicaps to control when the government first started moving west from the settled Central Division. "Control" has been achieved largely as a by-product to following up reports of raids and murders to make arrests; and when the Service got into the swampy deltalands in this pursuit the white officers were literally at sea. The guilty tribes did not wait to get caught. When they heard the Guv'men' was coming in their direction they left their villages and took to the marshes, where they knew the tracks and how to sustain themselves on swamp foods. And there they stayed until the Service, devoured by mosquitoes and leeches, had to retreat, from lack of provisions or illness. There is one yarn of a murderer the Service was looking for who presented himself to the officer, offering to lead him through the swamp paths to the culprit. The offer was gladly accepted; he was even paid his "presents" in advance, and after several day's "chase" through the miasmal bayous the murderer abandoned the police party, leaving it to get out as best it could.

When the Gulf tide is out . . . and about a twenty-foot rise and fall is average . . . the villagers themselves use planks laid over the mud to get up from the water to their clearing on the high ground. This was our means of entrance to the Vailala settlement. The impressive thing about this first Papuan village was the great number of people in it. Or perhaps it was because the clearing was not large and the towering bush all around seemed to make a crowded corral of it. Melanesian settlements are invariably small, seldom exceeding a population of two hundred, and less than a hundred being average. (Where there are more, as in Hanuabada and several of the coast mission stations, it is a modern collocation of two or even several villages.) But the Papuan, either for security in number or for economy of labor in clearing the bush, collects a whole tribe into a single village. Some of the largest of the past have had an estimated population of from three to five thousand. What a sing-sing or raid they could stage! Five hundred Papuans at a time were enough for us, for there must have been that many wet black aborigines waiting for us when we had clawed our way up the slippery planks to the bank. Above and behind them could be seen the façade of a regular skyscraper of a building that looked like the prow of a ship. We lost the missionary in the crowd immediately, and never found out whether this was one of those men's club houses where the youths are confined in the gloom anywhere up to two years while they learn the secrets of life, or whether it was just one of the Papuan apartment houses where the entire clan down to the last dog and pig lives together. The ridgepole soared to the height of the jungle treetops, and looked to be two or three hundred feet long.

We had difficulty making our way toward the house, for no path in the crowd opened before us. We had to nose forward something like a polite bulldozer. Scores of little wailing yellow dogs and tall muddied pigs tore around trying to avoid the milling feet; naked muddied children pried their way toward us between the legs of big wet men, while the women eddied around the outside edge of the excitement—which was ourselves. I got the rather unfamiliar sensation (for this country) of being pushed around inside a calliope of smells, the identifiable one being that of a small boy when he comes tearing in from the football lot, too late. Not exactly uncleanliness but certainly the fumes of escaped salts and mud. The villagers did not frighten us; this demonstration of enthusiasm or curiosity or whatever it was, was just the confidence built up by the Government. But I kept remembering inconsistently what Governor Murray had said about his

Papuans; that most of the Europeans murdered by them had been men who knew them well but trusted them too much. This was because Margaret had got ahead of me. With the bloodhound's indifference to all other smells when it is on a scent, Margaret had pushed her way ahead toward the longhouse, and in a minute she was shouting to me to come quick. She had found a "black widow." Margaret said afterward that the woman looked like a black sitting hen on her nest of grass skirt, but all I had time to see was that she was black. Her face and arms had been blackened with soot

or charcoal (which made her look like a minstrel darky, for
the rims of her eyes and lips were still pale by contrast) and
she was sitting in deep gloom on a shelf under the raised
floor of the longhouse.

Before I could get near, Margaret was backing off from
the woman before a blast of some Papuan idea delivered in
a shrill soprano. The woman was beating the air with her
black arms, clawing down in Margaret's direction, but she
did not move off her perch. In fact I got the impression that
she was not so excited as just vehement. It had a curious effect on the crowd. Only afterward we remembered that something had happened to the men; they were gone. There were
only women about us, and at first they were just looking at
Margaret with their mouths open. Then they began pushing forward until she was jammed in the center of a lot of
shrill naked Papuan anatomy. The women did not seem to
be angry, yet they were not recognizably laughing. It looked
like the clawing kind of enthusiasm one sees in a push of
autograph hunters or rationed goods grabbers, but without the
grab.

We retreated with enthusiasm ourselves, the backs of our
necks crawling—for the women followed and then nearer
the shore the men crowded them out and when we finally
managed to get down on the planks again, which now seemed
safe by contrast, the crowd on the bank was a milling turmoil.
It was somewhere along here, we recalled, that the great
Tamate, Reverend Chalmers, had left his head when he was
paying just such a friendly call. But that was forty or fifty
years ago. We reminded one another when we were back on
the *Chief* again and had had a sustaining drink. "It would be
just as well," the Captain remarked dryly, "if you didn't give
these people tobacco along here. If they know you have a
supply in your dilly bag and someone tries to filch a few
sticks you would resent it, and then something unpleasant

might happen." So that was what *he* thought of the racket; that there had been a cause.

The Vailala episode might have passed out of our minds like many another such encounter if something had not come up eventually to explain it. Meantime it served as a rather concentrated introduction to our new models. And at Kikori, the next day, we ran into another lucid illustration of the Papuan personality.

Kikori is the district government station of the Delta Division, one of the first to be established in the west, and for something like thirty years now it has been spreading sweetness and light, seasoned with justice, around the neighboring swamps. The natives are, or presumably were, well under control. We can confess now that our advance on this lonely station was not without guile. In fact we were stuffed with it. We wanted to get our Papuan studies here for the excellent reason that the natives were probably the "purest" we would find on the coast. They were far enough distant from the Melanesian areas not to have had even a recent admixture of that race, and there would be none of the Australian influence which has certainly had something to do with the type farther west. Remaining at Kikori depended on being offered lodgings, and the only dwelling was that of the Resident Magistrate. However, Governor Murray had given us a very generous safe-conduct addressed to "Papuan Officers" in general which requested that we be given "every assistance." This could not be interpreted as a command that we be bedded down in any officer's home, but if we presented the letter it was a good hint. Particularly if we hauled our camp outfit ashore and began driving tent stakes into the man's front yard.

Kikori is about twenty miles back from the Gulf. I cannot say inland up the Kikori River, because those twenty miles after you leave the Gulf are a succession of water-riddled sections of land, or land-riddled waterways, that is merely an extension of the Gulf when the tide is coming in. At any rate the government station is on one of the banks, and the steamer channel leading to it is a serpentine course winding up a canyon of towering jungle. At some points it becomes so narrow that the fat *Chief* just manages to squeeze through by going cautiously, and at other places it spreads out into a lake. The rain still drummed down on a river golden with flood silt, and the tide was rising; but every now and then, rounding a bend, we came on a mud flat where two or three crocodiles snoozed, still oblivious to our approach. We spent the trip up informing them of it with the Captain's gun. The rifle was an old Express which, lacking tomahawks, could have blazed a trail through the bush, and it should have exploded a crocodile. But even when they were hit . . . and we were close enough now to see our hits . . . they still whirled into the water and disappeared. There is a superstition among men who shoot at crocodiles that it is impossible to kill one unless you hit it squarely in the eye, but it is our opinion that a crocodile dies in places one at a time like a snake—and it just takes longer. When we came back down the river some time later we saw some natives towing to shore one of our hits that must have just floated to the surface. And I am not sure that it made us feel any better, for we had been potting at them just to see them jump, confident that we weren't killing wantonly.

But we could understand now why crocodile meat is so seldom mentioned on the native menu in this hungry land. In a few districts the natives have exceptionally long and heavy spears, and a number of these are thrown simultaneously and with great force at the crocodile, after which he is allowed to die thoroughly before anyone goes near him because the powerful tail, so long as there is a will in it, can still swing out and break a man's legs.

When we arrived at Kikori we found a Resident Magistrate snorting flames. But such conservative British flames at first that we failed to recognize them until they were roaring. While the men exchanged their mysterious men's greetings we cast a speculative eye about for a site on which to pitch our camp. Mud. The residence was up on a high bank of it and rain was beating down on yellow lakes all over the clearing. The clearing was small and hemmed in to the river by a semicircular precipice of jungle that must have been a hundred feet high, and the light in the place was like a well. We concluded that the R.M.'s rather terse manner was caused by claustrophobia. He had disappeared into his office, presumably to read his mail and answer important correspondence (because it had to be mailed out on the same boat); and when we heard him again he sounded as mad as a man piling firewood. For reasons of his own he had opened the Australian newspapers first, and he came out of the office waving them. "Cannibals," he blazed, "slau-ughter! Good god. Five hundred butchered. Why the crimson rags. Look at this, 'Whites Evacuating Kikori. Fear Uprising.' Oh-*o-o*." He held his head. "Well," the Captain grinned, "how many *were* et?" The R.M. was vague. He fancied twenty natives, not more.

But this was the real thing, a regular old-fashioned "cannibal orgy" with, we were told, about the average number of casualties for such an event. But this one had taken place only two weeks before and at rather close quarters, within "controlled" territory. That was the feature that was making the Guv'men' "wild." Natives in controlled areas are those who understand that should their village be raided by an enemy they are not to retaliate, because the Guv'men' will deal with the offenders. This disarms them and makes them entirely dependent on the government for security. Consequently should one tribe within the controlled area raid another also inside it, it does so a priori under the "protection" of the government. The R.M. should have his district under such absolute control that an accident like this in the Kikori district could not happen. A very unhealthy situation could arise out of such "remissness"; loss of confidence that might decide the natives to do their own retaliating thenceforth, and a consequent lowering of government prestige and authority, even resentment which might be justified. It would certainly take longer to regain the confidence of the natives than it had to gain it in the first place, and so on and on. Yet the thing had happened, the southern papers were making the most of it, and the R.M. was holding his head.

But as it happened this "affair" was not a raid. There was an old feud between the two tribes involved which had its origin, someone said, in the table manners of their fathers. In one tribe, the proper way to prepare a fellowman for eating was to cut him up in steaks, wrap the cuts in leaves, and roast. Or at least respectfully boil him in small portions. But it was the custom of the other tribe merely to toss the whole roast undressed on the fire. This was considered very bad taste by the steam-roasting school and, when they became the victims, was much resented. The government stopped their raiding one another, but the sons of the roasters were still casting jibes at the open-fire cookers, until, a fortnight ago, some well intentioned person suggested that one of the tribes give a feast for the other and patch it up for good. Village A therefore invited Village B over and, with the confidence of government protection, the B's accepted. And the A's simply ate the B's instead of the pigs.

The Papuan administration is always under fire of southern politics and press, because it is more interested in its native subjects as natives than as labor for "development" (by big financial interests) of the country. Consequently the slightest

evidence of lapse is seized on as proof that the country is being improperly administered and that it is high time for new
appointments. Any raid or "cannibal feast," no matter how
remote the district in which it has occurred, shows that the
savages are out of control and threatening the lives of Australians in the territory. "Never mind," we soothed the R.M.,
"think of what the American newspapers would have done
with that much blood to start with. They'd have had you
scalped too." "American . . ." He seemed unable to think
of anything adequate to add to that.

The authors of the cannibal feast had already been brought
in to Kikori and were even then at the station, locked up and
eagerly anticipating the excursion to distant Port Moresby
for their trial. We went over to have a look at them. They
looked about normal; no crumbs on their chins. There were
ten or twelve men, one an old fellow who spoke pidgin English and couldn't have been kept still anyway. He said the
idea of eating their guests hadn't been planned. It had just
come on them suddenly, when they saw their old enemies.
If they ate the pigs as they had intended, there would not be
much for each man, whereas if they ate the guests there would
be plenty, and even the women and children could have some.
This wouldn't be raiding, which they knew made the
Guv'men' wild; their old enemies had come to them. Asking
for it. Anyway, it had been worth trying. The old fellow
put the back of his hand up to his nose and sniffed, giving us
a mischievous glance over it that came as near a wink as we
have ever seen in a primitive. He didn't know that just that
savvy was what would give him and his fellows a reasonably
long jail sentence.

We were back on the *Chief* and under way again before
we remembered the governor's letter, still undisturbed in the
brief case. We hadn't even tried to drive stakes in the R.M.'s
yard. He was going back to the scene of the crime and count

bones until the *Chief* returned, when she was taking him and his prisoners down to Port Moresby. And we weren't yet sure enough about immortality to test it staying alone anywhere in Papuan New Guinea—however well controlled.

23

"Every twenty-four hours of the day," said the Storekeeper from Daru, "year in and year out, two hundred million gallons of water flow out of this Fly River into the Gulf. That makes . . . let me see . . . a little less than a hundred and fifty thousand gallons a minute. Lot o' rain falls up in those mountains." Properly impressed, we gazed down at the seas smacking broadside against the *Chief*, trying to realize that the silt which made them yellow even as far as ten miles out in the Gulf was some of the thirty thousand square miles of New Guinea through which the Fly and its tributaries flow. This was the nearest to the interior of New Guinea we would ever get, we were thinking sadly, sailing through its silt in the Gulf.

Early in the morning the Captain had announced that we were starting across the mouth of the Fly River and in mid-afternoon we were still passing the mouth of the Fly River. It is something like ninety miles from one bank to the other. But there had been no change in the scenery for three days, for we had been constantly passing the mouths of rivers. The steady rain still blocked out anything more than a quarter of a mile distant, but occasionally we glimpsed the solider gray-green of one of the scores of delta islands that strew the estuary of the Fly. The seas across this bar-littered stretch might have had something to do with our sadness, but also it was a comfortless thing to be seeing only bleak rain when we were passing a spot, for probably the only time in our lives, which intrigued us at least as much as the hereafter. It was not so

much what we knew about the great river as what no one
knew. It is only in recent years that the government has conducted any explorations beyond the waterway itself. And
not until Officers Karius and Champion traversed the island
to the north coast in 1927–28, using the Fly for their penetration of the interior from the south, was the position of the
headwaters determined. Up that river and in the mountains
beyond were people who did not know that any other world
existed, who would not believe there was such a human being
as one with a white skin. What treasures portraits of those
Papuans would have been! Every time an uprooted tree complete with foliage came tossing out of the rain from the north
we watched it out of sight on its way into the Gulf thinking,
ah, a paleolithic tree, no doubt. *It* had "seen Carcasonne."

We finally got by the estuary of the Fly, and very soon
afterward were swinging in toward Daru and facing our
Present, which was trapping and overwhelming Mr. Goodfellow. But first to become campers. And a more dismal prospect in this downpour I have seldom faced. I say I, not we,
because Margaret, so help me, was still pretending that living
in a wet tent would be "jolly." But that was because she did
not have a cold to make her nose hot as a pudding raisin.

"Now look here," said the Storekeeper consolingly just before we landed, "it isn't going to be so bad camping. We can
find a high spot for you above the tide where the mud isn't
quite so deep, and of course the snakes won't bother you.
That's what we've got the snake catcher for. The only thing
is, you'll have to have a real tent, with sides, because the crocodiles are nosy. But I can rig you up something out of sail . . .
or maybe the boys had better dig a trench all around because
the crocodiles have been known to chew right through canvas." But I knew him as a puncture-proof optimist that years
of living in Papuan weather had not suppressed. "Think of
what I would be like if I lived in Australia," he had said, "and

got all the good things to eat and didn't have malaria. Why, I sit down like a fried egg now, just on tinned food. I'd get *fat!*" He and Margaret came out of the same rainbow-hued bubble, and they were inseparable. And insufferable. It seemed curious, what with his fondness for her and the fact that we had made a gift drawing for him in Port Moresby, that he should let me go on suffering over the prospects of pitching camp in Daru when he presumably had a home here. And a home had a veranda, even if it did not have a guest room. But he and the Captain would have their little joke, and string it out until we were actually stepping onto the jetty of Daru Island. There we were met by the wife of the assistant resident magistrate, all prepared to take us home with her.

In our pursuit of the elusive Mr. Goodfellow next morning we unintentionally saw a great deal of the settlement. We did not count them, but there cannot be more than ten European buildings at the station. Most of these are residences, some of them long unpainted and all but the government-owned surrounded by tall weeds that harbor the snakes which are stalked by the snake catcher, who was a reality. The "business section" at the landing is two stores, the larger and cleaner and emptier of natives being that of a mission society with which we were to become unexpectedly well acquainted, the other belonging to our Storekeeper. Daru is a large enough island—two or three thousand acres—to give one the impression of being on a mainland, and there is none of that garden-of-the-gods charm of the other end of New Guinea. Anyway not in our season of the year—whatever it was. The site of the settlement is flat, with a number of tall wet trees left unfelled; and what is beyond it is hidden by wet jungle. Depending on the tide the shoreline before the clearing is either a narrow strip of deep mud or a wide one, and elsewhere around the island the coast is mangrove trees or mud. "A very thoroughly uncomfortable country," says one of the govern-

ment reports, a set of documents noteworthy for their understatement.

We spent quite a spell in the vicinity of the town mud, because Goodfellow's boat was anchored in the stream beyond.
Goodfellow must have seen quite a bit of Daru that morning
himself, because we followed him from store to store and
house to house, until it occurred to us that the populace had
ganged up with him for the sport. That made us retire to the
Storekeeper's, from whose elevated veranda we could drip
while spying on the entire waterfront.

The Storekeeper's shop was like a small cave, complete with
lake, and the Storekeeper came out from the back room like
an excursionists' barge, wending his way between walls of
stacked bolts of calico and cash boxes, coils of rope and barrels and boxes and showcases of stuff, under hanging hatchets
and knives and flashlights and belts and lanterns. A few tall
dark Papuans with muddy feet, who had contributed the lake
on the floor, crumpled back into the merchandise to let the
taubada pass, and he reached us beaming and uninjured, easily half an inch bigger all over with a new idea he had for us.
Little wonder: he proposed that we should make portraits of
the indentured natives of Daru and *charge for them*. And we
did, but I'll face that explanation later.

Meantime, it seemed the best of all possible wet feverish
worlds as we sloshed home to luncheon, in spite of Mr. Goodfellow still being uncaught. He could not evade us long on
an island the size of Daru, and anyway now we did not want
the date of our departure set too soon. We found ourselves
in a deluge of portrait commissions in the little settlement. The
Resident Magistrate had ordered "some kind of colored picture" of his wife and child, who were then well on their way
to Australia. We had caught a fleeting glimpse of them as they
embarked on the *Chief*, but what data my memory lacked
was to be supplied by some snapshots. Then we had a thank-

you drawing to make for our host, another enlargement of a snapshot. And finally there were our own Papuan studies and the portraits of the colored patrons whom the Storekeeper guaranteed he could produce, at five dollars a head. That business of rolling up the sleeves and rubbing the palms briskly together and the happy lover's sing deep inside, "everything is all right, just all right," that lasted until breakfast the next morning when a limp paper talk-talk was delivered from our ally, the Storekeeper. As Margaret read it, first to herself and then slowly aloud, it was the first time I ever noticed that she had moments of looking like Charlie McCarthy. The muscles of her face were set in a beaming smile, but her eyes were blank as she looked at me. Mr. Goodfellow, the note said, had decamped, cleared out for Thursday Island at daybreak!

24

The photograph our *Taubada* wanted enlarged was of a native, and a very strange South Sea islander indeed. He looked exactly like a Pharaoh of ancient Egypt, even to the long sawed-off bob and a short jutting beard like the false ones the kings of Egypt wore. But the nose had it most of all. It was the shape we think of as "Jewish," with a high thin bridge and depressed tip. The curious thing was that the face looked light-skinned though the body was native-dark and naked save for a huge loin shell that must have been held on by sheer magnetism, for there was no visible waistband. The man certainly had the features of a Mediterranean type, and with clothing and a haircut could have passed as a modern Arab or Armenian, or even a Spaniard or southern Italian.

The amateur ethnologist is always being stirred to the core by the discovery of similar customs, legends, and physical types in widely separated areas. Just as if Sir James Frazer had not spent a long busy life collecting just such data into *The Golden Bough* to show that there was no such thing as an original joke. Still we continue to be stirred, and when we find in the pre-missionary native legends of the Solomon Islands the story of the Flood with even an Ark and a Noah, in Rabaul paint an Egyptian red bench with carved dog-head bar ends and black and white "wave" designs, and finally come across a photograph of a living native who looks like a profile on an Egyptian frieze, then we amateurs think we have discovered something. We think that some of the migrations which populated this part of the world must have come from farther west than the Indian Ocean, and with very few stopovers.

Imagine then, after this gratifying conclusion, our discovering that the subject of the photograph was one of those mysterious Papuans of the interior, that he was a practising cannibal with his chops hardly dry from the latest feast, and that he was at that moment in Daru!

The man's name was Tauparaupi, and he was one of eighteen Suki tribesmen captured after conducting one of the most

ambitious headhunting raids that have come to government notice in the west in recent years. The Suki live in the vicinity of the Pink Lagoon, so named because of the pink water lilies that cover the marshes at a place about two hundred miles up the Fly River. Some weeks before, the Suki braves had set out down the river in a fleet of lagoon dugouts, slaughtering, feasting and collecting trophies of heads as they went. It was said that they had even planned to do a little tinkering at Madiri, which is the last white plantation up the Fly and only about fifty miles from Daru. Coming down the river on the current was probably easy, but the lagoon canoes are not built for rough water, and the lower Fly is the width of a great lake and is swept twice daily by the high Gulf tides. The Suki shells were shallow dugouts with both ends open, which made it easy to tip out water, but also made it easy to ship water on anything rougher than a pond. Then the paddles

were really only long punts with a blade of less than nine by twelve inches. Withal not a very seaworthy outfit, especially with a cargo. However, it appears to have been adequate for a certain distance according to one government report of conditions found at the village of Weriadai on the Fly: "The longhouse [communal dwelling] had been burnt . . . Legs, arms and entrails were lying about . . . Thirty-nine people had been killed, and the stench of the rotting remains was awful. The victims had been cut up on the spot, and the bodies and heads taken away by the raiders." This was only one village. At another, evidence shows that the Suki had begun to get particular about their cuts; they had left the torsos of the women minus the breasts, and with a degree of wantonness that attains the story-book level, they had driven stakes down through the headless torsos and scattered the unwanted arms and legs all around the clearing.

The raid came to an abrupt end in the river when a tidal bore swept up on the fleet, swamping the shallow canoes, drowning some of the feast-logged Suki and washing away their gruesome trophies and evidence for the government. When some time later news of the business filtered down to Daru the Service acted on it with typical finesse. The government launch with one officer in charge of a small detachment of police boys proceeded to the Pink Lagoon, where they anchored off the village that was suspected of having organized the raid. The surviving cannibals, not feeling in the least guilty, since raiding was to them just a hearty diversion, were delighted to receive the visitors, and though none of the police party could speak the Suki dialect, nor any of the Suki speak the coast language, gifts of tobacco and axes and knives made them immediate friends. It took only a short time for the officer to learn enough Suki words to be certain which of the tribesmen were the ringleaders of the raid; and these were invited on board the launch. The engine was already warmed up and was waiting to go; and without any further ado away sailed the government with its prisoners, even towing one of the bloodied canoes, which was the only concrete evidence of the raid that could be collected in the village. Convicted men, they were merely being held in Daru until they had learned enough Motu to be convinced that the white men were now the bosses and would not tolerate raiding. Meantime, they spent their days under guard, cutting down some of the jungle of weeds around the settlement, using machetes, incidentally, which they must have wished they had had earlier.

One would expect something rather spectacular in men with the appetite of the Suki, and for once we got it. Though it was not spectacular in the way you are expecting. When the barbarians were marched out for us to choose a model, we were standing on the high veranda of the R.M.'s residence like royalty reviewing the troops, and the big grinning Kiwai Island police lined the cannibals out in a row below us. We looked down, and they looked up. And never, so help me, have I looked on a row of more winsome, amiable countenances than these worn by the gentlemen who had driven stakes down through the torsos of women. Unless it was in a bathing-beauty contest. They were smiling pleasantly in a shy way, one or two were scratching like anyone who itches, and one tall fellow down at the end of the line was trying to get the rest in a neat row, as he must have learned from watching the drilling police. That they had not always been so charming was evidenced by their cropped heads. The threat of cutting off their hair has been found to be one of the most effective controls of obstreperous prisoners. But the Suki, not understanding the language of the threat, had had to be shown shortly after they found they were not going to be allowed to return to their village after the buggy ride down the river. But there was nothing dispirited in their manner; they were being educated, not humbled.

Tauparaupi in the flesh, fullface and without his Egyptian bob, looked a little less like an ancient Pharaoh than like a deeply tinted rabbi. His face was now, mysteriously, just as dark as the skin of his body. But he was extraordinarily Semitic-looking, even with the same sad-lidded, "hollow" eyes that we associate with a certain "Biblical type" of Jew. To strengthen the impression, his short beard grew in points up his chin with the same good lines repeated in his closely cropped mustache. (The mongoloid Melanesians are almost as hairless as the real Mongoloids, and consequently find hairiness disgusting. One never sees face whiskers among them except on the old men who have grown too indifferent to pluck out their beards.) Withal it was a strong handsome face, not in the least brutish, and the only departure from "normal" was an extremely high hairline. It looked like growing baldness or as if the hair had been shaved back, but this was normal for Papuans. Even the hair of the woman begins back on the top plane of the head.

The other physical peculiarity of these swamp people did not appear until Tauparaupi had taken off his new calico sulu, which was his pride and his prison uniform, and started posing for us. This was the disproportionate development of his upper body, including the arms, in comparison with that of the legs, which was the result of environment and occupation. Where the terrain is mostly marshland the only use the legs are put to is as a prop when standing, while the rest of the body develops normally, doing the navigating, which is by canoe. The feet of the men were also abnormal as a result of the watery environment, Tauparaupi's toes being so widely spaced that he looked duck-footed. All of the Suki walked as if they had corns—which they were just growing, in fact, for the first time in their lives. The natives of the mountains who spend their lives trudging the brutal earth have hard calluses on their feet that sometimes look like hoofs, but the soles of Tauparaupi's feet were still like the palm of a hand, despite his month on real earth.

From the moment the cannibal was elected to pose for us he began distinguishing himself as a personality. For the first few minutes after he understood that he was to remain with us he watched his fellows being marched back to the quarters with a rather doubtful look on his face, but then he turned to us and waited with simple dignity, spine erect, arms hanging straight down by his side, for whatever came next in this strange white man's world. Margaret handed down a stick of tobacco to him; and as he stepped forward to take it, palm up, one foot forward, he was suddenly the naked Christ that Manet painted, the same appealing gesture, the same deep wise look, almost the same features. Tauparaupi was never conceivably a "boy."

Anatomists tell us that the average primitive has the same brain matter, weight for weight, as the average white man; and to this Governor Murray adds that his Papuan subjects are "a very intelligent people" but at a low stage of development because of having been isolated from contact with higher civilizations. We can augment that by stating that after a few days in our company Tauparaupi's intelligence had developed to an embarrassing degree. To begin with, we had no way of communicating with him. We were left alone with him without a guard or even a houseboy who knew more of the Suki dialect than we did, but Margaret and he soon worked out a game for teaching one another their languages. It started accidentally when she held out a stick of tobacco to him and pronounced the Motu word for it, *kuku*. This was probably the first word Tauparaupi had learned in Daru, so he nodded his head wisely and gave the Suki word for it, which Margaret wrote down phonetically. After that she checked the names for things by asking for the object in her Suki word and having Tauparaupi point it out. Then gradually, without our being aware of when it started, Tauparaupi was the teacher, checking Margaret on her lessons and often finding her failing. For his part he seldom forgot a Motu word after he had heard it two or three times, and especially if it stood for some object that interested him.

There were many objects around us of European origin for which naturally there were neither Suki nor Motu names, as for example a simple chair. This becomes a "sit thing" in Motu, and to a swamp cannibal a very laughable object. I intended to make a careful drawing of Tauparaupi's head from every angle before painting him; and because I had a cold and did not want to sit on the wet veranda floor in order to be at head level with him . . . he was squatting on his heels as natives do when the ground is damp . . . we attempted to pose him on a kitchen chair. He got the idea of sitting on the chair readily enough, but doing it our way troubled him because the chair was "loose." That is, it was not attached solidly to the ground and it was high, at least higher than one's heels. Before that matter was solved we had discovered the real hazards of a kitchen chair. First Tauparaupi hooked his buttocks gingerly on the edge—but that portion of his anatomy was also without calluses or very much padding, and before long his muscles were trembling, trying to ease the weight. Margaret finally persuaded him to sit back on the chair in order to distribute the pressure; but he could not be induced to lean back. That was too dangerous. Eventually it was solved by allowing him to sit on his heels on the chair, his knees up to his chin, his chest resting on his upper legs in his normal spider fashion. Then he felt safe even up in the air, but he looked less like a Manet Christ than like a naked cannibal coming down a slide on a tin can toboggan.

The cold I had was a record breaker . . . every such minor affliction was exaggerated these days by our general condition . . . and it posed a number of questions in our relations with Tauparaupi. We were very anxious that we should not be the cause of spreading this white man's curse to a people who presumably were yet unacquainted with colds. And it seemed apparent that Tauparaupi actually did not know what was the matter with me. Every time I attended to my poor nose—which was often and lustily, first with toilet tissues which I carefully tucked into a dilly bag hanging on the back of my chair and then with a big handkerchief which I kept in my pocket—Tauparaupi would peer at me as if he had spectacles on, his absorbed gaze following the disposal of the tissues and handkerchief and then remaining fixed on pocket or dilly bag for some minutes afterward. "Sneezles and wheezles," I explained for lack of a Motu word. "S- . . ." Tauparaupi started to repeat, and then could go no further. He could not shape his Papuan tongue to manage two vowels in succession. But when I sneezed he looked at me alertly. "Asimana," said Margaret, giving the Motu word. Tauparaupi nodded his head and gave us a Suki word which along the lower Fly is the Papuan word for soul or spirit. This is interesting because in some localities on the coast a sneeze is the sound one's spirit makes as it is leaving or re-entering the body. There are two occasions when it absents itself, when one is asleep and during illness. Thus the sneeze would seem to have some association in the native mind with illness. For a salt-water native to identify the sneeze for what it is does not mean anything, because colds are commonplace among them; but when a native of the interior calls a sneeze a spirit, and we know the interpretation elsewhere, it would seem to suggest that he knew something about the common cold on his own score.

However, if the Suki had colds they were not the kind I was exhibiting, and Tauparaupi could never have believed that our treatment for it was anything but sorcerer's hocus-pocus. Every time I sneezed Margaret bathed the air, myself and Tauparaupi too with our priceless nasal solution shot out of a fly sprayer. Meantime I periodically stuck an inhalator up my nostrils, and finally went down from the veranda and made a pyre of the tissues in the dilly bag. Tauparaupi looked down through the railing, saw me burning the contents of my own skull—and when I saw his expression I burst into laughter that to him must have sounded demoniacal. Such an anatomist as himself could reach only one conclusion about this business; I was disposing of my dismembered anatomy so that it would not fall into the hands of an enemy who would take it to a sorcerer. In fact a houseboy we had in Rabaul, far more savvy than this innocent, once asked us why the "mastah" blew his nose into a handkerchief and then "saved" it so carefully by putting the handkerchief in his pocket if he did not fear to leave it about.

To call Tauparaupi an anatomist was no mere figure of speech. He had probably done more dissecting of human cadavers than the average European physician, and he was certainly a specialist of that part of the anatomy which was bothering me. There are two general schools of "head-craft" in New Guinea, one which esteems only the skull and the other only, to put it as delicately as possible, the extracranial tissue. In the latter the process is to remove the skeleton by an incision down the back of the head. The flesh is then dried by suspending it over the smoke of a hot fire, which also shrinks it, but does not destroy the hair. Clay is packed into the cavity, the incision is sewed up and the whole, which is now about the size of a grapefruit, is mounted on a short heavy stick. It is now a "dance stick," a "decoration" to be held in the hand in dancing. Occasionally skulls too make knobs for dance sticks, but in this case they are rattles. The brain pan is partly filled with pebbles and is sealed by inserting the wooden handle in the big foramen where the spine is attached.

Only enemies supply the dance stick heads but the skulls stored in a village may be either those of deceased clansmen or trophies of the raid, or both. So far as we know no distinction is made between the two in the method of making them fit to live with. The patient or lazy simply wrap the severed head in leaves and set it aside for the cockroaches and ants to

clean. But there is an art among skull fanciers, and in the districts where it is practised the process is lengthy, and some very handsome pieces are turned out. The severed head is first singed to remove all the hair, and then it is placed near a fire so that the flesh softens, after which it can be scraped away more easily. The decomposed brain, which is encased in the skull and cannot be reached, is next shaken and blown out of the ventricles, after which the insects are allowed to work on it. The end result is bone as clean inside and out as if it had been scrubbed. The next step is decorations. The surface of the bone is waxed to a high polish, and then is painted in bold designs in lampblack, earth-brown, sometimes blood or the crimson seed of the liquorice berry. Gray Job's-tears are stuck on in patterns with black tree gum, and frequently eyes of shell disks or green cat's eyes are inserted into the eye sockets. In the Western Division, a long false nose of wood and a Pharaoh's bob of plaited palm are added. Artists proud of their work will sign it with their "mark." It seems rather gruesome taste, but the decorated heirloom skulls are often beautiful. Whatever the wax used on the surface, as it ages it takes on a deep amber patina which is sometimes quite brown, especially since the bone also darkens. And this rich "background" with the restrained coloring of the designs and the handsome curves that God gives even the dumbest of heads when they are down to the bone, produces an object that does not in the least remind you of anyone you know and would probably be an artistic improvement on him if it did. Today, however, it is impossible to pick up any of these *objets d'art* along the coast. What past collectors have not helped themselves to the natives have hidden or disposed of by missionary persuasion. And of course the art is no longer practised, partly because it is abhorrent to these missionaries and partly because the government requires the natives to bury all of their corpses underground, for sanitary reasons. (A not uncommon practice was to place the corpse on a platform raised from the ground, and as it decomposed, to collect the "fluids" that dripped down and use them for ceremonial purposes.) It is doubtful if the old skulls of clansmen are ever discarded, however, because they house the soul of the deceased. A Service officer related how he entered a village to make an arrest and surprised the women scuttling for the bush with the heads of their relatives and ancestors clutched under their arms. For this reason, that trouble was started by visitors walking off with the clan spirits, the removal of skulls from a village by a white man is now unlawful. Buying them is also forbidden, because if the natives found they could get trade goods in exchange some, fearful of the clan stock, might be tempted to lay in a supply of fresh ones for the market. Nor, no matter how innocently acquired, may one have the evidence in his possession in the country. Unless one is a missionary. Which one wasn't, so when a very handsome piece of contraband goods came our way we quickly mailed it out of our possession—only to have it lost on some border customs because it lacked the proper bill of release.

This skull which Tauparaupi examined he declared to be that of a man. It takes an expert anatomist to distinguish the difference between, for example, the skull of a woman and that of a half grown boy, or between that of a large woman and a small man. Size alone is not a reliable guide; and where the faces of men and women seem to be almost equally "strong-boned," as they are among the Papuans, there is less of the phenomenon of greater delicacy in modeling and proportions to distinguish the female. And in any case the preserved heads seldom if ever include the jaw, which would be more positive identification. Yet Tauparaupi, after turning the skull around and fingering the muscle process in a manner of mild curiosity, pointed to his own head, indicated his sex and then tapped the skull. Margaret repeated the performance on herself, her face all question. The answer was no; it was the skull of a man, like Tauparaupi.

Whether seeing the skull had inspired Tauparaupi or it was just the helpfulness of the R.M., the cannibal came for his sitting next morning all decked out in "war" paint. He was a startling sight. His face and the entire front of his naked body were smeared with big careless swaths of yellow pigment. (Now we understood the light face in the photograph.) An aureole of sand-colored quills was on his forehead, a fat plug of bamboo in the septum of his nose, bundles of big rings made from the quill of the cassowary in his ear lobes, and for pants he wore a big nautilus shell. (Which was held on securely by a twine going around the hips.) Two black-plaited bands which were certainly not ornamental and yet appeared to have no use went around his body, over one shoulder and under the other arm. In India the same simple band worn the same way is the insigne of a brahma, but if the custom came from India the significance had been lost. Tauparaupi was all warrior. He carried a bamboo bow five feet long and a bundle of mean-looking arrows the longest of which was just under six feet.

Many of the arrows in this bundle we knew to be simple hunting or fishing arrows. They had hardwood tips, sharply pointed, and the rest of the head was spooled or flat with a thin wave edge. Then there were some with innocent bone tips, or the gouger toenail of the cassowary. But the ones with reverted saw edges of bone, sharp as knives, or reverted thorns or flying fox teeth in rows, or sliced-off bird legbones that turned back along the shaft, these were the kind meant to be retrieved after hitting their mark. They were for the man hunt. The shafts were bamboo painted with a design at each joint (sometimes a totem insigne or the mark of the artist) and every one was strengthened and made fleet and true by charms. Between a man and his good arrows there is everywhere the same mystical attachment as that between the primitive and his drum. These Tauparaupi brought were old, and must have found their mark many times. Yet, without any hesitation, he exchanged the whole handful for an equal handful of the new white man's kind of kuku . . . tobacco, if you don't remember. We soothed our conscience with the thought that he would never again use such arrows; the man hunting days were over for his whole tribe.

The pose for the painting was arrived at by the simple maneuver of having Tauparaupi teach Margaret how to shoot with a bow. It had a bowstring of split bamboo skin with a resistance of about a hundredweight; and Margaret, even with some good tennis muscles, could not draw it back more than about nine inches, and then only for a second at a time. Tauparaupi drew the string for a papaya tree at about sixty feet, and picked off the fruit as fast as we could watch by automatically swinging the arrows up into position with the little finger of his bow hand. The snap of the string striking his bark armguard was as punctual as the ticking of a clock. And we think the arrows might have carried true at a greater distance, though they lost altitude rapidly after fifty feet, no matter how hard Tauparaupi drove them.

When it came to posing in the position of shooting we counted on short poses and long rests, because of the great strain in just holding the arms outright. But Tauparaupi arranged that for us. He knew by some extra sense all about posing for an oil portrait, though it was hardly likely that he had ever seen even a printed picture of any kind. In fact he had the thing we call "native intelligence," which is a reasonableness that does not seem to have anything to do with experience or education. While he was aiming an arrow at the papaya tree we put a chalk mark around his feet and signed to him to "wait," the wagging of the hand that is universal. He waited, holding the position motionlessly until he got tired, then he squatted down on his heels to rest. In a little while we motioned him up, and from then on he rested and resumed his pose voluntarily. And this went on without interruption until the portrait was finished.

We tried all our tricks on the primitive, but for every abracadabra we showed Tauparaupi he had one as good and sometimes better. Our automatic cigarette lighter was our best property. It was really automatic and never failed to work, because Margaret spent her Sunday mornings servicing it instead of praying. "Atchison, Topeka and Sante Fe," said Margaret, "squeezing" a flame out of her hand. Tauparaupi whistled in surprise and then grinned. "Kwedidi kwedada na dangi bwa dongwa da dodoma do nango iye ko iye iy, jobu jawa pwobwo dangwo gumaga madaga." The sounds (which have no meaning) rolled off his tongue. The next morning he brought his own fire-making instruments. There was a simple stick that had been split at one end, and he wedged this apart by placing a pebble in the crotch, after which he stuck into the fork some shavings that looked like bark scrapings. (The whole outfit had been wrapped up in a dried leaf, and the tinder was in a separate little packet, evidently to keep it dry.) He then braced the stick upright against the veranda railing with his foot and started drawing briskly around it, in the manner of shining a shoe, a strip of bamboo skin at the apex of the split where the tinder was. In a few minutes the stick began to smoke and Tauparaupi, being double-jointed, leaned over and blew as he continued "shining." And in less time than it has taken to tell this a little flame had broken out in the tinder. We were never able to duplicate that miracle.

When it came to the completion of the portrait, however, Tauparaupi showed the same blank spot that other native models before him had revealed. He did not admire the picture; he did not think this illusion of three dimensions on a two-dimensional plane was the miracle that we ourselves always did. He accepted it like a child, only recognizing the extraneous objects, the bow and arrows, the headband and armguard and indicating it by pointing to them as one might say "that is my armguard." No doubt he failed to recognize his profile for the usual reason, he had never seen it. But we were determined that this intelligent man should have that experience. There was a three-foot mirror in the house, ample for reflecting the whole figure at a certain distance; and we brought this out. I held it up on the veranda railing, Tauparaupi was guided to it, and then Margaret held up our big mirror to one side and turned Tauparaupi until she thought he should see his whole profile. But the reaction was not what we expected. Tauparaupi would not be turned. That is, he let Margaret turn his body but he kept his face glued toward his reflection in my glass. He must have thought at first that the mirror was vertical water, for he reached forward as if to touch it, and then quickly snatched his hand back. Margaret was standing behind him, and after a minute his fascinated gaze moved from his own reflection to that of Margaret, and into his face there came an expression of such pure wonder that if ever mortal looked on the Transfiguration this was the look he wore. We did not, and still cannot, understand it—because a man living on water as smooth as glass, as he did, not only saw his own reflection daily but those of anyone near him. Also there have been found in New Guinea villages purposely designed mirrors of dark-colored stone ground out to contain water. Nevertheless Tauparaupi was hypnotized by himself. After staring motionless for several minutes he opened and closed his mouth, wriggled his tongue and examined his teeth, poked his fingers into his ears, removed the bamboo plug from his nose and looked at it in the glass, then ran his finger through the empty hole in the septum of his nose. Gradually he became more assured and stepped backward and forward, raising his foot and wriggling his splayed toes; and so on and on. I got tired holding up the mirror, so I set in on the floor and we left him there, tribesman converted into individual, squatting before this trick that did have him stumped. And us too.

Finally, it was the mirror that stole the show when it came to the "unveiling" of the portrait for the rest of the Suki. We had asked that the men be brought up to the house, so that we might observe their reaction; for they, at least, must recognize Tauparaupi's profile. They did—and the reaction, though brief, was refreshing. They whistled! It was a chorus of whistles something like the swell a sailor gives vent to when beautiful-girl-crosses-vision. But Tauparaupi was wagging his arms about the veranda, explaining to the men below that this was not the duplicate he had told them about. It was the mirror business he wanted them to see. So we brought out the glass and watched seventeen times the antics that Tauparaupi had put on. Until the party became so excited the guards had to herd them off, our model included.

It was not until we saw Tauparaupi trotting along obediently before the big Kiwai policeman that we remembered that the Suki was a prisoner too. It was raining, and his golden skin was washing down his calves in streaks and he was shorn of all glory. He had left his bow and arrows, his bark arm-guard and headdress, his fire-making implements and pants behind with us, and in his big hand hanging straight down at his side was the payment, a few piddling sticks of the tobacco that tastes like wet skating mittens. Then he was gone, lost to sight in the downpour. Only then, with the disarming personality of the Papuan removed, did we remember that the portrait we had was of a man who had eaten other men, who had cut off the breasts of women, burned dwellings and scattered the gnawed bones of children to the dogs, leaving in his path all the horror and destruction of the killing man. But he would learn from the white man, we thought, and sometime peace and security would come to dwell forever in this land that had run with blood for centuries.

25

As the time for the return of the *Chief* drew near we went about our discarding and packing as if we were disposing of the property of the deceased. No good taking back to the States the big heavy easel that had been made out of a planter's veranda railing in the Solomons. Except for sentimental reasons; it had been a stout friend, failing us only in the "blow" of Panasesa. The Skipper of the *Maroma* should have the heat-buckled records of the "Meanderings of Monte" that had delighted him so much, and the umba-umba should be sent back to that fat chief in Marovo Lagoon who had thought it would be so nice for his gondola. It was a depressing business.

We made up a basket of the round cigarette tins of boat paint that was still serving us for quick sketches. The Storekeeper's boys should appreciate that, with their recent education in art. The Storekeeper was still producing commissions, still protesting that his boys were ordering the drawings themselves. And, to be sure, those who sat for us did pose with less boredom than any native model we had ever paid. But a suggestion from a *taubada* is a powerful thing, and all of our patrons were indentured to the Storekeeper. In fact he paid us for each drawing, and checked it off in his books against the wages of the boy—who would not be paid his full wages until the end of his term anyway and who, according to our agent, would never miss a pound. We wondered if the boy would remember what he had received for that five dollars if he did miss it. To ease our conscience we had made the head in the drawings almost lifesize, at least twice as large as the thing our white patrons paid three times as much for, and we left out not a hair or a mole and, finally, mounted the results on a cardboard with a protection of waxed paper. This last was a chore and was suffered as much to save my feelings as to provide a conscience salve, because the first few drawings had not lasted their owners two days. The paper was ordinary thin charcoal stock, already saturated from the dampness, and the patrons had handed their drawings about to be looked at as if they were on wood. There was very little drawing left even before the interest had died down, and the paper looked like the rag it was. No artist can stand seeing his work treated like this, and anyway the patron deserved something less perishable for what had cost him over two months' wages. Hence the labored "frame." However, our first sitters did not appear to be particularly pleased with their portraits anyway. We finally discovered that this was because the heads stopped off at the neck in the drawing, questionable taste for a headhunting clientele, so from then on we attached a little body onto the neck in the manner of a cartoon; and that took care of that worry. But there were other worries in every commission. The patrons did not complain; they just looked worried or did not seem enthusiastic enough, and with our conscience in the state it was we worried around ourselves until we found what was troubling the fellow, and patched it up. If these black aborigines were being exploited, they made us sweat to do it.

The Storekeeper was floating around us somewhat like a soap bubble deciding to burst as we put our mark on the last portrait drawing . . . and we often chuckled at the idea of some future "intrepid explorer" as he braved the terrible jungle of blackest Papua coming on one of these signed masterpieces in the heathen village from which our patrons came. "Now look here," the Storekeeper was saying, "if you'll just

wait a little longer—just let this *Chief* go by—my own launch
will be fixed. The engine parts I've ordered from Sydney may
be on this boat, and as soon as they're in the launch *I* can
run you over to Thursday Island." But nothing could shatter
our sense of futility concerning shipments from Sydney. The
only way we had been able to get art supplies up from the
south was to order them mailed in small parcels or to have
Sydney-bound friends shop for them and put them on the
steamer themselves. The wharf lumpers down there had been
striking for years, over two on and off that we knew of, and
it might still be months before anything like an engine part
could be loaded and reach Daru. We could not stay on with
our present hosts for such an uncertain wait. Any more than
we could change hosts in the same settlement even if another
offered himself, or go and live in our tent. If there were just
some way of getting in touch with the *Chief* to see if by some
miracle the Storekeeper's freight were on it. While we were
groaning over the lack of carrier pigeons a strange white man
came into the store, but we did not wait to be introduced.
We went home to finish our loathsome task of packing, for
the *Chief* was due in the next day.

By seven o'clock of the second following morning our
cases and duffle bags, ourselves and everything we had discarded were on board the *Dogi* going, not in the direction
of California, nor even across Torres Strait, but *up the Fly
River*. And the thing that made it heaven-bound was that we
also had certain passage for Thursday Island in the future.

The explanation is that the strange white man we had
passed by in the store was the manager of Madiri, the last
plantation forty or fifty miles up the river, and the *Dogi* was
the plantation launch. The boat was badly in need of repairs,
and when a substitute launch came over from Thursday
Island she was to be sent across to dry dock. And we might

travel on her. Meantime, would we care to stay at Madiri while waiting? *Would* we! Even behind this invitation we saw the duplicity of the Storekeeper, may his tribe increase. For "Hamlet," it was obvious from the beginning, was not the expansive kind who thought up house parties overnight, which was the speed with which this invitation came. The Madiri overseer seemed shy and looked ill and dispirited. As who would not, living at Madiri.

White explorers have been coming to New Guinea for two or three hundred years, yet it was not until the early 1840's that the Fly River was discovered. And now we can tell you why. There are two deep channels past the estuary of the river, the North Entrance and the South Entrance, one on each side of long Kiwai Island; and in flood tide and on a clear day these are navigable by fairly deep-draught vessels if they keep their elbows in and the sounding leads going. For all across the entrance the water is littered with shifting sandbars that kick up seas which have caused this stretch of sailing to be known as the toughest anywhere around New Guinea. During the northwest season when the *guba* are piling up the Gulf to meet those flood waters pouring out of the Fly over the mud bars it takes a busy engine to make it past the estuary.

The South Entrance, separated from the west bank by a string of small islands, is not so rough as Toro Pass, between those islands and shore, but it is a longer route from Daru, and the *Dogi* took Toro Pass because time was important, more so than we knew. Hamlet was an uncommunicative soul and did not think it worth the effort to mention to us that unless we ran the estuary on the strong flood tide it would be necessary to anchor outside until the next flood. He had timed the trip to make it, for the *Dogi* was without a motor. It had an engine, but that was one of the things that weren't working. The boat also had a bottom; but we were not far out of Daru before the bilge was washing over the floorboards below. The reason we knew was because there was no shelter on deck, and when it began to rain inside our slacks and the wind was raising alps of gooseflesh we went below for shelter. But didn't stay long.

It was hours after Daru before we sighted land again. Curious hours. Margaret and I huddled clammily together under a tarpaulin on the forward hatch cover, sitting in a lake of water, all of which reminded us again of the disadvantage of clothing in this country. There were two native boys on board, one at the tiller and the other stationed forward, casting a sounding lead ahead in the opaque water. "By-de-mark two-oo," he sang, slowly noting the fathom depths on the lead line, "quarter less tree-ee. By-de-mark tree-ee." The two wore only the usual thin calico sulu, and the bullets of rain were bouncing off their oily hides and streaming away like water on a hot griddle. The minute it stopped raining (if it ever did) they would be dry and smelling sweet. Hamlet, on the other hand, was a nice illustration of the way we felt. He had no raincoat, refused ours and would not share the tarpaulin, so he sat with the rain blasting down on him, his thin ribs showing through his shirt and the bones of his legs through his cotton trousers. A felt hat pulled down to his eyebrows provided a watershed for his sallow face, making it look darker than ever. Hour after hour he sat there thus, not moving from the aft hatch but wrenching from time to time with the paroxysms of malaria chills.

One of the curious features of malaria is that while it is not infectious except by inoculation, its symptoms are catching. If you happen to harbor malaria wogs already and see someone else quaking and with a scarlet face, it isn't long until your own nose begins to feel hot and you are jerking yourself. So I jerked, first with vicarious chills and then with real ones. Tiffin time came and tiffin time went, with nothing provided to fill the gap in our middle except our thoughts. So went the long morning.

The first sound out of Hamlet since we left Daru came when he suddenly leaped to his feet with an exclamation of "Ca-ripes!" A minute before the *Dogi* had been lippity-lipping along on the yellow seas like a roped steer. Now she was bucking with her hind end in the air, her nose in mud. To all appearances we were in mid-ocean . . . though the rain was so dense we could not have seen land if it had been a block away. The boys hauled out some long-handled canoe paddles, and after poking around the boat they tried to pole us off the mud. But the *Dogi* could not be budged, so they calmly stepped overboard into about thirty inches of water and tried to push us off. But we were wedged in, and every sea that came up behind us nosed us in deeper. If Hamlet had been a talking man, I think he would have said something then. We knew without asking that there was nothing to do but sit until the tide rose enough to float us off.

We had been trying to get through a channel that was less than twenty-five feet wide in places, sailing blind, so to speak. There were a few widely spaced pole markers (we noticed them when later we came down the river on the trip out), but these were not visible in the rain. Nor were they always safe to follow, for the silt bars change position and size from day to day, the poles are washed away—and if it is very rough they are not apparent even in broad daylight. It takes luck, not navigation, to get into the Fly River.

The rain lifted after a while, and when we saw land about a mile off to the west it was as gratifying as a forest to a city dog. Hamlet did not look surprised when we asked to take the dinghy ashore, but he warned us that the tide would be full and would start running out in a little over an hour,

and we should be floated off before then. We would have to
make it nippy, for the *Dogi* was in a bad place without an
engine.

We had to take both boys with us, for several reasons.
There was too much current and the seas were too high
for us to handle the dinghy alone, and then when we got near
what we thought was the shore, the keel stuck in the mud
and the water's edge was still two or three hundred yards
distant. Beyond that was a shelf of flat mud about a quarter
of a mile wide. Both boys dropped overboard, and while we
punted with the oars they pulled like the Volga boatmen.
Then when we came to the mud one boy stayed in the
dinghy and we were towed the rest of the way on foot,
hanging onto the back of "Emperor Jones's" belt. We short-
ened this name to "Emp" later, when we got used to the
owner's disquieting visage. And then restored the boy to
full title when he lived up to his face.

On the far side of the shore was a wide sheet of trapped
tidal water, and the forest we were headed for was on the
other side of it. But a short distance down the shore the bush
grew nearer to the water's edge; and so, with our shoes tied
around our neck and leaving Emperor Jones to take care of
himself, we sprinted off down the stretch of water. Margaret
sprinted, and I clanked after her. But when we reached them
the trees proved to be just a thin screen separating the beach
we were on from a deep inlet beyond. And as we rounded
the point we saw tucked back in the apex of the cove a
huge longhouse. Our first Fly River "village."

There was not a sign of life about the place, not even the
howl of a dog; and this slowed us up a little. After all, we
were still pretty juicy eating, and we had neither our walking
stick nor the bludgeon flashlight with us now. We called out
two or three times in a pleasant voice, and then realized that
this was probably one of those abandoned villages. Some-

times the house is just worn out, and the villagers have built a new one elsewhere. Frequently a scourge of bad spirits forces the inhabitants away, or they all die in real epidemics. In the not-so-very-old days a stronger enemy tribe would slowly eat them up, down to the last man. Whatever the cause, this house had been long unused. Vines were already grown over and through the roof, tearing up the thatching and rafters. Tall grass and bushy undergrowth were so dense about it that not until we reached it did we see that the floor was on piles easily six feet above the ground. We could walk upright underneath it, and were doing that very thing to look on the far side for an entrance when we heard rustling. Snakes! That instant the rustle became thrashing. Pigs popped in every direction in front of us. Wild pigs and boars with curling tusks. They scattered, wheeled, and some tore back. Margaret and I leaped up, grabbed at the same piece of flooring and crashed with the rotten sapling in our hands. Perhaps it saved us, for the pigs wheeled off again. We bounded for a slanted log that ran up to a square opening, and hauled and pushed one another up the notches to the floor. It was like touching dynamite; we were so afraid it would let us down again. We finally perched on the heavier timber, and then we were safe. Except that the pigs stayed. Five grizzly animals that looked as tall as great Danes took up a station in a semicircle and stood looking at us, eagerly switching their long tails. We wrenched up rotten flooring, and hurled the pieces at them. The pigs crashed away—and came straight back. Finally all the rest of them returned, and after looking at us questioningly resumed their egg-laying or whatever it was they had been doing. "They must be domestic pigs left behind when the natives moved away," offered Margaret; "they just want us to feed them." "Preferably ourselves," I sniffed. "Did you ever hear of a native going away, even in death, and leaving a pig? Now what would Mrs. Martin Johnson do if trapped by pigs? I'm going to try a good helpless female scream for the Emperor." I screamed, and Margaret added her taxi-hailing whistle. The pigs looked up at us quizzically, and the sounds bounced back off the thatched roof as if we were in a padded radio studio. "I think it would be bonza to bring home a couple hundred pounds of bacon," said Margaret finally, and started back through the dark cavern, searching for a bludgeon. I watched cautiously for a while, waiting to see her crash through the flooring, but she kept to the heavier timber of the cross supports. It was when I hoisted myself up to help in the search that I discovered I had done something to the base of my spine when I landed on it under the house. It was probably just a stretched ligament, but it felt like a bastinado.

The great hall was an eerie, evil smelling place, dimly lit by the holes in the roof. The thatching and rafters were black with soot, and the acrid odor of smoke-drenched thatching mingled with that of its moldering. When people lived in this great house they not only roasted their food on sand ovens laid on the floor but kept smudge fires going continuously to thin out the mosquitoes. No smudge fire had smoked here for a long time, and there were generations of mosquitoes present, evidently having been sustained by the pig tenants below. But now they had us, and it was a feast day. All along the sides of the hall were little doorless enclosures that were once family apartments . . . the central hall was exclusively the men's . . . and the families entered these from the ground below. In case of raid the floor exits were handy. We found all sorts of wonderful rubbish that the occupants had left, decayed net bags, rain hoods of pandanus that had once been plaited, part of a necklace of Job's-tears still with its greasy string attached, and a club with a rudely carved head on one end, some of the red seeds that were its eyes still adhering . . . a garden stick to ward off evil spirits. This was too precious—and probably too rotted—to be used on the pigs. We were tugging at one of the uprights of an apartment . . . the lawyer vine binding still held stubbornly though all the other wood was decayed . . . when we heard the distant crack of a rifle. That could only be Hamlet signaling for us to return. It meant that the *Dogi* was afloat, and had to get away. Now what?

We had never heard of wild boar doing anything but furiously attacking humans and rending them limb from limb and, as a matter of fact, they do attack fearlessly. (We later on shot at some wild pig from a boat in a stream near Madiri, and one of the outraged animals, though uninjured, charged down to the water's edge.) But there was nothing to do but make a run for it. We gathered up armfuls of the largest chunks of flooring, smashed a hole through the wall on the water side of the building, threw farewell kisses to one another and dropped down simultaneously with a yell that must have rocked the *Dogi*. The pigs were under the house and they scattered, which was bad because then we did not know where they were. But we wasted no time. Still yelping and swinging clubs around our heads we ran like hell. As much like hell as the waist-high grass would let us. No pigs turned up in front of us, but when we reached the mangroves I tripped over a root and broke my spine from the front. I didn't even feel it then, I was so preoccupied. I had fallen into the gumbo, lost all my kindling; and Margaret was 'way ahead of me. Emp Jones was strolling up the strand toward her with all the alacrity of a colored gentleman on his way to work. And somehow that was gratifying to see. Though I still did not like his dissipated-looking face.

As night fell a New Guinea miracle happened; it stopped raining and blowing. And by and by the clouds broke over-head, and a half moon threaded its way serenely through them. Silently we were running wing-and-wing with a fine following wind, steady keel in deep flowing water, and trail-ing a wake of moonlight that swept to the invisible horizon. The river was like a lake, its east shore miles away. Our sails were almost white in the moonlight, and the shadows on deck were clean-cut and black. It was sweet sailing.

Hamlet slept sprawled on the hatch like a dead man; his day's fever was broken. I still had a hot nose and aching eyes, enough fever anyway to be "seeing things." We were sailing close to the west bank, and all along the shore in the black shadows under the towering bush wall I kept seeing lights. Not a light here and there, but a suffusing glow that beamed strong and then faint even while I watched. Sometimes a shadow would be black, and as we went past it would start glowing light. The thing looked so real I had a hard time not saying anything to Margaret about it, but she would start worrying if she knew I was having hallucinations—even though they were beautiful ones. Finally Margaret, sounding as if she doubted her own sanity, asked, "Do *you* see lights in those trees? . . . There is such a thing as phosphorescent fungus, but could it beam on and off that way?"

It must have been after midnight when at last we saw lights of the kind we recognized coming from civilized wicks. They were lanterns blinking on and off behind trees as they were carried down a path, high above where we had thought the bank to be. The tide was full again, but the jetty at Madiri was still ten feet above the *Dogi*. (We saw the river flowing over that jetty before we left Madiri.) At the top of the lad-der on the wharf was the assistant overseer of the tract. He, naturally, did not know that we were on board, and the greeting that came down to the boat was from man to man. "Caripes," he said, "I'm ba-loody glad you've got here. I've had the wind up, no fear." When he saw us he was so astonished he accidentally ripped out another and he was about to apologize when we said, "Cripes, what are those lights behind you?" He swung around as if he had been kicked, and then burst into laughter which, if it had been a girl, we would have said was almost hysterical. "Fireflies, glowworms, billions of them," he said excitedly. There were billions of them; they swarmed so densely that as we walked up the path with the assistant we had to keep our mouths closed. But lights no longer interested us. The assistant was spilling over to tell us why he had the wind up, and he was stuttering to get started when it became unnecessary. A sound like the hounds of Baskerville, half croak, half scream, rose from beyond the tall trees to the left of the path. It continued wavering up and down for a minute, then stopped dead on a high note. "That's it," said the assistant quickly, "that's it. The fellow's cranky, and I can't do anything with him. That's been going on ever since the boss left. He gets the other boys howling too. One more night and I'd have joined them. Cripes, I don't even know how to handle the sane ones yet. Their idea of a jolly time is to wade out in the river and throw rocks at me. Cripes, I haven't slept for years . . ." and so on. This was very interesting indeed. For we had heard that Madiri was one of those government-subsidized, mission-managed plantations maintained just for the purpose of teaching natives not to throw rocks at white people, but instead to learn the peaceful arts of husbandry.

In the screened living room of the residence, which was also the dining room, the assistant began fighting a primus stove into flame for hot tea. And in that bleak lamplight we had our first look at the English lad who was to become the bright light of Madiri. At that moment he did not look it. He had a thatch of dense reddish-brown hair that had not been cut for a long time and stood out in every direction as if it had just been massaged. Half of his front teeth were missing, and those that remained looked like stalagmites and stalactites crumbling away before the cave-in. Above the missing teeth was the sort of pink mustache a baby mouse wears, but above that was a good bony English nose, the one remaining feature that established the mark of breeding on this handiwork of the tropics. The assistant had not had a leave to get to a dentist in the two years he had been at Madiri. For the same reason he could not see very well. For on each side of the good nose was a blue-green eye which was enlarged to the size of a head-light by spectacles that must have been a quarter of an inch thick, and the glasses needed to be changed. Eyes usually go in pairs, we know, but the assistant's didn't. One went one way while the other stood still, or vice versa. Normally the assistant thought his cocked eyes as funny as anyone else did; but nothing was very funny that night, and the way he bog-gled first one eye and then the other around our heads made us feel as if we had bats ourselves. With every down thrust of the primus stove pump a corresponding wheeze came from the assistant. Finally he ran out of breath, coughed up the last dreg of it and inhaled as if he had springs for lungs. "Asthma," he explained unnecessarily. "It's always worse when it starts to rain." Finally he got the tea made, and that was it; simple tea, our meal of the day. When he took the tea things out to the house-cook we looked around in silence, and the air was dense with what we were thinking. There was a lot of moth-erly work to be done around here. "Yes," said Margaret, just as if I had spoken. "Alas, poor Yorick." And that was how the dolorous manager of Madiri happened to become Hamlet, Ham for short, and the emaciated English boy, Yorick. Names that delighted them, and stuck.

We did not see Hamlet again that night. We heard him stamping the mud off his feet as he made his way to his room somewhere at the rear of the veranda, then there was a screech of rusty springs as a limp body fell on them and silence followed. Not even the clump of the first boot falling to the floor. Yorick showed us to the doorway of our room, thrust the gasoline lamp into our hands and then fled, leaving us to our fate, which was a drenched bed covered by a moldering mosquito net. After exploring the high mud paths in every direction we finally found the toilet at the end of one, about a hundred feet from the house, standing in what appeared to be an endless opaque lake.

The bawling at the labor quarters had left off suddenly just before Hamlet came in, but the lights had not been out ten minutes before it began again. It was a chilling sound in these unfamiliar surroundings. The forest began not far from the house, a forest of rubber trees, we discovered later, but it looked like an other-world in the cold white moonlight with the fireflies in the shadows beaming on and off like chiffon ghosts in an unfelt breeze. Frogs whirred and bats chirped, and all around us the water drip-drip-dripped from the flooded gutters into the lake in which the house stood. When the scream started up we heard the rusty bed springs inhale as a body released them, and shoes clumped heavily down the steps shaking the whole house on its loose piles. The footsteps went squudge-squudging away in the mud in the direction of the labor quarters. A minute later the bellowing ceased, and presently a returning shadow traveled along the rafters above, cutting across the reflected moonlight from the pond around the house. Yorick was having a fit of coughing, and we could hear his breath rasping through congested bronchials. Finally he got up and in his bare feet began to pace the veranda, coughing until it seemed we must strangle ourselves. Bump, bump, bump, up and down, up and down. Sheep going up and down. I was almost asleep when it began to rain. It came suddenly in full force and then boomed across the iron roof in waves like the drum thunder of Valhalla. Presently came the voice of Wotan himself from the labor quarters. The springs inhaled, the feet stomped only as far as the edge of the veranda this time, and then stopped. There was a wait in which Margaret whispered, "He must have flown this time." Then came a sharp crack as Hamlet fired his gun into the air. A death moan from the blackness in the direction of the quarters, and Margaret snickered, "I think I'll sing us to sleep." And she did; at least she sang. She got her ukulele and lay in bed singing "Night and Day," the one ballad that can make me hurt more than malaria.

When morning came at last, a phenomenon made more apparent by the banging in the house-cook opposite than by honest daylight, we found the residence standing up to its knees in water. The lake which extended right up to the rubber trees all around us was sectioned off like rice paddies by paths that ran away at every angle from the house. These paths were built up a yard higher than the surrounding ground, so that one would not be marooned until it stopped raining. We were to discover that the water could rise over the paths in a few hours of rain, and drain off completely in as short a time after it had stopped raining. This wetness was the reason the living room was another screened enclosure inside the screened veranda. The area was one vast mosquito incubator.

Our hosts were already out of the house by the time Margaret had managed to haul me up to another day of fever. Then she announced our readiness for breakfast by sticking her head in the house-cook as we passed on the way to the dining room. There was a sudden cessation of the racket there, but then nothing whatever happened for three-quarters

of an hour. Finally a shrill whine announced the coming of
food, and sent our ears up. A female servant! It was. Her
name was Derivo, and she appropriately entered our lives
hind end first by butting the screen door open with that
projection of her anatomy, attempting then to back through
quickly with her tray before the spring snapped the door to.
She didn't make it, and was batted into her tray and the tray
into the doorjamb while Emperor Jones and Beremiki, the
cook boy, stood in the doorway of the house-cook and
bawled at her. The woman looked entirely naked from the
rear except for a G-string and a liberal coating of river mud,
but when she turned around she seemed even more so, for
there was more anatomy. Only a bundle of dried shredded
grass ornamented her sex. As she gathered up the china from
the floor her long bony fingers were trembling. With rage,
we thought, because a native resents being laughed at, and
her black face was sullen. But it was fear. She had never
before seen white women.

The presence of a native woman on a plantation, unprecedented in our experience, is explained by the fact that
Madiri was really a mission station in the guise of a plantation.
Ordinarily women may not be indentured, because the administration believes that this would accelerate the disintegration of the race. With the women leaving the villages there
would be no incentive for the men to return after their terms
on the plantation, and the end of it would be that the natives
would become homeless dependants on the Europeans. So
when it came to women Madiri was a mission station.

Originally it had been a kind of pay-as-you-save proposi-
tion. Local natives were hired to work the rubber and coconut stands, which produce paid for the support of the station
and at the same time provided a tidy congregation of heathen
souls to work on. At one time (as it still is in the other islands)
the competition between the different religious factions was

so intense that an unclaimed native was liable to be torn limb
from soul in the struggle, and in those days the plantation
mousetrap was a better idea. But Governor Murray had long
ago settled that mission feud by dividing Papua up into four
"spheres of influence" between the four contesting mission
societies, and today there is no open nabbing of converts outside the established diocese. The idea of a mission plantation
is still good, however, because now all the labor must be
indentured, and that means that the heathen is trapped and
taking orders for the term of his "paper," two or three years.
But there was no missionary at Madiri during our stay.

Until the rubber market crashed, Madiri's method was
a tidy business venture as well as a soul saver, for the mis-
sionary-managers were at least as practical as the next planter.
And they extended this efficiency into the business of saving souls. Sunday was really a holy day; and the indentured boys, instead of loafing around primping and allowing their fancies to lead them in the direction of the
neighboring villages, attended morning and evening services.
The work day was started off with prayer, meals were
blessed, the evening ended with hymn singing and the boss
boy was a deacon who kept the gang's hearts pure while he
kept their muscles working. Occasionally in the evening as a
special treat colorful lantern slides illustrating the Bible stories were shown. (These were still in the house.) And finally
the ancient and honorable custom of marrying only one
woman at a time was introduced. This was probably to keep
the boys from tinkering around the neighborhood. But if it
actually was an attempt to solve the moral problem the mission went at it in a rather curious way, for they limited the
number of wives that might live at the plantation. Theo-
retically the wives were housekeepers of the labor quarters,
and there was one for each seven boys. Derivo was one of
these housekeepers.

There can be no doubt, however, that Derivo was an honest woman; only legal matrimony could have developed such
freedom of speech with such ineffectualness. The girl was a
whiner. We could hear her out in the house-cook, her whining punctuated by breaking dishes and banging pans, under
the house as she swished the laundry around in the tubs, and
along the path as she went complaining to the quarters at
night. And why not; the unfamiliar work apart from her
sisters must have been deadly and it was certainly un-
rewarded, for all she got was abuse for doing it wrong. Davi,
the boss rubber boy, was her husband and both were of the
Gogodara tribe on the north bank of the river opposite
Madiri. The girl was a raw swamp woman. She had been at
the plantation only two months and had never been out of
her village before. We soon learned that she had just been
brought into the house from the labor quarters especially to
be our handmaiden.

Derivo was instantly slated for a portrait . . . as soon as
my feverish nose cooled off . . . and I planned to paint her
in the plaited pandanus rain-hood that she wore to and from
the quarters, but first the girl had to be acclimated to us. Our
presence was the one thing that could dam her whining, but
then she was alternately wild-eyed or black-visaged, and in
any case no subject for the hall of immortal primitives. So
we brought out that old theory that working together is the
quickest and most painless way to reach a comfortable relationship, and decided to put it into action on the house. What
this neglected bachelor establishment needed, we could see,
was a touch of beauty, the feminine touch with the good hard
hand of female efficiency in the glove. In the process Derivo
would learn something about housework that might make her
useful after we left, and at the same time she would find out
that we were harmless.

So we began. On the fourth day we saw Hamlet, never a

smiler even at his brightest, sitting in a puddle at the top of the steps holding his head in both hands. Yorick said he was crying. He had lost something and had been searching in vain for it for two days. It seems the man kept records of the horses he bet on (by mail) on the margins of magazines, and his valentines inside them. Our first act naturally had been to gather up these hundreds of moldy magazines and news-papers, some of them ten years old, which were on every chair and table, and have Derivo stack them in neat piles in the storeroom. We knew better than to throw them out, because papers are read and re-read until the ink is worn off. Poor man. We ourselves brought all the hundreds back into the living room, where Ham could see for his search. And we had barely turned our backs for a visit to the store down by the river when Derivo had returned the magazines to the spare room. Hadn't we *told* her that these papers must be put there? But how to qualify an order in sign language! And when we gave instructions to Beremiki or Emp to trans-late for us, they put our gentle words into a machine gun and fired them at the girl.

Margaret's personal contribution to the uplift campaign was a batch of jam. There were two or three kumquat trees back near the bush wall that were loaded with fruit, and one morning Margaret dressed in a bathing suit—a sight that sent the modest Ham and Yorick fleeing into the rain in the op-posite direction—and draped with net native bags for the fruit, waded off across the yellow lake to gather the kum-quats. She was followed by a glum Derivo modestly cloaked in the rain-hood that fell to below the knees. The girl was carrying nothing, for we had found it simpler to do things ourselves than to tell Derivo how in sign language. When the two came back they had the fruit, but Margaret's lips were white as her legs. Like the little girl of Silver Lake, she had met a water snake. All she had seen of it in the opaque water was its head, and as it was coming in her direction, when it disappeared she had no reason to think it had changed its course. The moral of this episode is that Derivo herself knew better than to wade in flood water but it would not have occurred to her to warn Margaret, to tell us anything. White people seem to do this even unwittingly to less assertive souls. Our very assurance that we are bright and right seems to beat them down, and the humbler they become the brighter and righter we think we are and the more assured.

The jam tasted fine, but it looked as if it had raisins in it, almost as many as a compote. It was Yorick who discovered with only one eye that they were flies. In the house-cook there was a table, but it was used mostly as a catch-all for cooking utensils. The kitchen staff and flies worked together in a crowd on the floor, and Derivo was useless in jam making until she was permitted to work squatting as she did in the village. Anyway flies could have no meaning to her as bacteria carriers. Two months before she had not only been eating with flies but eating vegetables grown in a garden fertilized by human excretions. And she was relishing such things (which we have no reason to believe are *not* tasty) as head lice, ant eggs, grubs, grasshoppers, snakes, lizards, bats, rats and, of course, dog. Doubtless a snack of flies would have been prized if flies came in snacks.

After the siege of jam-making Derivo *had* to take a bath. The flies clung to the spots of jam, and rode into the dining room on her. So far she had worn only her village rami, that shredded tangle of pandanus leaf that looked as if it had birds in it, and the dried clay on her backside was hard to look upon. While we are staunch advocates of native undress it seemed that if we could once get Derivo clean and in a fresh white sulu it would not only make her more appetizing as a waitress but would put her on a social plane with the white-skirted boys and perhaps inspire her to excel them as houseboys. But getting Derivo clean was not a simple matter. At first Beremiki as interpreter was charged with seeing that she understood the matter of washing oneself with soap, something she could not have known about. (The Yela Papuans use a sponge for bathing, but we never heard of another tribe that washed themselves with anything but their hands.) Derivo took the soap, disappeared whining in the direction of the river, and came back two hours later still whining, still smeared with mud. We called on Davi, her husband, and he sent her whining back to the river, but when she dried she caked again. Finally Margaret took over personally, accompanying the girl to the water. She reported back that Derivo and mud were like a dog and carrion. She didn't roll in it; she bathed with soap, rinsed obediently and then picked up handfuls of mud and smeared her thighs and as far up her back as she could reach. We decided then that she must be in mourning for someone. The mud shroud, especially on the face, is an old Papuan custom. We gave the girl a sulu to put on anyway, and then left her alone. Only a reincarnation can change the mind of a "sot" woman, and there's nothing sotter, we had discovered, than the mind of a primitive woman. Whether she was acclimated to us or not, Derivo should pose so soon as the holidays were past. Christmas, our third away from home, was only a few days off, and we were determined we should somehow make this one gay.

26

While Margaret worked on a Christmas tree and gathered stores for a feast I spent the days making drawings of Yorick, all handsome profiles, one for each of his four fiancées back in England. Our gift for Hamlet was an oil copy of a faded photograph of his deceased wife. She had died of blackwater fever on an island "in the east" where they had been living alone (except for the plantation labor). He had dug her grave himself, buried her alone and alone carried the news back to her missionary father in Australia. She was his connection with this mission plantation in New Guinea. While I painted he sat behind me and in his few words told me so vividly what was the color of her hair, her eyes, her skin and how she smiled in a certain way that I saw her alive and young again and had painted her so right that I was sorry. It was not a promising start for a gay Christmas, but it was the only picture he had wanted.

Christmas Eve dinner was to be a climax of island dinners, a meal of native foods to end all meals of tinned ones. We suspected, rightly, that it was going to take long preparation, so we rolled up our sleeves early on the big day. The first consideration was meat, so shortly after daybreak an excited Emp and Beremiki with one rifle between them set out with Davi armed with bow and arrows and a club. They had orders to bring in wild pig or wallaby and all the "pigeon" they could get. There was a good chance of their returning empty-handed, because Emp was only a fair shot and neither of the other boys had ever had a rifle in his hands. Davi had his alibi

all ready; he had to have his dog to give him the warning bark
when game was near, so he could keep to windward of the
quarry, and here he had no dog. So to be prepared for an
emergency, Derivo and another of the boys' housekeepers
were sent off to fish. It was the only time we ever saw Derivo
show any animation. The fishers of the Gogodara are the
women, but ordinarily they make and use basket traps of vine
and bark twine. There was no such trap at Madiri nor any
time to make one; when the women left, in the opposite direction from the river, they were carrying small nets and wore
wide smiles. We would have been as pleased to have gone
with them or with the hunters, but their primitive methods of
food-getting seemed so chancy that we still had to make certain of an emergency meat. The last resort was tinned meat,
to be found at the store.

The Madiri store was not the kind of grocery store you are
thinking of. It was a corrugated iron structure about as big
as a small trolley and shaped much like one. The principal
difference was that there were no windows at all, and only
one outside door. In front of the doorway was a mud plateau,
an island in a lake of yellow water. Standing there in the rain
were a score or more of tall wet villagers who had arrived in
canoes bringing coconuts to exchange for trade goods. The
women wore rain-hoods, and their naked babies sat under
the hoods on the back of their mothers' hips like baby monkeys. The coconuts, tied into bundles by their husks and
already counted, were stacked in a pyramid while the natives
stood patiently in the downpour, credit chits in hand, waiting their turn to get into the crowded store to choose their
"present." Howls of Nordic laughter were issuing from that
dark interior, and when Yorick saw us he came to the door
holding his nose. "Stinks," he said elegantly, and then went
off into gaffaws again. "You know, I'm gettin' so blinkin'
cockeyed. I just asked one of those blokes what he wanted,

and another one way down at the end of the counter answered." As he backed into the store a string of cheap lace edging hanging from a bolt of many like it stored in the rafters caught his spectacles and swung them from his face. Without the glasses Yorick was almost blind except for distinguishing light from dark, and while he waved his arms around in the air trying to catch the swinging spectacles (and we stood and laughed callously) the natives looked like children when Santa Claus takes off his whiskers. Yorick himself had carefully fostered the rumor that his unique eyes could see in every direction at the same time, even in back of him, because his customers had a habit of picking up anything they fancied and idly taking it with them. If they felt one of Yorick's eyes on them, however, they more often remembered to turn over their chit for the article. Proof of the high native intelligence of the Papuan is that it took only a few years of association with our brand for the villagers around Madiri to discover that they could pick up their trade coconuts right along the borders of the plantation, bring them in to the store and get goods for them, Madiri's own coconuts.

"They're making off with whole crates of tobacco," we shouted consolingly to the still-blind Yorick. We were in the storeroom, where we were helping ourselves. The old fashioned "bullamacow" of the islands is now labeled minced scallops, mutton pie, chicken à la king, beef stew, sheep tails and so on. The sheep-tail label comes the nearest to reality, for no matter what the label, the contents of the tin are usually mutton. We took a tin of each brand and then went over to the labor quarters and picked up some garden yams and ground-ripened bananas from the housekeepers. Anyone who expected to find ripe bananas on a banana tree in this land would find only the leavings of the fruit pigeons. The bananas are cut off while still green and buried until they are ripe. There was one imported orange tree on the plantation bearing puny little oranges, and for dessert we wanted to make a layer ambrosia of oranges, bananas and shredded coconut. To get the coconut shredded we had to bring one of the housekeepers up to the residence to see that she washed her hands thoroughly before she began shredding. Then while she was shredding, every time she scratched herself we made her wash her hands again. The fussy precautions we took to insure uncontaminated food, dysentery being the constant threat, were just so much witch's hocuspocus to the woman . . . as they might have been to many of our grandmothers and most of our great-grandmothers. We had found some half-ripe tomatoes in what Yorick had said was a garden (but at the moment was a yellow lake) and decided to have them sliced and fried, but they were dropped in hot water first just to be sure. As the day wore on we seemed to run up an egg-less blind alley every way we turned. And we needed lard, which will not keep in this tropical country, and condiments and other ingredients which were in the corner store seas distant from the steamy smoky house-cook up the Fly River. But by four o'clock we had pans of some of the food, either cooked or all ready for the stove, set out on the table and covered with bed mosquito netting.

At five Derivo ambled in, fishless but looking even more amiable than before. At five-ten it began to rain corrugated iron roofing and a few minutes later Emp and Beremiki came in almost dry-skinned, carrying a bundle of *flying fox*— bats to you—that could have been shot in ten minutes. Davi never appeared at the house at all but he was found later to be at the labor quarters, also gameless. It appears that we had just given the five a day's walkabout in the bush. So it was tinned mutton for the feast, after all.

Dinner was not served until nearly nine-thirty, an hour and a half after the usual time, due to the stovepipe coming down. We won't go into that except to say that the delay it caused was the reason for the party being a tremendous success. Everything had been ready for the usual dinner hour, Derivo with a clean white sulu in readiness to be put on at the last minute, her long nails chopped off, belly unmuddied and her mind freshly primed on the lessons in serving, for this was to be her debut as a proper houseboy. The Christmas tree in the corner of the dining room was a masterpiece of what our family would have called "make do." A palmetto had been turned upside-down, which gave the branches the proper tannenbaum swoop, an inch-wide bolt had been sawed off the edge of a roll of toilet paper and before it was unrolled tightly pressed in two or three joints so that when it was pulled out it was crinkled, and this festooned the branches, along with some of the red-and-yellow lace edging from the store. Margaret had mended all of Ham's and Yorick's socks as a Christmas present, and these were rolled into pairs, dipped in flour and hung on the tree as popcorn balls. A liberal sprinkling of flour snow was also scattered over the tree, and a big tin star nailed over the stub end at the top. But Margaret's lighting was sheer genius. She had arrived at it from hearing me working in the darkroom. I had decided to sacrifice myself and as a Christmas present print up sets of pictures from our films for Margaret to send home. Darkroom work is a chore even under ideal conditions, and the only way I could manipulate a darkroom was to work at night. As the darkest possible place I chose the rubber shed. But the fireflies came in, or were already in, and went beaming around, ruining a film I was trying to develop in a tray and generally making such a glow that they were endangering our remaining printing paper. Margaret went into a huddle with Beremiki over the firefly situation, and they came back from the river with leaves and pieces of bark which they tied on around the stalk of the Christmas tree. There was no effect until it began to get dark, and then the whole tree glowed with fireflies, which cooperatively stayed right among the branches. They were attracted there either by the leaves or by the ladies on the leaves, and in either case made the only truly astral light we have ever seen coming from a Christmas tree. In that soft glow, Margaret in white décolleté and lipstick looked as fresh and lovely as a soap advertisement.

The only thing we had been doubtful about was the apéritif. We were afraid we had a real one, in the medical sense and not the French. Being a "mission" station, there were no proper spirits available for the banquet cocktail; but in the back room at the store we had found part of a case of stomach tonic. According to the label it was almost as pure as Ivory Soap, and it was at least as tasty as some of the brews we had drunk from crystal in the barren years. The dosage advised on the bottle was one tablespoon before each meal, so we took one tablespoon straight and decided what it needed was a little water. And we were still experimenting an hour later when the men joined us. It seemed to us we had never seen two funnier looking persons. Their heads appeared to be ringbarked. They had spent the afternoon shearing one another, and had achieved haircuts that looked like those bad-fitting toupees the bartenders wear in Tijuana, with a strip of nude white skin between the hair and the weathering of their necks.

Not knowing that the stovepipe was on its way down we began pouring at seven-thirty, so that by nine-thirty when the dining room screen door banged shut in the way it had when the last fly had been shooed in, our palates were not only toned, they were nearly insensible. The chimney soot was the only flavoring that got through, and it just made things tangy. The meat course, which was supposed to be with stuffed instead of fried tomatoes, appeared in a porcelain wash bowl as cubed mutton in tomato sauce. What was intended to have been candied yams was ossified in the pan.

Only a cook will know what happened; we didn't care. Our carefully prepared native cucumber salad went untouched, because, as someone remarked, it looked like a mess of Yorick's eyes. And we were not very sure about the dressing ourselves, as the sealed bottle of oil had been in the storeroom since the days of the first Madiri missionary, and there are some things even vinegar cannot gloss over. But everyone cheerfully helped the weakened flies out of the ambrosia as discipline took its final leave of Madiri.

The kitchen staff could not have guessed the reason for our sudden animation, but like children they were quick to sense the abandoned moment and take advantage of it. Derivo, for one, showed that she did not give a damn how a civilized meal should be served, nor what a sulu was meant for. She had donned the white calico, but *over* her bird's nest bundle of grass, and then used it, the sulu, for a hand towel. When she removed dishes she stood on one side of the table and reached across to the opposite side, trailing her person over plates and through the bottles of sauces and seasoners that always stood around the lamp, Christmas or not. She had her tray on the floor near the door, and when it was filled with dishes she crawled past the treacherous screen door, then dragged the tray out after her. This was something she had been told not to do. She had also been told not to start screaming at Beremiki and Emp as soon as she began dragging the tray down the veranda to the house-cook. And the boys had been ordered not to laugh at her. Whenever Emp could manage it he would charge through the doorway just as Derivo was clearing the danger area, and let the spring door smack the girl into the room by her bottom. One of these contacts knocked the sulu right off her, and after that we had her semi-nude, which, however, only made a fascinating contrast every time she leaned over Margaret in her white décolleté. The house-cook echoed with whining and the banging of pans and dishes until long after midnight, and that, we might add, is about the usual advantage a domesticated primitive gets out of a Christian holiday; just a lot more work and confusion.

Meantime we triumphs of evolution were having one of the wildest parties Madiri had ever seen. First we had a magic lantern show of the old Bible-story slides, with a descriptive talk by Yorick, which was certainly the first of its kind ever to go with those pictures. Then there was a musicale, an asthmatic tenor, a flute whose notes kept slipping out of Ham's control, a ukulele with two strings, and a hand drum (my guitar had long since fallen apart) rendering, in the sense of inflicting on, all the old Christmas carols. Then Yorick sang something which he said was an old Australian folksong, so censored that it lacked sense. Something about a pirate who could be no bolder, who "snapped his fingers, ha-ha-ha-ha. He snapped the others, ho-ho-ho-ho. I don't care if, da-da-da-da. Once aboard the lugger and (censored)." After which Ham and Yorick wiped their tears and lapsed incongruously into hymn duets.

This was the usual Madiri Nights entertainment. When the two men were alone they sat night after night like this, the dark sick-looking man with his bony fingers working along the flute like piano hammers and Yorick, head back, cocked eyes closed, his jaggle-toothed mouth giving forth a fine tenor, making music in the metallic din of rain on the roof. Usually some of the plantation boys sat under the house, listening. Or while Hamlet added and subtracted his horses on the margins of magazines, Yorick wrote to the girls he was engaged to. Yorick had proposed to every likely girl he had known in England during his first homesick month at Madiri. The exchange of mail took a long time, and when the answers began coming in he found four had accepted him, cocked eyes and all, and the rest were still consoling him. Yorick wrote love letters as a woman knits, picking it up at odd moments.

By one o'clock we had laughed and sung ourselves out. Only the fireflies were still beaming with enthusiasm. We

turned down the lamps and stood holding the ones we took to our rooms, and while the rain drummed on the iron above our heads, spattering noisily on the ponds around the house, and while the fireflies glowed in the dusk, we sang soberly the song that closes every good British party, Auld Lang Syne. This Christmas our thoughts did not wander nostalgically the thousands of miles to home. We had been gone too long; we had learned what every good traveler must, to live our lives where we found ourselves.

I was first out on the veranda, and was surprised to see

the tail end of Emp just going down the steps. I meant to ask if he should not have been in his quarters long since when Yorick called out, "Anyone got a cigarette?" No one had. We began looking about, casually at first, then searching frantically. Finally Margaret found seven moisture-stained king-size Castles in a tin in my paint box. That was all the cigarettes there were at Madiri besides the stubs we gathered together.

Post mortem note: The stomach tonic contained its own antidote.

27

Just as Tauparaupi had been the best model we had ever had, the equally Papuan Derivo was also a superlative; she was the worst. A worse model is not one who jerks around while he is posing and never gets back into the original position, or even disappears forever in the middle of a portrait; it is the one who sits but never lets you have a good look at her face. Derivo sat cross-legged on the veranda with her peaked rain-hood over her head and falling around the back of her shoulders, and she kept her head hung over her lap so that the hood constantly hid her face from view. She was like an ostrich with her whole naked body vulnerable, the one thing hidden that we wanted to see. Her long bony fingers twitched unceasingly, and when she was released for a spell she would half rise and charge off the veranda as if she had just escaped from a torture rack. Periodically Margaret had to go out to the house-cook and slap down the ears of the house-boys in her best Motu, because we suspected that their hooting and yapping, ostensibly at one another, was really directed at the girl. She had been willing enough to pose at first, and this silliness had only developed after her first look at the unfinished painting. "She thinks you're taking away her ghost and putting it on the canvas," offered Yorick. To which we retorted, "Spinach," he had read that believe-it-or-not in some tourist's book about blackest Papua. But when we called in Davi, to get an explanation of the heavy cicatrices that ornamented his wife's chest, we also, incidentally, got an intimation that Yorick might have made a good guess after all.

Davi could speak some pidgin English, but he had little opportunity when Emperor Jones was around, because Davi had trouble understanding us; so Emp concluded we were the dumb ones, and he translated Davi's pidgin into his own for us. It was therefore Emp who said that the girl's scars were simply "flash," something for look good fella. Somewhere we had read or heard, however, that the keloids between the breasts were slashed to keep the breasts from becoming pendulous—a vain hope, for the breasts of these Papuan matrons were standard.

While this examination was going on, the subject of it was sitting on the floor whining into her lap. Finally I lost patience. "Goddam!" (pidgin exclamation, not profanity) I said, "what name dis fella cry all-a time?" Emp asked Davi, who asked Derivo, who replied at length; after which the boys looked blank. "Well," we insisted, "what name?" "No," said Emp. "No?" I asked. "Yes," said Emp. In case you don't understand English that meant; What is the girl complaining about? Nothing. Nothing? Yes, nothing. Nevertheless there was something—and just to make it confusing it was a something-nothing, a something for which there is no name. The girl intimated, however, that this painting business was making her legs sick. If her legs hurt—and she did not appear to be fudging her misery—it may have had some basis, for though she had probably spent most of her twenty years sitting in the position in which I was painting her, she was so tense that her muscles could have been cramped.

Finally Derivo's anguish made her altogether useless, for I could not keep my mind on my painting; and though the figure was not finished we gave her some tobacco as a dismissal present. And as usual when she was released she dashed for cover under the house, her whine beginning as her head dropped out of sight down the steps. Thereafter for a few minutes there was quiet, and presently the odor of tobacco smoke floating up indicated that she was squatting below enjoying the fruits of her misery. Then suddenly came a piercing howl followed by scream after scream. We tore down the steps, and were back up almost as quick. Ham had just reached the house, and in three seconds had trapped under a gasoline tin the first venomous foot of a three-foot snake. The snake had stung Derivo, not on the leg, but on her bare buttocks.

For a few minutes there was the wildest excitement. When the barefooted Emp and Beremiki rushed down the steps they too would have rushed back up when they saw the snake, but Ham ordered them into action. Beremiki was sent down to the quarters to bring back another native woman, and Emp was ordered to sit on the gasoline tin so that the snake could not get loose until something could be done about it. Then the three of us caught the hysterical girl. With no polite preliminaries Hamlet threw her face-down in the mud and then, straddling her legs as if he meant to give her artificial respiration, ourselves holding her shoulders, he slashed across the snakebite with his pocket knife. It was hard to find, because of the girl's dark skin and the usual coating of mud. Then we faced the embarrassing problem of who should do the sucking of the venom. Hamlet, of course, would have lost caste in the Fly River by any such action. Emperor Jones, being native, was the logical one, so to release him Ham passed along his pocket knife for Emp to cut off the part of the snake that was outside the tin.

The boy planked his big callused foot squarely on the head of the still live snake, and without further ado sawed. Then Ham could not make him understand about sucking. "*Rosia, rosia!*" he ordered, pointing to the girl's bottom. "Rosia" means to nurse. Emp just stood there boggle-eyed at this suggestion. I always very conveniently get nauseated when there is anything distasteful to be done, and Margaret was tightening her belt to get into action, when the plantation woman arrived. But she did not even understand "rosia," because it is a Motu word; and until Ham could make Emp understand and Emp could get it across to Beremiki and he in turn could convince the Papuan woman that sucking was the proper treatment for snakebite, the victim of it lay face-down in the mud waiting for death. Snakes are malevolent spirits, and there is no counteraction for their bite except another sorcerer to undo the work of the first one, who sent the snake. He ties on a ligature of vine rope, slashes the puncture with a sharp shell and applies a poultice of enchanted ginger leaves or coral lime to the wound.

The first thing Margaret's fertile brain had thought of was the stomach tonic, and while the Papuan woman was doing her best to rosia, about a half bottle of the tonic was poured into the girl's mouth. So she was probably just drunk when she refused to get to her feet after the mauling. But Ham had two unfailing remedies for everything. One was castor oil, and the other potassium permanganate. About half a bottle of castor oil was therefore added to the stomach tonic, and as there was no fresh solution of the potassium permanganate made up, Ham slapped some of the crystals on Derivo's bottom. That got her up with a yelp, thoroughly cauterized. After which she was turned over to her tribe with instructions to keep her awake by walking her until they had orders to stop.

Then we turned our attention to the viper. It was a land snake, and not the first we had seen at Madiri. The plantation was on the highest area of land in this part of the river, and as the rains filled the swamps all the snakes in the countryside scuttled in. Then as the water rose further they sought safety on the raised paths, and some found the two places that were usually above the flood, the toilet island and the square under the house. This latter was a place used as a laundry—where things were washed but never dried—and a close watch was kept for snakes by the boys, who were familiar with the danger. Either they were too familiar to have thought to warn Derivo, or she was too upset by her experience posing for us to remember when she squatted in the viper pit.

Emp showed a morbid interest in the snake, which did not seem to be much affected by being bisected. He picked up the end with the head on it and pinched it just behind the jaws, and the rest of the body wound itself around his arm just as if it were alive. Then he ran a match down the back of the tail section and the severed end rose in the air and turned about as if there were a head still on it. After which he picked up both parts, and he and Beremiki took them down to their housekeeper to have them made into snake casserole with rice for dinner. Eating snake will make one wise and courageous.

It was seven hours later, and we were finishing dinner, before anyone remembered; and then Yorick released one of his most explosive ca-ripes. We had forgotten all about Derivo. When we reached the quarters we found her still alive, and in at least as good health as her tribeswomen. They looked like the last marathon dancers in the ring. The women had been told to walk the girl, and they were still walking her—a task that was somewhat complicated by the castor oil and the antidote in the stomach tonic. But Derivo had a sick leg now, "true fella," and from then on she stayed in the quarters. We had failed completely in making a friend of her, even before the portrait was begun. Patience, kindness as we knew it, even an attitude of offhand good fellowship that will break down the barriers with a suspicious child, all these had had no effect. We had never been able to make her laugh or smile, or even look squarely at us. And we had tried very hard to think of her as another woman and to like her. The latter especially we had not been able to manage. There was not one likable quality about her, not even the humility or the bewilderment of a stupid person that can sometimes enlist one's sympathy. I, alone apparently among Europeans who are acquainted with primitives, am so convinced that their intuitive sense is specially developed—more exactly, less suppressed than ours—that I think this was the whole cause of our failure with Derivo. She sensed that we did not like her, and she suspected foul play, for that is the expected course of dislike in the village. And her expectations had been fulfilled.

The whole episode put us in bad odor in the community, and for a while we could get no other woman to pose for the unfinished figure in the portrait. A housekeeper could have been ordered to sit, but we preferred not to force the issue, as there was other work that could be done until time had cleared the atmosphere. This was a head of Emperor Jones.

Emp was native of the Vailala River district, where we had had the encounter with the "black widow," and though the boy had probably spent half of the last fifteen years on plantations, the law requires that a native return to his village for a period between terms of indenture (for breeding purposes), so he had not lost track of his village by any means. In other words, though he was savvy, the mud of his tribe still clung to him. And he was not at all beautiful. His Papuan nose was not the regal one of the ancient kings of Egypt. It was a big black wad on the end of a long stem, with a hole in the septum that hung down in a loop big enough to shoot peas through. His upper lip was fat and curled back sensuously, while the lower lip protruded and was thin, an arrangement that reminds me now of a shrewd observation made by the cartoonist "Ding," which was that a man can manage his lower lip to grow the way he wants it but the upper lip grows that way by itself, revealing the real character. But

Emp's character was revealed better in another way. He had rings under his eyes.

Primitives, even the aged or sick, do not often have this blemish of exhaustion or nerves that marks civilized man for a driven race. Either the high cheekbones take up the slack or the blue pigmentation that outlines our marsupial pouches is invisible in the brown skin and so makes them less apparent. With age or sickness the eyes of the average native just appear to sink farther back between the projecting brows and cheekbones. However, there is one common exception, the haggard lined face of the old sorcerer. For some unaccountable reason sorcerers look like sorcerers. And Emp had the visage of one, for the loose flesh under his eyes cascaded right over the ledges of his cheek bones. But there the resemblance ended, for he was neither old nor shrewd-looking.

We had nicknamed the boy "Emperor" because he was fully as big and black as Eugene O'Neill's Emperor Jones. He had hands like baseball mitts, and there was a thyroidal insistence in the way he jerked them about that had made me plow to shore hanging onto Margaret while she held onto the rear of Emp's belt when we went through the mud at the mouth of the river. Ordinarily I had no personal feeling about a native man. We sat on their locked hands to be carried over the surf and clutched their naked shoulders, a more intimate contact than one would ever have with a strange white man, and it was as impersonal as if the boys were horses. Not only to oneself but to the native. For contrary to fiction the white woman seems to have in the native mind a sexless status like that of angels if we can judge from his attitude. Emp's manner was exactly that of every other native, nevertheless there was something unwholesome about him. I was painting him partly because he was another type of Papuan but also as a little joke, because he looked so exactly the preconceived notion of the bruitish savage which is so far from the truth. Also we were curious about what made him so repugnant.

It was uphill work from the start, a fact I attributed to the storm which had begun at daybreak and was reducing my analytical centers to a vapor. This was a new kind of rain, a regular old-fashioned hot-summer electrical cloudburst with a flood of water and a banging and snapping of thunder and lightning which, however, did not stop with exhaustion after an hour or so nor yet move on to terrify other counties. "Change of seasons," said Yorick when he dripped in to breakfast. "That's bonza," we said, "We can stand some dry weather. Our scalp is growing fungus." "Oh, no," he answered, "we've just had a dry season. We're going into the wet."

As I worked, half my mind was on forest fires. The light was a curious yellow, and one could smell the ozone in the scorched air. Every celestial explosion rattled the iron over our heads; and Beremiki, who had ideas of such displays being ghost anger, kept a worried eye turned skyward as he jiggled nervously up and down the veranda on the pretext of sweeping it. Emp was twitching around as if he had grasshoppers, fluttering his big mitts and baggy eyes so that I had to forget what he looked like before I could remember what I wanted to paint. Finally Margaret came sloshing in, announcing that she had trapped a female model for me from among the housekeepers. "Well, give me a hand with this one first," I groaned. Margaret seated herself in front of Emp with her ukulele and began crooning soothingly, "Oh give me a home where the buffaloes roam . . ." Crash-bang over our heads. That was a close one. Emp began scratching the skin in one place on his leg with a long fingernail as Margaret's voice was drowned in the thunder of water all around and overhead. There was no light left to paint by. As I threw down my brushes I bawled at the top of my voice, "Jesus lover of my soul." Margaret joined me, and I noticed Emp look suddenly alert. We had the impression that he liked hymns. In the evening he stayed around as long as he was allowed, listening to our quartet.

We kept on singing while I mixed some paint, and when I looked up again I was startled by the change in Emp. He was now leaning forward rigidly, with his big hands fussing around his diaphragm. His eyes looked dopey, and the muscles of his crossed legs were trembling. "Boy sick?" Emp didn't answer, but he began clawing at his belly. We shouted for Beremiki. This wasn't ordinary malaria chills. As Margaret jumped up to go after Hamlet, she bumped into Beremiki. He was coming from the doorway of the house-cook and his eyes, focused on Emp, were out like doorknobs. "Belly don't know," he said in an awed voice. He was dispatched for the *Taubada*. By this time Emp was frightening. His creased face was contorted, his big mouth drooling as he muttered and panted. The excruciating pain was just below his ribs, for he kept clutching at the flesh there, pulling it out and letting it snap back as if to tear out the bad spirits. Whatever did one do for a stricken person in this doctor-less land—just sit and watch the death agony? The natives had been watching for centuries; perhaps their sense of help- . lessness was what had made them turn to mysticism. The thunder was rocking the air when Ham came up the steps. He was not hurrying; he strode deliberately across the ve-randa, grabbed Emp by his mop of hair and jerked his head back. He paused only a second to make sure, then gave the boy a blistering smack across the side of the head. The cure was instantaneous. Emp came out of it like a man who had been hypnotized, staring around him with bloodshot, stunned eyes. After which I went to the veranda rail and did what the *Varanus komodoensis* does when it is badly frightened.

Hamlet never explained to us how he discovered the treatment for belly-go-round, but it was obvious from the nature of it that originally he had regarded the spells as faked or at least self-induced. But I had previously observed two epileptic seizures, and for a long time I was sure that Emperor Jones was an epileptic and that slapping was a merciful therapeutic for a fit that modern medicine had overlooked. Then finally we read a paper called "Vailala Madness," by F. E. Williams, the government anthropologist, which probably gives the real explanation.

Some years ago a religious movement which had its origin among some ex-converts of a Christian mission started up in a village of the Vailala River, and in a short time it had spread like wildfire up and down the coast. Originally the cult was an independent native version of Christianity, having as its featured tenet the resurrection of the dead. At first just the adherents of the movement were promised resurrection as mortals, then all of the dead of the past were to return to life. By and by everyone was to reappear with a white skin, and finally white men were believed to be merely resurrected natives. So far the philosophy probably stayed pretty close to the mission version, which promised that in heaven we shall all be the same. But then the natives began to get some of the old whoopee into it. In several places a kind of "first supper" table was maintained, awaiting the return of the dead, and it was a white man's table laid with a cloth, metal service and dishes, and a ready supply of feast food. However the cult did not receive official attention until news trickled into Port Moresby that a whole shipload of deceased relatives was expected any day. The vessel was to be a real steamer and would be stocked with tinned meat, tobacco, knives, axes, *rifles and ammunition*, with which the natives would run the present white ghosts out of the country. If it seems inconsistent that one set of ghosts should aid the mortals against another set, that is because you are not thinking with a native mind. Or if it seems contradictory that natives who a few years later proved themselves loyal subjects of His Majesty during the Japanese invasion should at any time have entertained the idea of liquidating his white subjects, then it is only necessary to remember that the Papuan is of the genus *homo sapiens*. The same tribe which in defending its Christian way of life uses the very means most condemned by Christianity. The sapience is demonstrated in the capacity for expedience. When planters in the vicinity of the villages most violently affected by the cult began to get the wind up, the government was obliged to take action. An extract from the annual report explains why in one case: "At night when somebody imagined that the vessel was sighted there would be a cry of 'sail, ho!' and instantly the whole village would run out bearing torches, repeating the cry; and thus kept themselves in a ferment of excitement for weeks . . . even for months. The routine of the village life was disturbed, gardens were neglected, all regular work ceased, and instead of making copra or selling coconuts to the traders the nuts were being stacked in the villages until the arrival of the vessel. During the time the lunacy was at its height there was a considerable increase in sexual offenses. . . . All the natives most seriously affected were brought to the station, where they were put to work and regularly fed until returning to a normal state of mind, when they were permitted to go back to their villages."

The lunacy referred to was the basis for the name "Vailala Madness," and some of the manifestations described were identical with those exhibited by Emperor Jones. No one, least of all the adherents, can explain the connection between the fits and the philosophy, but the seizures were a regular part of the "services." Violent trembling was a manifestation shared by all who became possessed. Generally they staggered around the village clearing, brandishing their arms,

jerking their heads, falling to the ground writing and slob-
bering and frothing at the mouth. The fits were genuine
enough. There were those who received a "gift of tongues"
and went about shouting or muttering in a language no one
else could understand. Or they threw themselves into grotesque attitudes, while others joined in frenzied dancing and
chanting, the latter occasionally distortions of hymns. Large
assemblies were naturally the most violently affected, and it
needed only the contortions of a few to send the whole
village off into a St. Vitus's dance that sometimes lasted for
months. "An interesting parallel was provided only recently
in London," the account remarks, "when many individuals in
an audience of shell-shocked soldiers fell into contortions in
imitation of one of their number." But occasionally some
individual would become possessed when the village was
quiet, and would have his fit all by himself without anyone
else being affected. Another peculiarity was that a believer
could have an attack of the mania when he was far distant
from his fellow, or even long after the cult had appeared to
die out in the district.

The original Vailala Madness has long since been brought
under control in Papua, but cults having similar, though seldom so violent, manifestations are always brewing somewhere
in New Guinea. However, they do not always have their
origin in a village that has been under missionary influence,
so it is not necessarily a bounce back from hymn singing.
Nor is it positively known that they occur only in govern-
ment-controlled areas where the old forms of whoopee, raiding and terrorization, have been suppressed, because there
has been little opportunity to study what goes on beyond
the frontiers. The same writer, F. E. Williams, is of the
opinion that cult flurries are an old Papuan custom, starting
up easily, becoming violent and then dying away as quickly,
a new one from some other quarter sweeping in to take its
place. So it must be Papuan temperament.

The fact that the movements can become violent and that the physical manifestations are contagious made it all the more necessary to keep Emp's attacks under control. Because he might easily have attached some creed to his fits and had the makings for a fine kettle of fish at Madiri. The co-screwball who howled every night of our first week at the station was a ready convert to something, and we had seen for ourselves in the encounter with the "black widow" in the Vailala River village how quickly the mob could respond to the excitement of one. (It was not fantastic to think that the black woman had seen in Margaret the materialization of some deceased relative. It has happened to white men before—and in "civilized" districts.) But not until now, after seeing Emperor Jones possessed, did we realize what Yorick had been through those days he was alone at Madiri, nor the strain that Hamlet must have been under the week following. No wonder the one was wild-eyed and the other grim. They were quietly holding under control something far more combustible than an individual case of moon daffiness.

Employers in our land of the free may wonder why these two potentially dangerous boys were not discharged. One answer is that such lapses, if they are infrequent and can be controlled, do not incapacitate a boy for ordinary muscle work on a plantation. Emperor Jones's attacks seemed to come on him only during violent electrical storms, so Hamlet had only to hear thunder in order to be prepared. Another answer is that labor is scarce in Papua. The Papuans are not very enthusiastic about working for the rugged Australian planter, and the distaste for portering in the mountains is so widespread that even the government occasionally must resort to authority when the Service needs carriers for some emergency expedition into the interior.

A third good reason is that both these eccentrics at Madiri were indentured boys, for whom the plantation had paid some recruiter twenty-five dollars a head for a two-year contract. If the boys were discharged, the recruiter's fee was sacrificed. The only assurance an employer has that he is getting a normal healthy boy is the O.K. of the government, which passes on all recruits before they are signed on. The medical examination, however, consists of looking at the candidate's eyes and tongue and asking if his bowels are functioning, to which the answer is "Yes." There is nothing in the questionnaire that would reveal whether the native was subject to fits when it thundered or when the moon was full.

For Emperor Jones to have had a visitation while we were painting his portrait was unfortunate, for it was piling up evidence against Art at Madiri.

28

We made short work of the woman, another housekeeper, who succeeded Derivo as model for her unfinished portrait. She began posing for us one morning, and that afternoon she collapsed on her bunk with an indisposition which in our south would pass for just "cussed nigger laziness." She claimed she was unable to stand; there was something the matter with her legs. Ham went down to the quarters to get her up, and undoubtedly did, for he used castor oil, but as no further mention was made of the case, we got the rather undefined impression that the *taubada* himself thought Art was disorganizing his labor line. Whether psychological or real, the results were the same; our victims were incapacitated for work. So we turned our destructive forces on another quarter.

There was no lack of models at Madiri. Almost every day a dozen or more wet muddy villagers would paddle in to the landing and lug up to the store their coconuts to exchange for trade goods. There were whole families, the almost naked women carrying on the back of their hips under the rain-hoods their wholly naked infants. While under way, the youngster straddled the mother's waist and clung with his arms about her body like a baby monkey, but when at anchor he stood up on the woman's rump and peered over her shoulder, with his arms about her neck. Most of the women had their hair shorn to the bullet-shaped skull, but now and then a button of wool was left on the crown, apparently for the child to grip to balance himself. Occasionally a woman had a strip of hair like a cock's comb running from front hairline to back. Now and then one of the dour creatures smiled at us, not often. All of them had heavy keloids on the upper part of the body; these were on the upper arms, across the chest, and always between the breasts. The gashes, now scars, had been made with a sharp-edged shell and packed with clay to cause them to heal in welts. Curiously the scarification had been accomplished in such a way that the pigment of the skin was undisturbed and did not show the bluish-white that marks the scars from other wounds on a negroid skin. Some of the upper arm keloids were "family portraits." The characteristic long, waddy-tipped nose of the district is much admired, and the bigger the nose the handsomer the owner.* A young woman with a very beautiful parent will have the length of his nose marked off in cicatrices on her arm. Others of the keloid patterns were brands of ownership, or claim. Western Papua is that woman's para-

---

* This glorification of the nose by the monumental-nosed Papuans bears out our observation of man's irresistible preference for his own type of beauty. With unfailing regularity he will select some feature which distinguishes him from men of other races, frequently one we would consider the least becoming, and give it prominence. For example the Polynesians have a characteristic mouth; a narrower lower lip and a fat upper, which curls back acutely and in repose has an adenoidal expression. This upper lip is anything but inhibited, however. When the owner of it laughs, instead of pressing on the teeth, it rolls out like the lip of a sneezing horse revealing a wide strip of red gum. Yet the "Maori maiden fair" accents this mouth by not only tattooing the lips blue but decorating it all around with bold designs, the only tattooing on the face. The duck-billed Ubangi women do about the same thing with rings inserted into their full negroid lips. Orientals who are famous in cartoons for their buck teeth have them covered with gold when they can afford it, and their child-breasted women bind their chests in an obi to appear even more breastless. The almost hairless Melanesians despise body hair, but it grows in a dense bush on the head, so the rare bald Melanesian is a joke. The short fat feet of the French women trip along on the highest heels endurable to make them look even less efficient as feet, and the already ample women of central Europe would stuff themselves for greater girth, while their men regard as shapeless our divine Yankee spindle-shanks which we bare to the knee whenever the styles give us an opportunity.

dise on earth where there are more marriageable men than women, and as the age increases the disproportion becomes greater, because it is the women, not the men who die off first. There is consequently a great rush to claim girl children. The old men get there first, naturally, and at the time of be-trothal—the girls are not married until they become of "suitable" age—the brand of the contract is cut on the girl's chest. Only an acute shortage could make these Papuan women so sought after. Yet the ones who came in to Madiri posed willingly enough; and that gave them a kind of virtue.

All sorts of pictures turned up in a day's work; a thin brown little lad of ten or eleven going through his coming-of-age puncturing, the raw holes in the rims of his ears and the septum of his nose stuffed with tassles of dried grass to keep the wounds from healing closed. He looked queerly like a little old man with a ragged mustache. There was a fine-muscled young man the color of a ripe plum who wore fixed on the crest of his blue-black hair a pom-pom of some spiky plumage vividly yellow-green with a quill of vermillion stuck through it, and at his throat was a disk of nacre. He had a nose like a potato, so he was parfait indeed. Came a woman who would have been considered beautiful had she blossomed among the tribes north of the mountains, where tremendous hanging breasts are the ideal.

One day the government launch pulled in with a prisoner on board taken at Tirio just above us, a native settlement famous and much feared throughout the Lower Fly for its sorcerers. We had attempted to visit this village, and before our anchor was down had been scared off by a chorus of screams the source of which remained a mystery for a long time. The prisoner had murdered a sorcerer, a much mur-dered character in New Guinea. It was the same old excuse in this case; the sorcerer had boasted that he had done to death by witchcraft the prisoner's wife, so he had paid with his own life for what had been largely a boast. The prisoner was in his widower's weeds, on his head a Juliet cap of twisted and plaited bark twine from which fell a cape of shredded pandanus palm leaf. A long fringe of the same material wound

about his body and hung to his feet. Like Tauparaupi he had a short mustache and black Judus beard, and the bearing of a sheik out of the Seven Pillars of Wisdom. There was a kitten on board the launch, and while the patriarch was standing regally posing for us the kitten was dancing around his bare feet, playing with the fringe of his shroud. Finally the man glanced down, observed the cat, and with no wind-up whatever swung out sideways with the royal foot and sent the puzi flying out into the river, where it was swallowed up by the hundred million gallons of Fly water. Margaret bet that he probably got a month in the quod for that, even if he didn't for murdering the sorcerer.

One day there came to work on the plantation the strangest looking human being there is to be seen anywhere, a white "negro." He was an albino, almost "total." Albinism is not rare in New Guinea, and it is not a single-family strain. The boy in this case was a Papuan, and we had already seen two other white natives in the Melanesian east. These two, incidentally, were sisters and must have been twins, for they were so much alike that we called them the hiccough sisters. One always followed closely behind the other, and each was a minor shock. The Papuan's skin was not dead white, it was a scabby blotched pink that looked like a white man's skin when it is healing from a bad sunburn. His eyelashes and kinky hair were platinum blonde, very light but still with a yellowish tinge. And his eyes—we examined them by pulling back the eyelids—were red, the actual blood system of the eye, which is usually concealed by coloration. Most of the time the boy was posing for us his lids were nearly closed, for even the dull light inside the rubber smoke shed where we worked was too intense for eyes with no protective pigment. One wondered how the man stood the dry season when the equator sun on his uninsulated hide must have made him feel skinless. He looked startlingly naked as it was, not being brown. But if we had thought that the Semitic-nosed Papuans looked like "black Jews," as we had heard them called, we now had the comparison in a white-skinned Papuan to prove that a Papuan looks only like a negroid Papuan, no matter what the color of his skin. The hooked nose had wide flat nostrils, with the characteristic deep narrow groove at the root, and the face was huge by contrast to the narrow long skull. The man looked, rather, like a native painted white. Just weird. And he acted weird. He jerked all over and all the time, hunching his shoulders and clasping his arms about his body like a man who is suffering with chills, which he may very well have been, for skin pigment is also a protection from the cold. Even in repose his white-haired eyelids fluttered incessantly, and when he tried to look at us he would turn his head from one acute angle to the other, as one would if he had an eyeshade on low over his eyes. Even the boy's language seemed jerkier than the usual Papuan flapgabble. We know more about albinism now than we did then, and know that there was nothing wrong with the native's mind. But his nervous system was in bad shape, as a result of having no pigment protection from the sun's rays. The least of many disorders an overdose of ultraviolet rays can give one is neuresthenia . . . as I discovered for myself in time, being an inadequately pigmented blond. But at that time we did not know that the boy was not daft, and it was only desperation for a model that caused us to make a study of him. For by this time our reputation for damaging our models had spread to the village natives, and they would not risk posing for us even for store trinkets.

This boycott was irritating, but it would have seemed less so if I had not had a toothache. It was my first, and like a first baby I suppose it actually hurt less than I thought it did, but I got the vivid impression of tassels of unsheathed nerves hanging down in the back of my mouth, sensitive alike to wind and tide. Captain Voy, who had brought us to the islands on the *Mataram* . . . he was dead now; a stroke while playing tennis at Tulagi without any covering on his bald head . . . the Voy had warned us about quinine. "It'll rot your teeth if you keep on taking it," he said. "When you begin to crack up, it'll be your teeth that will go first. Get out of these islands then. Quick." This was still unproved, however, for Margaret had been taking her five grains of quinine daily for almost two years—and I was the one who had the toothache.

Yorick, who knew all about toothache, had given me a bottle of some brew that he said would kill the pain, without, however, telling me that the stuff improperly used could remove every nerve ending in my mouth along with the lining, and still not affect the original ache. After that experiment, we tried that old strategy of tying one end of a cord to the tooth and the other to a doorknob, but it was an adult wisdom tooth, and all we did was to extract doorknobs. Finally both Hamlet and Yorick had a go at trying to pull it. Ham had pulled those of Yorick's teeth that had not fallen out by themselves, and the implement for extraction was a pair of pincers such as we have seen blacksmiths use for pulling old nails out of horses' hoofs. The only way they could get the offending tooth was to take two others out with it. I was willing if they would just leave me my tongue, but they seemed unable to make even that selection. So the toothache had remained, held snugly in place by plugs of rubber latex that had to be replaced after each meal because latex and tinned mutton taste and chew up just alike. In any case, when the albino began posing for me his frenzied jerking more or less reflected my own state of mind.

We were using the second floor of the rubber shed for a studio these days, because the village natives were too wet and muddy to bring to the residence veranda. And anyway, strange natives were not encouraged to become familiar with the house. The ground floor of the shed was a smoke room for drying out the sheets of latex, a process that we will get around to presently. Meantime, the fumes that rose to the second floor from the drying room were those of a stable, ammonia and smoky steam and the "studio" itself reverberated with the whacking of Davi's huge machete as he sat on the floor on the dim far side of the room, trimming the yellow sheets of latex into oblongs for baling. I too sat on the floor, with my back to the open doorway, big drawingboard in front of me—and beyond it sat the blotchy jerking albino looking like a specter in that black interior.

As I worked I was wondering if the albino had sweat glands like other people's. Somewhere I had read that melanin, the dark brown substance that colors the skin, absorbs the ultraviolet rays from the sun, converts them into heat and the heat causes sweat which carries off some of the body toxins. Lacking melanin to promote this orderly process, could the albino eject his toxins? Obviously he did something. With two Papuans in the poorly ventilated room the human odor was that of insufficiently cured beef, the acrid kind that you can taste as well as smell. Margaret was up at the house making trade-tobacco cigarettes, and I wished she would get down with a few, so that we might neutralize the fumes in the room with something familiar.

By the time Davi spoke my nerves were sticking out in knobs, partly because the drawing was going so badly. The drawing paper was like a wet rag, and every whack of Davi's big knife on the floor reverberated in the core of my ailing tooth. Davi was Derivo's husband and I thought as I watched him "killing" those sheets of rubber that he was probably the reason she was a whiner. He must have been twice her age, and he had a coarse muscle-creased face, as obstinate look-ing as hers was petulant. Did I savvy this woman of his, he asked. Yes, I said, I knew the girl—and was her sore leg a good fella again? No, said Davi, the leg was a sick fella; and the silence that followed suggested that Davi was think-ing the whole woman was no good fella any longer.

Finally after a long pause punctuated only by the steady bumping of the knife, Davi asked if I remembered the woman of Eapi. This was the second housekeeper who had posed for us. Well, her leg was sick too. Phooey, I said, this woman was just "gamin'" to get out of work. Davi let that pass; but presently he rose to his feet, and still with his sword in his hand, he came over to our side of the room. First he looked long at my drawing, then he studied the epileptic model, and you could hear the wheels of his brain turn. Nothing could have been more eloquent than his silent conclusion that between portraiture and ill health there was a very close connection. And his woman was "no good" any longer.

I did not forget Davi altogether, but I was absorbed trying to figure some way of finding out what he and the other plantation boys would think of this strange white native; whether they would laugh at him for being different or grant him special esteem as being a little nearer than the white man. Perhaps they would think him possessed—as I did myself, then. At this point in my mulling I missed something. It was the bump of Davi's knife. He was not back at his place on the floor. How had he got down the steps outside without my hearing him? Then I smelled him, and my skin prickled. I saw his dim shadow on the drawing board as he moved a little. There was no sound except the rumble on the iron over our heads, but the albino had twisted his body at a grotesque angle, and with his head almost horizontal he was jerkily peering above me.

I know now what it is to be "frozen" with fear. I remembered afterward that I had had the thought of crying out, but had made no effort to. I did not turn around to look, nor even try. I just waited in a kind of timeless vacuum, not even consciously frightened. Everything had "stopped." I did not know this until everything began going again. "*Once* aboard the lugger and the girl is mi-i-ine . . ." Yorick, mortal man sloshing gaily through the mud below the shed on his way in to tiffin. I bawled out like a calf, and kept on bawling uncontrollably as I fell down the steep outside steps toward the assistant. It was nerve exhaustion, the brand of hysteria now known by the soothing appellation "war fatigue." If I had looked around, I might have found Davi scratching his head.

29

We four at Madiri (I wrote in the current installment of our non-stop letter) are like vestigia of a vanished world, perhaps the white man's world after we have annihilated one another and the tide of Color has flowed back over the earth. To the left of us are brown cannibals and to the right brown headhunters, and all between is water and desolation. Water races out of the place that was once a sky extending to infinity, pounding on the yellow lake that surrounds us and obscuring the forest—if there is one behind it. The stream flows under us in the direction of the river, and there always before us is that horizonless stretch of water beating eastward toward the sea. Forever and ever, night and day without end.

There is no wind, but the downfall is so furious that spray makes a pool all around the veranda like the deck of a ship in a storm; and through the rooms wet patterns of bare feet walk ahead of us. The mosquito net over our bed almost drips, and more than almost smells to heaven. The nights are pitch-black, without even the glowworms, nor the sound of frogs, nor lizards, nor bats. There is just the sound of water everywhere, the drumming on the iron above our heads that is as insistent as a stuck car horn and as the drip-drip-dripping under the roof. By morning we have pressed the wet sheets into accordion pleats with the warmth of our bodies, and our damp hair feels like a cold pancake on the head. Rust and mold coat every useless worldly possession, shoes, camera cases, bags, the emerald fungus growing as a man grows a beard, overnight. And all the insects that like wetness have come out and multiplied according to the will of the Lord; and we reflect on this our last refuge taken over for eternity by leeches and cockroaches.

One reason for this sense of isolation is that the last time-piece that was going, our watch, has stopped. It probably has moss in the wheels. Ham has to guess when to start the gang to work in the morning and when to stop in the evening, because the light is no clue. I think I'm a great help here because I have a dog's sense of what clock-time it is. Another reason for feeling ourselves abandoned is the continued absence of the relief boat from Thursday Island. It is now so long overdue that Ham admits that since it did not take advantage of the fairly safe weather of a month ago it will probably wait until we are well into the wet season, when the winds will be fairly steady again. Meantime we are running low on provisions, and Madiri is stuck with us and we with a tooth.

I leave the "ache" off the "tooth" purposely, because that syllable has been taken care of, temporarily at least. Davi and Beremiki went across the river to Akarina just before the heavy rains set in, with orders to come back with a medicine man who could take the "bell" out of my head. By that time you could see the bell. It had swollen out on my jaw like a tumor. The boys came back with a surprise for us; not only the sorcerer but all the Akarina braves, to put on a dance for us. Ham had enticed them over with promise of a rice-and-tobacco banquet.

There were about fifteen men in the canoes, and when they set out for our side they must have been painted; but it was raining, and they arrived with their bodies in streaks of black and white pigment of which only a few polka dots, the original design, remained. In the rear of their belts were stuck the first sugarcane leaves we had seen, and down the front was a rather original loin apron, big bunches of tobacco leaves hanging the way they are hung to dry on the planta-tion. A few wore drenched feather headdresses, and there were one or two drums; but most of the men clutched bunches of leaves in their hands, instead of dance sticks. The journalists who write about the wild savages should have witnessed the dance that followed. The only space large enough for all of them was a sea of yellow mud in front of the veranda, and when those streaked-black-and-white brown men got hop-scotching around in that gumbo—you never saw such a mess. The Akarina, who are born with long faces, were becoming more dispirited by the minute because we who sat in comparative dryness up on the veranda could not control our hilarity. And the more we laughed the funnier they became, waving their arms and leaping about, all with an expression of deep despair on their faces.

The removal of the bell from my head was a much more interesting business. The sorcerer as usual looked the part, especially with his face streaked with soot and lime, and his big hanging lower lip gory with betel-nut juice. To our great satisfaction we discovered that the medium of our cure was to be *gamada*. This is a rare form of vice in the Coral Sea islands, though it is extensively used in Polynesia, where it is known as *kava*. According to our guidebook to the primrose path (a government paper given to us for other reasons), New Guinea use of the intoxicant is confined to western Papua where the shrub *Piper methysticum*, from whose leaves and rhizomes the concoction comes, was once especially culti-vated for ceremonial use. But in recent years, the missionaries claimed, the natives had dispensed with the ceremony and were indulging in the drug for its own virtues—and to such excess that finally a law was passed (without His Excellency's entire approval), prohibiting its use. Now there was a penalty for even cultivating the herb, and patrol officers were instructed to destroy any wild specimens they ran across. There was a nice clear illustration of the leaves, from which we identified those the sorcerer took out of his sack. "Gamada?" we asked the sorcerer brightly, at which he did something so characteristic of medicine men the world over when a patient is getting warm on the identity of his hocus-pocus that though we could not laugh then we have many times since. He regarded me with a cold eye for a minute, and then ignored the question, busying himself with his potion brewing. He had cut off a section of root, and after removing his quid of betel nut he put the root into his mouth and was busily chewing on it while he made a sandwich of the light green leaves by placing them flat inside a folded larger leaf. When this was finished he spat a stream of mustard-colored liquid into the sandwich, took the mangled root out of his mouth and extended it to me, indicating that I was to put it in my mouth, at the location of the bell.

This juncture is probably where I missed out on a permanent cure, for the well sterilized root I softened up for myself certainly lacked enchanting flavor. It was some minutes before I got any reaction, and then I began to foam at the mouth with something like soap suds. The sensation was astringent, then burning, and finally sickening, the taste indefinitely nasturtium and sweetish. Following instructions I swallowed the flood of secretion with the impression that I was drinking mustard-colored dishwater. When some of the leaves, also well sterilized, were added to the quid we took a color test, and found I was manufacturing a rather unwholesome olive-green froth. So far there was no sensation but the burning peppery taste.

When finally the secretions were quite brown in color, the sorcerer had ready the "nest" which was to receive the bad fella spirit in my cheek. The foundation of this was a flat, almost round stone, chockful of magic. It had been heated

. . . over Madiri's primus stove, for the sorcerer did not have a proper bed of embers . . . and was laid on the floor with the sandwich of leaves placed over it, and my swollen cheek on top of the leaves. I now had my fourth quid of root inside my mouth.

For some time nothing happened. Though I thought I could smell scorched hair and flesh, and I could naturally feel some warmth, yet it was not excessive, and there was no smoke. The sorcerer just sat with the bags under his eyes and lower lip hanging, testing from time to time the relay rock that was heating on the rack over the primus stove. When that stone was hot enough it was exchanged for the one under my head. And so the treatment went.

"The alcoholic extract of *Piper methysticum* leaves," I remember Margaret reading, "when evaporated is as active in inducing local anesthesia as cocaine, weight for weight." Margaret examined me curiously. "How do you feel?" I turned my eyes at her and wagged them. They were out on the ends of flexible stems, and it was easy. "Like absinthe, it attacks the sensory fibers and motor nerves, which produces a leaden feeling in the limbs and an inability to move them." This was not so in my case. I felt stimulated, as if I should be able to shake my very skin like a horse. But, Margaret read, "It affects habitual drinkers more quickly than novices. The aftermath varies with the temperament of the drinker, but oftenest there is an irresistible desire to sleep. There is profuse and offensive perspiration, weariness and pins and needles in the hands and legs, with a notable loss of control over the limbs. . . . In time the appetite for food goes, resulting in emaciation. Excess produces inflamed eyes and a leathery skin blotched by large scales which fall off, leaving unpigmented spots that become ulcers. Before the discovery of synthetic substitutes the Germans used the drug to induce sleep and dry up secretions. As it is a cumulative poison the habitual user eventually sinks into an unwholesome lethargy with mental faculties so dulled he is unable to carry on his part in communal life." Margaret looked at me a little anxiously. "How do you feel now?" "Not even pins and needles yet," I think I said. "It feels fine. I can't feel at all." But I remember thinking something. It was as interesting as a dream that these reputedly "bestial savages," the Papuans, had been in possession of this narcotic and had known its effects for probably many generations, yet had not used it for any but ceremonial purposes until lately.

Somewhere along here I found myself sitting up, and the sorcerer had put a slender stick in my hand, the end of which had a wisp of smoke curling up from it. As quickly as I could move, following Beremiki's translated instruction, I got the gamada quid out of my mouth, located the wisdom tooth and shoved the hot tip of the stick up into the cavity. The fumes of frying nerves came out of my nose like a dragon's breath, but it didn't hurt much. Not any more than having a tooth pulled with novocain. The second day following, when normal sensation began to return to my head, we found the bell had departed.

But it was only temporary (I continued in my letter). Now I keep a supply of gamada root in my pocket, like an old witch, and at the slightest twinge tuck a quid into my tooth. One thing it has succeeded in doing is to banish any desire for cigarettes—which is lucky, there being none. At this minute Margaret and Yorick sit across the table from me, frenziedly trying to shred the un-shreddable trade tobacco and make it stay inside rolls of oven-dried newspaper. The seven Castles we found Christmas Eve were cut up into thirds, and each of us was rationed out a third after dinner daily for five days. All the stubs had been collected from all over the house and store, and we even found some out in the rubber shed that the boys had missed, and these were pooled, re-rolled in toilet paper, and smoked in bamboo holders just in case the tobacco was not as pure as it once had been. It does seem that we should establish cigarette smoking as a ceremonial in the way the primitive used gamada, or the

missionaries should do a little missionary work at home and have a law passed, for a man denied his smoke is a pitiful thing to see.

While the rest of us slave away Hamlet is entertaining us with the thin slipping notes of a flute. He is breaking our hearts. A few minutes ago a large praying mantis plopped down on the table near one of the candles. (We are saving lamp fuel for dinner time, just to be sure we don't run out.) The mantis stood for a minute like a centaur, the upright front body with the arms and three-cornered head turning this way and that to examine us, while the four-legged rear body remained stationary. Finally it located the source of the shrill sound, stared indignantly with its head on one side for a minute, then gave Hamlet a "Bronx cheer," rolling out a long spiral tongue and letting it snap back. Ham changed his tootling from a hymn to a hula-hula in time to the mantis's side-to-side swaying. The insect continued sashaying back and forth, posturing with "her" arms and tipping her head coquettishly. In a few minutes she got bored with this, gave Yorick's boxing finger a few rounds, rejected a dead insect that Margaret offered, and then herself discovered the still kicking ones in the candle saucer. She seized one of these in her saw-bladed arms, and was devouring it with the tiny mouth at the lower corner of her triangle head, when the candle caught her eye. Still with her mouth full she reached out and grabbed at the flame. "Ouch!" It took a minute to realize that that was a human voice. When I glanced up the faces around the table all peering at the little mantis looked the size of the giant face of the puppet master when he pops his head out after the performance. Even our thought-dimensions are reduced to the size of a grasshopper. This experience might make a Christian of me. We've read the *London Illustrated News* back to 1915 and are now on the Bib . . .

At this point the letter broke off. Ham and Yorick had suddenly bounded out of their chairs and grabbing the flashlight banged out of the dining room, down the steps, and tore away through the mud as if there were a raid alarm. Beremiki followed, trying to light the lantern as he ran; and Emp, making croaking sounds, jumped off the edge of the veranda into the dark without bothering with the steps. The labor quarters were singing out. Margaret picked up the newspapers on the table with Yorick's pile of laboriously made cigarettes, and threw them toward the roof. "Sail-o-o!" she whooped, echoing the chant from the labor quarters, "the Thursday Island boat. We'll sail away da-da da-da!"

Only it was not the relief boat, not the T.I. relief anyway. It was the *Vanapa*, one hundred ton burden auxiliary ketch engaged by the American sugarcane collectors to carry supplies to their proposed base camp at Everill Junction. Everill

Junction is the intersection of the Fly and Strickland River, about two hundred miles inland. And one bit of cargo not in the contract but delivered to the base was two rapturous American headhunters.

30

In an article that appeared in one of our glossier publications about the American venture in New Guinea sugarcane collecting, the staff of our expedition was referred to by the staff of the other as "stowaways" who had "wheedled" the trip up the Fly River from the captain of the *Vanapa*. We could smile this aside privately as mere scientific Puckishness, except that it serves to bring out into the air a point that may have been mystifying some readers. Just how much wheedling and chiseling, gold digging or apple-polishing does it take to hoist oneself around the world on his own petard? The answer is this: The means of getting something for nothing is the same abroad as it is at home; sincerely expect to pay for it. And it usually costs less to pay in advance, the way the natives do. For the generosity of mankind is such that though he will give any amount of help voluntarily he is rigidly opposed to relinquishing that which he suspects is being slyly pried out of him. And he often resents being openly asked for anything, because he may not be able to give it—and to be asked gives him the choice of appearing ungenerous or giving unwillingly. If we had a racket it was in this savvy. There is also something else, however, which we realize was an asset to us. Having a job to do has the same effect on spectators that an excavating shovel has. Bypassers pause to watch all that energy digging away, a few stay to see what is being done; and should the shovel break down or strike hardpan, there is plenty of advice and usually some good fellow willing to give the operator a hand. A mere wayfarer wandering through the world only to absorb can be as negative as a stalled dynamo.

The scientists of the sugarcane expedition were not on board the *Vanapa*. They were flying up from Port Moresby when camp had been established at Everill Junction. There were three white men who came up to the house from the boat that night. One was the captain of the vessel, sandy-colored and square, with arms and neck like a hairy oak; he had once known a girl named Ruby in San Francisco who had liked strahb'reys and cream for breakfast. And there was the "Gallant Commissary," the local men who had charge of supplies and camp organization. He had even been born in San Francisco, but there was no trace of it left in his speech, and the years in New Guinea had even made him look like the malaria-hounded Britisher. The third man looked like a large-sized Boy Scout. He was the government escort of the expedition, but not just any patrol officer. This was the Buffalo Bill of the Service, Ivan Champion, who with Officer C. H. Karius had accomplished that history-making first central transverse of the island.* And it was Officer Champion, the "Government," who brought us our Port Moresby accumulation of mail just as if he had expected to find us at Madiri. Then promptly following our introduction he had extended the invitation to join the *Vanapa*. It was the fastest wheedling on record. For a minute later Margaret and I had staggered out onto the dark veranda and were leaning on one another like an A, dazed to find ourselves going up into country that not even many white men have visited.

For stowaways we occupied a lofty position on the *Vanapa* when she got under way shortly after dawn next morning. There were two cabins on the vessel, one on each side of the companionway that housed the engine; but anyone who has gone to sea with both an oil burning engine and a weak

* "Across New Guinea from the Fly to the Sepik," by Ivan F. Champion.

stomach will know why we chose the roof of the cabins for our quarters when we were given a choice. There was air up there if nothing else, when we first saw it. But by mid-morning our hosts with the aid of about thirty natives—police boys, carriers and crew—had rigged up a camp on the roof with all the comforts that the United States Department of Agriculture could provide. There was an ample tent, and a wide ledge had been left in front of it for a veranda with a fly to shelter the natty deck chairs. It gave us a penthouse view of the river in all seasons. There was a table to lean our elbows on, and a trim little gramophone with a crate of shining records right out of a Washington store, and a whole box of sharp, unrusted needles. But the Commissary's best rabbit was a tin of real cigarettes. The Government's was some toothache wax with ether in it, which eventually succeeded in finishing up the sorcerer's work of killing the nerve in my tooth. Then the Captain brought out some old banjo strings, with which Margaret replaced the patched and frayed gut strings on her ukulele; and with that our last mortal need was taken care of.

It rained all of that first day, and except for the smoothness of the water we might have been in mid-ocean. The river was still about five miles wide, and neither bank could be seen, for we kept in midstream. But we were all snug under a big sail awning rigged across the wide beamed deck amidships. While I made drawings of the boys . . . there were both Melanesians and Papuans from all through the Possession . . . Margaret's ukulele provided the accompaniment for a quin-tette. We sang all of that wet day through and when twilight came and the *Vanapa* pulled in toward the left bank and anchored for the night we kept on singing, we were so pleased with ourselves. Sun-downers came up, served with relishes, cheese, olives, pickles, delicious tastes when we had almost forgotten that there was such a thing as flavor.

In a surge of gratitude we impartially toasted the American taxpayer and Papua's Lieutenant-Governor, whom we privately thought responsible for our being on the *Vanapa*. Finally, dinner over, we resumed our chorus while the boys sat in a quiet row along the rails listening, only the orange highlights on their skin making them visible against the black night behind them. This was their own idea of a Papuan Night's entertainment. And by and by out of the dark came a dozen or more village men from some nearby rain-hidden settlement. They tied up their canoes on a rope thrown them from the vessel, and the captain let them come aboard, so that we could sketch them. They were not different in type from the Papuans further down the river, but we were new to them and their childlike expressions of wonder at all they saw, and the expression of superiority with which our savvy boys regarded their wonderment was something which proves conclusively that no matter how far down the culture ladder you go you still have your tourists and rubes.

There is something mystically satisfying about a quiet vessel at anchor when finally all on board have settled down to sleep, some kind of agreement of purpose that is lacking in the day's activities. Especially when you are far distant from others of your kind, and all that is familiar is confined to this deck. Then as the last lantern goes out and silence falls, you stretch out full length with an unfamiliar feeling of security and Margaret whispers across from her hard damp cot, "Isn't luxury ni-ace!"

The second day aboard the *Vanapa* dawned, like every one thereafter, with a timber-shivering explosion of language underneath our deck. Something on a Diesel engine has to be heated to get the oil flowing into the engine, and for this step the Captain used a selection of seagoing terms that had taken him thirty years of sailing to acquire. The engine boy had exactly the same vocabulary, though without knowing what the words meant, and he used the same accent and tone as the Captain. But even relaying it took them half an hour to get the vessel under way. When we descended to breakfast from our penthouse, which would still be swaying from the blast, the Captain would say in his Oxford Gaelic, "I do hope you didn't hear us getting that engine started this morning." Then for breakfast we were given the nearest thing the *Vanapa* could provide to what Ruby had liked: fresh orange juice, real coffee without chicory in it, and *pancakes* with *maple* syrup. Frequently about halfway down through the second stack, we would remember a conversation that had come up through the floorboards of our house in Port Moresby. The boys were talking about the food of their villages and what and how much they were going to eat when they got home again. "Yes," said one boy in Motu, "we shall eat-eat-eat, until we vomit. Then we can eat again."

The rain stopped in the morning of that second day, and the stream narrowed so that we could see both shores. They were an unbroken façade of high foliage, mile on mile. On the barren treetops choked dead by the parasite climbers below, thousands of fruit bats hung head down, looking like a never-ending colony of wrens' nests. We were provided with two sporty light rifles and a stack of boxes of cartridges, and spent the long lovely hours with our elbows balanced on the table making the flying fox miserable. One would think a serious expedition would have something better to do than wake up bats; but we didn't.

By and by we began to pass stretches of sugar cane growing out of the water in front of the trees, and now and then there was a mud flat dotted with targets of snow-white or gray cranes. The Government climbed up to our deck and for a while sat watching our misses, then he asked casually, "I suppose you know what you'll get if you hit one of those birds." Yes, we said brightly, a feather for our cap and fresh meat for the boys. The natives were lined up along the rail watching, and every time we missed—which was every time we fired (throb of the engine)—a soughing of deep Papuan disgust wafted up to us. "No," said the Government, "no aigrette; a year in jail *and* a hundred pounds fine." "How

much for a bird of paradise?" "You'd hang for that," he said, "and we cut off your fingers at the second joint if you're even caught with the feathers in your possession, no matter how you got them." This was because the natives were still allowed to kill the birds for their own use, and so long as Europeans could have the plumes in their possession without a penalty the natives killed to sell the plumes, then the birds were still in danger of becoming extinct.

New Guinea has the distinction of being the only habitat of these flamboyant crows, the *Paradiseidae*, and we soon found that we were more certain of staying out of jail if we did not shoot at any birds. Because there are about a hundred varieties of bird of paradise, and only a few of the males might be recognized from the plumes on Queen Mary's hats. However, if you suspected two birds and one of them did a dance for the other, finishing it by hanging upside down, displaying what plumage it had, this would be a bird-of-paradise courtship. Something we weren't likely to run across to help us, for bird stalkers spend their lives hoping to see the dance and only a few have been able to report on it. Almost all the birds seen were protected, a goura pigeon whose smoke-blue crest was also once a millinery must, and aigrettes that looked like simple white or gray cranes standing in the marshy spots along the shore. However, we soon started the run through the Fairfax, or D'Albertis, Islands and on their mud banks were scores of responsive crocodiles to which no penalty for shooting was attached.

One of the unique features of navigation in the Middle Fly is that it is achieved almost entirely by feel. There are no detailed charts, and no dependable channels to chart. The depths, and even the islands, change from one season to the next in the contest between ocean tide and river current. Keeping off the bars hidden by the opaque water engages several persons besides the wheel boy, among whom is one who can read the ripples on the river surface and decide which is caused by the deepest current. This became a problem when we reached the narrow waterways through the string of islands. Then a boy was stationed up in the forward shrouds to watch far ahead and signal the direction down to the wheelhouse. Two other boys, one on each side of the bow, continuously threw ahead sounding leads and droned the fathom lengths marked on the lines. Slowly, cautiously, in an acutely serpentine course, we pushed on against a powerful current. The ceiling was still low but the light was glaring, indicating that the clouds were thin. We hoped for clear weather.

By noon we had left the islands behind and seemed to have clear going ahead. The tide was running in, and we gained speed. "By-de-mark t'ree," chanted Hayfoot. "Quatah-less t'ree," droned Strawfoot. "By-de-mark *two!*" It was snapped out, and there was a sudden commotion. A twelve-foot bottom; and the *Vanapa* drew eight. The engine was cut down, but too late. Before we could get into reverse our nose was in the mud. There was not enough current in either direction to help us off. Again, a wait for the flood tide.

The north bank was nearer, and we headed for this in the dinghy. Rowing was a police boy, and in the boat with us were two of the crew. The boys had obtained permission to go ashore to shoot "pigeons" until the water rose enough to float the *Vanapa*, and Margaret and I were along just as tourists. The police boy had his service rifle, and when we set out the two other boys were carrying our expedition rifles . . . just in case someone shot a five-hundred-dollar pigeon. The first bag was therefore a flying fox. As we neared shore a shot sent up a cloud of the hanging bats overhead, and against the glare of the sky they became transparent, the body and skeleton of the long arms clearly outlined in the thin webbing of the wings. Before they settled four or five of the animals were brought down, but they fell into the river and only one was swept near enough before it sank to be grabbed. It had a wing spread of over two feet and was truly an animal, covered with reddish fur and with a head like a little bear. It would not have been in the least repulsive if it had not been crawling with vermin and had such a musty personal stench, features that did not in the least dull the boys' appetite later when they ate it. It should have been tasty meat, for the bats live on fruit.

There was no open place along the shore where we could land, and we were hauled up a ten foot mud bank under the overhanging foliage. Then we were in the dense jungle wall of bushes growing up, vines hanging down and hurdles of aerial roots and mammoth leaves. For some distance we crouched along behind the natives who whacked out a tunnel with their machetes. Finally the undergrowth got lower and then we could see up to the lofty roof of tree foliage. The first shot there brought down an enormous goura pigeon. It was as big as a Thanksgiving turkey and had a superb crown of filmy feathers the blue-gray of cigarette smoke and the shape of a fan. The boys were again delighted with the prospect of fresh meat, but for us it was a moral crisis. Here was a taboo bird already dead whose crest would be burned off with the rest of its beautiful plumage as a preliminary to roasting; and yet we, being Europeans, could be penalized for preventing the destruction of those feathers. Did our status as an expedition collecting *materiae artisticae Papuae* permit us to salt those feathers away in the camera case? and return to the *Vanapa* with a bald-headed goura?

This matter being satisfactorily settled, the hunt was suddenly off. We were sped shoreward by one of New Guinea's lurking curses, leeches. One of the peculiarities of an attack of leeches is that you do not feel them until they have surfeited themselves, and the first warning was when one of the boys suddenly gave vent to a New Guinea oath (which sounded like ee-*yah*), and by that time everyone discovered his legs and even between the toes encrusted with the minute dragons. Margaret and I were in our usual armor against the mosquitoes, riding breeches and boots, and despite the legend that a leech can get through a zipper these garments saved our nether parts. However, we trapped one leech undamaged, just as it was getting its teeth into my neck; and Margaret folded it securely inside her handkerchief and put it in her pocket to examine later. It was thin as a string, about half an inch long and the color of half-green wood, perfectly camouflaged for its habitat. It behaved like a measuring worm, raising the fore part of its body and moving it around as if feeling for a pore.

We had another encounter before reaching the river, and if the reader does not believe this he at least has the company of everyone in Papua to whom we told it. Even the Government, who had some fantastic tales himself, listened with a cocked eyebrow. We encountered a "prehistoric monster."

And the only reason I am sure *I* saw it is because the others did too, though our impressions were suspiciously varied. The police boy was in the lead, following the path that had been sliced out on the way in, and I was close on his heels to keep from having the branches he pushed aside snap back in my face. My thoughts were quietly on leeches, and my eyes were glued earthward on the lookout for snakes. Though the earth could not be seen because of the undergrowth. Suddenly, with an exclamation, the police boy backed into me. As he whirled and pushed me I just had time to glimpse an enormous flat head, exactly like a snake's but big as a crocodile's. It was waist-high in the undergrowth, too high for a saurian. The mouth was open, hissing, and there were many teeth and a long forked tongue. The front of the neck, all that was visible of its body, was like a huge goiter and the mud-gray hide had the texture of small-plate jazerant armor. That was all *I* saw. The others behind us, as we in front mowed them

down in our retreat, each got his glimpse of the fabulous crea-
ture and added a two cents' worth to my conservative impression. One of the boys saw eyes, red like a ship's lantern,
and another saw a "hood" around the animal's face. The police
boy claimed he had seen its feet, and there were as many toes

as a man has, each with a great curved claw on it. "Toenail
all-a same cassowary!" he insisted excitedly. The huge claws
on a cassowary's feet can disembowel a man, so there was
meaning to that simile.

For a long time the identity of this monster remained a mystery, not only because there is no record of a New Guinea
land animal larger than a wild boar, but also because tales of
strange animals seen in the bush are so commonplace that no
one takes them seriously. Captain Monckton in his book,
"Some Experiences of a New Guinea Resident Magistrate,"
describes such a beastie as "five feet long, three feet six inches
high, has a tail like a horse and cloven feet, black or dark
skin with patternlike markings, a long snout, and calls with a
shrill note." That could be a New Guinea mosquito. But we
are now convinced that the animal we encountered was a

giant monitor, perhaps the same as the *Varanus komodoensis* which inhabits one of the nearby islands of the East Indies. This great lizard of ancient lineage and dreadful reputation was supposed to have become extinct centuries ago—until the tribe on Komodo was identified. Living specimens have been found there that measured ten and twelve feet long, including the tail. "The animal," our source of information states, "is fearless and extremely vicious and moves with great speed, so he is a dangerous fellow to meet in the wild state." Perhaps what saved us is that the monitor likes his meat already dead and prefers it decayed, when he "rends it voraciously with saw-edged teeth," doing fierce battle with any contenders for the carcass. The dragons also hiss nastily at one another and stick out long forked tongues. It puzzles us, what with the reptile's reputed keen sense of smell and sight, that at the moment of our mutual surprise he was facing us and had come up our path that must have been heavy with scent. It is not so surprising that he had not heard us, for the animal is said to be too deaf to hear even the discharge of a gun. But to have missed the wind of three Papuans shows even less than normal olfactories. There are two possible explanations: that he had no reason to fear humans, or that he was deliberately following the prey. But at sight of us he had not charged, speedily or otherwise. There is a good explanation for this. We had probably frightened him, and when a *Varanus komodoensis* is badly frightened he becomes nauseated. *I* could understand that.

Back on the *Vanapa* shock followed shock. Margaret discovered, with greater horror than the dragon had produced, that the leech she had brought back to examine had got out of her pants pocket and by a circuitous route into her pants. And all the time it had been contentedly slaking its thirst without her having felt anything. Her breeches were tight, and when she sat down it had squashed the leech, which re-

leased a stream that made Margaret look as if her leg were
bleeding to death. We were both in the shower stall conducting an exchange search for other unannounced leeches when
we heard a roar outside. It was a distant rumble like the sound
of an approaching airplane. We assumed it was the expedition plane, and were not much surprised when shouts started
up on deck. Then there was a great paddling of bare feet as
the natives raced about, making things fast, we soon discovered. The volume of sound grew until we looked out of the
port. But there was nothing in that quarter of the sky. The
roar was water. Around a bend in the river, some distance
below us and extending from bank to bank, came a wall of
water. It was easily ten feet high, a regular tidal wave and
making the sound of one.

Tidal bores along with waterspouts and northern lights and
fireballs are one of the irregularities of Nature that we could
easily get superstitious about. We had plenty of time to observe this one. The shelf of tide behind the big advancing
breaker had a surface five or six feet higher than the water
ahead of it, and it came on with the leisurely dream pace of
the Red Sea rolling back into place after its miracle. The river
above it was glassy smooth, and behind the vanguard surf was
a succession of low following combers keeping an even pace
and distance. It was like an ocean moving forward intact, not
rolling over but sliding ahead. A huge tree that had been
drifting downstream near the shore was lifted like a matchstick
and shoved up into the vegetation on the bank. We were wondering what would happen when the sea struck the stern of
the *Vanapa* with her nose in the mud, and envisioned our tent
and contents going up in the air like the tail of a bronco. We
were spread around as if we had been living on a houseboat.
Then the surprising thing happened; the bore died in its
tracks. The great wall of foam tumbled forward like a regular beach breaker, and simultaneously the following lines of

surf melted away. The bore had struck the lower end of the sand bar on which we were aground. But the tide rose so quickly then that the *Vanapa* was off the mud while we were still staring at the spot where the bore had vanished.

Two conditions are necessary to produce a tidal bore, one of them being a tide, naturally, and the other a funnel-shaped waterway. The Gulf of Papua is a huge bottleneck for the tides which forces them to run up the rivers, and the Fly with its wide open mouth at the far west end of the Gulf gets the full force of the volume of water that piles up twice a day. Serpentine as the river is and strong the down-current, the regular tides run inland over a hundred miles. Even at Everill Junction, the captain noted a regular rise and fall of two feet. And we were having a spring tide following the full moon, when the water rises three times as high as "normal."

The bore in Papua's rivers is the one thing for which even the imperturbable Service Officer admits a healthy respect. For while one may save his own skin in an encounter, there is no way—except being tied up to the bank—of preventing one's craft foundering with, naturally, a loss of supplies which is almost always serious. The river natives are well acquainted with the roar, and usually manage to get their canoes hauled or tied up and themselves on shore. But after we had seen a bore we wondered how even eighteen of the Suki cannibals had managed to escape . . . unless it was our San Luca holding them over to pose for us.

Someone was taking good care of the expedition.

All of the two hundred miles to Everill Junction we saw only one native settlement on the river. This was Weriadai, which was supposed to have been wiped out by the Suki, and here we stopped to buy canoes for the expedition. Obviously many of the inhabitants had saved their lives by the old Papuan strategy of taking to the bush, for on the beach alone there were at least half a hundred natives, men and boys, and back in the clearing was a new longhouse replacing the one that had been burned.

As the *Vanapa* ran in toward shore the beach was an exciting scene. Now we could see the source of the screaming that had frightened us off from Tirio, the hamlet of sorcerers down the river. A large pack of little yellow dogs lined the shore, giving vent to the kind of warbling howl tortured women and children would make. Added to the din were the shouts of scores of dark men and youth tearing up and down the beach. We, being tourists, assumed this was a Fly River welcome, but there seems to have been some question about it. The natives should have got into their canoes and come out to the ship, that being the custom when a village is friendly and familiar, as this one was, with white men. There was a long wait on board during which the men went into a huddle. Then finally the whaleboat was put over, all the police boys got into it (carrying their rifles) and we, not knowing that the Weriadai were upset, lined up with camera and sketching materials at the top of the ladder behind the Government. He was shouting "sambio, sambio" toward the hopping figures on shore. No one seems to know what "sambio" means literally, but it is a greeting of friends and seems to be a declaration of peaceful intentions. Apparently, however, the Weriadai did not believe this, for they continued racing back and forth along the shore while we, all but the Government, waited in silence. He continued to call out, and gradually the figures on the beach converged into a loose group. Then presently a single canoe was hauled down to the water, and two men got into it and pushed out. That instant the Government dropped down into the whaleboat, and they shoved off. When the two crafts met there was one of those Atlantic Charter conferences, very brief; and we saw tobacco changing hands. Then the whaleboat continued to shore, and the canoe came on out.

In the excitement that followed no one noticed what we two were doing. The minute the police party landed they were swallowed up in the noisy crowd and the whaleboat came straight out to the *Vanapa*. Again we lined up at the head of the ladder, this time behind the Commissary, and again he and his expedition boys got off without us. Everyone seemed to be in a powerful hurry. The Captain had remained on board, and was aft at the engine. And we noticed, without thinking very much about it, that the engine was idling. We were at last on our way down the ladder, waving the Weriadai canoe to the bottom of it with sticks of tobacco. The nearest man took the tobacco, let us get down onto the flat shell and then, obediently following our motions, started paddling for shore. When we reached the wide strip of deep mud the men got out into it, but we remained seated, indicating to them that they were to haul us up to dryer land, which they did. But the minute we rose together to step out of the canoe, there was sudden confusion. Margaret said afterward that she had heard a sound like cracking wood, anyway the two men began the wildest jabbering and flaying of arms. We got out of the canoe and away from them in a hurry.

Our little puddle of excitement did not attract any attention in the general bedlam. We could see the barrels of a few of the police boys' rifles sticking up above the heads of the milling natives in one spot, but there was no one we knew on the outskirts of the crowd and we headed back toward the longhouse on some business of our own. It was an enormous building on the lines of the abandoned one we had seen at the mouth of the river, and it appeared to be deserted. The only opening was a kind of Dutch door or window about three feet above a little landing which had a notched log ladder leading up from the ground to it. The opening showed a pitch-black interior, but as we approached we caught the flash of figures disappearing back into the gloom. We women recognized even that little as other women. "You know," said Margaret slowly, "I don't remember seeing *any* women in that crowd on the beach. Isn't that a sign of something? that there'll be a late spring? or a dark man will come into your life?" But neither did we remember seeing any weapons among the men—though even at that minute it sounded like a massacre on the beach—so we proceeded up the ladder to the entrance of the longhouse.

The reader will now return to the shore, leaving us standing before that aperture, perfect targets for anyone inside who wanted to throw a spear, holding sticks of tobacco aloft and calling "sambio" to the black interior. We wanted to get a sketch, or at least some photographs of these Middle Fly women whom the Suki had not eaten.

The explanation behind the Weriadai's reluctance to come out to the *Vanapa* was that she was the first "white" vessel to have come along since the abduction of the Suki cannibals. And these things get around. The men may have had their doubts that the white man meant "sambio" when he called it. And though the captured Suki were no friends of the Weriadai, the latter could have thought that the government made no distinction between the tribesmen it shanghaied. Anything but killing is not a retaliation in the Papuan mind. In any case something had gone wrong at Weriadai, the Government was aware of it, and he was proceeding with caution until the villagers were convinced that we were there on a peaceful mission. The racket on the beach was at first the excitement of suspicious men, then presents of tobacco were distributed and the commotion that followed was simply the bargaining over the canoes. The canoes are owned by several men, the owners had to be identified, and the agreement to sell and price had to be unanimous in order to avoid trouble. Avoiding trouble was the Government's specialty and they had been getting along nicely, making only happy racket, when our two outraged ferrymen managed to get through the crowd and report to the interpreters that we had done something dreadful to their canoe; we had split the bottom when we stood up to step out of it on solid ground. Then the Weriadai were upset all over again, not to mention the Government; for he had not known we were on shore. And by this time we had vanished.

Returning now to the entrance of the longhouse: at first there was no response to our overtures. But we had learned patience if not caution in this island venture. The women were there, and to bring them out into the light two things were necessary: first, to assure them that we were not white men; and then, to make them inquisitive enough to act on that confidence. We began by doing things we knew to be useless, just out of habit. Since we were trying to be pleasing and attractive, we could not resist smiling broadly. Whereas the native himself does not smile or laugh unless there is a reasonable stimulus, something that delights or amuses him. If you laugh at other times it is construed as a jeer, and has the opposite effect from our social smirk. Then I took the pins out of my hair and let it down. That had worked once in a village where there was some doubt about our gender; but it was a savvy boy who then identified us, because he knew that white women had longer hair than their men. This clue to our gender was lost on the occupants of the longhouse because the reverse is true of them; even the maidens are shorn to the scalp.

By this time our eyes had become somewhat used to the interior gloom, and what we saw was not especially reassuring. Spooky light shapes not altogether human in outline and yet having the general assemblage of the human form, one larger mass with approximate arms, legs and head, were spotted around on the floor level some distance back. We might have thought them carved figures except that the approximate limbs reached out each time we tossed tobacco into the hall, and we could see the sharp highlights of eyes glittering in the heads. It occurred to us that we might have run into a clan of albino women.

For the next half hour or so we must have looked like a puppet show, from the interior. First I became very fascinating, flicking the cigarette lighter on and off, then I demonstrated the camera, clicking open the automatic finder and flashing the whole glittering business around. No effect. Margaret took my place on the window ledge and sang "Looking through the knothole in father's wooden leg"—which did not get the usual response. Every now and then we tossed in more tobacco, like the medicine man scattering samples to hold his audience, but nothing we did brought any action.

We finally had to admit ourselves beaten, and I climbed up on the window ledge to chalk a legend on the log lintel above, "Through These Portals Pass the Least Visible Girls in the World," and when I descended the occupants had gathered into the area of light from the entrance. And they did not scuttle. Nor were they albinos. They were women, and they were smeared with big irregular swaths of white clay all over their bodies. There were patches of black and patches of white; hair, nostrils and the crack of their mouths were still black, and the only garment they wore was a pubic bundle of grass such as Derivo wore. For a while they just stared at us with those polka dot eyes, and then an old crone in the front line began "swearing" at us, talking "strong." We extended some tobacco toward her and then, ever so casually with the appearance of reaching her, we stepped over the sill and were inside.

When the Government arrived with the Papuan army and a vociferously protesting crowd of tribesmen . . . the longhouse is taboo to strangers . . . we gals were all sitting chummily on the floor inside the longhouse, the clay-plastered

Weriadai matrons acquiring charm by smoking Old Golds and Margaret and I yodeling the Hawaiian "Piercing Wind." Which *can* sound as if someone were dying. This was all a preliminary to getting the women outside, where it was light enough to photograph them. At the sound of the ap-

proaching multitude they showed that they no longer had any fear of any of us. We all crowded to the window together, and while the Weriadai men yelped at their women the women yelped back defiance, waving their Old Golds.

From that moment the atmosphere in the settlement changed. The canoe transaction was quickly completed—three twenty-five foot canoes, including the one we had damaged, which was left behind, were paid for at one ax, thirty-six yards of red calico and twelve sticks of tobacco each. When we left all the Weriadai, including the women, children, dogs and pigs, collected in a line along the beach and jerked their arms after us singing out "Bamahuta, bamahuta!" This is an introduced Motuan farewell, "may you sleep." We climbed up the shrouds to wave our goodbyes, mostly because we wanted to put off meeting the Government until time had removed from his face that expression we had seen when we first looked out of the longhouse. It promised that we should be put in irons. But instead we were congratulated. We had "promoted friendly relations between the natives and the government." Those were the officer's own words; and he added, to prove it, that no Papuan woman had ever waved at *him*.

On such simple things are great empires builded.

31

One night the Government told us a story which he admitted he might have laughed at skeptically if he had heard it from someone else. To be mistaken for a "god" by primitives who have never before seen a white man is an old traveler's tale. But future travelers to Bolvip, high above the Fly River basin, in the Dap Range, will have some foundation for their yarn.

It was on the second of his two attempts to get across New Guinea that the Government came to Bolvip; and there, sure enough, the natives asked if he had come down out of the sky. He said he "thought it best to reply in the affirmative" in order to increase the prestige of any Europeans who might later come this way. To do this he pantomimed the manner of his arrival, which was to be "with outstretched wings and a roaring sound." At that time the Government could not have dreamed that one day not far off whole squadrons of white men with outstretched wings would be roaring over New Guinea, but he knew that there wouldn't be many white men going that way on foot. Airplanes were the only practical means of exploration in this difficult country, for the risks and tortures of travel on old-fashioned feet made penetration of the interior altogether "impractical." On his final, successful trip over the central range, he had encountered above the headwaters of the Fly River sheer limestone cliffs up whose surface it did not seem a fly could crawl. Yet he and his carriers and police had had to find a way up. Only to be faced by descents where the depths below were lost to sight in the haze of distance. And they had gone down. Up and down and up and down interminably, hungry, thirsting or drenched, frozen and injured and risking their lives as they entered each infrequent and frightened or antagonistic village. Again and again on the descent down the north watershed following the Sepik River they had found themselves in a cul de sac of the river gorge and had to retrace their tortuous steps climbing back out of it. Wearily they felled trees, built scores of bridges and rafts that were only demolished in the furious rapids and whirlpools. Each time they lost more of their men and stores and ammunition. Then into the dripping rain forests with their treacherous moss and leeches and mosquitoes and finally through the lower regions of stinking gora bugs and heat, to come out at long last on the northeast coast.

All this country we had been traveling through with our elbows on a table, and the five or six hundred vertical miles ahead beyond the Fly basin, was terrain that the Government had inched over, a good part of it literally with the help of his fingernails. But now, just as he had promised the Bolvip chief, he was returning with outstretched wings and a great roar. Officer Champion was flying northwest toward the heartbreaking country in the expedition plane. And so was I.

When we first heard the sound of the plane we all thought it was another tidal bore, and scampered about, hastily gathering up and tying down our scattered belongings. Then Margaret and I raced up the rigging, our favorite place for taking panorama pictures. So, in a manner of speaking, we were stowed away when finally "Sugar," the head of the expedition, and the pilot came on board. It turned out that they had "just dropped over" from Port Moresby to see how the *Vanapa* was getting along and to "take a run" up to the Junction to see if the Government's old camp was above water. They had to be back in Port Moresby for tea. It had taken us three days so far just from Madiri, and we had another day to go before we reached the Junction. The Government's face was a study when they mentioned that tea engagement. But when he found that he was to fly up to the camp with them he looked more than ever like a Boy Scout, one that has just been awarded the Eagle. And he did his scout deed for that day by wangling me into the extra seat in the plane.

We were just off the water, and already I could see that those towering trees along the banks of the river which had given us the impression that we were navigating through a jungle were a fake. They were only a wall lining the river. Beyond it were almost treeless plains, or what looked like plains from the air. Actually it was almost limitless swamp. Mile on mile the cane marshes stretched out all around and below us, winding yellow rivers snaking through them with here and there deep clear lakes and splayed lagoons so shallow that we could see their emerald floors. And all across the subtle green tones were scattered the blue patterns of the clouds of our stratum, the tiny speeding shadow of the plane losing and finding itself in the vast panorama. Above us was clean blue sky, and all was right with my world.

"Sugar cane!" bawled Sugar with a pleased smile as he stabbed downward at the opalescent greens. But I had my nose pressed to the glass, and with straining eyes was searching for my own kind of pay dirt, human beings. Just a tiny stick of a canoe that would humanize that dazzling earth below. But there was nothing, not a circular clearing in any dark clump of green that would indicate a settlement, nor the plain brown oblong of a longhouse, nor any wisp of blue smoke coming from some woman's cooking fire. There are stretches of country like this in our own land, miles and miles of forest-cloaked mountains or desert that from the air appear uninhabited; but in New Guinea it is actually un-

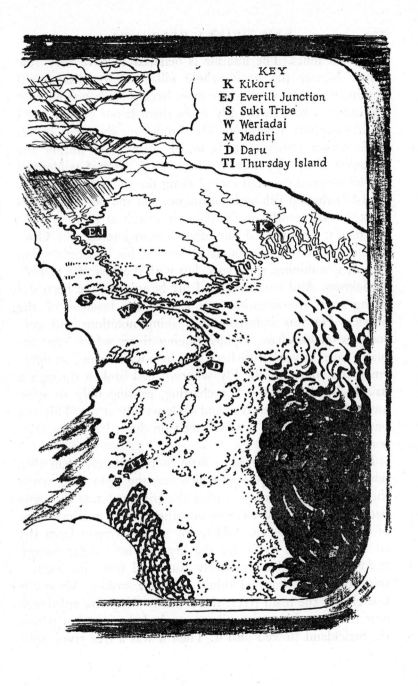

KEY

K Kikori
EJ Everill Junction
S Suki Tribe
W Weriadai
M Madiri
D Daru
TI Thursday Island

populated miles. The interior is believed to have very few tribes. Nearer the coast whole villages have disappeared within the memory of white men, having eaten one another up; but also here in the Fly basin there is not enough solid land to support a populous life throughout the year. In the rainy season much of it is under water, and during the droughts of the dry season it becomes a parched wilderness of yellow grass deserted except along the rivers by all except mud-hibernating fish and mosquitoes and the nomadic hunting tribes constantly on the move in search of food.

I finally remembered our other human interest, the Government, and turned around to look at his ecstatic shining face. It was shining, to be sure, but with the dew of a terrible seasickness. And any emotional lift he might have been deriving from the situation was lost to the business of the Service. He was industriously making notations and corrections on his chart, rapidly tracing rivers which may actually have "never before been seen by a white man," straightening the course of the Fly where it had broken through a hairpin bend since the last charting, pausing only to wipe away the dew of his travail and smile weakly at me. This was one of Sir Hubert's "outside" men on duty, long may they wave.

I have often wondered, a little more privately than this, what decided for explorers which was the main river when they came to a junction where the tributary was the same size as the river they were on and the distance to the source of each was unknown. And seeing a river system from the air did not solve it. So far the Fly had been a fat yellow snake that twisted convulsively back and forth on itself, a spine to which traveled other narrower snakes. Always it was clearly the main river; there was nothing else anywhere near the size of it—not until we reached the junction where the Strickland flowed into it. Then it was a tree trunk split into identical branches. In fact the Strickland continued in an almost straight course from the lower river, whereas the Fly made a sharp right angle to the west from the junction. Perhaps someday they will find that the Strickland is really the Fly and the Upper Fly the Strickland.

We circled over the camp at Everill Junction . . . six acres of clearing in the jungle on the bank of the river . . . and then zoomed down, almost shearing the barren tops of the tall trees. It sent up clouds of flying fox and in the rear of the compartment our stomachs rose up as one man and spoiled an otherwise great moment. The pilot prayed aloud as the day-blind bats circled and came back in our path. It would have been quite a bump had one hit the propeller. The clearing, over which were spread three large thatch-roofed barracks and some smaller buildings, was not only out of flood but gave evidence of having been drying out for some time. There were great fissures in the clay. We were apparently coming into another of New Guinea's seasons. Also the swamps of the Middle Fly seemed to have been left behind. The land all around the Junction was hidden by the solid green of the bush, and to my horticultural eye that meant solid earth for roots to grow in.

The survey was brief, and we were up and away, streaking northeast over the Strickland. About half a minute beyond the camp I sighted what I had been looking for, a narrow clearing on the right bank with little man-made blocks of huts. I bawled out that I wanted to drop down, but it was fish talk; no one heard me. Far in the distance to the north were silvery streaks of more water in the hazy blue green of forest. The government shoved his chart in my lap and pointed to the network of unfinished lines. "Lake Murray," I read. For a minute deep inside me was a hard core of hope that the pilot was heading for this big lake and meant to land. In our collection of pictures of race types there were a few

of the Papuans of Lake Murray. We had looked at them so
often that the faces, the expressions and poses were almost
as familiar as those of our friends. They needed only to be
articulated. I think the Government had the same hope, for
another reason. He had put a new roll of film in his camera,
and had his chart all spread out ready to finish some of the
hitherto unknown borders of the sprawling lake. Then Sugar
looked at his wrist watch. He tapped the pilot's shoulder,
showed him the watch, and the earth whirled beneath us, the
sun swinging to starboard. We soared up and up above the
bumpy stratum of clouds, following the river southward.
Taking Sugar back to tea. But the Government had his opportunity again later.

It was sunset when the *Vanapa* cautiously sidled in to the
camp clearing at Everill Junction and tied up fore and aft to
the bank. At that moment the deck and bank were exactly
level, and it was only necessary to put a plank across to
walk ashore. The clearing was not at the actual junction of
the rivers but a short way up the Strickland, where it flowed
due west. The water in that direction, ordinarily an opaque
gold with silvery highlights in full daylight, was now a wide
lane of crimson reflecting the sunset sky. There was a deso-
late sense of openness about the spot that had so far been
lacking in opulent western Papua and which had not been
observable from the air. A few trees had been left for shade
throughout the big clearing, but they were scrubby, and in
the jungle wall surrounding the area and that of the opposite
side of the river about a quarter of a mile away, there were
gaps and thin places in the foliage that suggested open country beyond. This was not the case, of course; I had seen
only wooded country from the air. The explanation was soon
apparent; we were surrounded by mangrove swamps. And
the tall scrubby trees that were not mangroves were drowning.

The minute we were tied up some of the realities of life in the interior of New Guinea descended on us. In swarms. I happened to be taking a shower at that historical moment, and I don't care who knows that it was the last total bath I took in that part of the world. All the mosquitoes from the swamps for miles around crowded into the shower stall with me, and from then on we were as intimate as the contents of an egg. And as darkness fell, instead of thinning out they increased. At dinner there were strangling smudge pots going under the table, boys fanning at our necks, and above board the air and our food were periodically sprayed with Buzzoff. Yet the "mozzies" were so dense we were slapping them in the parts of our hair, picking them out of our ears and even eating some. They rode into our mouths on the forkfuls of food. After dinner the captain sat with his massive arms folded over his chest, and counting his bared neck and face there was about a hectare of exposed skin outside of his shirt. Most of it was overgrown by a jungle of hair, and when the mosquitoes got down in this undergrowth and had swollen up with their fill, they couldn't take off. The captain just left them stumbling around in the impenetrable forest while others unaware of the trap swarmed in to their doom. Nothing is ever said about mosquitoes in these mosquito countries, any more than flies enter the conversation of our farmers, but it wasn't long before we were shouting our remarks at one another—even when it was only "pass the salt." For reasons which are now obscure we spent that night on shore in one of the huts. I think it was with some idea that by going somewhere else we would leave something behind, but there was no escape. We just added insomnia and sand flies to our other itches.

As night cooled a thin mist settled down on the river, hugging to the earth the miasmal steam and mangrove stench that was all around us. Soon the black recesses under the trees were glowing with fireflies and luminous fungus. Tree toads sang and frogs croaked, and the bats screeched and flapped around the clearing. Then a cold white moon rose in the lonely sky and the clammy air filled with cries of strange night birds and the dolorous and incessant cou-cou-cou of the mourning dove. In every eerie sound was the note of uninhabited distance. Near by, the guard, rifle on his shoulder, paced the bank on silent bare feet, the only mortal sound his frenzied slapping and scratching. And around our stretcher nets the demented "mozzies" never left off whining.

32

When the *Vanapa* finished loading, her business at Everill Junction would be done and she would return to the coast with her stowaways aboard. Before that time we had a lot of work to do. First of all we must make portrait drawings of our hosts when they could spare the time to sit. Then, with the hope that we might run across a lagoon with pink water lilies, we had brought along Tauparaupi's portrait so that he might have his proper background painted around him. In any case, lilies or not, the background had to be painted from this part of the country. Finally, we must somehow get to the native settlement I had seen from the air and get at least drawings and photographs, if not paintings, of the women. We now considered ourselves high-voltage charmers of Papuan women and anticipated no difficulty in inducing them to pose. But the Government presented a problem in transportation. He had just given us one of those Boy Scout smiles when we mentioned having noted the village, so it looked as if we might have to reach our models under our own steam.

Short of swimming there was no way of getting out of camp, for only a leech can go overland through mangrove swamps, the whaleboat was too much for us to pull against the heavy current, and we could not have boys to paddle the Weriadai canoes even if these salt-water boys had known how to handle the shallow dugouts. By mid-afternoon we had to face the fact that we were stymied indefinitely in camp unless some miracle moved us. And we resigned ourselves to jungle wall and sugar cane as a background for Taupa-raupi's portrait. That was the scene directly across the river from the clearing, so we brought out the big canvas, set up studio on the wheel deck astern, and started to paint with the racket of unloading clumping around behind our ears. And what should we presently see emerging from their cocoons among the expedition shipment but three portable canvas canoes. The commissary fitted one with an outboard motor, had a little gasoline put into the tank to try it, and then lowered it to the river and left it there unguarded while he and his boys moved back to the rear of the clearing to do their shouting and banging.

All that the canoe lacked was *enough* gasoline, for I judged the settlement to be about five miles up the river; and if the current were as stiff as it looked we would need plenty of fuel to be safe. But we could not find the drum from which the commissary had taken the gasoline, and it did not seem necessary to bother him to ask what he had done with it. Lined up along the bank alongside the *Vanapa* were one thousand drums containing ten thousand gallons of airplane gas. In the morning that gasoline, standing in the hot sun, had begun to boil, raising a fine din of bumping and gurgling even after water had been thrown over the tanks to cool them. Now they were sheltered under palm fronds, and all we needed was a can opener or a marlinspike. And in ten minutes we were off upstream, keeping close to the bank, five gallons of reserve gas on board, drawing materials, camera, and tobacco with which to charm savages.

Anyone who knows anything about automotive combustion knows how far an outboard motor will go on high-test gasoline. But we didn't. When finally Margaret thought the regular fuel might be running low, which was at a point about a mile and a half or two above camp, we pulled in along the bank and filled up with the airplane gas. And after a little fussing the motor started. But we had just reached midstream, crossing to get into quieter water . . . the heavy current swings from one bank to the other on the river bends . . . when the motor stalled. In an instant the keelless canoe was swept like a whirling leaf down the breast of the current to the opposite shore and straight into the overhanging branches of a tree. We both grabbed, caught them, and nearly had the light canvas boat swept out from under our feet. Which would have left us hanging out on the end of a limb in the interior of New Guinea. If the limb held. *That* put the fear of God into our defaulting hides.

For a good many miles up to this point we had been saying uncomplimentary things about the island launches that set out to sea with an ailing motor, often insufficient fuel and seldom any oars or paddles. But now we were getting our come-uppance. We too had failed to put paddles into the canoe. So for the next hour or so Margaret tinkered with things that had the impressive names of intake valve, adjustment screw and manifold, while I hung onto the bough with my head in the foliage thinking I was being devoured by leeches because I couldn't scratch. The sight of Margaret's ears below me were enough to make one itch. The rows of mosquitoes nibbling away at the rims were so big they looked like those tortoise-shell plugs the Solomon Island bushmen wear for ear decorations. Meantime there was not a murmur from the outboard motor.

We finally decided to inch our way downstream from bough to bough. This was after we had made one hair-raising attempt to float home and this time keep the prow forward with the rudder. But the current was too swift for the flat-bottom canvas boat . . . it had been imported for use in the quiet lagoons . . . and before we could get our weights adjusted to give both the prow and rudder leverage, we had been swept, luckily, into the bushes again. However, we were getting along well enough, braking our speed by holding onto branches until we came to the first stretch of cane along the shore. Here there was a backwash or whirlpool in the river, and the current was coming upstream toward us. For a minute we were stymied. And during that minute, while we rested under the boughs of the last tree debating the matter, we heard something that made our eyeballs pop. It was native voices coming from upstream.

If we have ever heard a party of men out for a lark, these voices had that note in them. Almost immediately four long flat-bottom canoes shot into view around the bend above us. There were at least twenty-five or thirty natives standing in the canoes, using their long-handled paddles to keep the dugouts guided along the breast of the current. They shot by us so quickly that after they had passed all we remembered about them were their huge white loin shells, like bull's-eyes, and the excited chatter. "They look like a lot of young fellows out for no good reason," was Margaret's reserved comment.

We waited a while to be sure no more canoes were coming . . . for somehow the idea of meeting strange natives this way, with a dead motor and a cargo that might be regarded as good loot, was not particularly appealing . . . and then began painstakingly pulling ourselves ahead by the cane. The stalks were rough and the leaves stiff and sharp-edged, and the girls were suffering, but we finally got past the canebrake, back into the branches, waded around a mud flat that had the imprints of crocodiles on it, picked up a piece of driftwood with which we poled into quieter water, back into the bushes and mosquitoes, more cane, a bad stretch where the high bank was washed away and there were no boughs hanging over—where we had to let go and pray—then more flat mud, and home. No one had missed us.

The men were just coming on board the *Vanapa* for tea,

and the first thing we asked was why in the name of something they had not stopped and held for us the canoes of natives that had gone down the river ahead of us. They stared at us for a minute, and then the captain and the commissary laughed. No one had seen any natives! not even the guards. But the Government did not laugh nor even pause to question us; he sent a police boy up the shrouds, who immediately began wagging a piece of red calico and bawling "sambio." The natives were at that minute hiding under the overhanging foliage up at the bend of the river. Margaret and I had passed along the outside of this stretch of growth, within feet of twenty-six natives in three long canoes; and they were so perfectly camouflaged by their dark skin, and so quiet, that we had not known they were there.

So far as anyone knows the natives themselves had not known the camp was occupied, and they had been surprised into hiding. Even so, it was fifteen or twenty minutes before one canoe ventured out and then presently, encouraged by the entire camp bawling "sambio" they all came slowly downstream. But they still had to be enticed to the side of the ship with proffered sticks of tobacco. This shyness, or suspicion, seemed peculiar to us because the Government himself had built the camp on his first attempt over the island, and only government parties had used it since, which was guarantee that there had been no mistreatment of the natives. They should have been, on the other hand, fairly familiar with the sight of white men, and friendly toward them. We could only conclude that news of the Suki abduction had filtered up from the Lower Fly.

Half an hour later the Government, assured that the visitors were harmless . . . they did not even have fishing arrows with them . . . went back to his work in the clearing, and we were left alone with them for our experimenting. The first thing we did was to start making a collection of loin shells. These shells were different from those the Suki wore, which was a whole nautilus, the penis being inserted into the outer chamber. The Strickland model was a huge curved slab cut from a shell that must have been the size of a football. The largest were about nine inches wide and a foot long, and they were ground down to a quarter of an inch thickness. We handed down three sticks of tobacco and each man, grinning widely, removed his pants and handed "them" up for a boy to take. When we had four men standing there naked as Adam, we paused to reflect on the moral angle of this transaction. Such shells as these must have taken years to work their way up the two hundred miles from the coast. They were traded for arrows and spears from village to village and tribe to tribe, some doubtless remaining years with one owner, until a native from farther inland offered for each something too irresistible to be refused. Many shells were the loot of raids, others were heirlooms that had passed down from father to son, and in any event they were all acquired the hard way. No man picked up his pants from the beach in this part of the country, nor had a change that he could don when we had swindled from him the shell he wore.

So we turned to something constructive, which was procuring a model from among the visitors. There was an age distinction in coiffures, we noted. The older men had short hair and wore the little plaited "beanie" with a peak in the middle which made it look like the cap of an acorn, and it was the younger men with sparser whiskers or none at all who had the Cheops haircut such as we had seen in the photograph of Tauparaupi. Actually the hair was still short, but the raffia had been plaited into it and it hung in scores of tiny braids down to below the shoulders. And it was this "hair" that we wanted to paint into the portrait of the Suki cannibal, Tauparaupi. We did not know that the local natives were not allowed up in the camp clearing, but the visitors must have known it, and we had to bribe them with tobacco to leave their canoes and come up the bank. And it was the business that followed that brought the government back apace.

For the moment we had forgotten that Tauparaupi's portrait, which was full-length and almost lifesize, would be a novelty to these natives. And their expressions as they came over the top of the bank made us think we might have made a mistake in inviting them. Each grinning man as he caught sight of the picture behind us stopped in his tracks and stared with a wild-eyed expression, then half turned as if to leave. But more men were crowding up the incline, and by-and-by the whole group were standing in a semicircle, so absorbed in the painting that for several minutes they said nothing. We finally persuaded one man to step over the rail onto the deck and examine the canvas, even to put his hand on it. Instantly he became very animated, and whatever it was he said to the others induced them to step over onto the deck also. Soon they were crowding around the canvas and really giving it rather rough treatment, for some wanted to look at the back, while others in the rear of the crowd wanted to get up to it. Meantime we were pouring gasoline on the fire by repeating Tauparaupi, Tauparaupi, and pointing to the head in the portrait. They knew the name for they repeated it; but whether they recognized the figure as one of the terrors of the countryside, or as a native who had been taken away by the white men to reappear flattened out in this fashion, they were very excited about it. A few of the bold ones began to scratch at the paint with a fingernail; and that, naturally, was the limit of my curiosity about their reaction. We motioned them back from the canvas. But they were paying no attention to us now. We tried pushing, gently at first and then with force, and we raised our voices on the old theory that if you speak it loudly enough, anyone can understand English. It was at this point we discovered that the Papuan is personally unpushable. He just eases around to the side and even gains a few feet. We then tried to order the men off the boat, but they didn't want to get off the boat. A few of them were even poking up through the passageway between the cabins. Finally the boat boys, attracted by the rumpus, came into the fray shouting the "bush pigs" toward the rail, while the bush pigs shouted back. From the rear of the clearing it might have looked and sounded like a massacre. Anyway the Government arrived with his police boys, and they very firmly pushed the visitors right down the bank and into their canoes, and then made them shove off from shore. After which the Government left a police boy on guard and took his headache back to his work in the clearing.

Now we had to patch up a bad job; restore friendly relations, at least long enough to paint the straw hair. The canoes had moved off only a few yards from the ship, so we threw the men a rope to hang onto. Then Margaret quickly brought down the gramophone and kept playing it while I painted straw hair from any man who happened to have his head turned in the right direction. And if some future explorer, thinking he is treading New Guinea where no white man's foot has trod before, comes across cannibals singing Bye-Bye Blues like the Mills brothers, it will be the memento of our passing that way too. Margaret tried other records, the whole roster from talking and singing voice to tom-tom-jazz and symphony, and they all produced that baffled look with which the men had greeted Tauparaupi's portrait. But the Mills brothers they really liked. They kept the slightly wild-eyed expression, head on one side like a listening Victor dog, but looked so let down when the Blues stopped that Margaret kept on playing the same record over and over until I had finished painting.

The sun was just touching the tops of the trees down the river when the Government returned to the ship. He found us waving *bamahuta* to the departing visitors and looking very smug. With the help of the captain we had just made arrangements with the natives to return on the following day with their wives. It had not been easy. The men were to go home (a: business of waving them up the stream) and sleep (b: head on one side, eyes closed, hands under cheek). Next day (c: arm rising up with sun in the east) they were to come back (d: reverse of a). And bring women. Up to this point the men had been following us, nodding in complete understanding, but now we came to a comma: there is no motion for "bring" except a hooking movement of the arm, and unless there is something in the hand to show what should be brought even the verb is not clear. We had to get ourselves into the hand somehow. The only pantomime for woman that we could think of was the burlesque motion of running the hands over the figure, and I think the thing that fogged this vignette for a while was that the captain was also outlining his two hundred pounds of muscle, giving himself a Victorian bust and bustle, after which he rolled his eyes to heaven lasciviously. The natives studied the three of us for some time, looking like any substantial citizens watching such a business; then suddenly one man nodded his head briskly, said something to his fellows, and then made motions with his hands over his body. It was a crude imitation of our pantomiming, but it showed that he understood what we meant. The other men were now laughing delightedly and when we went through the figures from a to e (women) they imitated us, all of us flaying our arms like windmills. After which they paddled cheerily off to b, and we turned to the Government. His face was a study. "All the Papuan Service needs," we said brightly, "is a bust." And what he said in a quiet voice was, "Best let me know when you want to leave camp again." To the well-brought-up British child that would have been the final warning before having his ears twisted off.

33

We were much chagrined when the following morning passed without any of the tribesmen returning. In camp the captain was the only one of the men not busy, so he sat for his portrait, and through that sitting we inadvertently learned the reason the Fly River natives smear themselves with mud.

The sky was overcast that day, but it was almost insufferably hot. The mosquitoes were so sticky that after about an hour's work I was almost crying. It is a confession of weakness, but we had reached the end of our resources for combating them. The captain was impervious, because the mozzies did not have beaks long enough to get through to his sensory nerves, and Margaret could sit with a mosquito net draped over her while she crooned her lullabies to the captain. But I could not see nor work through a net, so all the camp pests settled on me. "If I just had a tail like a horse," I moaned. "Well, why don't you roll in mud like a horse," the captain suggested. And that is approximately what I did. I took river clay and smeared it all over my face and the backs of my hands, and when it dried I was encased in a porcelain shell through which no mosquito could get his stiletto. But it was my resemblance to the Weriadai women that explained their use of the clay. The superficial explanation for the custom of smearing the body with clay is that it is a mourning shroud, and admittedly the Weriadai were in mourning for the victims of the Suki, but Derivo's use of the clay, smearing it on her back especially, which would be hard to keep clear of mosquitoes or to scratch, was certainly a mozzie preventive, and a good one.

Meantime we had not suffered in vain in making a sketch of the captain. The Government and the Commissary declared that they had ordered the drawing (they had mentioned wanting to give one to the captain) and insisted on paying for it. While the captain contended that he was so flattered that *he* must pay for it, and of all the five-way salaaming and insisting and protestations of deathless gratitude. At three o'clock that afternoon we were laboring away at the background of Tauparaupi's picture when we heard the captain speaking to his Diesel engine. A few minutes later the wheelboy came back on our deck and before my very eyes the model for my portrait background across the river moved away downstream. The *Vanapa* was taking an excursion up to the Strickland village.

The settlement proved to be not five but seventeen miles above the Junction, and we must have gone half of that distance when, clearing a sharp bend in the river, we came out on a spectacular sight. In a long line ahead of us, shooting down the breast of the current in our path, was a whole fleet of canoes. There must have been fifty or sixty men aboard them, all standing up, and they were smeared with yellow and black "war" paint like that which Tauparaupi had donned for his portrait. Also there were all the other fancies, feathers on their heads, rings in their ears and bamboo plugs in their noses. And on the shallow bottoms of their canoes were bows and long arrows. For a minute there was the wildest excitement as the crafts maneuvered out of the path of the ship. One of the canoes was caught in our wash and went over, and the men were swept downstream and out of sight. The rest were shouting as they reversed their direction and tried to keep up with the *Vanapa*. We happened to be standing with the Government in the bow, and he was looking puzzled. After our jovial parting the day before, this greeting apparently was not what he had expected.

When we arrived at the settlement it proved to be only a temporary sago camp. A string of rude little huts lined the narrow clearing along the high bank, all with their floors head-high above the mud. There was a great stir in the settlement, dogs wailing their dirge and men shouting and racing about, much as it had been at Weriadai. By the time the *Vanapa* had maneuvered a turnabout, the canoes had come in—and then the din increased. Finally the personage who must have been the chief disentangled himself from the crowd on the water around us, and he and two other patriarchs were permitted to come on board. They were, in the manner of the Service, hostages for our safe trip ashore. As before, the Government went ahead with his police boys; but we did not follow this time until we were invited.

Americans as a group are, I suppose, no more courageous than other peoples as well fed, but there seems to be evidence that we have a harder time learning fear. This may be because most of us grow up in a fairly safe environment where the untamed elements, weather, wild animals and men, are not a major threat. Violent deaths are common enough, but they happen to other people; it is strange names in newspapers who are killed in motor accidents, who get "bumped off" by gangsters, or in "love nests." It takes an effort of imagination to be afraid for ourselves—until the day we break our neck skidding on a waxed floor and so confirm the insurance company statistics that the most dangerous place to be is at home. But until that fatal moment we can come near it again and again without learning whole-hearted fear, without believing that a Stone Age Papuan is not just a dark-colored white man.

I am not sure just when we became separated from the police boys and Government, but when we did notice that they were still on the bank at the place where we had landed, that was where we wanted them to be. We were about half way to the end of the clearing and had just discovered stuck under the floor of a hut two complete pairs of bird-of-paradise plumes. They were mounted on bamboo sticks, and one was henna red and the other the rare golden cream that looked like a flash of sunlight on that dull day. Margaret had hauled ashore her "bitich bokkis," a net dilly bag containing empty tin cans and liquor bottles. All down the line we had traded the rubbish for anything we wanted, cassowary-plume dance sticks, cane armguards, arrows and even ornaments the men were wearing. The excitement had not died down when we came ashore, and now it increased when the natives found that glass would cut. One of the bottles had been broken, and after this discovery everything loose was thrust under our noses in the frenzy to obtain this precious cutting material. (We did not see any hard material like stone or shell used in the weapons in this mud-surfaced country.) So when we came to the paradise plumes it was not a question of the legality of possessing them but how much of a portion of a Haig and Haig bottle the owner should get for them. He would have been happy with just the neck, but abiding by our principles of non-exploitation we gave him the whole bottle and then showed him how to become a capitalist by breaking the thing into splinters for him.

By this time the racket around us was pandemonium, and we eddied along as the nucleus of a body of yapping milling men and boys who smelled like seals. There were no children, no women. Among them was a lanky bearded native with an enormous mouth and a yellow smeared face who made himself conspicuous by always being right in front of our feet; and, as we have said, the Papuan cannot be pushed around. Finally, he further distinguished himself by suddenly reaching down into Margaret's bag and snatching at a bottle. Just as quickly Margaret gave him a smart whack on the hand with the camera tripod. It may have hurt, because he did not look pleased about it. A few feet further, and we decided that it was time to return to our own. We were almost to the end hut, and just wanted to have a look there to be sure there really were no women in the settlement. But before we reached the hut we were stopped. The lanky one was in front of us again, and others of the men had crowded close to him, and they were all facing us, jerking their arms and jabbering at us. It was clear: we were not to go any further. Nor did we want to. But we could not retreat either. The natives were packed in behind us. For an instant I glimpsed the area beneath the hut beyond the men; there were three women squatting under the floor, all staring toward us, jerking their arms and shrilling, fright in their faces. Then the figures between us closed together, shutting out the scene. And I looked back to see the tall yellow-faced native bending down over Margaret. He had his wrist between his teeth, his big lips were curled back, baring the strong white dentures, and he was staring straight into Margaret's startled face. One could hardly mistake that pantomime. It is the code throughout known New Guinea for man-eating.

I do not know what happened immediately after that, for like my friend the Varanus of Komodo I was being very ill. Margaret must have shouted, for next thing we were being hustled through the shrilling crowd toward the whaleboat, with police boys around us. The natives were like ants in a disturbed nest, milling faster, making more racket and jostling the police, an uproar to which the pack of dogs added the final note of tortured infants. Somehow we were down that bank and onto the deck of the *Vanapa* and the *Vanapa* was off downstream full speed ahead in a matter of minutes and without our seeming to have made any physical effort in the transfer. No one shoved us nor ran himself, but for a dignified withdrawal it was one of the nippiest on record.

There were no *bamahutas* at this parting on either side. The natives rushed to their canoes on our very heels and, still whooping, paddled along with the *Vanapa* until we had outdistanced them. And it wasn't until the last canoe was out of sight that Margaret and I realized that we were sitting across from the law—each of us with a wand of bird-of-paradise plumes stuck in the back of our belts, the feathers framing our white faces.

The only other faintly amusing feature of this encounter is the misunderstanding that occurred when we asked the visitors of the first day to return with their women. When we made swathing motions over our figures they must have understood us to mean that they were to smear on their "war" paint, and they were obligingly returning so smeared when we met them on the river. This paint was what must have puzzled the Government, for there had been no sign at the parting the night before that the natives were going to put on a show. But that won't be cleared up in the Government's mind unless he reads this, because it was not until we started writing it that the explanation for the paint occurred even to us.

No one knows why the big native bit his wrist in Margaret's face, but it is my opinion, now that my blood has warmed a bit, that he was not necessarily threatening us. There may have been the remains of a cannibal feast in the hut beyond, and he was simply describing them . . . standing in our way to do it. Our favorite theory is that one of the women under the hut was ill or in labor and could not escape to the bush with the others, and the two other women were assisting her. Though ordinarily, at least in Melanesia, parturition is more private than this. In any case we know that since there were no other women in the settlement these three had not stayed behind voluntarily, and for some reason they were not receiving visitors. There was a rather shaky angle to this theory in the fact that the men would seem to have been protecting the women. Ordinarily I believe the Papuan woman is left to do her own protecting, which is a matter of running fast enough with the babies to keep from getting trampled on by the men in the general rush into the bush when the village is being raided. But here they appeared to be guarding their females according to the most modern dictates of gallantry. By a long stretch of the imagination the big fellow's action could be construed as a warning that if we tried to go any further we would get "et."

However it was, this encounter succeeded in making us Americans thoroughly fearful of something, the uncurried primitive—though remembering Tauparaupi even that fear did not seem so durable. It was just a matter of getting acquainted under the right circumstances.

34

As we came down the river we faced a problem. We could remain on the *Vanapa* and return to Port Moresby and there transship for Sydney. And be home within six weeks. . . . Home. We could even remain on the *Vanapa* indefinitely. San Francisco Ruby had builded well in the captain's heart for all American girls to follow, and the copra-collecting itinerary he offered us on the *Vanapa* sounded like the one we had dreamed on the charts before ever we left the United States. The Bamu River, the Turama, and Kikori and the Purari and up the Vailala. Even nine months ago this invitation would have been like one from Saint Peter. But now we were faced west. And we must get on with it, get to the Indies and finish up the job. Before we cracked up. I could feel it coming. So when the *Vanapa* pulled in to Madiri she loaded up with the plantation's accumulated shipment of copra and rubber and left us still to wait for the Thursday Island relief boat.

This brings me, rather belatedly, I must admit, to a subject that had been influencing the course of Art ever since we had been in the islands, particularly New Guinea. And it was, indirectly also, to play a role in our future. The subject is rubber. And the reason we have not dwelt on it before is because it was not until we returned to Madiri that we had achieved the right mood, amount of information and leisure to give the subject our best. I did not paint again at Madiri; I did not feel like painting.

The rubber tract at Madiri had not been very conspicuous

393

even before the heavy rains set in, for the stand was not old and neither the trees nor the manual part of the production had any particular artistic appeal. Also most of the tapping is done in the dry season. But there were still a few trees giving out, and we examined these as a tourist duty. These young trees had trunks of only about seven or eight inches diameter, the bark of which was slashed for tapping in a herringbone pattern with a central upright "stem." At the bottom of this was a cup to receive the fluid that seeped out of the top cuts. A new diagonal cut was made above the old one every third day, and this had to be done very carefully by an expert boy, for too deep injures the sap-circulating "skin" between the tree and its bark. It is only the bark that exudes the fluid containing rubber latex, and this oozes forth so slowly that even a mature tree (over ten years old) produces only about an ounce of latex a day. Then when the whole bark has been tapped up to easy arm-reach of a boy, the tree must rest for three or four years to grow a new bark. Thus, counting vacations, a rubber tree gives the best years of a long life to just one automobile tire.

Automobile tires while still liquid latex in a vat in the rubber shed look heartbreakingly like heavy butter cream to butter-hungry headhunters. The fluid actually has the construction of milk, being globules of something suspended in water which also, like milk, contains carbohydrates and proteids. The shed even has the good old barn odor previously mentioned, the source of it being the formic acid solution which is stirred into the vat to separate the latex from the water. When this mixture is allowed to stand, a curd of latex forms on the surface; and these thick pliable "biscuits" were, at Madiri, run through a roller turned by hand and came out the other side in thin waffled streamers about a foot wide and six to ten feet long. When they were hung from the ceiling racks in the smoke room they looked like the crowded laundry lines between the tenement windows in New York. And they soon acquired "that tell-tale color." The smoke room dried out the remaining moisture but in the process turned the snow-white sheets of latex amber brown and semi-transparent. The last stage was when Davi whacked the streamers into eighteen-inch slabs and bundled them at which they became "commercial" rubber, "not worth the cost of production."

This phrase, and "not worth the cost of the labor," was frequently heard among white islanders. In the Solomon Islands it was applied to copra, because that is the principal export of the group. In the Territory of New Guinea we heard gold prospectors grumble it because the big companies with machinery and airplane were the only ones who could make gold "pay." We had heard no mention of rubber there, yet it was outside of Rabaul that we visited our first rubber plantation. In 1913 the Germans exported about thirty thousand dollars' worth of rubber for the territory, a fifth of the value of their copra export; so it was a coming produce. But at the time of our stay in Rabaul, the Australians were exporting so little rubber that the produce was not even included in the index of the government's annual report. Yet the rubber stands were still there, fine old tracts of trees in the prime for both quality and quantity of production.

The tract we visited was of several hundred acres, perhaps half a century old, and for sheer beauty outranked anything else we saw in the islands. There is no other tree so clean-looking as the rubber tree with its waxy light-gray bark and big shining deep green leaves. And there was a limitless forest of these great old trees set out in wide avenues that extended in every direction farther than we could see in the gloom. High above us the dense foliage grew solidly in a level roof that shut out all the hot sun and made the "interior" as cool and dim as a great cave. There were no birds up there, and below no leaves on the forest of gray branches, nor any undergrowth between the trunks. Our footfalls made only the sound of rustling leaves, for the surface was spongy with the years' accumulation of humus. The thick taupe columns of trunks were covered with spiraling scars of the old tappings that made them look like pillars in a Moorish palace. But it is the color, the curious lightness of gray smoke suffusing the forest, and the loftiness and quiet that are unforgettable. Yet it was a cemetery, an abandoned man-made place, and had nothing paintable in it for us.

This solitude in a rubber tract had no special significance for us until we met our first rubber planter in Samarai. Rather, he was an ex-planter, on his way out. For some reason which we decided afterward must have been one of those involuntary muscular contractions of the expiring, the man had ordered a portrait drawing of himself. And while he sat for the picture he told us about the rubber business and why he was departing from Papua a failure. It was because of Uncle Shylock, he said.

This was not his version of it, but it seems there was once a thing called the Stevenson Plan, a cartel ostensibly devised for the "organization" of the rubber industry. It was a simple plan. It was based on one of the soundest principles in financial usage, that of getting the money from one's creditor with which to pay the debt owed him. For the Plan originated as an effort to enable Great Britain to help pay off her war debt to the United States. We should be interested in this efficient means of paying a national debt, because it is something we shall always have with us, whether owed by governments to one another or owed to the citizens by the government. It shows our great financial minds at work, the only minds that are heartily international in scope.

In the case of Great Britain, the Englishman Stevenson who devised the Plan was able to show that British subjects were the owners of the majority of rubber plantations in the world, while the United States was the biggest consumer of rubber. All that was necessary to make this situation amount to something was to run up the price of rubber, and this could be done by limiting the supply. Then from the increased export tariff payments of the debt could be met with greater ease. So all the British planters reduced the production of their tracts to one-third of normal output, and in a few years the price of raw rubber had soared from twenty cents a pound to a dollar twenty. And Great Britain was managing nicely with her payments, the while, incidentally, bestowing on ourselves the title of Uncle Shylock for accepting those installments. However, by paying six times as much for every baby-bottle nipple, hot water bag, automobile tire or rubber band Americans individually were paying much of that British debt. Or, having already contributed the loan in taxes, they were now paying up a second time in excess costs of rubber goods. There was nothing unethical about the scheme, according to Business; it just smelled from an aesthetic point of view, which is ours.

This period of highest prices was when little Papua began to have dreams of grandeur as another Malaya. Rubber trees thrive best in moist soil and air, and in this respect the territory was swimming in luck. Our Samarai plaintiff, along with a number of others who gambled on continued Yankee endurance, leased extensive coast acres and set them out with rubber cuttings imported from the Malay States. These pest-free sprouts, incidentally, being impossible for parties outside the cartel to obtain from any British source.

American rubber buyers meantime were not taking the Plan lying down. In the final analysis no one can outsmell the member of a society of rugged individuals if he gets the idea that it is a competition. Private companies, unwittingly aided by the American taxpayer, took up huge land concessions in Liberia which were set out with rubber, and others started tracts in South America. But it takes even a healthy tree ten years before it begins to produce either high-grade or very much latex; and everyone, with the exception of the investors, was delighted when the Amazon venture began to fail because of a lack of immunity to the rubber-tree diseases that had been weeded out of the Malay stands. Then the Liberian venture had its wings clipped when the opposition brought forth charges of "out-and-out slave labor" in the American concessions. These charges were investigated by a League of Nations commission and, true, were found to be so odoriferous that, while every important newspaper throughout the Empire gave front-page space to the findings, very very little appeared in our *Clarions* and *Heralds*. Lincoln's ghost must be kept from walking.

In the end it was a combination of factors that broke the Stevenson Plan. Holland had never joined the cartel, and while on the one hand her East Indies plantations were profiting by the rubber boom she was letting American rubber buyers fondle the other, serving as what would now be called a "black market." But the price of rubber started to slip seriously when U.S. manufacturers began using reclaimed rubber. In the end it was that which caused raw rubber to zoom from its high of $1.25 to less than three cents a pound! If we had had the ears of the big bad wolf at the turn of the depression decade we might have heard the air going out of rubber dreams all the way from Mandalay to Matapi in the Coral Sea.

No one in the United States noticed a corresponding reduction in the cost of girdles then or since, naturally, but the rubber growers felt the recoil; and inasmuch as such things as the Stevenson Plan have no provision for failure it was each planter individually who "took the rap" for Great Britain's attempt to make an "honest woman" of herself. Meantime in the Netherlands Indies, as the plantations began to lop, the rubber buyers on the front lines were quick to see the golden opportunity, and the best possible American support was pumped into the failing tracts. By the middle thirties our interest, at least that of a few of us, in those then-distant lands was far from impersonal. We were up to our necks in anything that happened in or to the European possessions in that now-not-so-very-far East.

There was to come a time when Great Britain, the Empire, was to regret the Stevenson Plan even more than the growers did at the apex of their suffering. If the curtailment of rubber production had not continued so long under the Plan, if instead rubber plantations in New Guinea had been enlarged at the normal rate and new ones started in all these islands so well suited to the growing of rubber trees, by the time the Second World War came along the loss of the Indies and Malay tracts would have been nowhere near so serious. Australia, at least, might have been kept rolling on its own rubber. If . . . well.

By the time we little Yankee carpetbaggers arrived on the scene there was only a trickle of latex coming out of the Coral Sea trees. The old plantations like the one outside Rabaul had first cut down production to keep prices up and then discontinued altogether because there was no price. In the Mandated Territory alone there was at least thirty thousand dollars a year less than at "normal" times for squandering on American-made portraits. For however much an artist likes to think of himself as elevated above the dirty marts of trade, his financial health is good or bad in direct ratio to that of the commoner clay around him. It is possible that the failure of the rubber barons had some bearing on our own little failure in Rabaul, but it was not entirely responsible. There was a financial depression all through the islands and in New Zealand and Australia long after we in the United States had begun to recover from our crash, and it was everywhere believed to have been caused by the long-since-canceled War Debt. Just as we ourselves never could see the connection between the First World War and that depression, the British refused to recognize the fact that you cannot blow up millions of dollars in ammunition and work-hours, and escape paying for it. Uncle Shylock had drained the world dry and was abandoning it to the wolves. There were persons like the ex-rubber baron in Samarai who in their wretchedness and bewilderment accused Americans personally. It was a barrister in Auckland who gave us our first copy of "Honor or Dollars," and a newspaper reporter in Darwin our last.

It says much for the sportsmanship of the British that they were so generous with their hospitality and help when many of them must have felt that we were gnawing on their very bones. There is little doubt, however, that the general attitude had a bearing on our attempts to help ourselves. Without presenting any new data, there was the commission for the portrait of Sir Hubert Murray which we have reason to believe was lost because of the combination of a financial depression and our being the cause of it. And in the end as we came to quit Papua no one was less surprised than ourselves to find that Mr. Goodfellow, he who fled to Thursday Island without us, was an ex-rubber baron reduced to recruiting.

Obviously no individual can escape responsibility for the shady deeds of his countrymen and their government—not so long as he can influence ethics in free speech and press and can vote. Nor, for that matter, can he take credit for the glory unless he avails himself of these instruments for guiding his destiny.

35

When the *David Pitt* set sail for Thursday Island from Madiri no "pirates" could have been gayer even if we were not bolder. Yorick was sailing with us on his long-needed holiday to get new teeth and glasses in Australia and repair his riddled lungs with a long rest, and the boy was spiritually cured from the moment we cast off. (A substitute assistant, a real missionary this time, had been sent up to replace him, so Hamlet was not left alone with his flute.) It had been decided that the *David Pitt*, which was the relief boat, was to return with us to T.I. because the *Dogi* was much too risky for the weather, it being the bad end of the guba season. The new boat was a 38-foot cutter manned by four big black grinning Torres Strait islanders of whom Robin, the biggest grinner, seemed to be the boss boy. (The natives of the Strait islands are classified as Melanesian, but the ones we saw were as tall and almost as dark-skinned as the Australian Aboes, yet had the Papuan nose and kinky hair.) The quarters of the crew were the forward hold, which Yorick apparently intended to share with them, but never did. Ours were aft, in dimensions not quite long enough to stretch out full length on the floorboards without hanging our feet in the soup nor quite high enough to kneel upright without cracking our heads on the cover of the headroom. But when the boat was on a steady keel we could squat.

It soon became apparent that we were not to have a steady keel on this journey, not even in the river. We set out in a driving rain at daybreak, but had a stiff head wind and the flood tide. Sailors will appreciate the going from the fact that we made only twenty-three miles in thirteen hours. The last tack just before it got too dark to see took us in to a spot on the north bank just about five yards below the place we touched on the previous tack. The reason we recognized it was because there was a crocodile sleeping on the mud spit, and when we came back he was still there and a family had grown up around him, two smaller crocodiles. We decided to anchor here for the night and nosed in with the bow projecting over the crocs without their hearing us. Yorick had made some tea on the primus stove, and he poured the scalding remainders down on the nose of the nearest crocodile. That was the last funny thing that happened that day. It was too rough to heat a dinner on the primus stove even if anyone had wanted to eat, and it was too rough to sleep. Yorick kept falling off the headroom above us and crashing down onto the deck as if he were coming through. The crew had closed themselves in the forward hold and sealed down the hatch-cover after them leaving Yorick out in the weather by preference. He said he needed air to live, and curled up with his asthma on the roof above us covered by a tarpaulin. So in the morning we were a little less gay, but deep in our hearts was still a song to be on our way.

The first casualty came late the next afternoon, after a similar day of weather. We had all crowded down into our compartment and succeeded in making some tea by holding the pan of water on top of the primus. Another pan of water was put on to heat and had just reached boiling when Margaret let go for something, a sea came over and sent the blazing primus, boiling water, bilge water, ourselves and everything loose into a jam in the far stern. It was some minutes before we got arms and legs and stuff re-sorted, and by that time I knew whose leg had got the full pan of boiling water on it. When I peeled off my breeches the hide came with them, leaving a big raw circle on the right knee. The tea leaves for easing it were handy anyway; they were all over our sleeping blanket. That night Margaret spent searching for the source of a burning odor, thinking the primus had set fire to the blankets and that they were smoldering under us. I could have told her they were too wet to burn, but it didn't seem worth the effort. But night after night she searched for that fire—until we found that the smell of smoke was coming through from the forward compartment. The crew had a corrugated iron pan of embers going, by which they kept warm and lit their pipes.

It was dusk of the third day before we reached the estuary of the river, and on the approach the men debated trying to get out that night. But there was an ebb tide to help us, and we of the superior race were so weary that we persuaded the crew to make a try for it. Once out we would have a tail wind and tuck right along to Daru. Robin grinned doubtfully but kept on going.

No soundings were taken on that tack. The combers were coming over the silt shallows like a succession of tidal bores, and after one look Margaret and I lay down face up on the hatch, decided that if we were going to drown we wouldn't have to hang anyway, and it was no good to watch it coming. There was a small bird, about swallow size, trying to alight on the masthead; and it never did catch up. The minute we got into those rollers the deck was awash and the mast began making violent zigzags and sweeps across the clouds that made the bird look as if it were being jerked around on a string like a "bumble-puppy" ball. We shipped water, and pretty soon the little cutter wasn't rising to the seas. A comber seeming half as high as the mast would come rolling slowly toward us and we would nose right into it and the wave would foam down the deck, lifting us bodily between our clinging hands. Twice we had a close call; the men let fly the mainsheet just in time to keep us from keeling over. Yorick kept exclaiming "Ca-ripes, ca-ripes," but there was not a Melanesian curse out of the crew. They lived on the little reef islands and this water was "old stuff"; and any-way, there is no profanity in the language. But if we had been sailing the *Dogi* we would have foundered, "no fear." As tight as the *David Pitt* was, our belongings were awash in the hold, and that included paintings and drawings on paper. But it didn't go on for long. Before any of us could get our anatomy organized for seasickness we were clear and lifting along westward, still trailed by the persevering bird.

As we neared Daru we tailed and then overhauled another light vessel that dropped anchor within calling distance of our berth. "Sail-o," sang out a European's voice in the dark. "Wha-name?" "The *David Pitt* from Madiri," Yorick an-swered and then asked the other's name. When we heard it Margaret and I nudged each other with the last nudge we had in us that night. It was Goodfellow. He had set out that after-noon on another run to Thursday Island and had had to turn back because of weather. The sissy. "Got some passengers, I see," came the next question, because he couldn't see any more than some extra blobs of white. What he wanted to be sure of was who, for he knew very well that we had been at Madiri. We kicked Yorick just in time and all he answered was, "Yes"—a brevity that never seemed to be resented by the British but always sounded discourteous to us. Our plan was to beat Goodfellow across the Strait; and if he knew we were on board he would certainly take off before us in the morning.

When we cleared at Daru, Yorick was signed as skipper because the Australian law requires a white navigator no mat-ter who does the actual skippering on a vessel. And we "went through the customs," a brief oral questionnaire in which we declared we had no illegal plumage, heads or skulls in our gear. "Well, if you have," we were informed pointedly, "they'll find them at the other end." So we were saved then from having to open our bags and look at the damage caused by their soaking. The business delayed us, nevertheless, and Goodfellow's cutter was nowhere to be seen when we cast off. If he had sailed at daybreak he had about three hours' head start; but Robin, our real skipper, was an old master. He knew the waters, was keen on the race and set a course outside the Warrior Reefs which, if rougher, was a shorter and faster route than the regular passage. We thought we could stand anything that would shorten the hundred and fifty miles of reef-strewn waters ahead of us.

Great Barrier Reef, which strings along the western border of the Coral Sea for over a thousand miles, terminates at both ends with landmarks having significant names. The southern pile just northeast of Brisbane is called Wreck Reef and the northern, opposite the mouth of the Fly River, is Bramble Cay. Whether the Cay was named for some Mr. Bramble or because it is a prickly spot, the fact is that today the black hulk of a coaler is piled up on that coral marking the beginning of dangerous waters for vessels. (For a long time the *Papuan Chief* picked up her coal from this dump, and the natives from the nearby mainland are still eating the descendants of the ship rats which have managed to survive on the shellfish of the reef.) Captain Cook was the first to report the dangers of the area, for he had a close shave on the *Endeavour* when he was poking around the reefs discovering Australia for George III. Then Bligh with his eighteen faithful men from the *Bounty* wandered around for something like two weeks in their open boat before they found a passage through the reefs to the Arafura Sea. Today the maze has been thoroughly charted, especially along the Australian coast, and here there are safe channels for large vessels. Still the storms blow. Somewhere along the southern reefs in this "safe" passage an X on the coral marks the spot where a brand-new liner on which we later traveled went aground in one of these "blows." The field is a graveyard of ships.

There seems to be a divergence of opinion regarding the formation of the shelf. Some scientists say that the area of the Coral Sea was once land that incorporated in a huge mainland Australia and all of the islands now surrounding the Coral Sea. Those who hold to the subsidence theory believe that the reefs will sink out of sight in another eon or two. At one spot near Cairns where they bored down to about six hundred feet nothing but ooze was found, and at another place farther south the sea floor is known to have dropped a thousand feet in less than seventy-five years. Others believe that the coral polyps are in the process of filling in the Coral Sea to reverse the picture. In any case the reefs must have been there when the Indonesians were invading Melanesia; our trip across the Strait gave us a vivid explanation for their having taken the longer route around the north of New Guinea for their migrations. The sole entry in our "log" for the journey is "Saw some birds."

No one with a spark of life left in him could have failed to note those birds. They appeared out of a driving rain, flying east like a long black cloud low over the water. They were small birds, and there must have been thousands of them, for they were in close formation and went over us for about ten minutes, so near that we could have bagged them with a butterfly net. The air darkened under them and the sound of the wind in their wings was a cosmic sing such as you imagine fills the stratosphere. Later we learned that these birds were a sign of dirty weather, but we did not need signs when we had the facts.

At dusk we anchored in the lee of some reefs with mile-long breakers thundering on the windward side some distance off. It was not a very sheltered place. There was a bitter gale driving cold rain from the direction of the Gulf, but we managed to get some soup and meat out of tins and to heat the mess on the primus stove below deck. However, we couldn't eat it there and keep it down; and up on deck, no matter which way we faced, the wind whipped the stew out of the spoons and into our faces before we could take it in. The kettle was cold by that time, anyway. That night Margaret and I finished a job begun long ago on a fishing sampan in Hawaii, that of wearing down our hips to fit boat planks. We were down to the bone by morning.

Whenever an outfit of mixed genders and races travels on a small boat having no accommodations whatever there are bound to occur situations that might baffle Emily Post herself. Ordinarily good taste restrains the narrator from reporting these choice tidbits, and thereby half of the flavor of the journey is lost for the vicarious traveler. All of which is preparation for the following.

When we started out on the *David Pitt* the attitudes of civilized society still prevailed among us. When Yorick felt something coming up he would stagger forward to the bow for privacy, where the seas washing over the side would return to him full in the face that which he had given forth. When our turn came we would dive down into our compartment and Robin, grinning with all his teeth showing, would hand down the freshly washed gasoline tin, a receptacle, we learned too late, which was the only thing of its kind on board. In other words, when we had the tin—and we kept it through the night—no one else had it and the rest were deprived of a private outlet for anything that struck them. Men alone on board would not have needed privacy, but a Melanesian crew is delicately refined when there are women, and especially white women, at close quarters. Just after we got under way that first morning at sea Margaret "strolled" up to the bow, where she stood for about three-quarters of an hour breathing deeply of nature. Another of her theories about seasickness is that if you let the rhythms of nature establish the tempo of one's own rhythms there won't be such a conflict in one's stomach. I noticed that the three natives back at the tiller were chuckling, and the minute Margaret came aft two of them rushed forward and, reaching over the side, pulled up a half drowned seaman. He had been sitting on the guys that ran from the bowsprit aft to the side as the only private place left to him. The keynote of this anecdote is that the modest Melanesian would evidently rather drown than have a white woman discover he was only human.

The second incident of this nature, also caused by a shortage of equipment, might have been more serious but it couldn't have been funnier. Margaret and I had been down in our stateroom all morning (with the gasoline tin) and evidently everyone thought we were stowed away for the day. This might have been the case if there had not been a sudden thumping and shouting on deck. The next instant the hideous grating of coral on the bottom right under our heads sent us scrambling out on deck. We had scraped over, without damage, but that was a side issue to the spectacle we saw by emerging so quickly. We towed a dinghy astern and Yorick for some reason—perhaps he thought distance and the curtain of rain would lend him privacy—had chosen it as his cloister, sitting hooked over the stern. At the shout of "reef" he had half risen, his trousers were at half-mast and while we watched, spellbound, a comber swept over—and when it passed Yorick had vanished.

When our friend's head reappeared he was thrashing away for dear life, swimming like a mermaid, for his pants had turned inside out and were trailing from his ankles. And he was headed for the great open spaces of the west, because he had lost his spectacles and couldn't even see the cutter. That dunking actually liquidated our skipper. His seasickness and

fever took on the wretched violence of gastric malaria that
stretched him out for the rest of the journey.

Late in the afternoon of the second or third day—a vague-
ness that indicates the flow of life up until that moment—
it stopped raining altogether and blowing quite so hard, and
in the comparative lull we at last fell asleep. When we woke
it was still daylight and there was a strange quiet. No motion
to the boat, no sound of booming water. For a minute before
I opened my eyes I thought perhaps I had died and was feeling relieved until I heard Margaret up on deck sounding like
a calliope. When I popped my head out I saw why; we were
anchored in a sea of color. All around us as far as we could
see in every direction were clumps of low reefs, and from our
anchorage on, the coral shelf did not appear to be under more
than a foot of water. Water that was as level and motionless
and transparent as if we were fixed in a great slab of crystal.
It was crystal over color, magnifying it, intensifying it beyond anything we have ever seen that was not in the sky.

Off in the distance were the *David Pitt's* boys walking, to
all appearances, on the surface of the sea like Jesus. They were
fishing with harpoons, and when we shouted Robin came
after us. We were going to wade with bare feet as the crew
were doing, but Robin advised shoes—and the minute we
were over the side the reason was apparent. There were
patches of sand, snow-white sand, between the clumps of
coral but no patch large enough to put your foot on without
stepping on some living blob of color. Lying on the bottom
were sea anemones with fleshy aster "petals" in flower forms
of sapphire blue, rose, delicate flesh pink, vivid emerald green
and even brown growing out of olive green "foliage." The
tentacles can give a painful sting to a human, and as for their
marine victims they simply enmesh them close over and absorb them. There were sprawling leathery starfish brilliantly
blue or coppery red with yellow encrustations, and great fat

bêches de mer with a lavender highlight down their black satin back. There were shells and shells with and without living tenants, "leaping" shells, "spider" shells with horns on all sides, and something that looked more spidery, a shell which was all slender spines frozen in mobile forms. There were chambered nautilus shells with a nacre throat and pink

striped back, and shiny cowrie shells in innumerable lovely tones and patterns. Margaret was babbling in Latin. There were succulent seaweeds growing like cauliflower, like lettuce or slit heraldry flags, and streamers and tubes and hairy bunches of just "things." Color, color, color. And there were clams. We thought we had seen the Paul Bunyans of mollusks in the lagoon between New Georgia and Vangunu of the Solomons, but Barrier Reef clams grow to weigh as much as a man and they have purple, midnight-blue, forest-green or fawn-colored jaws with lips that look like shirred velvet glittering with jewels. There was a spotted reef eel that fought and tore at Robin's spear with its sharp teeth when it had been harpooned. Robin said he was a bad fella—by which he meant to kill as well as to meet. Specimens measuring up to eight feet have been found in the reefs. One other respected form of reef life which I recognized from once having stepped on a member in our own southern waters was a black

sea urchin. Its foot-long spines are set in a ball-and-socket arrangement, and when we poked at one with a harpoon all the
poisonous needle-tipped quills turned toward the attack ready
to break off in anything that brushed against them.

All of these living colors and thousands of indescribable
others are forms which are simply superimposed on the reef
rock. The coral itself outstrips for variety of pattern and
color any other one species that lives on it. There are patterns that look like fragile lace, like snowflakes on stems or the
branches of trees, sponges or fingers, and that most curious
kind of all, the great convulsive shapes of the "soft" coral that
has a lime deficiency and as a result lops in curling forms like
human intestines—if that makes it any clearer. There are
textures that are knobby or warty, and the "brain" coral that
resembles the convolute surface of a brain. Or sweetbreads.
The colors are not brilliant, but instead every soft lovely
tone; coral, pink, shades of violet and raspberry, chamois yellow, subtle flesh tones, pink-tinted grays and "off" whites
that deepen to rose and brown and queer greens. There is
not a restful form or surface to anything (except the water
itself) in all the eighty thousand square miles that constitute
the coral shelf. We saw it under a gray sky, when every
detail is apparent and when hues are intensified to their full
strength by the absence of glare. The very expanse of it lifts
the heart, and in such a still hour, when the pools had become
mirrors reflecting a violet twilight, it seemed that all the
anxiety and small discomforts of our long headhunt had been
worth it to have come this far and seen the glory of "the
world's largest curtain of coral."

One of the boys was poking around the clumps of reef
trying to stir out a favorite kind of shrimp when suddenly
the water clouded dark. He laughed and said something to
the others, then plunged his left arm down into the center
of the opaque spot and held it there with the expression of

feeling around. Almost instantly the pasty white tentacle of an octopus appeared above the surface, curling around the boy's arm. The native still grinned, still held his arm under. The ends of two more tentacles appeared—and still he waited. Finally there were six suction-cupped snakes of pure sinew wound around the native's arm, which left two tentacles to be accounted for. That number seemed to satisfy the boy, however, for he then pulled his arm up as far as it would come, reached under the water with his knife, and cut off the two remaining tentacles that were clinging to the rocks. When he drew his arm up there was the octopus, self-caught. All dead in all its arms and nightmarish face and spread out, it had a span of about four feet, too old and tough even boiled to be edible, and even if one were desperate for food. But there was no scarcity of fish meat here. The pools swarmed with recognizable fish as well as some you couldn't tell from a chunk of coral. The very water itself seemed part fish, loaded with color. There were formless transparent masses of color, schools of minute swimming things that were almost invisible except as flashing bits of iridescence, schools of larger little fish browsing like bright birds among the coral branches, and so on up to the fish that Robin presently pulled off his harpoon. It was a parrot fish and must have weighed between fifteen and twenty pounds, a great fat blob of brilliant color. From a pure yellow belly the large scales changed to blue-green and from green to sapphire blue on the sides, which in turn became purple, depending on the way you held it. Besides the parrot coloring it had a bony parrotlike lip for nipping off its food from the coral trees. "Good fella kaikai," said Robin with a mouthful of raw fish, then he spewed sapphire-blue and purple scales and grinned, showing all his enormous white teeth. That was my picture of a Torres Strait Melanesian if we still had the health to paint it when we

reached Thursday Island. In the parrot fish and Robin were all the extravagant colors and proportions of the region.

To project our history, we did paint that picture; at least we painted Robin at Thursday Island. To the amazement of the local white citizenry and the great amusement of the natives—"hap-cas' " children, Chinese and goats—that make up the waterfront traffic of Port Kennedy, Robin posed standing ankle-deep in the water off the beach in front of our hotel, a kitchen chair hooked on his harpoon to weight it down in lieu of parrot fish. For no parrot fish was available without going back out to the reefs for it. Nor did we have Great Barrier Reefs to pose for background, for they too meant retracing those painful steps. So for over a year the portrait of Robin searched for a background, finally obtaining it in the far western end of Java. Even then it was not without incident. At the fish market of Batavia we learned why the good fella kai-kai cannot be obtained except among the reefs. One reason is that it spoils so rapidly out of water that it cannot be brought in as far as the market. The other reason is that some of the parrot fish that browse on coral reefs are poisonous. The fish that posed for Robin's picture was taken from the tank of the government aquarium. To get it painted before the colors faded, we attempted to do it in the aquarium garden. It was suspended by a twine from a tree branch with a gasoline tin of sea water below in which it was dunked periodically to keep the colors fresh. But that sitting ended when a pet stork on the grounds attacked first it and then ourselves when we tried to save the model from being devoured—and a stork's beak has the penetrating quality of a bayonet in an argument. The end of it was that we put the fish into a gasoline tin of formaldehyde and took it back to the mountains where we were living. We were driving, and on the trip the formaldehyde slopped out of the tin, leaving the already damaged fish half exposed. Nevertheless it was the only parrot fish in captivity in Java, and our last opportunity, so it had to be painted. We can now confirm the attribute of its rapid deterioration. At that time we had as pets a baby gibbon ape, an armadillo and a little *babu*, a Javanese maid. When the parrot fish had been hanging up for about an hour next morning the good-natured babu would not come up onto the veranda, the armadillo had gone into a corner and smothered his nose in his belly and the gibbon was hanging from the latticework at the ceiling, whistling his terror at the odor. Margaret stayed away on important errands all morning while I worked with plugs of cotton in my nostrils, breathing through my mouth.

When it came to painting the reefs we had one of our close shaves of the expedition. The nearest reefs from where we lived were down on the west coast where Sunda Strait separates Java from Sumatra. Karaktau, the volcano island that back in 1883 made "the biggest noise ever heard in the world," lies in the Strait to the northwest around Java Head and it had lately been bubbling in a minor eruption. The reefs I chose to paint were about a third of a mile out in the bay, and we had some natives take me out in their fishing outrigger and leave me there; Margaret was to have them come back for me when I signaled. At that moment there was ample space on the shelf in which to set the canvas up and still have distance between myself and the clumps of coral I wanted to paint. But as the hours wore on the tide rose, the shelf got smaller and smaller, and the breakers started rolling in and then over my island. But I wanted to finish the damned thing and intended to keep on working so long as my model reef was above the surface. Presently I heard a roar of water far louder than any before and turned to see what looked like a tidal bore bearing down on me. Karaktau must have belched it our way.

When I came up the first thing I looked around for was Robin, and I was relieved to see the canvas floating shoreward from where I was. That was better than I was doing. I think I must have been on the point of heat stroke anyway before I was swept into the water—and it was cold by contrast. The minute I tried to swim my legs were locked in cramps. Margaret had seen me go off the shelf and was standing on the beach (probably grinning) waiting for me to swim in. I thought I made her understand the fix I was in by jerking my arms wildly, and only afterward discovered that she had thought I was motioning her to get an outrigger and go after the picture. Anyway she did not hurry, and she had trouble getting the natives to launch their shallow canoe in the tide surf. Then they had their own difficulties getting out past the pounding breakers, and once that was done they made a wide diagonal tack to pick up the portrait, which they admired lengthily and only afterward started in my direction. I meantime couldn't use any wind to call out. I had kept my lungs inflated and was floating with the aid of my arms, but I didn't know then that each comber as it swept over me was not going to be my last. There was a lot to be lived through before then, some of it the remainder of our trip in to Thursday Island.

On the last day of that journey the sun came out, warming our chilled bones and by the same token giving us a sunburn that came close to the record of the Port Moresby races. Our top facets were cautiously covered, but the reflected rays from the water were almost as intense as those from the sun itself. In spite of it we might have got some rest that night if we had not run into one of civilization's plagues. We anchored in the lee of a wooded island a few miserable yards from a clean steady beach and were not allowed to put foot on it because of a quarantine for influenza. Along about midnight we saw a light toward the north, and when the boat came to anchor near us a voice shouted across, "Sail-o! What name?" Goodfellow!

If we had had our health we would have enjoyed that race the next morning. It was a superb day, with great white bundles of clouds floating in a lupin blue sky. And already in the air there was the something that indicates the proximity of a continent. We were still less than eleven degrees below the equator, only a little farther south than the muggy Solomon Islands; but in the wind was that clean brisk quality that comes after a storm on land, the smell of earth in it that must have warmed many a battered sailor's heart in the past.

Goodfellow was already out of sight when we cast off in the morning, but in two hours the crew had sighted his sail on the dazzling horizon. We still couldn't see it ourselves. By that time we had left the reefs behind, and the sea all around was littered with distant blue islands; Traverse with huge Banks far to the west, then Double and Wednesday with Tuesday Island on the other side of it. Captain Cook had certainly run out of poetry by the time he got to this quarter of the world.

Little Thursday Island was squeezed in between big Horn and bigger Prince of Wales. We never did find Monday, nor did we care. With T.I. in sight we were overhauling Goodfellow with a smart quartering wind that gave us the edge with no cargo. Goodfellow must have been carrying some copra and he had a few recruits, for there was a dark lump of figures on the foredeck. But we did not want to pass this boat that had abandoned us too quickly. We wanted to look at it. We wanted to run alongside it and look quietly at Mr. Goodfellow, though I still thought the occasion warranted thumbing our nose with impunity or both thumbs if we felt the impulse. Robin, understanding this and grinning, close-hauled to get on the weather side of the other boat and blanket his sails . . . take the wind from them . . . and we rose to our feet to strike poses like the Victory of Samothrace. That was as far as I got, rising. When the *David Pitt* passed the other cutter I was down in the hold with my head in the gasoline tin, and grateful to be hidden. And that over, I never did rise again.

In arriving at Thursday Island we had reached a long-sought goal; but there was no relish in it. The halt, the lame and the blind leaning on one another staggered together as far as the land end of the long jetty, then we went our separate ways, Margaret to engage a room at the hotel, I to a half-caste dentist (Australian Aboe and white) who pulled my infected tooth with bare fingers and without novocaine, and Yorick to the hospital. Before we parted he stood there a minute waving in the breeze, his coffee-red hair standing on end, blind eyes cocked in different directions and his bony English nose blue and more pinched than ever. We were good friends and did not expect to meet again, and the moment was awkward. "Well, anyway," Yorick said finally in an off-hand way, "I can still snap my fingers." And he did, just once, and tried to grin. Then big Robin, so muscular and fit, the survivor of generations in this hard land, led the broken white lad away. He was a blithe spirit, was Yorick.

36

If this chapter reads like the synopsis of a misspent life it is because we are merciful; we are trying to crowd a year's activities, not many of them funny, into a few pages so that the weary reader may see us safely home from our long head-hunt. We started to go home from Thursday Island. It was time, and by the rarest luck there was a small freighter going through to the Philippines after calling at Port Darwin. But when we reached Darwin we disembarked, by request. There was no doctor on board, and no other women passengers; and the captain was afraid to risk us as far as Manila. But like every captain before him he was chivalrous; he returned our full passage money. Out of his own pocket, we suspected. Without it we might have been in a tight spot, caught between seas on the far northwest coast of Australia.

Darwin was momentous for a number of things, the first being a record for flies, goats, dust and heat. It was the dry season, and the hundreds of miles of Great Sandy Desert south of the hills of Arnhemland were making of the flat corrugated iron town a fireless cooker. Next was the fact that our baggage was searched for a second time, though we had cleared at Thursday Island, an Australian port, were disembarking at one and had called nowhere in between. They were searching for narcotics. As the newspaperman told us, we could make a pound or two bringing it in for some Oriental on the freighter. However, the customs would not have been so inconvenient if it had not been for the wharf lumpers' strike. Even the town's one taxi driver would not touch our luggage, and an idle native whom we asked to help us would have risked his hide if he had had the courage to try. Even in normal times in "all-white" Australia no aborigine is allowed to do the work that a white man will consider, and anything paying a living wage is "organized" work. The aborigines are not permitted in the unions. So while strong men sat on their fundamentals in the shade along the customhouse wall we dragged bag after bag to the cab after having unpacked and repacked the mountain of gear, even including the rolls of paintings and hundreds of soaked drawings which were leafed through individually. "No fear," we were back in the land of equal rights. And how we missed those courteous and cheerful slaves of New Guinea who would rather have eaten us than refuse a request. (Governor Murray tells about two Papuans who were brought into the Central Court on the charge of murdering an old man. The victim had asked the two to carry him across a stream and as for some reason they were unable, or unwilling, to do it, they killed him!—because, as they said, it would have been too impolite to say no.)

Ample compensation for all the rest was our Darwin hostess, a friend of a New Guinea friend who took us, unresisting, from the hotel and for a month until the next steamer arrived, gave us refuge and warm friendship and good home cooking. She even dug up a few portrait commissions and through the nearby native compound at Point Myilly arranged an aboriginal corroboree for us to paint. But we were through with spectacle sing-sing pictures, and for our Abo canvas and last portrait of the South Pacific we chose a nice quiet grave with a solitary figure squatting beside the colorful graveposts. It was symbolical. This stood for the last of the Mohicans, the last of the Tasmanians and what will soon be the last of the full-blood Hawaiian Polynesians, and the Maoris and the Aborigines and possibly the Melanesians and Papuans and so on. For this is the twilight hour for the earth's exclusive tribes.

We left Darwin just in time to keep from being female counterparts of The Man Who Came to Dinner. The *Mindini* was not sailing east, the way we wanted to go, but to

Singapore by Java ports and we took passage anyway, expecting to transship immediately for the Philippines and home. There was just the little matter of funds for the longer trip, but we'll get around to that presently. The master of the *Mindini*, long primed by Captain Voy of the Solomons run, had been expecting to pick us up somewhere—but not in the shape we were in. He had us moved from second-class to first-class quarters and sent in the ship's doctor. When we arrived at Surabaya we were taken first to friends, who put us up in their guest house, and then to the hospital for examinations. Our only visible symptoms were protruding skeletons, the cavity of island sore on my knee and the patches of *kukikuki* that Margaret was still fighting. It was the invisible things that sounded like a Latin recitation. In my case everything was traceable to long-standing malaria, the most inconvenient of the by-products being anemia. Though Margaret had so far shown no symptoms of malaria, she was deficient just from the long siege of heat and food lacking in blood-building minerals and vitamins. All my attacks of nausea, the chronic headaches, hysteria and muscle cramps and ailing teeth, now plural, were signs of the general debility, while the general cussedness was caused by an enlarged spleen which in turn was caused by the malaria. The Dutch doctor advised us to take our American millions and go up in the mountains to one of the rest sanitariums, but he made that even less possible with his bill. And when we had got through with the clinic and pharmacy (which also thought we were cruise tourists), they had us on their hands; we did not even have enough money to take us home from Singapore.

In the end we lived almost a year in Java, most of it in a little village up in the mountains of the west, the part called Sundaland. It seems now that it must have been a dream to have lived in such beauty and peace. We were so grateful just for physical comfort. It was a quiet little life in the remote annex of a hotel that had once been a tuberculosis sanitarium for Europeans. All around our second-floor balcony were the fronds of coconut palms and the red-tiled roofs of natives' houses. Across a green plaza was the Mahometan mosque to which came on special days the Sunda nobility with their gold umbrellas, and hadjis in sultan-sized turbans with dresses and long flowing coats of plain colors in combinations like mulberry and robin's egg blue, dull gold and green, and copper and pink or purple. At day-break when "the Hunter of the East caught the Sultan's tur-ret with a noose of light" we would hear the muezzin's voice from the top of the minaret calling the faithful to prayer. Then below on the village road the shuffling bare feet of men passed and soft gongs rang out in the pale blue glow of morning.

The gamelangs of some Hindu wedding or puppet show that had gone on for days and nights would still be sending forth their strange haunting dissonance when the first lumbering bullock teams ambled past on their way to the rice paddies. Then came the sweet odor of hot coconut oil as our native neighbors fried their breakfasts in the little bamboo huts across the road. When we went out on the veranda the sun would be flooding across the mountains around us, turning the blue mist in the valleys first lavender then pink, then into nothing, and all the terraces of rice paddies down the hillsides as far as we could see would be a thousand rose-colored mirrors reflecting the rising sun. A canal ran behind the huts on the other side of the road, and by-and-by the families would be in it bathing naked and unabashed while upstream others began pounding their laundry on the flat stones along the bank. The lush green along the canal still with the dew on it was like an emerald flame in that clean morning air. Then the breeze warmed, the laughter and chatter down in the road began—and it never left off all the long day. The last to appear was always our little babu. She would come staggering up the steps under a huge tray of breakfast, her round golden face beaming and a crescent of fragrant white flowers in the big knob of her patent-leather hair.

All around us was the rich background with which those ancient Indonesians had sailed into the Pacific, most of it to become lost in the race evolution in Melanesia. Here under our noses were all the odors, everything tempered with coco-

nut oil, and all the colors, the golden brown skins and patterned sarongs, gaily painted rice carts heaped with Biblical
sheaves of rice, the luxuriant tropical flowers and bizarre
foliage, and the sounds; the squeaking of the great wooden
wheels of the carts, the lively shouts of the water buffalo
drivers, the tinkling bells of the food venders and roll of
the two-inch drum of the cloth vender . . . a different
"sing" for each kind of merchandise . . . the chirping and
whistling of "rice" monkeys and the screech of cockatoos,
and on Sunday morning the zither serenade of the fat blind
musician who would sit on the grass and play for an hour for
a few pfennigs while his wife stood with her hand outstretched, her leprosy-eaten face turned up to us still val-
iantly smiling. From down the road came the shouts of men
around an unlawful cockfight or a ramfight, and behind all
the other sounds was the obbligato of the gamelang as persistent as the odor of coconut oil. Now and then a fantastic
coming-of-age procession would come down the road, the
young men dressed in women's garb, their faces painted
white. Then there were the block-long dragon and fireworks
of the Chinese New Year, the wayang shadow shows of the
Hindu myths, and the enclosure where at night the pros-
titutes sang in a high-pitched nasal twang, posturing with
their arms and double-jointed fingers and never looking at
the men who danced like cocks around them. Back of the
huts the housewives pounded the rice in a crude mortar like
a Melanesian drum, then shook it in flat baskets to separate
the kernels from the chaff. They wore only a sarong below
the breast and were as beautiful as the Bali women, and more
friendly. No native ever passed without a greeting and a
smile, and some stood off at the side of the road with head
bowed, coolie hat in hand. There was no humility in it;
it was simply courtesy, perhaps the gentlemanliness that the
Melanesian inherited.

This rich experience was made possible by a combination of factors, the first being that Sir Hubert Murray had given us letters of introduction to a number of Java friends, among them an Englishwoman living in Surabaya and the Governor of the Netherlands Indies. The former persuaded us to use the letter to the Governor, whose palace was in Buitenzorg, a few miles up-country from Batavia. She thought that a portrait of His Excellency would produce other sizable commissions which in a short time would enable us either to take our rest cure in the mountains or to proceed on home. Also the American "colony" was in Batavia, those high-salaried rubber and oil company executives who were "throwing their money around" (in the faces of the low-salaried British, we took it) and among them we would be on home ground for portrait work. So we proceeded to Batavia, but not without misgivings. Despite the legend that artistic genius thrives only on ill health or some form of insanity, we lesser fellows turn out our best work when we are in our right minds and the pink of health. And the few portraits we had attempted in Surabaya had been dismal failures. However, there was nothing to lose in the move; we already had our passage, and the Englishwoman gave us letters to American friends to help us on the way toward Buitenzorg.

There was a peculiar atmosphere among the Americans in Batavia. We did not know whether it was because of our having lived so long among the more reserved British or because these Americans had not lived long enough as superiors in a caste society with their homes staffed by long lines of inexpensive servants. Anyway, they seemed giddy in a kind of Flaming Youth pattern of the Prohibition era. And they were throwing their money about—though little of it came in our direction. No one had time or the patience to sit for a portrait; there was always a large party in the offing or they were recovering from one, or off for a long week-end in the mountains. And in any case there were no children, our best customers, and our few speculative portraits were as dismal as those we had attempted in Surabaya. It did not look promising for our designs on the Governor at Buitenzorg.

Then at low tide everything happened at once—as it almost always had in the affairs of the headhunt. It began with, of all irrelevant things, a Russian ballet company that was touring the East. It performed in Batavia, and after it had moved on to Surabaya and the champagne corks and orchids had been swept up, a big American automobile assembling plant looked around and found their advertising artist missing. He had fallen in love with one of the Russian ballerinas, and the two of them had eloped to Singapore. There, it developed later, they became a dance team, entertaining at the Raffles Hotel. The plant had been just on the point of making up a pamphlet to introduce the new model of a car, and they found themselves without an artist to illustrate it!

Our arrangements to do this work were so hasty and eager on both sides that the company never asked if we had done anything for reproduction before, and we failed to ask what we should be paid for it. Painting for reproduction is a highly specialized job, and we knew nothing whatever about it. Moreover, like many another professional artist, we cannot draw a straight line nor a fine curve—and there is nothing else to illustrating a motor car. However, we had *carte blanche* and were preparing to strain it for all it was worth when the second godsend arrived. This came embodied in a tall impressive mandarin clad in Dutch "whites" and bearing a note from mutual friends in an American oil company. Briefly, the American *Noña* had told the Oriental that we were in need of a change of climate, he owned the hotel at Sukabumi, "the paradise of the world" in the mountains, there was an unoccupied annex and if we cared to stay there until our health "felt well," our caller would be very "grateful."

Put that way, it made it difficult to descend to the vulgar question of rates; but we were still paying our way in gulden while it lasted. It developed later that the visitor owned, as well as a few hotels, two or three mountains of tea, coffee and rubber plantations, but he settled with us for about sixty cents apiece per day in the paradise of the world. That probably did not pay for our meals, inexpensive as eating is in Java. But he felt great *freundlichkeit* for everyone and everything American. His son had gone to Iowa State Agriculture College, his brother to Columbia Medical and another brother had married an American-educated Chinese girl from the Malay States. The poorest of us was not too humble to receive his homage.

So we were moved, bag and bundle, to the mountains with our *carte blanche* and photographs of the new car and Margaret began posing for the figures in the illustrations. For the wealthy Javanese and Dutch, and especially the halfcastes, had to be sold with the idea that this inexpensive American car was really a high-caste white man's motor. First Margaret was the happy wife driving along beside her happy husband who was also herself; then she was the modern young thing driving herself, finally she was a kind of allegorical beauty in a bathing suit accenting with her curves those undrawable straight lines of the machine. And in the middle of this standing pose I looked up to find Margaret, not sinking gracefully to the floor in a movie swoon, but going over like a telephone pole. She had not fainted; she had simply collapsed. After three years of tenderest consideration for our native models I had gone on painting with no regard for Margaret's endurance. And she had posed until she had literally dropped.

But this was not just fatigue. It was a symptom of a serious type of malaria, a kind attended by pernicious disorders and a more or less continuous fever of long duration. It was not until some time later that we were satisfied ourselves that

Margaret's illness was malaria, because it had begun without the warning chills that I so dreaded. It then developed that she must have been harboring the plasmodium fully as long as I had; the symptoms had been held in abeyance by her daily doses of quinine. These had been discontinued in Surabaya, and now the chilly nights in the mountains had brought out the disease in its most virulent form short of being fatal. Luckily she weathered the highest fever (of the first three days), and the doctor member of our Chinese family sent in a competent native nurse, which allowed me to get back to the streamlines of the Super-duper Six.

Three weeks later I sent down to Batavia the last of those ghastly paintings, convinced that they would be rejected. If I had been a praying woman I would have prayed those next few days. Margaret was delirious part of the time, and kept talking about home, which showed how intensely she had been longing for it. But never a word about it before. It did not seem that any portraits of any race, however vanishing, were important enough for such a sacrifice.

The check came on the fourth day with three and a half florins income tax (about $2.00) already deducted for Her Majesty, Queen Wilhelmina. The balance was *one thousand and twenty-two American dollars and two cents.*

37

A proper book, the experts tell us, should have an introduction, a climax and a conclusion presented in about that order. Anyone who has stayed with us this far, having been launched hind end foremost in the first few pages into the only possible climax for a tale of New Guinea today, will hardly expect a formal summary of the work here. I am not so sure it has a tangible sum anyway; the war has altered values. Moreover explaining the work that has already been presented is where the book writer and the picture painter come to the parting of the ways. *His* creation, the artist insists, should stand on its own for whatever the spectator can get out of it—and without any supplementary diagram. This is why one sees so many stunned-looking people in art galleries. (Some of them are artists themselves.) The ones who are muttering are the art critics, and what they are saying is that the artist himself paints his picture and then rationalizes it afterward, if he can, so how can he expect anyone else to know whether he was driving at anything? Nevertheless, if the painter has any conclusions he paints them into the picture, and this is what I have attempted in the foregoing. The only thing left is the final accent to bring out the contrasts.

The way out of the jungle of trees and back to the one of skyscrapers was as much an adventure for us as the other direction had been, for now we no longer took anything for granted, not even the familiar. The two thousand five hundred new florins added to the remainder of our other funds made a fortune, but it was not just money. It was a steamer, assurance of safe passage home whenever we wanted to go. But first it was time in which partially to repair our damaged health, and then more time for completing the expedition work.

The Solomon Islands and New Guinea canvases had to be put into professional shape so that they could be exhibited in New York, and there was no cheaper place to live while doing this work than where we were. Moreover stretchers had to be made by a carpenter, the paintings tacked on them and then frames had to be built; and nowhere else would these things cost so little. This architectural feature of painting—frames—is usually a headache for the artist, for not only do they cost more than all the other materials that went into the picture, they can sometimes make a masterpiece look like something less or, oftener, with luck in choosing, make a second-rate job an acceptable decoration. I think we had luck when we thought of bamboo frames. Nothing else could have been more appropriate nor blended better with the subjects and colors. A native carver living in a nearby village was engaged not only to build the frames but to burn on them a linear design copied from the smoking *bau-bau* we had brought from Hanuabada. He gave us a price of forty dollars (American) for forty frames, or about an acre of burned design on a grove of bamboo that he was to supply himself. It must have been a heartbreaking contract, but also the Java man has never heard that *tempus fugit*, so the frame-making stretched on for weeks and weeks. Finally the artist went all to pieces like the men on the mass-production lines we hear about and took to drinking rice wine. When we drove over to the village to see how things were getting on we would find wayang figures posturing among New Guinea crocodile tracks, and the artist would be doing the work with his feet while the workshop would be filled with his friends talking *sina* and *sana*. Rice wine is very weak, and he must have drunk gallons of it to get such relief, but sympathetic as we were something had to be done to speed up the frame-making. It was therefore as much to keep a watchful eye on that as for the portrait that we began painting the carver.

Up to this point I had not been concerned about obtaining Indies types to finish up the Melanesian collection, because I hoped to return later to the country. Not only were there some half hundred distinct physical types in the group that would keep me painting happily so long as I could see, but Java then seemed to offer everything that we wanted in this life; sweetness in the people, a vigorous climate, and rare beauty in the mountains—and especially the sense of security and peaceful industry that emanated from the populous countryside. But this idyllic picture began falling apart even in the workshop of the carver. Before we left the country the paradise of the world had become merely another, though still lovely, part of the real world.

The Sundanese of western Java have a language of their own but many Malay words have crept into it and in the carver's shop where all the idle men of the village loafed and talked, confident that we could not understand them, the words we heard often and did understand were the Malay "sina" and "sana." Literally translated they mean "here" and "there." To the Indonesian they mean more: "Sina" is "here, we Indonesians," as against "Sana," "there, the Government in Holland." They are political terms.

It had been our impression that the Dutch had established a rule in the Indies that was one of the most successful of all administrations of native countries. Their policy of encouraging inter-racial marriage, legitimatizing half-caste children, deliberately creating a middle-stratum populace that would act as a buffer and channel of communication between the two races showed an intelligent understanding of the problem and a sense of justice. For if a non-native power is to extract revenue from a possession the one thing that can elevate it above rank exploitation is for the aliens to dig into the soil with the producers. We have no reason to change our minds regarding the virtues of the Dutch administration; it was as liberal and executed with as much interest in the improvement of the natives as vested interests would permit. In any case the problems of white occupation of a native country seemed to have been happily solved in this instance. Yet suddenly in 1926, without warning, there was an uprising of the natives of Batan.

In the arrests and investigations that followed it was discovered that the nationalist movement behind the Batan rebellion was afoot all through the Indies. In its condensed version the people wanted Sina, self-determination, and Sana, freedom from western domination.

And now up crops that old boogieman, communism. It was held to be responsible for the nationalist movement. (For if the people could rid themselves of the present government their nationalism could take any form.) Much of the propaganda was seeping into the Netherland Indies from South China via agitators posing as coolies—these, ironically, being imported as cheaper labor than the Indonesians for work on the plantations and in the oil wells and tin mines. But also at that time as many as sixty thousand Indonesians annually were making the pilgrimage to Mecca, and there the Third International maintained a school for the instruction of educated natives and for the general dissemination of their world-revolution doctrines. There the innocents first learned of Egypt's final independence, of the successes of Iraq and Transjordania and others in self-government, and the failures of Western powers to govern as in India and elsewhere. The pilgrims returned to the Indies "sold."

In other words the great crusader, now in another garb, was abroad again nosing out a situation that had nearly if not entirely achieved harmony, saving, uplifting, liberating and "bringing order to," imposing *his* ideas of salvation et cetera and in the process destroying customs and ideals that have survived in older civilizations because generations of usage have proved them livable in those set conditions. It could have had any label in the dictionary, been any doctrine in the world and it would still have been motivated by that old meddling missionary spirit that seems to be almost exclusively white. As the other half of the expedition has been heard to observe, "If any fox did smell his own hole first he'd bide a while and clean it up. Hounds might die out."

In any case the idea of Sina and Sana did not die out with the suppressions in 1926. It was still going strong during our stay in Java. By the time we were ready to leave the country one of our best reasons for returning had vanished. For the peace on the surface was only skin and the lightheartedness of the people just one facet of the spirit that was straining its seams to express itself in another manner.

Much of our information came from a German engineer who was a neighbor in Sukabumi, our friendship being based on the fact that he had lived in New Guinea up until the First World War, and his for us being a simple white man's enjoyment of the company of white girls, and especially that of Margaret. (He had spent most of the four years of the war in a concentration camp in Australia, and he loathed the British with a bountiful loathing.) That he was active as an agitator in the Sina-Sana movement is somehow doubtful, or he was being highly indiscreet in revealing so much. He knew a great deal about the little clubs and organizations of the natives, though not suspiciously more than might be expected of a resident of almost two decades. However, he did a rather curious thing at the time of our departure. His business was building bridges and the big machinery for the sugar refineries, and it seemed to be prospering nicely since he had the three East Indies rewards for success, a house with a marble floor, an American car with chauffeur, and a half-caste mistress (who absented herself in Batavia during the week). Yet he suddenly sold everything and left for Germany. His explanation was that he wanted to go home, marry some "nice" girl and have children like a normal man. It would have been a more acceptable reason if he had not acted on it so abruptly.

Going through Batavia on our way out we saw only Americans, and after the long quiet months in the mountains our kind seemed more than ever the most restless of mortals. Many changes had taken place during our absence, executives had been shunted to different posts and a few men had even been recalled. Our "oil" friends were on their way up to Bangkok, a "rubber" friend had already been transferred to

Singapore and wives had departed on holidays. This had no meaning to any of us then, even the shunted, but it was being accepted as change always is by the American, with a lift of spirits. It exhausted us, for we had fallen behind the tempo, and we were glad to leave it behind.

The ship we sailed on was a British freighter taking forty-two days to New York, including a three day stop-over in Singapore for loading, and scheduled calls at Port Swetten-ham and Penang up the coast of Malaya, then a few hours in Ceylon. The route west was around South Africa. But instead of three days in Singapore we lay over for ten, waiting for something. And it proved not to be freight, for when we finally sailed, on a few hours' notice, we had taken on very little.

One afternoon in Singapore we were having tea with some friends in the Raffles Hotel . . . regretful that we were not to see the Russian ballerina and her artist whose dear love had given us this safe passage home; they had moved on to Manila . . . when a young man seated at a table a short distance down the terrace suddenly leaped to his feet and strode rapidly in our direction, smiling as he came. It was a dazzling grin, showing teeth as even as if they were false, and as white as the well draped suit on the *Esquire* frame. On the whole, while there are a great many young men in this part of the world, men of character and men of charm, there are very few real beauties. I looked in back of me to see who this dazzler was greeting so enchantingly—and the tables were empty. Dark sun glasses covered his (probably beau-tiful) eyes, but there was something about that bony Eng-lish nose that reminded me of someone . . . who? And the hair, the red-brown of coffee. At this point he reached Mar-garet's chair, put his hand up behind her ear and snapped the fingers briskly. Yes, poor Yorick—but no longer "alas." This was the lad who could be engaged to four girls all at once, still cockeyed but re-dentured and his asthma, hair, language and malaria well under control after a year on a cattle station in Australia.

Yorick was on his way home to England, not to marry the girls but to "join up." "It's no good," we warned him, "the Boy Scout motto is 'see far' and there's a flaw in your beauty." "Ah, but not in my eyesight. I can still tell a lovely girl when I see one." He was looking at Margaret, at least with one of his eyes. "They'll take me for my talent at figures." But what had decided him on a military career, we wanted to know; we thought he had had his bellyful of life on the front at Madiri. "Oh the clouds is bankin' up down west," he grinned, "looks for an early wet." Some of our senseless Madiri patter. He was blither than ever, certainly a young man relieved of the boring routine of a cattle station and away on a grand lark. He rattled us too.

The freighter skipped Port Swettenham, waited only overnight at Penang, again without taking on much freight, skipped Ceylon, and then without consulting us bounced off west across the Indian Ocean and into the Gulf of Aden. We were not going by South Africa. Christmas, appropriately, was in the offing when we started up the Red Sea, the pagan East behind us and the Christian West ahead. The wind was high, filling the air with desert dust that seasoned our food with grit and swept through the freighter a scourge of Holy Land fleas that rivaled the sand flies of the Coral Sea. Caravans of loaded camels were strung along the violet sands hurrying north as if late for the Nativity. All the way from Aden through the Mediterranean, gray warcraft spotted the foggy seas guarding the Crusaders' loot. We bucked bitter winter storms from Ireland on.

The freighter was three weeks late when she berthed in New York; the Singapore delay, the Atlantic storm and then three more days in the Narrows waiting for the fog to lift enough to let us run up the Bay. Margaret lay on her berth motionless, her cheeks scarlet, while the ghostly voices of buoy foghorns and other stalled ships moaned incessantly in the yellow opaqueness.

The result of this delay was that no one was at the dock to meet us as we came in, though there were two fur coats waiting—which was a good second best. For New York was having a typical pre-Christmas cold snap with a month and a half without a snowfall. The weeks' accumulation of furnace soot and just the powder eroded from the pavement by thousands of wheels and feet lay like a gray shroud over the city, blowing up into little whirlwinds with gum wrappers and other rubbish in the crevices of the shabby waterfront buildings. For these, not the marble and chromium monuments of Fifth Avenue and Wall Street, are the architecture of our progressive society. There was not a sprig of green nor other thing left that God had made, except humanity.

Our gear was being trucked into the warehouse by one member of the species, a full-blood Negro. Naked he might have looked like some Coral Sea islander, but in his shabby all-dark clothing he only looked like a black specter clanking through the big gloomy warehouse. The soles of his enormous shoes were worn off at the outside edge, and though holes had been cut in the top leather for his corns to pop out of, he shuffled along as if the boots hurt. He was still young, but his knees were angled like a boomerang. When we greeted him he did not look alert like a Melanesian. In a Deep South accent he asked sadly, "Where you wan' me take these . . ." He hesitated. "Portraits of a vanishing race," we supplied. "Gotta get em outta here anyway, Miz," he apologized, "this is just for movin freight. Wha' you wan' me do uth them?" "I think I'll give them to you," we said. "They're your relatives." "Oh, no," he looked alarmed, "ain' got room fo' no mo' relatives. I live in on'y two rooms, an' I got my wife an' baby an' her mother an' sister, an' sister's got a baby. We ain' got no room for relatives on the wall even." One of us, we decided, must have given him a corpse to hold for them.

At this point another native approached, and the first nipped away on his frozen corns. The newcomer was of a different tribe, probably Harlem born, for his speech was clearer and only the bags under his eyes were as dark as the skin of the other Negro. He was the shrewd boss boy or sorcerer type. His black hair under the hat was straight and shiny as patent leather, and a row of decorative metal pencils extended from the breast pocket of his overcoat. He took one of these out to write down the address to which our freight was to be sent. We wanted to leave the canvases in the warehouse until arrangements could be completed for their exhibition, at which they would be sent straight to the gallery, but this was against the rules. Then we reverted to type. We opened the coin purse wherein still faithfully reposed the weary Heffalump, and took from him one of the last of the bills we had exchanged in Singapore for our florins. Nothing was said as we slipped the chief the money. It took a hundred and fifty years to achieve this fluid rapprochement between the most backward and the most progressive. Build up, in the mind of the simple fellow who has always found a cheap lead pencil adequate for writing, a desire for the colorful shining kind (that will have to be loaded with lead) and you have the basis for such a happy understanding, especially if you are prepared to supply the means of a more beautiful life in a stock of such new pencils.

The cab drove into the warehouse for our baggage, and while the Deep South native loaded it up I went to use the telephone. I noted the driver, and out of force of habit was trying to fit him into some race category. He was an American; at least he had no foreign accent—unless Bronx English

is exotic. But he had a "European" head, and I wrote him off
as one of the unclassifiable Jews. He might have been a
Mayflower Bostonian or a whooping Iroquois for any difference it makes in this encounter. He was out of the cab
when I returned from the telephone, and as I approached
I heard him say slowly and intensely, "Why, you go-o-d
dam-mn nigger!" The "nigger" had scraped some paint off
the cab fender in putting one of our unwieldy cases in. That
might have passed off pleasantly enough except that the Boss
Boy had heard the exclamation and like the striking indentured
natives of Rabaul who had dropped all intertribal enmity for
the combined blow at the white employers, he went into the
fray on the side of his color. What he said in effect was that
no "kike" could call any nigger a nigger. Before we were
driven out of the warehouse (in another cab) a half dozen
totem factions were exercising their primordial rights to the
hilt.

Outside in the taxi the clamor and speed dazed us. Roaring trucks and squalling cabs raced one another in all directions through the labyrinth of piles of the elevated, trains
rumbled overhead and trams clattered bonging down the
center of the tunnel of iron and steel. At Times Square the
traffic signals changed, and we came to a catapulting stop,
first in line as two torrents of humanity burst from opposite
curbs and surged together, crossing in a solid pack before
us. The natives had ghostly white faces, their only feature
in common. Not until now did we realize how uniform the
primitive type that has developed in isolation is. Here there
were tall ones and broad ones and squat, thin, fat all over
or in places with a variety of head forms and faces, matching
or contradictory. Hawk-nosed, buck-toothed, chinless, lip-
less or neckless, with ears like *lakatoi* sails, eyes of every
shape and color, with and without bags, and on every tenth
set a pair of spectacles. There were women with mouths red-

der than the juice of a betel-nut quid, with plucked eyebrows like a Yela cannibal, on their heads strange and wonderful creations that would have made a sing-sing dancer gape with awe. There was baldness and grayness and so much white hair, the latter never seen on primitives. There were walking gaits that defied gravity, shoulders hunched and body bent forward, the loose arms and legs thrashing ahead as if they must come away before long. Where was everyone bound for in such haste? Others followed their bust or stomach slowly, like tanks, with arms dangling. So many limped. Some looked hungry and dreadfully cold, and the feeble and aged were like leaves floating slowly at the sides of the stream while logs swept around and over them. Now and then one of these eddied along in the backwaters with the dignity of the aged cannibal. Now and then there was an unbelievably beautiful girl—we had forgotten how beautiful a young white girl can be with her exquisite legs and feet, the shell-blond skin and satiny hair. Or what an ornament to the earth one dressed in perfect harmony of color and line. There was a healthy young traffic officer mounted on a horse as proud, and one thought of these as average of our people and it inflated the self-esteem. But there was also a Derivo in the crowd, her pasty sullen face bent forward as she shuffled along to her unpleasant work, and Mrs. Tabora still yammering and flaying her arms, her red crooked hair the dyed and permanent-ed triumph of years of experiment by painstaking scientists. Dignified Ahuia, gentle Sarli and wise old Gomai and Tauparaupi all passed. And there were big pleasant faces like Robin's ready to laugh, contented-looking little ones like that of Sarli's doomed wife, and so many helpless wistful little girls like Ninoa, pluckier or harder or less sensitive little girls than Ninoa. They were all there, just people.

Newsboys were bawling their wares on the traffic island next the cab, and when a paper was thrust up to the window we took it in. Blazoned across the front page was the banner headline JAPAN WARNED. We failed to find what act of aggression had been committed against the United States (that day long before December 7, 1941) nor, if the provocation were directed at China as the news indicated, just why this purely Asiatic matter concerned our nation so much— enough to risk the necessity of using force to back up the warning. Was it a greater love for China than for other victimized Asiatic nations? India, say. If the warning were in defense of international law and treaties, then why were they jeopardized by permitting private U.S. companies to send war material to Japan for her aggression against China? Unless it was that free enterprise was a law unto itself having supersedence over international law and the obligations of treaties. There was no answer to these questions in that issue of the news—if they had answers. Nevertheless we had by now guessed why the outlanders on the other side of the world were gathering to the clans and why Java, including (and especially) the Americans, was like a disturbed ants' nest. The clouds *were* banking up. The tribes had commenced raiding, and other tribes were smearing on their war paint—crusading.

Margaret continued scanning headlines as the cab bulldozed a path across town. At the first pause she folded the paper back to an item and handed it to me, quoting from a Chinese proverb we had stuck inside the lid of my cigarette-tin drawing box. "Two Co-eds Clubbed Unconscious," I read; and failed to see the connection. "Read on," she ordered. "Police Club Anti-War Strikers," the caption continued. Students a hundred thousand strong in colleges and universities all over the country had united in a mass demonstration to secure for their future that illusory promise of Civilization, peace. Wise Gomai, an old man himself, had said that it was the elders of the tribe who kept the feuds alive and incited the youths to battle, none of whom had ever thought to renounce the excitement of the raid and so sacrifice the admiration of the girls. And here it had occurred to them, to a hundred thousand young men and women. Such a thing had never happened before in history. It was a *good* thing to come home to.

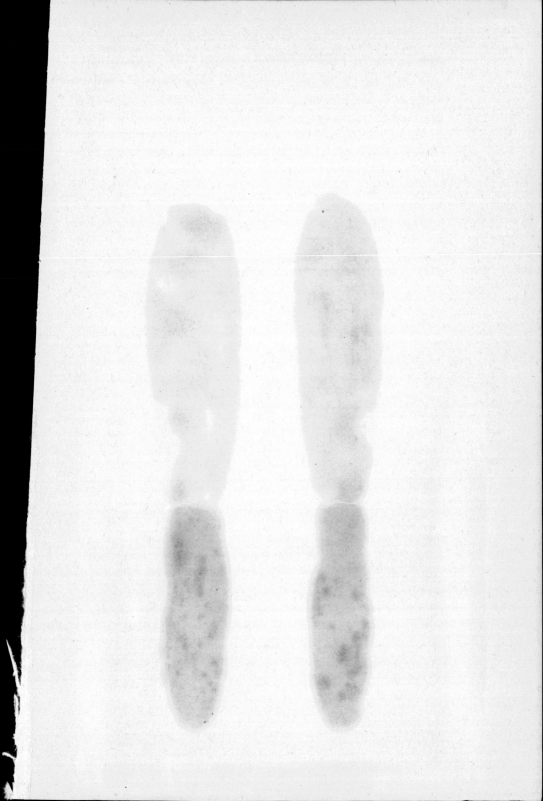

3/13/47

DATE DUE